This is the riveting true story of Paul Martelli, a fifteen-year-old German-Italian, who fought in Pomerania, on the Eastern Front, in 1945 as a member of the *33.Waffen-Grenadier-Division der SS 'Charlemagne'* and, later, as a soldier with French forces during three years (1951-1954) in the Tonkin area, Vietnam.

Paul recounts his time at the Sennheim military training base, where he was introduced to the rigorous discipline of body and mind: he then goes back to 1940, during the German invasion of France, when he was still a boy in Lorraine, hinting at his motivations for enlisting with the *Waffen SS*. He reveals his and many young soldiers' exciting and often humorous escapades at Greifenberg, his first love with a German girl helping refugees, his experiences and feelings during the combats at Körlin, during the strenuous defense of Kolberg, while regrouping at Neustrelitz and at the German defeat. With a companion he ends up at a castle delivering a group of women camp prisoners to a Russian officer, living in disguise among enemy soldiers until he escapes and surrender to the Americans.

After his sentence, imprisonment, evasions and military service in Morocco, Paul is sent to fight in defense of bases north of Hanoi, Vietnam. He survives three years of fierce combats, assaults, ambushes, night patrols, fatal traps and mortal risks but, deep down, he compares his service with the *Waffen SS* during the last year of war with the inefficiency of the French Expeditionary Force in the Far East and comes out deeply frustrated. At almost 26, he has fought and lost in two wars, both against the communists, be they Soviet or Viet Minh. Unemployed, and with the ideals of a 'Nouvelle Europe' in pieces, he briefly joins the French Foreign Legion, his last hope, but in the end choses another path.

This is a unique memoir, packed with incident and recounting the story of one individual caught up in a series of life-changing events.

Vittorino dal Cengio wrote books about climbing in the Dolomites that were published during the 1980s. He also wrote articles and short stories for a magazine and for Italian newspapers in Canada. After an interlude, in 2008 he resumed writing books, this time about social history, authoring three in recent years. He moved to Canada in 1977 in the spirit of adventure after his military service with the Italian Alpine Corps. He holds various technical diplomas from Italy and a BA (joint major in French, History, Political Sciences) from Simon Fraser University.

ON THE DEVIL'S TAIL

IN COMBAT WITH THE *WAFFEN SS* ON THE EASTERN FRONT 1945, AND WITH THE FRENCH IN INDOCHINA 1951-54

Paul Martelli

With Vittorino dal Cengio

Helion & Company

Helion & Company Limited
26 Willow Road
Solihull
West Midlands
B91 1UE
England
Tel. 0121 705 3393
Fax 0121 711 4075
Email: info@helion.co.uk
Website: www.helion.co.uk
Twitter: @helionbooks
Visit our blog http://blog.helion.co.uk/

Published by Helion & Company 2015
Designed and typeset by Bookcraft Ltd, Stroud, Gloucestershire
Cover designed by Paul Hewitt, Battlefield Design (www.battlefield-design.co.uk)
Printed by Lightning Source Limited, Milton Keynes, Buckinghamshire

Text © Vittorino del Cengio 2014
Images and hand-drawn map © Paul Martelli 2014
Other maps © Helion & Company Ltd 2015

ISBN 978-1-909982-09-3

British Library Cataloguing-in-Publication Data.
A catalogue record for this book is available from the British Library.

For details of other military history titles published by Helion & Company Limited
contact the above address, or visit our website: http://www.helion.co.uk.

We always welcome receiving book proposals from prospective authors.

Contents

List of Photographs

List of Maps

Introductory Notes

The Origins of the *Waffen SS*

Initially, the *Schutzstaffel* (*SS*) was a small, special force of paramilitaries with the mission of protecting Nazi Party chiefs. It consisted of bodyguards assigned to major cities such as Munich where they maintained order during political gatherings but they also carried out more menial chores such as billposting. By the time Hitler took power in early 1933, the membership of the *SS* had risen to around 50,000. These were men bound by oath to the *Führer* and organized on military lines under the leadership of Heinrich Himmler. The *SS* were regarded as protectors of Hitler's dream of a Nordic brotherhood of peoples with 'pure blood'. They performed police duties, served as guards at concentration camps and took part in the by then ubiquitous military parades. In September 1939, they were ready to fight beside the *Wehrmacht* during the invasion of Poland and later again in Holland, Belgium and in France. In March 1940, those members of the *SS* who took part in combat missions were designated '*Waffen SS*' and fully equipped as military units. At that time membership of the *Waffen SS* was voluntary and restricted to those individuals who met strict criteria of height, health and racial origin and for the most part, in the early stages of the Second World War, these were German nationals, *Reichsdeutsche* with Nordic physical characteristics. At the beginning of 1945, the *Waffen SS* divisions were in dire need of reinforcements but the reserve of Aryan manpower from all over Europe had already been sacrificed. Consequently, the ethos upon which the selection of *Waffen SS* soldiers had been made was relaxed to include those of virtually any ethnic origin who were willing to fight against Bolshevism and for the establishment of a 'New Europe'. Towards the end of the Second World War, the ranks of the *Waffen SS* included more than sixty percent of foreigners many of whom did not match the Nazi's Aryan ideal and amongst these were the Frenchmen who enlisted in the *33.Waffen-Grenadier-Division der Waffen SS 'Charlemagne'*.

Division 'Charlemagne'

In September 1944, the *Waffen-Grenadier-Brigade der SS 'Charlemagne'* was formed from the remnants of other units including *Sturmbrigade Frankreich* veterans (whose ranks were decimated during combat in Galicia and in the Carpathians), L.V.F. legionnaires (French Legion Volunteers), French militiamen and nationals who were members of the *Kriegsmarine* and

Luftwaffe and men from other, minor units. Then, in February 1945, the brigade was upgraded to divisional strength and renamed *33.Waffen-Grenadier-Division 'Charlemagne' (französische Nr. 1)*. The command of this new *Division 'Charlemagne'* was entrusted to General Edgard Puaud, a former colonial officer from the Foreign Legion and veteran of action in Tonkin, Morocco and Syria, but he was appointed only at *Oberführer* level in the *Waffen SS* hierarchy. Transforming this disparate group of men into a coherent and homogeneous *Waffen SS Division* was a task assigned to *General Brigadeführer* Gustav Krukenberg who insisted that *Division 'Charlemagne'* was to serve on the Eastern Front to circumvent the possibility of French soldiers being asked to fight against their fellow countrymen on the Western Front.

From the Greifenberg military depot and the Wildflecken training camp, the soldiers of *Division 'Charlemagne'* were sent to Pomerania to help stem the Russian advance. Without consistent support, and deprived of heavy armament and adequate supply of materiel, *'Charlemagne's'* first clash with the overwhelming Russian forces was a disaster. More than 1,000 soldiers were reported missing and 500 left dead on the battlefield before the division had the opportunity to regroup. Then, in the first days of March 1945, a regiment of *'Charlemagne'* was surrounded and annihilated near Belgard. Other units manage to escape but with grave losses. A few hundred survivors belonging to a *Bataillon de Marche*, having fought furiously at Körlin and at Kolberg, succeeded in reaching Swinemünde by sea where they re-joined the remnants of their once 7000-man-strong division. Many of these survivors met their death in Berlin during a strenuous, last-stand defense of Hitler's bunker while a few others — perhaps only sixty or so — were able to escape. Of these, many fell into the hands of the Western Allies only to be condemned to stand in front of a firing squad. Paul Martelli is therefore one of the *very* few soldiers of the *33.Waffen-Grenadier-Division 'Charlemagne'* to have survived both the Second World War and its aftermath.

The French Presence in Vietnam

French intervention in Vietnam starts in 1847 with the bombardment of the port of Tourane (present-day Da Nang) in order to protect traders and French missionaries persecuted by Emperor Minh Mang. For the same reason, Napoleon III orders, in 1858, the landing of French troops who, once having occupied the town, are themselves placed under siege. From this port, with the help of Spanish warships and Filipino fighters, the French occupy Saigon, a small city lying to the south of Tourane. Saigon (present-day Ho Chi Minh City) was important strategically because of its rich agricultural produce and as a penetration point into Cochinchina.

Within a few years, France controlled the Cochinchina peninsula and the territories of Annam and Tonkin and established the Federation of Indochina with the capital first at Saigon, then at Hanoi. From this last city, the French built a railroad towards China and improved agriculture in the south. The French language and Catholic religion were adopted by the most rich, learned and prominent members of the local population who, after the First World War, then opposed French colonial occupation.

At the start of the Second World War, when France was occupied by Germany, Japan took the opportunity to invade Indochina although it left the administration of the region to the French. In 1941, Ho Chi Minh formed the Viet Minh, a group of communist rebels, intolerant of both the French and Japanese presence. As the end of the Second World War approached, the Japanese invalidated the Vichy's Government's authority in March 1945 and placed Emperor Bao Dai at the head of an autonomous Vietnam. In August of the same year, after having conquered Hanoi, the Viet Minh deposed Bao Dai and on 2 September, the day of Japanese capitulation, declared the foundation of The Democratic Republic of Vietnam. Following the Allied victory against Japan, however, Vietnam was entrusted to the British and Chinese governments who in turn ceded Vietnam to the French, who then forced the Viet Minh to retreat to the north.

After an inconclusive treaty offered by Ho Chi Minh, and as a consequence of Viet Minh attacks, the French bombed Haiphong in 1946 thus commencing the First Indochinese War. To combat the superior military technology of their French enemy, the Viet Minh utilize their guerrilla-warfare experience and, after the communist victory in China in 1949, receive Chinese support and armaments. The following year, the Viet Minh launched an offensive in the north-eastern part of the Tonkin region, on the Red River delta and along the Chinese frontier using heavy artillery. The French response in 1951 was ineffectual and in 1953, the Viet Minh invaded Laos. Disaster awaited the French in April and May 1954 when at Dien Bien Phu, the Viet Minh inflicted huge losses on the French defenders. The French government, forced into negotiations at Geneva, surrendered on every issue and signed the Geneva Accords which ceded those parts of Vietnam north of the 17th Parallel to the Viet Minh while the area south of this line fell to ex-Emperor Bao Dai, with the agreement to hold a nationwide general election in 1956.

The United States and South Vietnam rejected the Geneva Accords on the grounds that a free election was not possible in the communist held North thus opening the way to the Second Indochina War. In spite of American support in Vietnam the *Corps Expéditionnaire Français en Extrême-Orient* (CEFEO) was disbanded by General Pierre Jacquot in 1956.

Pseudonyms

The names of many of the characters close to Paul have been changed to protect their privacy.

Glossary

Waffen SS Ranks and British Army Equivalents:

SS Obersturmbannführer	Lieutenant Colonel
SS Sturmbannführer	Major
SS Hauptsturmführer	Captain
SS Obersturmführer	Lieutenant
SS Untersturmführer	2nd Lieutenant
SS Standartenoberjunker	(no equivalent)
SS Hauptscharführer	Battalion Sergeant Major
SS Oberscharführer	Company Sergeant Major
SS Scharführer	Platoon Sergeant Major
SS Unterscharführer	Sergeant
SS Rottenführer	Corporal
SS Sturmmann	Lance Corporal
SS Oberschütze	Private First Class [US rank]
SS Schütze	Private

Other terms:

Ausbildung	training [German]
Davai	'hurry' [Russian]
Du meine Fresse	'bloody hell!' [German]
Fils de salop	'son of a bitch' [French]
Heeresgruppe	Army Group [German]
Karrotenkopf	red-haired person, meaning 'carrot head' [German]
Kriegsmarine	navy [German]
Kübelwagen	German military vehicle similar to jeep
niaqué	Vietnamese female farm worker
Matrose	naval rating [German]
Maudit	'goddam or damn it'[French]
Munitionschütze	soldier responsible for keeping a field piece supplied with ammunition [German]

Ostarbeiter	a worker from the east – often Russian [German]
Panzerfaust (pl.Panzerfäuste)	a rocket-propelled anti-tank weapon [German]
Pioniere	field engineers [German]
Porco boia	Italian expletive
Prévôtè	Provost [French]
rez-de-chaussée	the ground floor storey of a building [French]
Richtschütze	gun-layer [German]
roulante	mobile field kitchen [French]
Scheisse	'shit' [German]
Soldbuch (pl. Soldbücher)	German soldier's identity and pay book
Sommelier	trained wine steward in an expensive restaurant
Sigrun	the angular double 'S' symbol used by the *SS*
Standartenoberjunker	most senior rank of an *SS* officer candidate
tholang	Vietnamese head of a village
tirailleur	Senegalese rifleman
Truppführer	troop leader [German]
Volkssturm	German reserve force composed of male civilians
Zeltbahn (pl. Zeltbahen)	waterproof tent quarter carried by German soldiers

1

The *Waffen SS* Volunteer

Choosing Sides

It was after a long rail journey in 1943 that I arrived in Marseille to work for *Organisation Todt.* A billet had been arranged for me on the outskirts, at Septèmes-les-Vallons. As the train slowed on its approach to the platform, it passed wagons smashed by bombs, and broken, twisted rails, curling into the air like broken springs. One of the jagged spikes had pierced the chest of a woman who hung there in tattered clothes, as if frozen in a writhe of agony.

Guards lined the rails on both sides, protecting them from sabotage by the *Maquis.* The Germans feared them, these French partisans, and often changed train routes at the last moment. Sometimes they attached civilian wagons at the front of the convoy as a deterrent.

Oberleutnant Wödl was a friend of my family from my mother's side; he had fought in the First World War and now lived in Marseille, in a villa not far from the *gendarmerie.* He was a very serious gentleman, around fifty years old, bold, of normal height but thickset and short-sighted. He gave me his telephone number which I could use in case of trouble.

After work, I liked to stroll along the piers of the old port. Many young people were arriving at Marseille in search of adventure and, like most seaports, the area was swarming with all sort of pedlars, including ones selling bread coupons. I bought some of those coupons, and the following morning stopped by the bakery at Septèmes-les-Vallons in order to exchange one for a hot, crispy loaf.

"Hem! Wait here," the baker told me after turning the coupon in his fingers again and again, examining it very carefully. "I have to ask my wife something, she's in the back shop."

I realized he was suspicious and so I examined the coupons I still had in my pocket: they were stamped with the date of the following month so they should not have been in circulation. Only then did it dawn on me that I had bought them from a black marketer.

The baker returned. "My wife thinks they are not good," he said after a couple of minutes, showing his face from the back room. "You know, we could have problems in case of controls but I could offer you some bread...I have some just out of the oven...a delight if you are willing to wait."

To hell, I thought. *This fellow is selling me a pig in a poke; he only wants to gain time by keeping me here.* I slipped out of the shop but it was too late to avoid two *gendarmes* who grabbed my arms and then took me to the police station in Marseille. There they frisked me, confiscating everything I had in my pockets, money included. "You'll be stuck in prison for years," a tall and skinny *gendarme* told me, gloating, "for coupon trafficking… up to twenty-five-years forced labour."

I was flung into a seat. A bright light was directed into my eyes. Hours of interrogation followed with every word I answered typed by the skinny *gendarme's* assistant. It was now past five o'clock in the afternoon. Through the interrogation room window I looked longingly at the fresh, autumn sunset. Finally, the clatter from the typewriter ended. They forced a deposition into my hands, which was impossible to read because of the blinding light, and told me to sign it. "May I phone my father?" I asked in a low voice, tired and nauseated.

"Your father is here?"

"And he has a telephone?"

I spelled out the numbers and the '*lamp-gendarme*', after shutting off the light, dialled them on a phone. The tall and skinny *gendarme*, who seemed to be in command, waited with his arms folded.

I heard *Oberleutnant* Wödl's authoritative voice in the earpiece of the phone in the *lamp-gendarme's* hand. "*Was! Was! Was fehlt Ihnen den?*"

"Your father… is he German?" stuttered the skinny one, his face suddenly pale.

"Yes," I answered, "an *Oberleutnant.*"

With a trembling hand, the *lamp-gendarme* passed me the receiver. As soon as he realized I was the one phoning, *Oberleutnant* Wödl wanted to know where I was. I didn't explain anything about the circumstances because he, as an officer, was very rigid and inflexible and had strong ideas regarding principles of military and civil justice. I continued, however, with my little comedy; I would give those *gendarmes* tit for tat. I held the earpiece a little way from my ear to make sure the *gendarmes* could hear what was being said. "I am at the *gendarmerie* because I have declared that I work for *Organisation Todt*," I said in German.

"Don't move! I will be there in a minute," the *Oberleutnant* said. I heard him calling his orderly: "Otto, Otto, come quickly!" The *gendarmes* heard him too, and though they couldn't understand his words, the *Oberleutnant's* tone told them that he was far from happy.

Assailed by a growing sense of panic, the *gendarmes* suddenly became much more affable. But it was too late. Their office was located on the second floor and, just minutes later, the boots of the *Oberleutnant* and his orderly stamped heavily on the stairs; and they were in a hurry. They burst into the office. *Oberleutnant* Wödl set his monocle over one eye, holding it with his thick eyebrow in a manner familiar to me, and asked, "Were you ill-treated?"

"No, but I've been here all day," I answered.

The *gendarmes* stood at attention, even though they didn't understand a word of German.

"You!" said the *Oberleutnant* pointing at the skinny one, "Do you want to be thrown into work making cement for the coastal defenses?"

As I translated, the *gendarmes* became even stiffer. The skinny commander mumbled, "No, no…ehm…there seems to have been a misunderstanding." Then, turning to me, continued, "Tell your…"

"Silence!" thundered the *Oberleutnant* . "Another word and I will send you to forced labour immediately. You scoundrels! Is it in this way you demonstrate your gratitude for all the work we do for you?"

I translated again and then I asked for my documents back. They rushed at once towards the desk, clumsily holding out what I requested. Otto stood looking on, his legs slightly apart, his arms folded. "My money, too," I said.

"Of course! We did not have any intention of keeping it," the commander apologized while his assistant quickly gave me the signed deposition which I put in my pocket.

"Good!" said *Oberleutnant* Wödl. "You have been warned!" He turned on his heels and marched out, followed by Otto.

Cowardice dulled the eyes of the *gendarmes*. I didn't say a word of criticism to them but the incident made me wonder which side I was on.

※—※

I spent the winter of 1943/44 working for *Organisation Todt* and then, in the spring, for a local engineering assembly company. Often, heated arguments about politics broke out, creating a tense and unpleasant atmosphere so, in April, I said goodbye to *Oberleutnant* Wödl, who suggested that I enlist in the German Army, which I was free to do since Prime Minister Laval had signed a decree in July 1943 allowing young Frenchmen to join *Waffen SS* units, the army of a 'New Europe'.

I took a train from Marseille, on the coast of the Mediterranean Sea, 600 kilometers north to Nancy, still undecided about my future. At the station in Nancy, crammed with civilians and German soldiers coming back from or going on leave with their pack-sacks bulging, there was the most incredible confusion. Porters, calling their clients, were barely able to move. Everybody yelled to make themselves heard over the babble of noise, a counterproductive response that only added to the chaos. The stationmaster had lost control.

As soon as a train arrived, everybody rushed to it, pushing furiously. A young mother jammed her foot on the wagon's footboard, letting her small son fall down to the platform. A *gendarme* selfishly tried to push past her while the stationmaster looked on, ignoring the child who was in danger of being separated from his mother. Silence followed two shots from a pistol; a *Luftwaffe* lieutenant put his smoking pistol in its holster then stepped forward to the wagon door to help the mother and son get inside. He then called the *gendarme*, saying, "It is not so difficult, after all, you see?" Encouraged by his calm smile, and by his watchful eyes, the passengers boarded the train in good order, without jostling.

I left the station thinking about that *Luftwaffe* lieutenant, his cool nerves and his display of authority in a difficult situation. Then, on a billboard, I noticed a poster with the headline: *'WITH YOUR EUROPEAN COMRADES, UNDER THE SS INSIGNIA YOU WILL WIN!'* And the more I thought of *Oberleutnant* Wödl's advice, the more sense it seemed to make.

❧—❧

At the *SS* recruiting office I was very well-received, but there was a snag: being still a minor, my recruiting papers had to be signed by one of my parents *and* it had to bear the stamp of the police superintendent closest to my village. A German officer gave me a route-paper for a two-way train ticket from Nancy to my home, and a pass as a soldier of the *Reich*.

In a waiting room at the station in Nancy, I was still mulling over the decision I had just taken when a man dressed in a leather coat caught my eye. He approached me bit by bit without raising undue attention and sat beside me. He offered me a cigarette and promptly I lit up his, thanking him.

"Out of work?" he asked, speaking with the cigarette moving in his mouth.

"At the moment," I answered.

"Travelling alone?"

"Yes."

"Interested in defending our Motherland from the invaders?" he asked point-blank, searching my eyes.

"And how?"

He took the cigarette from his mouth, rubbed his untidy beard and said: "Ever heard about..." he swallowed, taking a short pause: "...the Resistance?"

"*Maquis?*"

"Ssst!" The bearded man's eyes darted from side to side. "I see we understand each other."

"I'm too young."

"But no…we have messengers that are even younger than you and…"

"I can't." I interrupted, showing him the raised palm of my hands for good measure.

"Everybody says that at the beginning, it's natural. But think of this, it's a noble cause…"

"The fact is, I've just made up my mind," I answered, displaying under his nose my route-papers and my pass. "I'm enlisting in the German Army to fight for a different cause, a noble *European* cause."

Half an hour later I was striding proudly across the platform to a train bound for Longwy, to a wagon at the rear, reserved for German troops.

"Hei, you! Those cars are reserved for the *Boches*!" the French stationmaster scolded me, guessing my intentions. I went back on my steps, waved my pass under his nose. "I am one of them now," I told him in a calm voice. He made a hasty, awkward military salute, and then turned in the direction of the locomotive.

In the wagon, German soldiers were happy, singing and joking; that cheerful atmosphere enveloped my spirit. I was on the verge of manhood and all of a sudden had the right to other people's respect — even from a stationmaster.

Back home I explained to my father that I had found work, that I would learn to drive trucks in Germany. He signed my recruiting papers. At the police station it wasn't so easy: as I expected, they wanted to ask questions but I told them that I was in a hurry and risked missing the train. They stamped the necessary permit and let me go, but not without remarking about my young age.

The following day, the goodbyes to my family were brief. I shook hands with my friend Dodek, wishing him good luck — he had, he told me, chosen to fight for the Resistance.

On my route-paper, the next address was that of the Marine Ministry, Balard Square, in Paris. There, between medical checks, eating delicious soups at the mess and restful sleeps in the dormitory, I learned how to differentiate between the various traits of character amongst the volunteers: there were skilled, small-time thieves; intellectuals; farmers; adventurers; pimps and veteran police inspectors.

During the frequent night-time air raids, English planes launched phosphorous rockets in order to illuminate bombing targets. German anti-aircraft cannons, aided by searchlight beams, promptly responded to the threat. Civilians took refuge in underground shelters — the one in Balard Square had a steel door that closed automatically. Inside, an elevator descended deep underground, to the lower floors which were equipped with air conditioning. There was an occasional day-time alarm too, with sirens giving their warning with ear-piercing, prolonged wails. Each room in the shelter was crammed with up to twenty people. Once inside, I couldn't wait to escape the claustrophobic atmosphere.

Our departure from Paris took place at the Oriental Station. Representatives of civilian authorities and officers in German military uniform with medals on their chests gathered around us, the recruits, speaking in French while a photographer was busy taking snapshots of us before we boarded a train that would carry us to Sennheim. Singing broke out amongst the recruits; some of them made faces and hurled insults at the stationmaster as we were photographed. Others scribbled on the wagons' walls. Rations, which included bottles of wine, were distributed at the last moment and so the racket increased. I stood apart, not appreciating at all that kind of misbehaviour.

From Thann to Sennheim

I arrived by train at Thann, 13 May 1944, at fifteen years and ten days old, and was immediately attached to a gathering of Belgian, Flemish and Dutch recruits, some wearing camouflage clothing. We were arranged in groups according to nationality and everyone received an old First World War uniform to wear. Thereafter, because the Sankt Andreas camp near Thann camp did not have mess facilities, we marched to the base at Sennheim for soup. This march served as a training starter and a means to 'stretch one's legs'.

Our every action was conducted under strict and omnipresent discipline. Waiting for the soup, aligned in squads at the mess' entry, we looked forward to our turn in silence while remaining nearly still alongside squads of German soldiers from the *Kriegsmarine* and *Waffen SS* who had, naturally, priority. In the mess, the long tables, each accommodating about twenty men, were filled in a hurry by young soldiers with healthy appetites: the white, one-and-a-half-liter ceramic bowls held a very hot soup made from tomatoes, potatoes, lentils, carrots and grated bread.

The Alsatian attendants in the kitchen were good cooks, despite being detainees serving out their sentences by working at the pots. We, Thann's recruits, had to eat quickly in order to vacate our places for the following squads but, before leaving, we cleaned the table to leave it as spotless as we had found it. Once outside we aligned in formation and, singing, marched towards the Sankt Andreas camp, a few kilometers away. As soon as we arrived at the camp, our stomachs were already empty. I was still hungry and would have gulped down with pleasure another bowl of that soup before we began group discussions followed by hours dedicated to gymnastics, theory, explanation of the *Waffen SS* hierarchy and the drill commands given by non-commissioned officers.

In the evening there was a distribution of bread with margarine and two cigarettes. I was carefree and happy in the pure air of that camp at Thann but the pre-training lasted only about ten days before we made our last march to the Sennheim base. Like all other recruits, I too was visibly skinnier. I had shed several kilos but my shoulder muscles and biceps remained the same as before — rather well-developed for a fifteen-year old. I was tall with black hair and eyes the colour of dark amber.

At the Sennheim base, the command formed new companies and assigned us to dormitories in the barracks. These had an entry door and, opposite, an exit one; there were douches and toilets. On the wooden bunk beds lay mattresses wrapped in sheets and sleeping bags coloured with narrow white and blue stripes. In every dormitory there was a metal coffee pot and a flask with a handle and a large flared spout for tea. The orderly *Sturmmann* watched over the corvée soldiers whose duty was to fill up the refreshment pots in the morning, after cleaning the dormitory. When they issued mess tins, I noticed that mine was not clean; here and there it still had traces of grease and those of my companions were in the same poor condition. Without hesitation, we went to the courtyard in search of a handful of sand to scrape the mess tins properly and to rinse them under the outdoor taps. I was surprised at this little setback; at the base everything was tidy and cleanness reigned supreme. This might have been, on the other hand, a ploy to test us, since inspections were frequent and rigorous — as I would find out during one of the first evenings, at bed time.

An U.v.D., or orderly non-commissioned officer — pronounced by us as *uvedé* — waited patiently while a corvée soldier counted the number of recruits present in the dormitory. On hearing that everything was as it should be, the *uvedé* slowly moved, checking to the right and left, between two rows of soldiers standing at attention. He touched the knuckles of a hand on the mattresses, examined the uniform of a companion and then arrived at the window where he ran a finger over the sill, looking for dust. He came back towards the center of the room, stopped in front of a locker and opened it. There was a total and grave silence. The *uvedé* pulled out a heavy belt and threw it to the floor, then a shirt, a pair of pants and other clothing. "All badly arranged!" he said in a disparaging, irritated voice. Raising his tone and assuming an imperious stance, he ordered the guilty soldier: "Face to the floor!"

The unfortunate recruit immediately complied.

The *uvedé* stared into the soldiers' eyes as he paced between the two rows and said: "If there is a night air-raid you won't waste time searching if everything is in order. Push-ups… for everybody!"

We threw our hands forwards, lay on the floor and continued to perform the exercise until ordered to stop.

The *uvedé* returned to the door, looked at us sternly and said before leaving, "Strip all cots…dormitory review in precisely ten minutes."

Frenetically, we worked around the bunk beds.

"Nothing is ever perfect here," someone blurted.

"Perfection is a rare thing," somebody with a calm voice answered from the opposite bunk bed.

"Quick! Hurry up!" the corvée soldier urged.

All this was to prove as nothing in comparison to the test we had to pass the following day. We were warned to prepare ourselves for tank training.

A Test of Nerve

They called it the 'nerve test'. Nearby there was a large field with some casemates where they selected the best soldiers, the most courageous ones.

"Dig the deepest hole you can…as fast as you can…and keep your heads down," the *Sturmmann* instructor yelled.

They had thrown into our hands a short shovel — the rest was left to individual ability and creativity. In the background a tank manoeuvered, its powerful engine roaring as it accelerated in bursts. Plumes of dirty smoke snorted from its exhaust pipe, reminding me of a furious, charging bull. A doubt, a weakening of my resolve, flitted through my mind but I discarded it immediately, paying attention instead to the shivers of dread running down my back. We waited for the command to start digging. I was clasping the shovel's short handle, thinking that the farmers among us would have a good advantage but nevertheless sure that anxiety weighed on all our faces in equal measure.

The *Sturmmann* instructor gave us another prolonged look, perhaps to make sure that nobody would give up at the last moment and scoot off. As usual, the wait was longer than necessary. This had become a common feature of life inside or outside base; often we stood for hours waiting for someone or something. By now we were used to it but here, in front of that tank, there was no evident reason to prolong the wait. Beads of sweat from my forehead ran down my cheeks to be absorbed by the leather of my helmet's chinstrap. *They want to wear your nerves down even before starting the ordeal*, I thought but I was determined to go through this test, at any price. I would show everybody how much valour was packed into my fifteen years. Didn't I volunteer to go to the very end? I would become a model soldier; that I was determined to achieve. Someone might lose their nerve but it wouldn't be me. I would stay in the hole I was about to dig even at the cost of hearing the tank's tracks rolling over my helmet. I wanted to be among the chosen ones, among those who would be destined to participate in special missions.

My companions and I, lined up in the middle of the field with shovels in our hands, had been previously picked and represented only a small part of the entire company. Those who did not feel up to this test were not forced to endure it.

The *Sturmmann* instructor gave the signal to begin with a wave of a red flag. The tank shook with a muffled vibration as its metal tracks clanged over pebbles and hard soil before stopping abruptly about one hundred meters from our group with a slight bow forwards, as if to offer us a sort of salute. Then I noticed some holes on the tank's armoured body, under the turret, which were probably the scars of past battles.

The *Sturmmann* instructor pulled out a small notebook and a short pencil from his shirt pocket while the waiting tank maintained its engine revs at a constant and high level, ready to leap forward. Tension filled the air like an electric force-field. We had been positioned in two straight rows, spaced at regular intervals from one another, and there we had to dig around our assigned spots. My foxhole would be one of the first to be run over.

The *Sturmmann* waved his red flag once more, yelling at the top of his lungs over the engine's rumble, "*Los!*"

We sprang into action in unison, digging and shovelling wildly. The veins in my wrists stood out, bulging with the frantic effort.

The tank began its slow approach, rectifying its direction by slightly lifting its rear-track treads, from which it sent out a stream of soil and dust. I jabbed at the ground with the tip of my shovel, throwing the soil behind my back. The ground was soft enough on top but deeper down it was compacted and harder to dig. I heard only the roar of the engine and the screech of the tank's tracks, hardly daring to cast a glance at that steel monster —there was no time for that! I rammed the shovel into the earth again and again.

The metallic clanging of the tracks drew closer, sounded more strident. My heart throbbed almost out of control; the veins at my wrists were on the verge of bursting. A few more seconds and the tank would be on top of me. I lobbed another blow with the shovel, then another, again, and then a last stab before tossing it away at the last second. I crouched in the pit gasping for breath, sucking dust into my dry mouth. I cast a quick glance at the cold nose of the tank but when the shadow of its cannon fell across me, I pressed my body to the bottom of my refuge as if my life depended on it. A deafening roar passed above. I pulled on the rim of my helmet, forcing it down onto my head. My knees pressed into the fresh soil, as if about to take root, burrowing deeper. Darkness! I closed my eyelids, wringing them tight. The ground trembled. As the interminable seconds went by, the dry soil around the margins of my hole collapsed and flowed into it, falling onto my back and shoulders, a suffocating, heavy, pressure. The soil had the smell of clay, a kind of freshness — *maybe that was the sensation felt by the dead when they were being buried*, I thought. After a few moments, I could bear the unpleasant feeling no longer; I needed to breathe the fresh air. I managed to move with some effort, pushing with my knees until I forced my body into the open air. I shook off the soil and dust as I cast a glance back-wards, towards the rumbling tank which was running above the last of the foxholes. One of its tracks had left a clear imprint on the loose soil, before and after my pit. The test was finished.

I breathed deeply but was happy and proud as I walked towards the edge of the field where I lined up with the others, some of whom still clung to their shovels. A few bled from minor wounds to their arms but every face was made pale by dust-encrusted sweat.

The *Sturmmann* instructor looked at us with a half-smile on his lips, a little flicker of pride in his men.

Kameraderie

Our training became ever more demanding and we were kept busy with one exercise or another; grenade launching, target practice, assaults with bare hands. And then there was the marching — often at a brisk pace and more than thirty kilometers a day — in full kit including helmet, rifle, bayonet, full ammunition pouches and infantry packsack. The first time we returned to the barracks after such an outing, we were dusty and tired from the heavy load and long kilometers. As evening fell, our company drew near the small city of Sennheim, our helmets scratched and nicked as a result of impacts from the debris thrown up from grenade explosions during training.

"Almost home, at last," Martin, a companion marching at my side, said. I had known him since the first days after enlisting. When he arrived in Thann, he was rather skinny and frail with jug-handle ears covered in small, blue veins. With his timid glances and hunched shoulders he seemed much shorter than I in spite of a marginal difference in height. However, after a short period at the base, his physical appearance improved visibly: now he had strong-looking muscles and a rosy complexion. Out of uniform, before going to bed, he appeared younger than his years but one could see that he was perfectly fit and of acceptable appearance. More or less of the same age, we talked often.

"I can't wait to take off my boots," I replied.

When the soldiers marching at the front of our column reached the first houses, the heavy sound of our footsteps attracted the citizens' attention; some leaned from their windows to watch as we passed while others stood at the entrance of their houses, the doors ajar behind them. Suddenly the battalion's brass band appeared alongside and began to play the march *Lisa Lisa* while we marked time, singing, in order to let the musicians parade in ahead and lead us into the base.

"Hei Paul!" Martin said, smiling in response to the melody.

I too let the music pour into my soul, lift my spirit, restore my aching muscles. I forgot about the sores on my heels and returned Martin's smile. Reinvigorated by the music — especially by the following piece, *Erika*, — we glowed with undisguised pride as we marched past the admiring onlookers. With our heads held high, we crossed the town, our energetic and resolute steps resounding over the cobbled streets in unison with the march-time beat of our brass band. Among the crowd on both sides there were many old folks who, hesitant at first, saluted us by stretching their right arms forward.

"We're making a good impression, don't you think?" Martin said with satisfaction.

"It is a good show for the locals," I answered.

On the courtyard at the base, the last notes vanished, drowned by the order to dismiss, absorbed by the enveloping sunset. Once in the dormitories, we went immediately to wash our feet while a nurse went about with scissors and a small bottle of tincture of iodine in his hands.

"Ah, what a relief," I sighed, lying down on the cot.

"Ooh," Martin echoed from the bunk above me as he caressed his toes.

"And now Gosse, it's rifle-cleaning time," said another companion, Jean, rising from his cot.

Jean and Gosse occupied the bunk beds beside Martin and me and had become our friends; we understood each other well, the four of us, and not only because we were all under age. Jean was as tall as I, with curly, copper-coloured hair and inquisitive eyes that were always in motion. His hint of a double chin was covered with sparse hair he defined as a 'beard in waiting' and his nose was straight and protruding—a mathematician's nose he once said. In fact, he had studied for a few months more than I did and was very intelligent, always ready to come up with an answer to any problem. Gosse, on the other hand, bragged about his street-smart experience and his well-developed common sense, which he claimed made up for his lack of studying. Olive skinned and dark haired, Gosse was robust and well-muscled. Everything about him gave the impression of an accomplished rascal.

"I'm still deafened by the explosions of the grenades," Jean said, inserting the index finger of one hand into an ear and slapping his head with the palm of the other hand. Satisfied by our good performance during the training exercises earlier in the day, before marching back to camp, we all enjoyed Jean's comical demonstration as we cleaned our rifles.

"I almost left the skin of my hands on the red-hot barrel of that MG 42," I said.

"Misery! Those barrels really can cause painful burns," Gosse added, showing us a livid tract of skin on his wrist.

"Yes, but when the hot barrel is substituted, it is a good and reliable weapon," said Jean, who was already an expert on firearms. "That's it," he declared, finishing his rifle-cleaning.

In a little more than a minute we too disassembled the trigger housing, stock, bolt, barrel and other parts our Mauser rifles. After cleaning and oiling certain parts we reassembled them with mechanical-like movements of our hands. During training, we studied the Mauser's mechanisms in minute detail, even before receiving them from the armoury, and soon learned to strip and assemble the whole thing in a few seconds while blindfolded.

After cleaning our rifles, we hurried down to the mess for the evening distribution of bread and cheese before returning to the dormitories.

"*Achtung*!" somebody shouted just as we were preparing to go to bed.

A *Hauptsturmführer* from another company came in. "At ease!" he said when he saw us standing at attention.

As we returned to our leisure activities, our eyes were drawn towards a soldier sitting on his cot near the window. He opened a felt case and took from it a violin.

"Well, Joseph, what will you play?" asked the *Hauptsturmführer*.

"A waltz?" Joseph proposed. He was a model soldier, attentive, diligent, polite and well-learned, who commanded everybody's attention when he spoke and, with these attributes, he reminded me a little of Jean.

The *Hauptsturmführer* sat on a cot nearby and beat time with his foot as Joseph played. The sweet and vibrant notes reached all corners of the dormitory, drawing us closer to their source, inviting us to sit near, some smoking cigarettes, others sipping wine from a bottle passed among us.

"Slower Joseph," the *Hauptsturmführer* said, "the Viennese waltz has to be played slowly."

We listened in perfect silence until the end of the piece, and then it was the officer's turn to play. This happened frequently and the two soldiers, although separated by around ten grades on the military hierarchy, clearly enjoyed each other's company and mutual enthusiasm for good music.

The following day I struggled to pull my boots over my blistered feet before rushing down to the muster and flag-raising ritual. After a few steps I felt better, although my feet were still smarting.

"Form ranks! Move!" an *Unterscharführer* yelled, in an unyielding voice. He ordered us to attention, to stand at ease, march, mark time, repeating the orders until growing tired of yelling. He turned to the *uvedé* , a *Scharführer* who also was responsible for company liaison duties and who recorded in his black booklet anything unusual, including incidents that took place during the previous night. As if expecting someone, the *Scharführer* turned to look towards the guardroom near the entrance of the base. From it came a *Hauptsturmführer*. Resolute and stiff, he strode towards us followed by a civilian who, dressed in worn-out clothes and clasping his Basque beret in his hands, hurried on behind with timid steps. The civilian was, it was clear even from a distance, a good and humble man who felt extremely uncomfortable on finding himself in the midst of the flag-raising ceremony. When the *Hauptsturmführer* stopped abruptly in front of our ranks, the *Scharführer* saluted. In the background the civilian, hesitant and awkward, moved back a few steps and waited. Now that he was closer I could sense the man's fear. *Perhaps he was a prisoner*, I thought, *one of the many Maquis captured during recent search operations and transferred to the guardhouse on our base.* Incidentally, on one of these operations, a comrade nicknamed Tyrol disarmed a *Maquis* by confiscating his 7.65 calibre pistol. With the excuse of examining the weapon, or rather with the intention of trying it out, Tyrol accidentally let go a shot that grazed his own belly. Of course he was awarded the *Verwundetenabzeichen* (wound medal) but one with the helmet effigy only — the two crossed bayonets had been removed because the wound was not inflicted during combat.

The *Scharführer* saluted again. "Ready for flag-raising."

The unfurled standard touched the top of the flagpole making the upper cord-ring tinkle in the wind. At the end of the ceremony we stood aligned, at stand easy. "Ahem… hem…." The *Hauptsturmführer* cleared his throat, evidently very annoyed at having to wait. He acknowledged the civilian's presence by turning almost imperceptibly towards him. "Somebody asked to see me this morning, and for a valid reason," the *Hauptsturmführer* continued, "this farmer, a good Alsatian civilian, complained about broken cherry-tree branches and insists that the persons responsible are among you."

A heavy silence reigned among the squads.

"Guilty persons — one step forward," snapped the *Scharführer*.

I rolled my eyes without turning my face, curious to see who would accept the accusation. *Ahi, ahi*, I thought, *forget about the stolen cherries but the broken branches, now that's a different matter. Any farmer would be furious…no cherries the following year.*

The Alsatian farmer's knees touched, his legs now trembling for all to see; perhaps he had dared too much.

"You see!" the *Hauptsturmführer* concluded with a firm voice, "I know my men…if they were at fault, well, they would have denounced themselves." He turned to the farmer, the palms of his hands upturned. "This is all I can do for you."

The poor farmer apologized by mumbling some broken words, then left in a hurry to be out of that excruciating situation.

The incident seemed closed, at least from the civilian's point of view. However the *Scharführer*, boiling with anger, warned us with a resentful and harsh voice. "I know that the guilty ones are among you. You have until evening muster to come forward."

The following eight days were gruelling and miserable. Alarms sounded night and day and we spent the time endlessly running and assembling ready for action. Equipment inspections were held twice nightly. The *Scharführer* commanded us directly though even an *Unterscharführer* wouldn't have bothered with such a trifling matter… *and* he wore a smile when he warned us that he was in no hurry to resolve the matter. On the ninth day, during morning muster and after the flag-raising ceremony, the same *Hauptsturmführer* cleared his throat once more and said: "I know that you are good soldiers, the punishment is lifted. I would like to know, however, and only for my personal interest, which squad was responsible for breaking those branches."

The silence among us seemed almost an act of defiance.

"You have my word as an officer that nothing will happen to you."

Still no one stepped forward.

"Very well," said the *Hauptsturmführer,* but let me say that I am nevertheless proud to be a commander of soldiers such as you. Dismiss!"

Amidst our chatter and the clanging of our equipment, we went towards the barracks passing close by the officer who I heard say to the *Scharführer*: "This is what I call good, healthy comradeship and bonding, typical among us, *Waffen SS.*"

The *Scharführer,* not at all convinced by his superior's assertion, made an effort to agree and saluted.

Oath Under Fire

"I swear to you, Adolf Hitler, as *Führer* and *Reich* Chancellor, faithfulness and valour. I solemnly promise..."

The growl of a Merlin engine rattled the air, deepening in tone as the Spitfire swept past low over the courtyard of our base at Sennheim

"...to you as our chief, obedience until death, with the help of..."

The Spitfire swooped again, this time firing its machine guns. Bullets ricocheted from the ground, their trajectories intersecting in mid-air as they whizzed between the officers in the visitors' stand and us, the perfectly aligned new soldiers of the *Reich*.

Engine revving, the plane effortlessly gained height.

Our formation, standing motionless, seemed like a colossal mechanism, jammed at that moment, with every recruit bearing his rifle in the 'present arms' position. I had the feeling that my companions' inscrutable eyes, in the shade of their helmets, were, like mine, following the plane's maneuver. In front of the visitors' stand, undaunted, an officer climbed up to a podium, ready to deliver his speech at the end of our swearing-in ceremony.

Now a mere dot in the sky, the plane turned. Screaming like an angry gnat, it plunged towards us again. "Damn!" I whispered with good cause — I was in the rank on the most exposed side.

"Cursed English pilot!" I heard someone behind say, gritting his teeth.

I had the strange idea that a bullet would hit my back. I tried to hold back the anxiety that came over me in surges, starting in my legs. In spite of being of the same height as the soldiers around me, it seemed that I had forced myself to become as small and incon-spicuous as possible, to seek protection among my immediate companions.

The plane's machine guns flashed. Bullets rained down in a fan-like pattern, tearing the air, lifting debris and dust that followed their slipstreams after ricocheting from the ground around the stand. An instant later, the plane's fleeting shadow fell across the visi-tors, momentarily dimming the glitter of the decorations on their chests.

I mentally examined my body: there was no pinpoint, burning pain from my back, no stinging sensation. The tension left my shoulders. I always believed that I would be able to react and survive were I hit in front, or in the arms or legs — it was a personal conviction of mine.

A hail of bullets burst against the nearby tower above which flew two flags — one with a cross, the other bearing the white *SS Sigrun* on a black ground. The two sentries were still there, as if nailed to their platform, silhouetted against the sky, as impassive as ever.

The airplane began to turn back towards us once more. A subdued murmur among the officers revealed their concern.

Our eyes focused on the base's anti-aircraft emplacement which, to our relief, began to fire. The plane's wings shook as if troubled by a violent gust of wind. Its engine screamed as the pilot sought the safety of height before drifting away, zigzagging lightly on the air. The officer on the podium continued his speech, ending it by reminding us about the inherent significance of the ceremony. His clear and curt words resonated from a loudspeaker: "You have become *Waffen SS*, unconditionally, for the 'New Europe'. You are tied by the sacred bond of your oath to the *Führer* until death." The officer stretched his arm forward. "*Heil* Hitler!"

"*Heil!*" we responded with a yell that rang more vehemently than usual; a release of the pent-up tension of the previous moments. Even among the officers, some still-pale faces seemed to display the desire to be somewhere else, oath to the *Führer* or not.

"Right form! March forward!" a non-commissioned officer yelled, stressing the cadence, "*links... links... zwei, drei, vier, links...*" The first platoon led the way, the second followed and so on. As I marched in perfect synchrony with my companions, towards the dormito-ries, a jumble of thoughts occupied my mind; I was confident that I would perform well as a soldier of the *Waffen SS* having successfully completed my training at Thann and at the Sennheim base but was nevertheless aware that the situation I was about to enter would be far more serious than anything I had so far encountered in my young life.

New Friends

After the completion of the swearing-in ceremony, the base was swarming with officers and there was the possibility of being found too slow to salute them properly and in accordance with the regulations. To avoid this, and any consequential punishment, I thought it prudent during my time off-duty to visit the nearby town. I hoped to encounter my three friends in the courtyard but met only with Martin.

"*Ohilà*, Paul! Are you going out?" he asked, approaching me with his head held high, proud and smiling. "I'll keep you company if you are."

"I was thinking of it. But where are Jean and Gosse?"

"Jean prefers to read in his cot and Gosse said he needed to take a rest. I bet he's still in fear of that English plane."

"Well, to tell you the truth I was afraid too," I admitted.

"We have our passes and our uniforms are impeccable," Martin said, "surely we'll be allowed to pass the guard post this time."

As we approached the entrance to the base, the sentry stepped down from the doorstep of the guard hut to place himself at the center of the cobbled exit, waiting for us, his legs straddled. "Halt!" he said in an assertive voice. He examined our uniforms from head to foot without complaint, nodded with satisfaction when he saw the shine on our boots. "Stand at ease...your passes," he said, holding forth his hand.

We presented our *Soldbücher*, our military identity booklets, to the sentry who leafed through them briefly. Then, obeying the sentry's orders, we completed turns to the left and to the right and saluted the guards as we passed through the main entrance onto the street. Usually there was a small train transporting soldiers to town; we had taken it a while earlier to go watch a tightrope-walker who crossed the main square on a rope stretched between the bell tower and the tallest house on the opposite side. But there was no train on this occasion so we set off on foot. Martin rummaged in one of his pockets, found two cigarettes and offered me one.

"Thanks. Did you trade your candies for tobacco?" I asked.

"Two handfuls — half my ration," he answered, coming close while shielding his words with a hand held at the side of his mouth in a conspiratorial way. "I almost gathered an entire pack of cigarettes." He struck a match on the sole of his boot, lit my cigarette and then his own. We walked side by side in silence, inhaling the smoke as if we enjoyed it. Being so young, we were issued special rations which didn't include cigarettes and so we traded bread, honey, butter and candies for tobacco.

"Did you have any problems enlisting?" I asked. The minimum required age was seventeen and Martin was just sixteen.

"No! I'm a son of Mother France… no parents, no relatives, no need of their signatures on forms. Simple, eh? And you…your parents have signed for you, no?"

"Of course! My father's an Italian immigrant…he signed because he doesn't know German," I replied, chuckling. "I told him they needed his authorization because I wanted to learn how to drive trucks. Luckily my mother was not at home…she works with a *Todt* unit as a maid and cook and speaks and writes perfect German…she was born and raised in Germany.

"Never knew my parents," Martin said. "And I don't care neither!" he added with a shrug.

"Before the war my father applied for French naturalization but was always refused… then as soon as the war started *gendarmes* arrived on our doorstep asking him to sign the papers to become a full French citizen. My mother — you should have seen her — she sprang up like a viper saying to them that if her husband was not worthy of citizenship before, he wouldn't sign the forms now. She's a woman of exceptionally strong character and very proud."

"Huh! She did right, answering in such way to them pimps. All they wanted was to slam your papa into the front line, and all for a lousy signature on a piece of lousy paper. Are you their only son?"

"No, at home we were a big family, that is if you include my grandparents who live with us," I explained.

"Your grandparents are from the German side?"

"My grandpa served with the German Army and when he was a bit tipsy he used to sing in his language on the streets of Longwy and at Villerupte-Cantebonne, where my family lives now, in Lorena."

"Ah…a few steps from the Maginot Line," Martin said.

Martin hadn't learnt that information on the school benches, if he ever went to school. He had, I think, recalled the observation of a non-commissioned officer who had asked me about my village one day in the courtyard at Sankt Andreas. "Exactly!" I confirmed. "And the store keepers gave him credit for bottles of Schnapps because they were picking his brains, asking what would happen when the war started. And so my grandpa was continuously gulping down the stuff — he knew very well that he wouldn't have to pay. In fact, he incurred debts everywhere because war was imminent."

"Well done! Very well done!" Martin, amused by the idea, quipped. "A good lesson for those parasites!"

"Grandma was full of rage at his behaviour, especially when people came to ask him for advice. Everybody feared the worst but grandpa told them to wait for the Germans."

"What a guy!"

"The villagers were always asking him questions...when should we leave, when do you expect an invasion, where should we go? Grandpa told them that when the Belgians passed through, the Germans wouldn't be too far behind. If one had to die, he said, it was better to stay at home tasting good wine and not kicking the bucket on a road, like a beast."

"The old guy was right," Martin said, flicking his cigarette butt to the roadside. "Good for him! Ah, we're almost there...now it will be our turn to drink some beer," he said, nodding towards a bar on the town square.

People were crowding around the tables set outside. We sat facing the street so we could see the pretty girls pass by. The fresh foam at the brim of our beer jugs moistened our lips, dry from the long walk. We sipped silently, relaxing on the comfortable little chairs, watching and following the coming and going in front of us. Many passers-by saluted us; some lifted their hats, others nodded their heads but the girls, they gave us short but frequent glances of admiration.

"Now I feel like a real man," Martin exclaimed emphatically as a girl caught his eye.

"It's the uniform," I said, "it creates a good impression."

"Being treated with respect...that's what is needed!" Martin said, tapping a hand on the table top. After another sip of beer he continued in a low, determined voice, "Never ever... never ever stray like a dog. I've had enough of that life...the wooden clogs, the rags for clothes, the continuous humiliation. Anything might happen to me but I will not return to that!"

"I understand," I said. "Dignity is a very important thing to a man and as long as we wear these uniforms, you will never lose it."

"Dignity," Martin smiled bitterly, lighting another cigarette, the muscles of his face flickering with a series of nervous twitches, "lost it long ago...at the orphanage. The food...when there was any...was revolting. And then, I thought I had escaped the shrew without scruples. She used me, made me toil with a bent back in the fields from daybreak till dusk without a drop of water...the bastard!" Martin made a show of gulping down several mouthfuls of his beer, almost as if to challenge onlookers from preventing him doing as he pleased. "To be free and respected...that's all I want from life," he said, flicking his cigarette butt into the middle of the street.

"I'm with you my friend...one hundred percent with you!" I assured him.

"As far as I recall, the first hot and satisfying meal I ever ate was given to me at the base, my first cigarettes too...and shoes. I get paid decent money and can spend it as I want. All these things are mine now and nobody can take them away from me."

"It's the same for me...at least with the pay, I mean."

"I know nothing about politics and care even less about them," Martin went on, sipping beer, "but my salvation occurred because of a billboard. I was exhausted and hungry and hardly able to read it because of painful stomach cramps. I could not believe what it said. Then I stepped back to read it again, trying to comprehend. I was tired of eating fruits from trees and stealing bowls of food from dogs just to avoid starving to death."

"Go on," I encouraged, moved by his story.

"And then I thought about the institution, the orphans, the wardens, the nuns and priests…and the *gendarmes*. Hah! I could see myself in place of the soldier on the bill-board. What ill could the *gendarmes* do to me then, I thought?"

I sipped my beer. "So you decided to enlist?"

"I ran to the nearest recruiting office. It's the best thing I've ever done in my life."

"It was a billboard that attracted my attention too. It began: 'WITH YOUR…'"

Martin waved a finger from side to side, as if scolding a mistake. "No, no. The one I saw said 'YOU TOO!' Sure, sure, me too, I thought, why not? 'YOUR COMRADES ARE WAITING FOR YOU IN THE FRENCH DIVISION OF THE *WAFFEN SS*'. And it proved to be true."

Stable Duty

Taking the *SS* oath marked the end of the greater part of our training. We no longer had to sit in the open listening to an instructor's efforts to explain the laws and principles of eugenics and tell stories about the *Führer's* youth, the First World War and contemporary history. The days spent perfecting our marching were now only a faint memory and soldiers who made a mockery of themselves during drill maneuvers now had reason to breathe more easily. The only inconvenience keeping us on our toes was the presence of the many officers who we had to salute promptly to avoid the risk of being punished for lack of respect.

The base commander at Sennheim was Heinrich Hersche, recently promoted to the grade of *Obersturmbannführer*. This fellow — a man of few words, a cavalryman from the 'old guard', tall and wiry with a face criss-crossed by authoritarian wrinkles — used to ride often, returning at any hour of night or day. He was in the habit of showing up without warning, obliging everyone to snap to attention. One early morning, while I was on corvée duty to the dormitory, he appeared suddenly in front of me when I opened a window that, like all the rest, had been covered with black paper to keep us invisible from the night fighters. "*Achtung!*" I shouted in shocked surprise. The few soldiers who were awake dropped what they were doing and the others, combatting the lingering desire for sleep, jumped up to attention from their cots wearing only their underwear.

"Relax! Carry on!" said our venerable commander in his strongly nasal voice before simply walking away.

With the end of training came new tasks, one of which was looking after the horses. This work was given to the youngest soldiers so Martin, Jean, Gosse and I found ourselves posted to the stables which housed around forty magnificent specimens. Some of the horses carried a mark in the form of an oak leaf — these were animals reserved for the higher officer grades. Each of us was now responsible for the daily care of one or two of these magnificent animals and I found myself in charge of *Obersturmbannführer* Hersche's pure-bred.

The German stablemen briefed us about the routine — or perhaps more accurately the ritual — we were to follow. In the morning, the horses were to be groomed until not a speck of dust remained on their hair. This was achieved by first currying the horse's coat; the stiff curry comb loosened the dried-in dirt and mud on the coat and spread the skin's natural oils. Then the coat was brushed — always in the direction of the hair growth — with a bristled brush. Finally, a softer brush settled the hairs and soothed the horse before the mane and tail were combed. This grooming process was followed by an inspection of the hooves for small stones which if present were removed. The animal's eyes and ears were then examined for the first signs of problems and the teeth were checked and cleaned to remove the remains of grass or hay. This process was repeated diligently after the horse had been worked. After a couple of days, the four of us were experts in the art of equine maintenance, an activity that we found most enjoyable.

During daily practices, the horses were let out in groups in the morning, afternoon and evening and, because the brass band members rehearsed on the other side of the wall separating the stables from the rest of the building, they liked to move in time to the music. Gosse too enjoyed the music, often joining with a favorite melody by singing very loudly… toreador, tatata-tata, toreador tatata-tata. To finish off the daily exercises, we took the horses for a trot around a circular track then for canter along a straight course.

In the evening, after a long shower, tired but satisfied, we returned to the dormitory to pass around a small bottle of Nivea cream which we rubbed into the bruises picked up during the day.

"Ah! This is what I call life," Martin sighed, stretched out on his cot, drawing the smoke of a cigarette deep into his lungs.

"It isn't too bad if it keeps going like this," Jean said.

"You doubt that it will?" I asked.

"Well, as long as it lasts, we must make the best of it," Gosse added.

Our lives continued on this pleasant course, day after day, repeating the ritual, sometimes with quiet moments spent sitting on hay bales after exercising the last group of horses.

At first I thought the rumbling noise was distant thunder. Then the alarm rang and I looked up, into the blue of the sky, through the open door of the stable. American fighter planes were closing quickly. They tipped their wings as they drew near, one after the other, breaking from their tight formation to swoop like hunting raptors. Flashes of fire danced on the leading edges of their wings; the high-pitched crackle of their machine guns penetrating the roar of the engines. They spat bullets over the road, 800m from our base, riddling a military convoy and nearby civilian vehicles. Amidst explosions and smoke, survivors ran towards the edges of the road, trying to dodge the storm of bullets from successive waves of attack. Satisfied with their work on the convoy, the planes then lifted their noses and veered tightly towards our base. Streams of bullets raced over the courtyard unzipping with ease, it seemed, the hard surface. Fragments of stone flew in the air. Bullets, distorted by the impact, ricocheted in cacophony of whines and screams. Our tethered horses caracoled nervously, tugging at their reins tied to wooden bars in the stable; those of the non-commissioned officers were separated only by ropes and so were bumping into each other at their shoulders and flanks and becoming more and more skittish.

"Untie the ropes!" Jean shouted.

"Cut them! Cut them!" I shouted, running towards the frightened animals. There was not a second to spare.

"*Alé, alé*! This way…you're free now," Martin said as he released the first horse.

"Easy, handsome, calm down," Gosse said to soothe another. "I'll take you out…good boy."

In a mad rush I helped free several horses and then, clicking my tongue in order to soothe *Obersturmbannführer* Hersche's pure-bred, I grabbed his reins and mounted him by standing on the wooden dividers. I directed him outside, pushing among the others, pressing against the flanks of Gosse's horses.

Gosse looked at me and said: "Heck! It had to happen right now didn't it…I've just finished currying them."

"Go, go!" I yelled above the neighing of the spooked, close-to-panic-stricken animals.

Finally we were in the open. We spread out in a fan-like shape, galloping unrestrained towards the road. I kept my head low, hunched over the back of my pure-bred, conforming to his gait as he galloped in great strides.

"Look out Paul!" Jean shouted.

I dodged the fender of a charging truck by a hair's breadth when my horse jumped onto the road but he continued in full gallop towards the cover of the nearby woods. The horses were still frightened because our anti-aircraft pieces were firing but they would soon be in the thick of the woods, where they would feel reassured. Only when I felt the first low branches scratch my helmet, did I pull on the reigns to slacken my horse's pace.

"That was close," Martin said, pairing next to me.

The drone of aircraft engines faded into the distance.

"Hell! I don't like it at all...this riding without saddles," grumbled Gosse as he too drew alongside. He looked around. "Where's Jean?"

We had slowed to a trot but the horses were still panting, shaking their heads, still agitated. A wheeze came from the wide-open mouth of Jean's horse as he came out from the shrubs to join us. I whispered in one ear of my pure-bred in an effort to calm him down; he stopped and puffed noisily from his dilated nostrils. I dismounted and caressed his flank which was covered with foamy sweat, ripples ran across his hide. "Poor beast, you're still trembling," I said in a soothing tone.

"We have to hurry to round up the strays, it'll be dark soon," urged Jean, his voice hoarse from shouting during the attack.

We returned to the stables in good order in spite of the debris strewn on the road and pungent smoke billowing from numerous burning vehicles. The horses went to their individual stalls practically by themselves, their legs still trembling, their muscles rippling in sudden shivers.

"Ah, more work," Gosse said.

"Yeah! Brush work!" I said, laughing. "It'll help them to settle."

A *Sturmmann* appeared in the open doorway. "There's a mare struggling outside, she's with her colt...one of you, quickly."

"I'll go," I offered. I had seen them earlier and had an idea of their whereabouts.

"Make sure everything is in order for inspection as soon as possible," the *Sturmmann* added as I passed.

I went around a group of prisoners who were already working at a trench in the courtyard, guarded by a squad of Flemish SS. A hundred meters farther on, the mare and colt were moving lazily, idling around. Walking slowly, I reached the mare. I stroked her throat with my right hand and took her bridle with my left. She let me mount easily and then, pressing my knees at her flanks, I kicked her on at a gentle trot. The colt followed, keeping a certain distance. As we passed the prisoners something startled the mare. She let out a loud neigh then went on a sudden gallop. I tugged her reins, trying in vain to bring her to a stop, grasped her mane with both hands when she jumped over a two-meter-deep trench, skimming across the heads of some prisoners. Rocks and soil fell on the shoulders of their striped uniforms. A soldier standing in front of a tent fell as he jumped to the side to escape being charged to the ground.

"*Achtung! Achtung!* Escape!" I heard a guard yell. I saw rifles raised in my direction from the edge of a trench. Prisoners were running around in zigzags seeking cover from the spooked mare's fury. Thankfully the guards, caught by surprise, did not have time to shoot in that confusion. The mare stopped suddenly, puffing her nostrils. I jumped down, turned her with my forearm pressed against her muzzle until she saw her colt. I whispered to her, "Take it easy...you're fine now." With him, she calmed down completely.

"She's very nervous, she doesn't like the prisoners," I said, apologizing to the guards, who now had me at the center of a semi-circle of pointing rifles.

The guards broke into a chorus of boisterous laughter, finally returning their rifles to their shoulders, relieved that the whole thing was nothing more than a false alarm. My friends at the stables also laughed; from there they had followed the action without being able to help me out.

I might have been reprimanded for the little accident with the soldier near the tent but he evidently thought it was not worthwhile raising a complaint. After all, everybody knew that we, the youngest soldiers, were well-looked-after by *Obersturmbannführer* Hersche.

The evening following the strafing, I was on duty at the stables, checking the horses. It was a peaceful scene with the horses chewing methodically on their fodder and snapping their tails from time to time to rid themselves of troublesome flies. They were tethered in a double line at a rope strung between posts with the pure-bred specimens separated from the others by divider planks. Everything was quiet except for occasional rattling snorts from their nostrils. I lit up a cigarette as I wandered over to the guard booth. Inside, I placed my rifle within easy reach and lay down on a mattress that was kept there. In the absence of a pillow, my helmet served as a place to rest my head. Sleeping, of course, was not permitted. In event of an air raid, we had to be ready to deal with the horses, especially the more unpredictable ones that had a habit of chewing at their ropes. I finished my cigarette with a last, deep puff and squeezed the butt with my fingers. It was almost midnight. I felt drowsy, my eyelids heavy from lack of sleep. A long night stretched ahead, my spell on duty lasting until the morning.

A horse's neigh woke me up. I looked at my watch…it was five in the morning. I jumped up from the mattress, grabbed my rifle and went over to the stables where everything seemed to be in order. I let go a sigh of relief but thought it best to make a thorough inspection starting with the officers' horses. It was then that I noticed that a stall was empty. I rubbed my eyes to make sure I wasn't still dreaming though I desperately wished I was. *Obersturmbannführer* Hersche's mount was missing! My heart pounding, almost leaping from my chest, I hurried to the exit door and found it already closed. *Maybe his rein was left too loose*, I thought; *maybe he got himself free and was among the other horses*. A thought kept repeating itself in my head; *what an imbecile I am!* By now I was only too well aware that this was no dream and I began to worry about the form my punishment would take. *Oh why did it have to be that horse?* The pure-bred *had* been in his stall; I clearly recalled caressing him and now he was nowhere to be found. Then a clip-clopping on the cobblestones in the courtyard caught my attention. I rushed out into the blood-red dawn, felt a wave of relief flood my over-tense muscles. The pure-bred was trotting in my direction with a rider — *Obersturmbannführer* Hershe. I took the reins from him, leaned against the front legs of the horse to limit its movement until the commander dismounted, helped him free his boot from the stirrup but forgot to give the regulation salute.

"Dry him up and then cover him," said the *Obersturmbannführer*. "And after one hour give him some fresh water to drink but not before, is that clear?" He completely ignored my failure to salute him.

"*Jawohl! mein Kommandant*," I answered, with a spring in my legs, at attention, the best way I could with the reins still clasped in my hand.

White and gray foam covered the pure-bred. His nostrils flared in rapid, rhythmical movements. Although still incredulous, confused and astonished by the surprises of the last half-hour, I ran a hand along his neck, squeezing the thick sweat downward as I talked to him in a low, calm voice. "Poor beast! Who knows for how many hours you've galloped, eh? Sometimes the commander behaves in a strange way." My nerves were still jangling as I picked up a large bathrobe to spread on his back, pressing it against his soaked hair. I continued to mutter to the animal like a mad fool. "You know, this area is not so safe now, with all those *Maquis*. Hersche knows the risks…with his outings…at night, but maybe he looks for danger eh?" The horse seemed to understand how frayed my nerves were and answered by rubbing his muzzle over my shoulder. I dried him down to his hocks and fetlocks and finished by caressing his muzzle, telling him my story. Somehow it felt as if the pure-bred was an accomplice to my misdemeanour, almost as if he could speak up for me.

The morning after my scare with the *Obersturmbannführer's* horse, after the flag-raising, the *Scharführer* addressed our assembled ranks, already much reduced in number because of the many departures for the front. *Obersturmbannführer* Hersche was standing to the side, at attention. He appeared fresh, as if he had slept well throughout the entire night. His eyes were fixed, looking into the distance, as if he were staring at the roofs of the buildings beyond the courtyard. Jean, Martin and Gosse, who I had already told about the incident at the stables, glanced towards the *Obersturmbannführer* from time to time to see if they could spot signs of his intentions regarding my punishment. I was on my toes.

"By order from our commander…" the *Scharführer* bellowed.

I held my breath, anticipating an announcement about my misdemeanour the night before.

"…as you have been told several times," continued the *Scharführer* ,"if any among you have had a change of mind and no longer wishes to be part of the *Waffen SS*, the exit door is waiting for you." The *Scharführer* allowed a few moments to pass but our ranks remained steadfastly silent. "You are free to return home. This is your last opportunity."

Now my turn for punishment would come.

"Dismissed!" snapped the *Scharführer*.

"Nothing?" exclaimed Martin and Gosse as we drifted from the parade ground.

I turned to them, surprised but not at all convinced about the final outcome. "They'll probably call for me later," I said.

"Maybe! But this is a good sign," Jean said.

"I bet that Hersche has already forgotten about you!" Gosse chipped in.

"I don't think so…he's protecting us youngsters," Martin concluded.

My fear of punishment was indeed unfounded. Hersche completely ignored, or forgave, my failure of duty on night watch at the stables.

Left Behind

At the base, there was a continuous coming and going; various companies were leaving for Germany and convoys of motorized *Waffen SS* units passing through Sennheim stopped for a few hours in our courtyard for refuelling and restocking with supplies before resuming their journey northwards. There remained only a few horses in the stables and so we were assigned to additional duties at the base.

"What a misery!" said Martin, sitting on the edge of his cot. "Look at the orders they give us now. Why don't they let *us* leave?"

"Special rations for those going to Germany," sighed Gosse.

I shook my head. "We've worked like mules until now. Are we destined to rot surrounded by these walls?"

"We have to do something to get out of here," Martin said.

Silence fell among us as our brains hunted for a solution.

"I got it!" I exclaimed. "We ask for a meeting with our commander…what do you think?"

"Could be a good idea," Jean said, "but the only thing that worries me is this: what are we going to ask for?"

"Simple, we go there and ask outright why we are not leaving," suggested Gosse.

"And he will tell you he needs soldiers for corvée and guard duties. No. It won't work," Jean said. "And who will do the talking?"

"I can do it," I said. "I can remind him that after all the training we went through we want to fight like any other soldier, in the end we are inferior to no one."

"It could fly," said Jean.

The day after, all lined up at attention in the impeccable office of *Obersturmbannführer* Hersche, I took to the floor. "*Obersturmbannführer*, my friends and I would like to carry out our duty to defend the *Reich* and join the fighting, if it is possible."

This officer clasped the knobs on the arms of his seat, pressing his bony hands around them. For a moment he seemed lost in his thoughts and then slowly rose, clasping his hands behind his back. I looked him in the eyes.

"Germany is undoubtedly in need of you," he said in his Swiss accent, "but you have to be patient...you have still to learn, to form yourselves, to become men. Your turn will come, as it came for the others."

I didn't have the courage to insist.

Obersturmbannführer Hersche left Sennheim while we remained at the base, now minus a pure-bred in the stables.

One morning at muster, I was on the first row when a *Hauptscharführer* called my name. I immediately took three steps forward and noticed then that his right hand was grasping a horse-whip.

"Attention!" he barked.

I wondered what I could have done wrong but at that moment nothing popped into my mind but, from the vexed expression on the non-commissioned officer's face, it seemed he was about to reprimand me on a very serious matter.

"Right turn!" he shouted. "March!"

While marching I had time for a rapid review of my conscience. Then it came to me... *it's about that bunch of grapes.* I had jumped over a low wall to pick that cute, single, little bunch with its juicy, dark-red grapes. That vineyard, on the outskirts of town, was bountiful. What difference would a single bunch make? I had hidden it under my shirt, thinking nobody had seen me.

"About turn. Halt. Arms above your head...higher!"

I felt defenseless, at the mercy of the man at my back, a man with a whip. I tightened my shoulder blades, closed my eyes and clenched my teeth.

"You do not take other people's property...understood?"

I was about to answer *jawohl* when I heard the whip slice the air. It smacked against my back and I flinched with the pain. A well-aimed kick directed at my buttocks lifted me from the ground.

"Follow me!" said the *Hauptscharführer*.

So I followed him obediently, to the offices of the battalion command.

"Wait here!"

So I waited there, in the corridor next to an open door of an office, my eyes shifting from the polished floor to the oil paintings hanging on the walls. I could smell the scent, of tea, of coffee.

"Send him in!" croaked an irritated voice.

Then I found myself in front of a personnel officer sitting at his desk wearing a white cordon on his epaulette — the decoration worn by sharp-shooters. The *Hauptscharführer* clicked his heels and saluted before turning to march out of the office.

The personnel officer looked me in the eye and said with a sneer, "A soldier of the *Reich* does not behave like a common thief." He sprang to his feet, beating the desk with both hands. "Such behaviour is contrary to the culture of the *Waffen SS.*"

I felt the blood flush up my neck and behind my ears. He was right: the fault was mine.

"We, the *Waffen SS*, must show a good example to the people of Alsace," he said in a more subdued tone. After explaining at length my responsibilities as a soldier of the *Waffen SS*, the officer dismissed me and in response I gave a perfect salute.

As I made my way along the corridor I felt a wave of relief sweep over me; I had escaped with only a light punishment and the matter, which was not recorded in my *Soldbuch*, was quickly forgotten. And this, I believe, was due to the influence of *Obersturmbannführer* Hersche whose benevolence almost certainly pulled me out of that sticky situation, in spite of his absence. I considered him as a second father. I admired his calm, surly and almost disdainful way of commanding. He sometimes appeared harsh and inflexible, steely, but we, the youngest of the *Waffen SS*, knew we were 'his' boys.

The Human Chain

The air raid alarm sounded in the depth of night.

"*Achtung*! Paratroopers!"

Dreams were forgotten as we pulled on our uniforms and ran down the stairs of the dormitory still trying to fasten our helmets. In less than a minute we had dressed and were in the courtyard, ready for muster.

"The lights in the dormitories, they're still on," Martin whispered.

"Someone's for it," said Gosse.

A few minutes later, with much cursing and pushing amongst themselves, a squad from the French militia who were staying temporarily on the base gathered in a disorderly alignment in front of us, one of them smoking a cigarette.

"*Nicht rauchen!*" A *Sturmmann* was not happy.

"It is nothing, only a little cigarette."

The militiamen continued to talk, to call each other by name, to joke and to laugh scornfully, unaware that there was nothing worse in a *SS* base than disorder and insubordination. Our *Sturmmann* ordered us to step backwards, separating us from the disorderly bunch of militia men and we remained there, standing ready for action, for more than one hour. Then the shooting in the distance gradually diminished and the machine guns on the perimeter of our base ceased firing. This was a portent of things to come; the Americans and their allies were coming closer — air incursions became increasingly frequent.

For a few days we also hosted *Wehrmacht* units coming from Normandy; besides their own motorized transport they were also using Jeeps and amphibious tanks captured from the Americans. Naturally, since food at our base was not abundant and hunger was keeping constant company with us, we were attracted by their trucks, loaded with supplies, that had been left untended. The four of us, Gosse, Jean, Martin and I, each 'investigated' a different truck to minimise the chance of being spotted before regrouping to report our findings.

"American and English cigarettes, fifty by the cartoon!" Gosse reported.

"Chocolate, preserves and soap," said Martin.

"I heard the quartermaster didn't have the time to distribute all the foodstuffs, that's why there's plenty still on the trucks," Jean said. "I saw all sorts of nice things…bread, sausages, oil canisters…you name it."

"Inside the one I spied there are packs of German cigarettes and bottles of French wine," I reported.

"A real treasure," exclaimed Gosse, rubbing his hands.

"So, what are we going to do?" Martin asked. By now saliva was seeping from the corners of his mouth.

"We'll scrounge up, no?" said Gosse, making movements with his hands like a cat about to strike a blow with its paw.

"Hei, hei," I intervened. "I still carry the marks on my back for that bunch of grapes. Can you imagine what will happen to us if we are caught?"

"Let's reason with calmness," Jean said. "That Paul, was outright theft, pure and simple…you stole from a farmer."

"Think of it this way…all this stuff is already ours…it belongs to our army," Martin reasoned.

"Exactly," Gosse said. "It already belongs to us…we are only going to use some of it before it is distributed."

I was beginning to worry. "Hei…you guys…don't even think about it."

We turned in the direction of a Jeep where two soldiers were busy unloading eggs, butter and milk.

"You could give us a hand, right?" one asked with a gesture that encouraged an affirmative answer. For us, it sounded like an order so we hurried to help.

"There," one of the *Wehrmacht* men pointed, "the guys from the auxiliary services, behind those trucks, they need you for the hand-to-hand chain."

By good fortune the human chain, starting at a truck, wound its way upstairs to a storeroom beside our dormitory. There, a quartermaster diligently noted down on a small booklet every item as it was brought in. Gosse and Martin looked at each other and smirked. I opened the dormitory door and took up position there. Martin was before me in the chain, at the corner of the corridor. Gosse stood behind me, inside the dormitory, waiting, and Jean was the next in line, after me…this gave us strategic control of a section of the chain where it would have been difficult for others to see our movements.

"Shht," It was Martin's signal that the next item was for us. He passed me a can of marmalade.

I gave him an assertive look, nodded and deftly passed the can backwards, into Gosse's eager hands, before Jean quickly replaced it with another article to maintain the steady pace of the chain. Our maneuver lasted for a good twenty minutes during which we diverted chocolate, sausages, small pieces of processed cheese, bottles of wine and an entire carton of French cigarettes into our possession.

When the work was finished, Gosse joined us in the corridor, in time for the quarter-master's thanks. The corvée soldiers, who made up the majority of the chain, showed their gratitude for our help by donating to us a loaf of bread, one sausage each, and a handful of cigarettes to be divided equally among us.

In our dormitory there were sausages sticking out from under our pillows on the cots and bottles jamming the doors of our lockers.

"I didn't know where else to stuff things," Gosse said, shrugging his shoulders in apology.

Gosse uncorked a bottle, pouring the wine into our canteens though I must admit it was with a feeling of guilt that I drank it.

Some days after, on account of the cigarettes and other trades, I was able to barter for a pair of sturdy leather boots and a Luger P08 pistol. I was just fifteen years and four months old, but now, I felt I was finally a man.

Harsh Lessons

One morning following muster, those of us remaining at the base each received rations for three days.

"Get ready to leave," a *Sturmmann* ordered.

Here we go, I thought. *Our war is just about to start.*

At Sennheim station, we lined up on the platform to wait for a train that was still manoeuvring to attach wagons, each with a pair of sentry boxes, its wheels screeching on the rails because of the sharp braking. Finally, it shunted against the buffers at the end of the track. Machine guns were installed in the sentry boxes. Political prisoners, who were gathered tightly on a pavement not far from us, were stuffed into cattle wagons, pressed in so as not to impede the sliding doors which were immediately closed and bolted. We, instead, climbed into freight wagons where the doors remained wide open, about thirty per wagon. Together with Martin, Gosse, Jean and other companions, I waited for the stationmaster's whistle.

"You are so serious, Paul," Jean observed, sitting in front of me.

"I am only thinking back to a similar situation, some years ago," I answered.

"In a train station?"

A sharp blast of a whistle irritated my ears; the train moved, clouds of steam billowing around its wheels.

"Yes, it was in a small village…we were refugees. I was with my mother and a sister of mine. We were squeezed into a cattle wagon too. It was lucky for us that we had an uncle on duty at the station…he found us a decent place in a corner of a wagon with dry straw and extra food rations. We were travelling southward."

"And this one is northbound," Jean said.

"To Wildflecken, I heard," a companion interjected.

"No! To Greifenberg, in Pomerania," someone else said.

The Alsatian countryside slipped by, past the open door of the wagon. We waved at farmers, bent at work, who returned our greeting with great enthusiasm. Girls on bicycles, pedalling on a narrow road alongside the track, fluttered their handkerchiefs at us, smiling.

"The Alsatians are with us," Jean said. And we believed him…he was the most judicious among us four comrades; his reasoning was logical, and he had a sensible answer to almost everything.

The overloaded train rolled on, the wagons swaying heavily, rattling and jolting at every joint in the rails. Then, while slowly approaching a small rural station, we heard a shot from somewhere farther up the track, towards the head of the train. A few seconds later, just at a crossing, we noticed a man in uniform, collapsed on the ground, motionless.

"What was it?" Gosse, who was busy trading some item, looked up at me.

"Somebody took a shot, at a railwayman," I explained.

"We'll know something in a bit," added Jean.

The train slowed, scratching and scraping on the rails, until it stopped. A *Scharführer* jumped from his wagon and approached a *Feldgendarme* who stood with the stationmaster.

"Who fired the shot," the *Scharführer* shouted towards the wagons.

"It was I," a *Sturmmann* instructor from Sennheim bellowed from his wagon's open door. "At your command, *Scharführer*."

"The reason?"

"Our soldiers saluted him, but that imbecile answered with an obscene act, *Scharführer*."

The *Scharführer* accepted that motivation with a slight, assenting nod.

"I thought necessary to even the score," the *Sturmmann* added, showing his rifle.

The stationmaster scribbled some notes and then, with the *Feldgendarme*, went to his office to make his report.

The train started moving again after a pause of about twenty minutes, accelerating laboriously, and clanging. "A similar thing happened during the invasion of Lorena," I said after a while. My friends and the others around listened attentively. "One evening, in town, the bar belonging to a woman I knew was full of German soldiers. One of them, dead drunk, bothered a civilian."

"And then?" Martin interrupted, impatient.

"Then an *Obersturmführer* went up to the drunkard, commanding him to get to his feet and to behave as befits a soldier of the *Reich*. The drunken soldier threw his arms forward, tried to salute, mumbled something but was unable to stand up."

"And then?" Martin repeated.

"The officer told him he was an idiot, drew his pistol and shot him in the head."

My shocked companions went back to lie on the straw in silence, thinking no doubt of the incident they had just witnessed…and of my own little tale.

French Lack of Spirit, German Kindness

I leaned at the open door of the wagon, looking out over fields so vast they seemed to fuse with the distant horizon, thinking of incidents from my boyhood which had just so abruptly ended…

I had lived close to the Maginot line, and played there often with my Polish friend, Dodek, before the start of the war. We lost our adventure playground when the Maginot Line's artillery came into action, in May 1940. One night, in my bedroom, violet-blue flashes of light danced wildly on the walls when the cannons fired. I sunk my head under my pillow, plugging my ears, when an emplacement close to our house started to fire. Just a few days later, the French soldiers prepared to leave. There was chaos in the village. I recalled a lieutenant trying to give orders. He was on horseback, cursing the drivers of carriages, vans and *roulantes* from the baggage train in an attempt to smooth the flow of traffic but was met with whistles of disapproval and crude invectives.

As my grandpa had foretold, the first Belgian evacuees started passing through our village, some walking, others on bicycles. Some families even travelled on carts pulled by cows. So, some days later, my father decided to join the exodus using a handcart to carry our few furnishings and some household utensils. We were in full flight. There was a rumour circulating that German soldiers were cutting off boys' hands and distributing poisoned candies. Then, in the first days of June, Stukas appeared in the sky. They dived on the convoys of refugees, strafing them, bombing them, leaving people and animals pierced by bullets and maimed by explosions. Soon the whole countryside buzzed with the flies visiting the corpses and carcasses. The civilians desperately tried to find transportation to escape that carnage but the French soldiers beat them to it. With my father, I helped push a stalled Renault C4 to a downhill section of the road hoping the French officers who had commandeered the vehicle would offer a ride to me and my mother, since there was ample space in the car, but they shooed us away without even a word of thanks. Before arriving at Saint Dizier's train station, we saw those same officers, their eyes directed at the ground, prisoners of the Germans.

In the station I found soldiers I had met while I played near the Maginot Line, members of the 27th Company, defending it with machine-gun emplacements. During an attack, I helped them by carrying ammunition. Unfortunately, some of them, who I knew by name, died there. I recall their inflection when speaking, accents from Bordeaux, Toulon and Marseille. My parents came in search of me, yelling and calling out my name, terrorized by my disappearance.

My family found refuge, after a brief train trip, in a village defended by some hundreds of soldiers who appeared indifferent and demoralized. It seemed that nobody cared anymore and there, the most total disorder reigned and I was able to wander unhindered into stores and tobacco shops. In a deserted bar, I poured myself a beer and tasted Martini for the first time.

In the morning, a company of German infantrymen accompanied by two light tanks arrived in the village square. The soldiers stopped beside the public fountain to wash themselves, shaving, boiling tea, talking with civilians and some French officers. Intrigued, I approached them and discovered the Germans to be polite but also straight and proud.

"They seem good fellows," whispered someone near me.

"Look at how well-equipped they are," another pointed out.

By now, a small crowd had gathered around them. An infantryman took off his helmet, revealing his well-cut, blond hair; he inhaled the last puff of a cigarette, left the fountain and went towards a woman wearing a black headscarf and holding the hand of a four or five-year-old girl. He took something from one of his pockets, stooped towards the girl and then stretched his arm saying in German, "Take it! You'll like it?"

The girl ran towards the soldier, smiling.

"No! For the love of God!" cried the woman.

The little girl stopped dead in her tracks.

"You don't want it?" the soldier asked, surprised by the girl's sudden, mute refusal.

"My daughter! Give me back my daughter!" implored the woman. She threw herself on her knees, sobbing.

The soldier, confused, didn't understand a word of French.

"Paul," my mother called, coming over at that moment, "are you always following trouble?" she said in German.

The woman turned to the crowd and, seeing my mother, begged her with pleading hands, "Tell him, please."

"This woman…why is she screaming?" asked the blond soldier.

"He was trying to poison my daughter with his candies," the woman sobbed.

The soldier looked at my mother and shook his head, "What is she saying?"

"She thinks the candies are poisoned," mother said.

"Oh," said the soldier, "I'm sorry."

"Don't mind her, they are all afraid…it's only gossip," said mother.

The soldier looked at the woman before turning to mother. "Please tell her that back home I have a little girl that looks like her daughter. I was missing her."

I recalled too, the German infantrymen rounding up the French soldiers without them firing a single shot. They used a nearby church as a temporary prison, with only one sentry at the entrance. And back home for the evening, I found my mother exhorting a French soldier to exchange his uniform for civilian clothes.

"It is useless," he said.

"You cannot wait any longer," insisted mother.

At that moment two German infantrymen knocked on the door and asked mother if there were French soldiers in the house. "No," she answered convincingly, speaking in German.

The two left after saluting.

The French soldier, showing his timid face round the kitchen door, asked, "Are they gone?"

"Yes! Now put these things on."

"For what purpose? We've already lost the war."

"But at least you will be free," said my mother.

I stared straight in the eyes of that soldier and I saw that his spirit was broken. He shuffled out of the house to give himself up. My mother was furious; she had lied for him, risking severe punishment if caught. I felt a twinge of shame — this soldier, and those that gave up just as easily, had let their country down.

On the way back to our village, after my father was released by the German local command by merit of my mother's intervention, we saw French prisoners lined up in columns ready to march and escorted by only a few German infantrymen. The two light tanks I had seen earlier rolled over the weapons my countrymen had laid down, crushing them under their tracks.

Only two men remained in my home village but there were several women whose number swelled when evacuees from the Gironde began to arrive. The Co-op was allocating free food, soap and other staples but soon suspended this service. In the school, which had a large hole in one wall, I found chocolate bars, biscuits, numerous artillery uniforms and French soldiers' hats or kepis, the sort of things that interested me as a child. One day, I dressed up in one of these uniforms and put a kepi on my head, then ventured out onto the road where I ran into a German soldier who simply walked on by. Soon after, two *gendarmes* stopped me.

"Hei you! Come here," one called. "Where did you get that uniform? Take it off right away."

He made to grab my elbow but I pulled it out of his reach. "No! It didn't trouble the Germans…why should it bother you?"

The *gendarme* raised his hand to slap me. "If I see you again you're in big trouble," he hissed…

❧—❦

My comrades were now stretched out on the floor of the swaying wagon. Martin looked tired, Gosse bored and Jean yawned frequently, politely covering his mouth…all Frenchmen who had thrown their lot, their future, in with Hitler's *Reich*. I went back to my thoughts, to my village, to that strange period of the war…

The school remained closed for a long time in the summer of '41 and to occupy my time, I often visited the old French military emplacements on the Maginot Line with Dodek. Gradually, the Germans set about bringing the area into proper order. Prisoners defused mines, raked the soil and helped repair armaments. Factories reopened. They requisitioned fields for agricultural use and, true to the German's love of efficiency, they reduced the number of French civilians working in municipal halls to that which was strictly necessary. Even the school reopened, with lessons including talks about Marshal Petain who, judging by the respect everybody felt obliged to demonstrate, I thought must have been a great man.

When we left school, Dodek and I joined a German firm that was demolishing the Maginot Line as part of a plan to reinforce the 'Atlantic Wall' defenses. Everything metal was salvaged. The hard, manual labour was carried out by Russian prisoners. Under my command, they rolled up old barbed wire and pulled looped-iron pickets from the ground, all done meticulously and in good time. For this, I received praise from my German boss who appreciated my organizational skills. I began to a feel like a valued, almost accomplished, member of the community.

A good proportion of the Russian prisoners were big, muscular men, and great workers. Others felt the need to go to the latrine at every hour. Those with some schooling assumed police duties and, as a reward, received double rations; they were diligent and did not hesitate for an instant to inflict punishments on their compatriots when necessary. This system worked perfectly and they accepted it. I soon learned not to trust the loafers; when offered a cigarette they demanded the entire pack. I was also greatly helped by the prisoner-policemen who told me that if I was having difficulty with a particular prisoner to: "give us a nod...we will show him a big stick."

The train trundled onwards towards Greifenberg , into the gathering dusk. Thinking of these events, which happened only a few years earlier, it seemed natural to find myself wearing a German uniform.

Arrival in Greifenberg

It was early morning. Sunlight sliced in through the gaps between the slats of the wagon's walls. The train was slowing. I rubbed the sleep from my eyes and sat against the side of the wagon listening to the grind of the brakes. There was a jolt as the train came to a standstill. Soldiers' voices on the outside drew closer. The sliding door opened wide. I heard names called out and soldiers jumping from neighbouring wagons. When I looked from the open door I saw a board carrying the station's name — Brückenau. Most of those who had travelled from Sennheim were gathered on the platform waiting for transport to the camp at Wildflecken, not far away. None from our wagon were called out. The locomotive's shrill whistle sounded; its wheels screeched on the rails, searching for grip. Our journey was not yet over and the train travelled at an exasperatingly slow speed.

Hours later, we passed through Leipzig and eventually came to a halt on a siding where our train waited. Eventually, in the distance, a locomotive's whistle sounded. Gradually, the slow clunk and rattle of an approaching train grew louder, stirring us from boredom and indolence. A long train was passing just a few meters from us, on the main track.

"Look — it goes slowly to avoid the shakes and jolts," Jean said.

I shuddered at the sight passing before my eyes. The cars were crammed with wounded soldiers. They lay on straw mattresses, arms dangling. Some were stretched out, their heads wrapped in blood-soaked bandages. Others sat with their eyes staring into the distance like ghosts from another world. We waved as they drifted past our waiting train.

"Look at them," Martin remarked, sadness in his voice.

"Poor guys," Jean whispered.

Some of the wounded answered with faint hand movements, their faces grey.

"The misery," Gosse said, clearly perturbed.

The wounded had a gloomy and dreamy appearance. One, with a bandaged arm, was doing everything he could to comfort a companion who lay on the floor wrapped up in bandages like an Egyptian mummy; another sat with his elbows on his knees, his dusty cheeks streaked with tears.

"I think we are going to take their place," Gosse murmured.

"That's a depressing thought," Jean said.

"Even *Waffen SS* soldiers die in war," I said.

Our locomotive hissed a cloud of steam. Buffers collided, the wagons moved backwards until they were beyond the shunting levers. From there, the train restarted its forward run, puffing energetically in Berlin's direction, as if determined to distance itself as quickly as possible from the one carrying the wounded. In the open country, women and girls at work in the fields greeted us with joyful and enthusiastic waving, a pleasant and uplifting distraction from the gruesome sights we had recently witnessed.

"What do you think of them, eh?" Martin asked.

"Not bad looking at all," Gosse observed.

"You might even say beautiful," Jean mused.

"And quite plump," I chipped in, moving from the open door to make room for my comrades who were shouting gallant phrases improvised at the moment. I smiled at their exultation, at their new-found exuberance. They were almost all twenty years old and their carefree happiness lifted my spirit, restored my strength. The beautiful and seductive feminine faces had dispelled the images of the wounded that were now no more than a fading memory.

Several times, the train stopped for long hours before we reached Berlin in the darkness of late evening.

"It's just like all the other stations I've seen," Martin observed when the wagon door slid open. "I was expecting something different."

"Maybe we are at the commercial depot," Jean said.

Gosse leaned out of the door to look along the platform. "Hei, supper is coming!"

Red Cross nurses were working their way along the open doors of the wagons, filling up the mess tins held in outstretched hands. As soon as ours were filled, the chatter in our wagon was replaced by the sound of my hungry comrades slurping or blowing to cool their soup. "Ah! So good," exclaimed Gosse. Everyone else nodded in agreement as their spoons went rapidly from the mess tins to their mouths.

Another Red Cross nurse appeared at the door of the wagon. "Coffee...who wants hot coffee?"

I could not resist the pleasure of being waited on by this beautiful, blond girl. I stretched out my arm, leaning out of the wagon with my mug, almost brushing her cheek — and close enough to smell her delicate, cyclamen-scented perfume above the aroma of the coffee. She looked into my eyes and with a conspiratorial wink, fluttered away like an elusive butterfly to serve my comrades who, imitating me, were leaning out of the wagon in the hope of attracting her attention.

With that pleasant interlude fading into the night, the train gained speed. The sliding doors were now almost closed, leaving only a long slit to allow the entry of fresh air. In the darkness, only the lateral jolts revealed changes in our direction of travel. I dozed off until the sound of two voices on the platform outside woke Jean and me. They were discussing a recent bombing raid as they passed by.

The train started moving at walking pace but stopped again after a short distance. I jumped down from the wagon for a short stroll to stretch my legs and wandered across to a squad of engineers repairing a section of track illuminated by flashlights and the locomotive's powerful headlamp. Close by stood an *Oberscharführer* instructor who had fought at Stalingrad, as strong as a bull but very kind. I lit up two of my American cigarettes and offered him one. He took it from me and inhaled its smoke, deep into his lungs, savouring the flavour. "You are a good soldier, Paul," he told me, stepping away, humming happily as he made his way to his wagon.

Late in the morning, the train arrived at Greifenberg, three days after our departure from Sennheim. We lined up on the platform, grouped in echelons some of which were destined to travel onwards to more eastern bases. An officer called out all the youngest by name and so I found myself in a group set to one side.

"The hell! Do you want to bet they'll keep us here?" Gosse cursed.

"We don't know that," Jean replied in a calm tone.

"Maybe they'll send us to the officers' school," Martin joked.

"Or into some special mission," I added.

Gosse was still annoyed. "So much for Hersche's word, eh?"

"Gosse," Jean said patiently, "he told us loud and clear that we are still too young for the front line, no?"

A *Scharführer* came towards us, busily turning pages in a folder. "You young fellows are assigned to an 80mm mortar section but at the moment you will take up guardhouse duties at the base," he said before leaving.

"I told you they would keep us here in Greifenberg," Gosse complained.

"But only for the moment," Jean said, "didn't you hear him say 'mortar section'?"

"I wonder if this is Hersche's way of protecting us," I added.

2

The Greifenberg Base

Orders are Orders

The base at Greifenberg was vast compared with the one at Sennheim. At the middle of one side of the rectangular perimeter wall was an entrance gate and, proceeding clockwise, were prisons in the cellars of 'Building A' where soldiers serving their sentences stayed for up to fifteen days. The inmates, relegated to corvée duties, were guarded by one or two soldiers. On the adjacent side, a building included a room for gas-mask training, a chapel, infirmary, orderly room and a horse-handling area with stables. On the opposite side were kitchens and, separated by a courtyard, the Military Justice's offices with prisons and officers' quarters on four floors. The guardhouse was beside the entry door. On the roofs of the buildings, a row of dormer windows completed the austere geometry. The whole base was dominated by a central, vast courtyard capable of holding thousands of soldiers.

Obersturmbannführer Hersche had moved into his apartment, near the offices, with his wife and daughter, two beanpoles as skinny as he. From a window facing the road, he could observe the sentry box at the guardhouse entrance. There Gosse, Martin, Jean and I, together with some other comrades, spent two-hour spells of guard duty, keeping an eye on the base and also the prisoners in the Military Justice cells. These prisoners included militia men, sailors and L.V.F. soldiers who normally worked on local farms but had absconded to Berlin using falsified permits. Others had been caught trafficking on the black market. These were a motley group of stragglers, gathered from various fronts, who were always whining, some about one thing, some another.

Contrary to the initial impression of order created by the systematic layout of the buildings, an air of confusion permeated the Greifenberg camp. Like the prisoners, the base's effectives were also something of a motley bunch. Some had previously served in elements of the armed forces of the *Reich* — *Sturmbrigade, Todt, Kriegsmarine, Nationalsozialistisches Kraftfahrkorps,* and *Flak* units — and were used to working under German command while others had been members of the French Militia, a force set up to combat the French Resistance. Those who had fought in Russia as members of the L.V.F. were proudly independent. This mixed bag of men could hardly be called a cohesive unit but *Obersturmbannführer* Hersche at once began to rectify this deficiency. He kept us young guards apart from the others and in such position as to be able to control everyone. Security measures were tightened; prisoners were forbidden to face the windows and guards had the order to shoot at those who did on sight. *Obersturmbannführer* Hersche also arranged to have some of his *Waffen SS* men as orderly officers or non-commissioned officers. The hours spent training were extended with everyone participating in weapons handling and rifle maintenance.

Not everyone appreciated the new rules: adjutants, sergeants and lieutenants of the L.V.F. were not used to the rigid discipline of the *Waffen SS* units. In the evening, at the guardhouse, it was often something of a comedy show when they came up for off-duty, walk-out permits.

"You! Where's your regulation uniform?" the *Sturmmann* sentry once asked a legionnaire.

"You'll find it in tatters on the Carpathians."

"Come back when you find it then."

"Hei, come on. After risking my skin in combat, I'm denied a…"

"Silence! The regulations are clear."

"But it's an…"

"You're punished! Three days. Guard! Inform the orderly officer. Next."

The *Sturmmann* looked the next in line up and down. Satisfied with the appearance of the legionnaire's uniform he said: "So, let's see the salute. Face the sentry, stretch the arm, hand in horizontal position, at eye level."

The slender legionnaire stepped up wearing a pained grimace. The *Sturmmann* made him repeat the salute maneuver three times. "What's wrong with you man? Keep your hand stretched too."

"I got wounded in combat."

"Where?"

"In Russia."

Exasperated, the *Sturmmann* shook his head. "It's the whole thing that doesn't cut it… the uniforms… the slovenliness. Here, we are not in Bourbaki's army."

The *Sturmmann* sent the legionnaires back to their dormitories. After another week of training, with new-found courage, they came again to the guardhouse. "It even seems like you went through Sennheim," said the *Sturmmann*, pleased at the improvement in the legionnaires' attitude and appearance. "Passes granted."

Gradually, the confusion disappeared and what had once been the atmosphere of a holiday hotel regained the semblance of a *Waffen SS* base. Order and rules were established; at the mess, for example, a member of the kitchen staff controlled the access stubs. There was still, however, a major problem: there were French officers who didn't speak German and *vice versa*. Having returned from the front without their original commission and companies, which had been decimated and reconstituted elsewhere, these officers were assigned to instructor duties.

A group of elderly German civilians accompanied by a squad of Hitler Youth with its band, flags and insignia, lined up in the courtyard, between the kitchens and the prisons of the Military Justice's building. The civilians were about to swear allegiance to the *Führer* when I heard a shot. I ran out from the guardhouse while the ceremony, now in full swing, continued with a crescendo of drums and trombones.

A guard in the courtyard pointed to one of the cells. "I took a shot at one up there."

"At what?" I demanded.

"I saw a prisoner facing the window."

Somebody, meanwhile, was shouting in one of the prison cells.

"I only tried to warn him, but maybe he got wounded," said the guard.

It had to happen when I'm the head sentry, I thought. There were two soldiers on corvée duty, sweeping the courtyard. "You two…with me," I ordered. They left their brooms and followed me upstairs.

I heard the voice of a terrorized prisoner call out from the cell where the shot had struck. "Get me out of here!"

"He is gone crazy, in there," a guard on the corridor warned.

The *uvedé* reached us with the key to the cell. "Watch out," he said, his fingers unbuttoning his pistol holster. After a turn of key in the lock, the heavy door squeaked on its hinges. Inside the cell, one of the two prisoners was staggering around, sobbing. On the walls and floor, bright-red blood was spattered, amongst it pieces of greyish brain tissue and fragments of skull bone. It was a shocking sight.

The *uvedé* officer didn't venture into the cell but stood at the threshold of the door as he took notes for his report.

"Please…I want out of here," moaned the sobbing prisoner. He was now crouched in a corner, shaking and shuddering.

"Get the place cleaned up…it was an accident," the *uvedé* said before leaving.

The corridor guard pointed his rifle at the terrified prisoner. "Let's go, there is an empty cell further on."

The poor prisoner, dazed by fright, followed like a lamb, keeping his hands firmly on his head.

A few evenings later, in the dormitory, the guard who had shot the prisoner was preparing his packsack with precise, almost studied, movements. He put his personal garments into a bag with great care while those around him pretended to read or to clean boots. In spite of his efforts to appear normal, I could sense that he was yearning to hear a comrades' voice dissipate the silence which seemed to weigh on him like a condemnation.

Eventually a comrade sitting on the edge of his cot asked, "How many days leave did they give you?"

"Fifteen days on a holiday camp. I'll do some swimming in the pool, I hope," he said with exaggerated, mock cheerfulness as he continued to assemble his things.

Jean, looking out of a window, asked, "What reason did they give?"

"For carrying out my duty."

The disdain for the man who shot the prisoner was palpable. We had to shoot on sight, yes, but who among us would have anticipated that one of us would shoot to kill a comrade? Even if the order didn't specify it, its demands could easily have been satisfied by firing against the wall as a warning.

Respect

I reported to the guardhouse where an *Unterscharführer* was waiting for me to accompany him on his night rounds which sometimes extended beyond the confines of the base. I asked him where we were going.

"Tonight, we are on duty in town."

This, in my eyes, was a pleasant change from the usual routine. We pressed the 1938 model black helmets down onto our heads and buckled the belts with bayonets over our official uniforms before making our way to a movie theatre near the center of town.

"So," said the *Unterscharführer* before we entered the theater, "we'll take a section each. Beware of hotheads. And remember, there must be silence during projections…and smoking only during breaks and only in the foyer."

Everything went smoothly until the interval when, in the huddle to reach the foyer, two men bustled in front of me. I told them to mind their manners. One was unshaven, his ruffled hair touching the raised collar of his threadbare coat. His older companion, skinny and with an aquiline nose, was equally shabby.

"Let the armed force go by," sneered the younger of the two, in Italian.

I looked them up and down slowly before demanding their documents in German. I leafed through them. "Civilian prisoners?"

"*Ja*, mister soldier," the young one answered, with a scathing look on his face.

"What kind of work?"

"Butcher… and kitchen," he said with difficulty, in German.

I raised my chin at the other.

"I carry the milk in the morning…and coiffeur," he stuttered.

"You know that prisoners are forbidden to go to the movies?"

"*Ja*," the milkman said in a trembling voice.

The butcher, looking at me hard in the eye, complained to his companion.

"You! Tell me something," I asked, addressing him in Italian, "what did the 'armed force' do to you?"

His mouth dropped open. "Nothing, nothing…I was talking so…I didn't think that…" he stuttered.

"Sorry, many sorry, mister soldier, he didn't mean to offend," the older man intervened.

I handed back their documents and in a curt manner said in Italian, "You may go."

They started towards the exit door, turning for a last glance. "Who would have thought it, in perfect Italian…an *SS* soldier," whispered the butcher.

"Shut up, shut up…if you want to save your skin," the milkman said, dragging his companion by the arm.

I smiled spontaneously, pleased that my standing as a *Waffen SS* soldier had help subdue that pair of roughnecks.

At the end of the film, I met the *Unterscharführer* in the foyer. On our way back to base, he led me to the tranquil corner of a bar where we enjoyed a beer and smoked a cigarette as we sat close to a burning stove exchanging stories from our youth. It was cold when we left but I didn't feel it; instead I felt a sense of camaraderie, a warm sensation that dispelled any doubt I had about my decision to volunteer for the *Waffen SS*.

Praise from Hersche

The male and female civilian personnel employed at the base left late in the afternoon as usual, laying the keys of the rooms in which they worked on the table at the guardhouse. We had the order to search their bags or satchels before they left but this rarely happened. From my position in the sentry box, I watched them disperse from the main entrance, onto the street, until I was alone.

Around five o'clock, it started snowing. Large flakes fell softly onto the ground without melting which soon made the scenery seem strangely static and unreal looking. In winter, at home in Villerupte-Cantebonne, I used to play with Dodek, rolling snowballs until they assumed gigantic proportions. Sometimes we made snowmen that had the grimace and likeness of villagers which often struck a chord with passers-by and made them laugh. *Lately*, I thought as I stood at the sentry box, *I had got to know people whose likeness would be perfect, imprinted on the round face of a snowman.* There was *Karrotenkopf,* for example, a German kitchen attendant who controlled the entry stubs at the mess. His nickname — a most appropriate one — meant 'carrot head'. He had red hair, small eyes set in a white face sprinkled with freckles, a long nose, jug ears, a falsetto voice and a strange laugh. With these unfortunate attributes he was the subject of much ridicule. Each day, with his comic and eccentric demeanour, he marked a cross with a pencil on the stubs presented by everyone entering the mess to prevent some 'smarty pants' from entering twice. *On the mouth of my imaginary snowman I would,* I thought, *insert Karrotenkopf's pencil instead of a traditional pipe.* I laughed to myself as the cold nipped my cheeks; my leather gloves protected me, though, from the iced barrel of my rifle that I held with the stock on the snow-covered ground.

The muffled trampling of footsteps on the snow diverted my thoughts from snowmen and *Karrotenkopf.* The distinguished figure of a woman wrapped in a fur coat was approaching in a hurry. As she drew close, I noticed her clear, blue eyes and her blond tresses hanging out from under her headscarf. In spite of being so heavy clothed, I could see that she was rather shapely. I tightened my pose, extending my body at attention. The woman passed by, ignoring me and, without stopping, entered the guardhouse. I pushed the alarm button on the wall of the sentry box: a guard appeared in the internal portal of the guardhouse to block her way.

"I have an appointment to meet someone," I heard her say in an impatient, arrogant-sounding voice.

The head sentry, an *Unterscharführer* from the mortar section who passed into the *SS* ranks from the *Wehrmacht,* joined the guard in the portal. "You've business here?"

The woman, clearly vexed by the guard's refusal to let her through, took a document from her purse. "Here it is…my pass."

At that moment a voice called from an open window of Building A, "What are you doing? Let her through!" It was an L.V.F. sub lieutenant, gesticulating in our direction. I didn't budge, nor talk, as was expected from a sentry on duty.

The head post too ignored the man at the window. "Your pass expired three days ago," he explained to the woman.

"But I work here as a secretary," she insisted.

"Not anymore," said the *Unterscharführer.*

"You…down there," the voice at the window called, "I'm on my way to deal with you… right now!"

The beautiful blond is looking to rendezvous with her handsome officer, I thought.

The sub lieutenant appeared at the guardhouse door. "What's in your stupid heads, eh?" he said angrily. "Let her through."

The *Unterscharführer* made a quick sign with his eyes and the woman went in, strutting beside her sub lieutenant as they went towards Building A.

Soon after, from inside the base, a trampling of heavy steps that ended at the guard-house reached my ears and, after a minute, the head sentry, accompanied by a guard appeared in front of me — it was Jean who was taking over sentry duty. "Get ready for the worst," he whispered. "Hersche wants to see you."

I didn't have time to ask Jean for an explanation. I went inside the guardhouse and took the ammunition from the loading chamber of my Mauser before placing it on the weapons rack. Moments later, I was in the commander's office, flanked by the *Unterscharführer* and the sub lieutenant.

Obersturmbannführer Hersche was red in the face as he began our dressing down. "What kind of idiots are you? *SS* guards behaving like cretins...unacceptable!" As the *Obersturmbannführer* continued, his hand slid over his pistol-holster, caressing it. I glimpsed as surreptitiously as possible at my fellow culprits and noticed how pale their faces had become. The commander then addressed me personally and, in tone of voice that was now suddenly mellowed, said: "Well done young man. I saw everything from my window. *You* have given the others here an example of *Waffen SS* discipline. You are dismissed."

I saluted before leaving the office but in the corridor, I stopped to prick up my ears.

"It will be no great loss for the *Reich* to lose a sub lieutenant such as you. Consider your-self a free civilian worker. Coming to you, *Unterscharführer*...make yourself available for the disciplinary decision. Let's see where we go from there."

The Russian Front, I thought as I hurried out of the way.

At the guardhouse, I took my turn again in the sentry box, my chest swelling with pride after the praise I had received — from Hersche himself. The blond woman, coming out from the base, gave me a withering glance. "I would never have expected to be betrayed like this by a Frenchman," she commented bitterly. Being a model of *Waffen SS* discipline and a diligent sentry, I ignored her scorn, kept my eyes strictly to the front. She turned away from me in disgust, flung her scarf in another pass around her neck and left.

The following day we had strict orders for those on guardhouse duty regarding the entry of unauthorized personnel; rumours had it that there had been enemy sightings in the vicinity. From that moment on, we were in permanent state of alarm.

Close Calls

At two o'clock of an icy, moonlit morning towards the end of 1944, I was patrolling a straight line in the courtyard, between the kitchens and the Military Justice's offices. I tightened the collar of my heavy winter coat, braced myself for the final, coldest hour of duty. My orders were to shoot on sight anyone failing to stop at my instruction or not giving the correct password — Berlin — issued the previous evening. There was also another side to the prevailing strict discipline: a superior on an inspection round who surprised a sentry sleeping on guard duty could exercise his right to execute him on the spot.

I was already looking forward to warming up inside the guardhouse when I thought I saw a shadow move in the bright moonlight. "Halt! Password!" The shadow seemed to melt behind a wall. I rubbed my eyes in disbelief, perhaps I was mistaken; after all, the imagination of a cold and tired sentry on night duty could easily play tricks on him. Then the shadow reappeared. "Halt! Who's there?" I shouted, lifting my rifle, pressing it steady against my shoulder. The outline of a man loomed up in front of my eyes, of uncommon height, a spectre wrapped in a greatcoat. Whoever it was didn't seem to have any intention of stopping. My heart was pounding. Had I waited too long? I took aim at the center of the silhouette stepping unperturbed towards me. As my finger touched the trigger I recognized *Obersturmbannführer* Hersche. I lowered my rifle and presented myself.

"Why didn't you shoot?" demanded the *Obersturmbannführer*.

"Well! I recognized…"

"And if I had been a paratrooper?"

"But…" I was speechless. I thought for an instant that I was embroiled in an absurd dream. The commander turned to continue his inspection round. I heard him rebuke harshly a pair of guards in the distance. Not being the only guard to have been chastised made me feel a little happier. *Obersturmbannführer* Hersche knew very well the risk he was taking for the good of those of us in the base. For the remainder of my spell of guard duty, and for those that followed, I made every effort to stay fully alert.

Later the same morning, with Gosse, I was on corvée duty at the prison cells and, as usual, we lined up the inmates along the corridor ready to go to the washrooms to empty their buckets. During those moments, they exchanged messages and took advantage of the little time they had to smoke and barter razor blades or tobacco. Although it was strictly forbidden to let them talk to each other we usually turned a blind eye to this in exchange for absolute obedience on other matters. I left my rifle with Gosse and made an inspection of the empty cells while he kept the situation under control in the corridor. When I had finished the inspection, and safely locked up the prisoners again, I went up to Gosse who was standing at the end of the corridor. As I approached him he whirled my rifle with one hand, like a cowboy with a six-shooter.

"Here have a go," Gosse said, returning my rifle.

As I emulated his demonstration, my index finger got stuck inside the trigger guard. The rifle recoiled as a shot rang out, echoing from the bare stone walls of the corridor. I was astounded.

"Shit," exclaimed Gosse, his face suddenly pale.

The barrel of my rifle was still smoking when the head sentry arrived. Without saying a word, he looked at the ceiling to locate the hole made by the bullet. Then he looked at the floor and prodded the flakes of plaster that had fallen with the toe of his boot. He shook his head as he looked me in the eye. "I think you'd better have a look upstairs," he said.

Strangely, I was not fearful as I ran upstairs. I had already convinced myself that I was in line for some harsh punishment. In the corridor above the one where I had accidentally loosed off a shot, I approached the door of a Military Justice office that corresponded with the shooting angle. Inside a *Rottenführer*, his elbows resting on his desk and hands gripping his fat jaws, looked at me and muttered, "Uh."

"Come in," said an officer standing beside another desk. "Are you the reckless one?"

I nodded, lowering my head.

"Come, come, have a look at this," the officer invited with a gesture of his arm.

"Uh!" repeated the *Rottenführer*, still sitting but turning towards me.

The bullet had left a scar of splinters up the back of his chair, missing him by a few millimeters before imbedding itself in the ceiling.

"I'll have to make a report," said the officer.

Without a word, still stunned, the *Rottenführer* passed me a form in triple-copy. I filled it in, my hand trembling as I committed the account of my misdeed to paper. Where there was space on the form to describe the motive of the transgression, I wrote: *accidental shooting.*

"You away with it," said Gosse, smiling, in the dormitory that evening.

"Lucky for me…no punishment," I answered.

"No, that's not what I mean…you had a close call. I could have killed you if a shot had gone out of the rifle when I showed you how to twirl."

We both decided it would be best not to dwell on the matter.

Karrotenkopf's Dignity

We from the guardhouse were not required to wait in line before entering the mess which presented us with the opportunity — which soon became a habit — to return for a second ration once everybody else had eaten. But the prospect of success for this maneuver depended on the personnel on kitchen duty. Besides *Karrotenkopf*, who controlled the entry stubs, there was an L.V.F. cook, a dumpy man of few words who always wore a serious expression on his face. All this fellow cared about was getting through the day so that he could walk away from the kitchen without a second thought with a piece of meat wrapped in greaseproof paper — or a slab of margarine, or simply some bread — hidden at the bottom of his satchel as he made his way to visit his girlfriend off-base. When he reappeared at five in the morning, his satchel contained tradable items such as cigarettes and chocolate. We at the guardhouse closed one eye — and sometimes two — at his coming and going and, in return of this favor, he turned a blind eye to our appearance in the food queue for double rations.

One day, Martin was disappointed when we found *Karrotenkopf* on stub-duty. "He does things by the book. No second helpings today," Martin said after we finished our food.

"Not so fast. Here…give me your stubs and just leave it to me," Gosse said, leaving us.

When Gosse reappeared from the dormitory, he was wearing a different helmet and had erased the marks left on our stubs by *Karrotenkopf's* pencil on our first visit. Gosse led Jean, Martin and me to join the last line of soldiers still waiting to enter the mess.

Karrotenkopf gave us a suspicious stare but nevertheless checked our stubs, marked them with a cross and let us in.

"A simple trick — rub out his pencil marks and wear a different helmet as a disguise," said Gosse, triumphantly.

"That dummy didn't even notice the erasures," said Jean.

We supped a second bowl of soup and when we had finished, Gosse put on his combat helmet and left the table to pop up again in front of the last few men in the queue at the door.

"*Ach!*" shrieked *Karrotenkopf*. "So you think you can cheat me?" His face suddenly turned red. "I am going to call the…the…"

"What's with him? Why is he jangling and bleating like a goat," asked Gosse, turning to the soldiers still in line.

"Let him pass, get it over with! We're hungry!" they called to *Karrotenkopf*.

"Hurry up! I have to report back to the guardhouse," Gosse urged.

"You don't fool me, smarty pants, miserable loafer!" Saliva sprayed from *Karrotenkopf's* mouth as he spoke.

Our friend, the L.V.F. came out from the kitchens, obviously concerned by the turmoil. He didn't want trouble and couldn't care less who was in the right and so let Gosse in while poor *Karrotenkopf*, incapable of expressing his anger in any other way, threw a bunch of stubs into the air.

The soldiers in the queue couldn't resist poking fun at *Karrotenkopf* as they entered the mess.

"Is this cross your signature?" a soldier asked.

"May I have your autograph?" another laughed.

"On your ass! I'll give it to you there!" *Karrotenkopf* aimed a kick, deftly avoided by the soldier, that had his leg swinging out of control, propelling him into a comical pirouette. The whole queue doubled up in laughter.

From then on, *Karrotenkopf* checked in minute detail every stub coming into his hands: he scrutinized them, turning them over and over. One day, though, Jean and I saw him at the mess entrance, his big mouth stretched from ear to ear in a sardonic smile. He was chuckling and muttering to himself, shaking his head in the manner of a man who was very, very pleased with himself. His pencil went to his mouth before crossing off each entry-stub — he was armed with an indelible pencil.

"He's forgotten about that smile stuck on his face," said someone in the mess queue.

"He's just carrying out his duty," another said.

"He thinks he's the provisions and supplies minister," a soldier said, his remark causing general laughter.

Karrotenkopf's master plan went smoothly at the beginning of mess call but, after marking dozens of stubs, and the continuous dampening of the pencil with the tip of his tongue, his lips had turned a dark-violet colour.

When Gosse and Martin arrived they burst into laughter. Gosse got close to *Karrotenkopf*, right under his nose. "But where are you going in such a mask. It's not Mardi Gras today," he teased in French.

Annoyed by the banter in French, *Karrotenkopf* cried for silence, "*Ruhe!*" which of course attracted even more jokes because of the violet slobbers dribbling from the corners of his mouth.

The commotion attracted the attention of the *uvedé* who, at the sight of *Karrotenkopf's* face, guessed the reason for the disturbance. "The head of the kitchens, where is he?"

The L.V.F. cook appeared as if from nowhere. "At your command, *Unterscharführer!*"

The *Unterscharführer* nodded towards *Karrotenkopf*. "Replace this man immediately."

Karrotenkopf, his plan in tatters, left with a dejected look on his freckled face.

"He was right, the *uvedé*, to replace him," I said, almost as a question.

"You're right Paul, in the *Waffen SS* we don't let anyone trample over a soldier's dignity," Martin said…his voice oozing with irony.

An Unfortunate Accident

In a beetroot field, Slav prisoners formed a semicircle, motionless, silent. I gave them a glance, signalling with my hand to keep a safe distance. I was the first to touch the pilot's scorched body; the other guards didn't have the stomach for it. A car stopped beside the site of impact. Two *Waffen SS* officers and representatives of civil and military authorities stepped out. One of them picked up a leather boot at about fifteen meters from the corpse. I saluted the *Waffen SS* officers before kneeling to raise the pilot's head for them to see. For a few seconds, they stared impassively at the battered, dirt-soiled face of the pilot whose yellow eyes, still attached to their optic nerves, hung out of their sockets. One of the officers gave a little nod — the signal for me to lower the dead man's head — before starting towards the smoking fuselage of the Messerschmitt 109. He caressed the swastika on the intact tail fin before moving to the dislodged engine which was almost buried by the force of the impact of the terrible crash.

The second officer scribbled in a little black book then turned to me. "Wrap him in his parachute for transport back to the base."

The men accompanying the *Waffen SS* officers continued to collect data while the first officer addressed the prisoner in charge of the work detail. "When did it happen?"

"Half an hour ago."

"Did it explode in mid-air?"

The prisoner stretched out his arms. "The wings were swaying."

"It left the squadron?"

"Yes, a few seconds...then bang!"

"The fighters were escorting military transport aircraft," explained the officer to a civilian standing at his side.

"It looks like the pilot died on impact...hurled out from the cockpit when the plane nosedived," added the second officer, having inspected the distribution of the crash debris.

Another vehicle arrived. Two soldiers got out carrying a stretcher just as the officers got back into their vehicle. The prisoners resumed their work while we took care of the corpse. I passed my hands under the pilot's armpits to lift him. His disfigured head flopped to the side to rest on my arm, soiling the sleeve of my coat. I felt a strong urge to vomit but managed to hold it down.

A comrade took the dead pilot's legs, to help me lift the body onto the stretcher. "His neck's broken," he said.

"This poor soul doesn't have a single bone unbroken," I replied.

Through an open window of the vehicle, I gave the smoking remnants of the plane a final glance. The driver accelerated on the narrow road, in the direction of our base, three kilometers away. It was a relief to get away from the smell of burnt flesh and spilled aircraft fuel.

Unfortunately, it fell to me to guard the pilot's body during the night vigil. The corpse still smelled of scorched cloth and blue gasoline, the type the fighter planes used. I lit up a cigarette, filled my nostrils and mouth with tobacco smoke hoping, but failing, to neutralize that smell of death.

Mignon's Revenge

As well as guardhouse duty, Gosse, Martin, Jean and I continued to participate in the training exercises involving the 80mm mortar section that we had been assigned to on our arrival at Greifenberg. We practised navigation on foot with the aid of a map and compass and shooting with the Mauser rifle and MG 42. *Panzerfaust* anti-tank training, which was fun, took place inside an area surrounded by an embankment of earth. Gas mask training was however something of an ordeal; jumping over obstacles, ramps and barriers wearing this unwieldy piece of equipment was an uncomfortable experience and so was learning to change its filter with closed eyes inside a gas chamber, a nerve-wracking one which, if not carried out strictly in accordance with instructions, left the eyes tearful and swollen. Nevertheless, all this training — and the frequent departures from the base as comrades were called to the front line — stimulated my eagerness for action.

Among those leaving for active service was the *Scharführer* of our mortar section whose place was filled by a young *Unterscharführer* not even in his twenties. When speaking, this newcomer blushed for no apparent reason which attracted everyone's attention and exacerbated the poor fellow's problem. This young non-commissioned officer strove to command with authority but his pink, baby-face undermined his efforts. Furthermore, he didn't express himself very well in German, so much so that when he issued orders, he only succeeded in creating confusion and it was up to us to save our section's honour by correcting them ourselves. After a few days, he was substituted by *Unterscharführer* Tron, who had fought in the Carpathians. Tron was not without his faults either; his imperfect German had a strong Bordeaux accent and he displayed something of an I-don't-give-a-damn attitude. Nevertheless, we accepted Tron as a competent leader of our section.

And then there was Mignon. Now, Mignon was a beast of a man, big and tall and very hairy. His thick, short neck and massive shoulders reminded me of a bull. This magnificent specimen of strength proved too much of a temptation for the bolder members of our mortar section who could not resist the challenge of playing tricks on him, which he usually took in apparent good humour. The authors of these pranks were, however, always very careful not to expose themselves by bragging about their exploits.

Once, somebody had the courage to pour water into Mignon's helmet in his absence. The giant took this prank in less-good humour and, his hair still dripping wet, warned everyone in the dormitory, "If I catch you in the act, I'll squash you. See these," he said displaying one bulging bicep after the other, "and these," he added, clenching his two massive fists in front of his chin like a boxer. "If you're man enough, reveal yourself!" He underlined his warning by smashing a fist on a table. We hid under the blankets in our cots until he cooled down. Only Jean dared taunt him sometimes, but he too had to be careful to take on the mighty Mignon at the right moment.

Mignon, without realizing or intending to, had his revenge on all of us in one go… during live-grenade training. Tron opened one of the wooden boxes set up in the training zone; inside were eight stick-grenades arranged alternately head to tail. He picked up one of them in his right hand and unscrewed the cap on the end of the handle with his left. A porcelain ball on the end of a cord fell out. "Pull the cord and the grenade will explode in five seconds…throw the grenade…then take cover," *Unterscharführer* Tron cautioned. Tron pulled the cord and threw the grenade with a long, lazy-looking movement of his arm. We dived for cover, burying our faces in our arms, under the protection of our helmets, and waited for the explosion. Bang! When it was Mignon's turn to throw, Tron repeated his earlier instructions, just to be on the safe side. "Pull the cord…remember this has to be done with confidence…bend back and twist your body a little to get leverage… like this…then toss the grenade and drop to the ground. Understood?"

Mignon nodded and confidently unscrewed the safety cap on the handle. He pulled the cord and leaned backwards, ready to launch the small but deadly bomb. He swung his arm. Our mouths dropped open when we saw it stop at the top of the arc of his throw, then fall to his side. Smoke from the fuse spiralled from the hollow handle of the grenade and up Mignon's arm. *Unterscharführer* Tron looked at him with eyes as round as cart wheels.

"Throw it!" screamed Tron.

"I'm left handed," Mignon said calmly.

Unterscharführer Tron hit the ground and we followed his example.

Mignon looked around as if he had all the time in the world, swapped the grenade to his left hand and threw it. Before it reached the top of its trajectory, it exploded. BANG! Shrapnel whizzed above our heads.

Unterscharführer Tron got up slowly, shaking his head in disbelief and looking at us as we brushed the dirt from our uniforms with our hands. "Thank God no one is hurt."

"That was a helluva long five seconds," Jean said.

Gosse sniffed the air like a curious kitten. "There's a funny smell around here," he said, touching his behind. Everyone laughed. And Mignon…well, he smiled his big, meaty smile.

Traitor in our Midst

The frequent departures and arrivals unsettled the fellows in our mortar section but at the guardhouse, now in a permanent state of alert, we maintained our usual rigorous discipline. Then, one evening, two policemen approached the head sentry with a suntanned individual under their guard. The policemen handed over their report to the *uvedé*.

"Looks like an Arab merchant," Gosse remarked, as we removed the prisoner's hat and coat.

The prisoner remained steadfastly silent. A lock of his long, black curly hair dangled on his forehead as his dark eyes searched the room.

"Who knows what underhand dealings he's involved in," I said.

"Where you come from?" Gosse asked in French.

"Marseille."

"Oh! So you do speak," Gosse remarked sarcastically.

"Very well! Are you a thief, a trafficker or a deserter?" Martin asked him.

The Marseillais didn't answer. Like a frightened dog, he shuffled towards the head sentry, who came from the waiting room with the report in his hands.

"He was apprehended in Berlin," said the sentry who read the report aloud, lingering over the main charges. "Suspicious and equivocal connections with French prisoners in Berlin. Irregular personal status. Prime suspect as information source of K.G. — boh, don't know what these initials stand for — from which secret data are transmitted to France. At the moment of arrest, found in possession of a list of names concerning the effectives of Brigade 'Charlemagne'..."

The Marseillais' cold-chapped lips began to tremble. A grave but short-lived silence came between him and us.

The head sentry slapped the prisoner's face. "Dirty spy!"

"Lousy skunk!" Gosse thundered, drawing his bayonet.

"Easy, easy Gosse," Jean said. "We have all the time we need now that he is in our hands, no?"

"So you are a spy and a traitor eh?" I said, clenching my teeth.

The Marseillais turned his distressed eyes from me to look at the others, as if seeking assistance. His lips quivered but he remained silent. At that moment Mignon arrived to take his turn at guard duty. Mignon's face revealed a fierce sneer when he smiled, his short nose almost disappearing between solid cheekbones. He was not the sort of fellow to solve a problem by the power of thought. The Marseillais turned pale.

"Who is this?" Mignon asked, staring at the Marseillais.

"You see...we too have our own methods," Gosse said, alluding to the arrival of the giant Mignon, evidently savouring the unfolding scenario. He prodded the prisoner's shoulder with a fist. "So...worm of a spy...how many names did you pass on to the *Maquis*?"

"And for what reason?" I said, supporting Gosse, but already guessing the answer.

"It's not...it's not my fault...they forced me...you must believe me...I swear it," whined the Marseillais.

"So now you tell us why," roared Mignon, clamping a hand on the young man's neck and lifting him clear of the floor.

"Let me…I tell you…I swear it," he gasped, his face deformed by the giant's grip.

Mignon lowered the unfortunate young man to the floor.

The Marseillais sobbed as he rubbed the pain from his bruised neck.

"He is trying to gain time, this bastard low life," blurted Gosse, holding the blade of his bayonet to the spy's throat. "Now…tell us…what happens with the names."

"They are transmitted to the *Maquis*," the Marseillais confessed.

"And then?" asked Gosse, pricking the prisoner with the tip of his bayonet.

"Then the *Maquis* try to contact their parents or relatives…to advise them of the danger they run. Don't you see you are on the wrong side?" The man broke down, sobbed as he pressed his hands together as if in prayer before composing himself at little. "You are French," he said, "like me…like your parents at home in France, your…our Motherland." Encouraged by our silence he continued, "You are fighting for the *Boches*. It is a lost cause, believe me!"

We hesitated, stunned by the prisoner's words.

"I have no father and no mother and don't want relatives neither!" Martin cut in.

"Coward of a traitor," Gosse shouted at him, hitting the prisoner's head with the flat of his bayonet.

Jean, logical Jean, intervened before the situation got out of hand. "Hold it Gosse. Let's get down to the point here. This charlatan is switching his tune." Jean turned to look hard into the Marseillais' terrified eyes. "You've given the names to the *Maquis*?"

"Yes… but…"

"And the *Maquis* go to seek out our parents?"

"Yes…to warn them," the prisoner said.

"Or to kill them in cold blood," Jean yelled, blobs of his saliva spattering the prisoner's face.

Every muscle in the prisoner's body was quivering now. "No no…only to…"

With anger swelling in my heart, I pulled Gosse away from the petrified man. "You tell your friends in the *Maquis* to seek vengeance because their sons are *Waffen SS* men, right?"

"Believe me…it's not like this…it's not true…" he groaned.

"Poisonous snake! I'll tear out your tongue!" bawled Mignon as his powerful hands stretched towards the man's throat.

Jean and the head sentry grabbed Mignon's arms to restrain him from throttling the man right there and then. The others, with their hands free, tossed the Marseillais about with blows from their fists and wild kicks. I knew this was wrong but my judgement, blinded as it was by my smouldering anger, told me it was also just. I thought of my family, of my parents being tortured then killed by the *Maquis* because I was a *Waffen SS* soldier and there was nothing I could do to stop my anger igniting into blind fury. I elbowed my way between my comrades, clasped the prisoner's throat and smashed two blows with my fist into his face. As he recoiled, my boot sunk into his belly until he slumped to the floor. "The game's up for you, you bastard," I screamed, as Martin and Gosse joined me in giving this skunk exactly what he deserved.

Jean intervened. "Hold on my friends. He's had enough for now. Military justice will take care of him."

We dumped the traitor in a cell, bloodied and bruised.

Forgotten Faith

Toward the end of December, together with some of the other guards from the 1st Company, I was often on patrol duty in Greifenberg. Our task was to keep order on the streets which were choked with refugees from the east, fleeing from the Russian Army. Mostly they were women and children bundled up in layers of clothes, pulling overladen handcarts or pushing bicycles. A few had their possessions piled up on wagons pulled by small Pomeranian horses, their backs whitened by iced sweat as they strained to overcome the resistance created by the thickening snow. Our words of encouragement, of consolation, were countered by the refugees' lurid tales of rape and sickening, depraved barbarity perpetrated by the Russian 'soldiers'.

Toward evening I came across an eight or nine-year-old boy, trembling with cold and hunger, holding the reins of a horse at the shaft of a cart. Sitting among a few items of furniture on the cart was an old woman, her hands at the cusp of the flame of a little lamp; beside her sat a girl on a plywood box and, at the back, an old man pushed. I grabbed the bridle and led them to the already crowded gathering center for refugees where I made sure they had hot milk and a dry, warm corner for the night; one frightened family amongst the tens-of-thousands fleeing the encroaching enemy. Their plight touched and angered my soul, aroused a yearning to go to the front, to fight, to play my part in stopping these Bolshevik hordes before it was too late to fulfill what I felt to be my destiny.

Late in the evening, after being relieved by the next man on the patrol rota, I was making my way back to the base when I was attracted by the yellowish light coming from the partly open door of a church. By this time a heavy frost had set in, covering the snow with a myriad of sparkling ice crystals. I pushed the door open and entered, trying to limit the clatter of my hobnailed boots on the shiny marble floor by taking careful steps. Curved over the benches, motionless in their meditation, a handful of worshipers chanted a prayer with the pastor who knelt on the steps of the altar. Some turned to look at me with sombre eyes. The pastor, at the end of prayers, came down the aisle, ignoring me, a silence that told me my presence was incompatible with a place of worship. But the pastor's pointed refusal to acknowledge my presence did not trouble me. I felt a calmness flood into my troubled mind, a moment of peace among the turmoil that was war. I felt a spiritual energy take hold of me, stir the ashes of my forgotten faith. I went out into the cold of the night thinking of the boy and his family that I had helped, thinking too of the time my own family had been forced to flee. I tightened my collar to keep out the cold and hurried back to the base.

Childhood's End

On Christmas day 1944, *Obersturmbannführer* Hersche gave a speech in French to the companies assembled in the courtyard in which ended with: "Your families are thinking of you when you are away from home and no more so than at this special time of the year. And you too will be thinking of them. But there is something else that we *Waffen SS* soldiers have to think about and that is faith, faith in our ultimate victory and your return to your homes, to your families, at the end of the war. *Heil* Hitler!"

"*Sieg Heil!*" we answered in a resounding chorus.

At the end of the speech, every one of us received a gift box from the *Führer* and we went back to the dormitory eager to open them.

Martin sat on the side of his cot, slowly turning the unopened package over in his hands. "I will tell you something my friends," he said, "this is the first time in my life I've received such gifts."

"Same for me," Gosse added.

"Thinking about it…I don't recall having any either," Jean said.

"Do you think they'll be the same for everyone?" Martin asked, still fiddling with his gift.

"I think so," answered Jean.

"Then we'll open them together," I proposed. I cut open the lid with my bayonet and from the straw-like green and yellow wrapping paper, lifted a small bottle of liquor.

"Hei…a pack of cigarettes," Martin exclaimed.

"And razor blades," said Gosse.

From the calls of delight from our other comrades in the dormitory, it was clear that every one of us received identical gifts.

"So, they consider us to be *Waffen SS* soldiers, complete and ready on all accounts," I said.

"Even though we are the youngest ones," said Martin.

"Sure, this is proof that we have the same rights as our older comrades but we will soon face the same dangers," Jean said in a subdued voice.

The war was closing in on Greifenberg; we slept fully dressed, with satchels and pack-sacks at the side of our cots, ready to leave at a moment's notice and, on one of the last days of the year, we mustered in the town square. Snowflakes, beautiful, big snowflakes fell as an officer delivered another pep talk. I stood at attention only half-listening as he did his best to whip up an *espirit de corps* but it was his last words that shook me back to reality: "…an exemplary punishment for traitors and deserters." I thought of the oath by which I was bound — '*loyalty unto death*'. This was not a game of soldiers.

While on patrol in town, I was drawn to an attractive blond girl distributing milk and biscuits to the children of refugees. Her knees were bent, her body leaning forward as she talked to a small boy. She ruffled the boy's hair then hooked her shoulder-length hair behind her ear as I approached. In the magical moments that followed, I discovered her name was Heidi and somehow managed to secure her promise to meet me that evening at a restaurant I had already visited several times and which was favored by soldiers from the base. My spell on duty dragged intolerably but I consoled myself by thinking of her beautiful smile and her perfect, little nose.

At last I found myself at the door of the restaurant, waiting for her, the blood rushing through my veins. And when she appeared, she was even more beautiful than I had remembered. Our entry was greeted by a waiter's perfect military salute. I helped her with her coat and hung it on the row of coat hooks near the entrance, beside my helmet and bayonet. As usual, the place was busy so I asked the waiter for a small table I knew of, the one shielded from the rest of the restaurant by a screen where I could enjoy her company with a degree of privacy. Soon we were exchanging the sort of stories that young men and women do when they first meet.

"What will you do after your studies?" I asked.

"I was training to be a nurse…but now I am helping with the refugees. With all that's happening in this crazy war, I haven't yet finished my courses. And what about you…the front is getting closer with every day that passes?"

"We are still at the base because we are the youngest ones but soon…" despite feeling that I could trust her, I stopped myself mid-sentence because we had orders not to talk to civilians about military matters. With a delicate movement, tilting her head to the side, she rearranged her hair in a way that somehow evoked the impression that she was surrounded by a field of golden wheat on a warm, sky-blue afternoon.

A voice interrupted my daydream. "Hei, Paul!"

It was Martin; he was standing with Gosse at the bar. I answered him by waving my hand.

"So this is where you're holed up," Gosse said, as the pair made their way to our 'private' table.

"We were looking for you everywhere," said Martin, though his eyes were fixed on Heidi.

"Paul, you must introduce us to this beautiful young lady," Gosse said before making a neat bow.

"Sit down with us, please," Heidi invited them, after I had made the introductions.

"Where do you work?" Gosse asked.

"At the *Luftwaffe.*"

"There's room," Heidi said, renewing her invitation.

I could see by Gosse's manner that he would have liked to join us but he replied saying, "No no, we have to go…and besides, we don't want to disturb you."

At the exit, while they put on their coats, Martin exclaimed, in French, "Wow! Did you see her…what a pair of boobs…big and round like…"

"Like the best milking cow from Brittany," Gosse interrupted, chuckling.

Heidi launched an inquisitive glance at me.

"Those jokers, they're always looking for trouble," I said.

"They're nice though," she added, titling her head alluringly.

Alone again, we continued the boy-girl chat when we finished our meal, our eyes meeting frequently, our fingers touching across the table. "It seems the entire base is here," she said after a while.

I felt my pulse quicken. "Would you like to take a walk?"

She smiled as she began to rise from the table, "Why are we waiting?"

We strolled along a path in a park, holding hands, in the ice-cold moonlight.

"It must be wonderful here, in summertime," I said.

"In peacetime, it is beautiful."

We came to a bench and, without a word, sat down together, listening to the splashing of a little stream nearby. I was aware that the night was slipping by in a hurry and that I would soon have to return to the base. I plucked up my courage and put my arm across her shoulder. She turned to face me, moving her mouth towards mine and, in a moment of sheer bliss, our lips met. One kiss flowed into the next as we held each other in a passionate embrace. Time, the war, seemed irrelevant as our hands found the warmth of the other's body. I was losing myself on a rising wave of ecstasy when the trotting of an approaching horse demanded my attention. I pulled away from Heidi; laid a hand on my pistol. "It's Hersche," I said in a hushed voice. I sprung to attention as Hersche's horse leapt over the stream and pulled up in front of our bench.

"At ease young man. We are in the depth of night, don't you think?"

"*Ja mein Kommandant.*" I relaxed and took a step forward to rub the pure-bred's warm nose; he let go a loud puff from his nostrils — he recognized me.

Hersche warned me in French about the danger I was running being isolated from my comrades at such late hour before he prodded the horse's flanks with his spurs and disappeared into the shadows.

Heidi took my hand, "What did he say?"

"He was telling me about a soldier that was stabbed with his own bayonet one night, while he was separated from his comrades."

"Oh," she exclaimed with sincere concern, "poor soul!"

"Well!" I cut short, "Now you know my commander."

Heidi giggled as she linked into my arm, "He chooses a strange hour for riding."

"A magnificent evening!" I was able to tell Gosse and Martin when I got back to the dormitory.

"Magnificent blond more like," Martin answered from his cot.

It took me longer than usual to fall asleep that night. I kept thinking about those sweet eyes and the oasis of peace, of light-heartedness, that seemed to surround Heidi wherever she went.

Tomfoolery and a Test of Courage

I jumped to a sitting position, scratching my armpit. "Damned beasts!"

On the cot a few steps away Jean lifted his head from the pillow. "What is it Paul?"

"Fleas!"

"Eh," said Jean, "sleep tight...they've invaded all the cots...it's just that yours are still hungry."

"Where did the little bastards come from? We didn't bring them from Sennheim, for sure," I said scratching now at my waist.

"They're Russian fleas," Gosse said, peeking over the edge of the upper cot.

"Damn the Russians, their fleas, lice and whatever else they bring along," I said.

"You're mistaken my friend," said Martin, "The fleas are brought in by the L.V.F. soldiers returning from the front."

"But they washed the sheets and disinfected the cots only a few days ago. These bloodsuckers should have gone, no?" I moaned.

"Eh my dear," Gosse said, "the dirt can be washed away but not those little beasts, those stay."

Jean made an astute observation. "I'm convinced they want a ride back to the Russian Front and they've chosen us as their means of transport."

Martin yawned. "I've heard we're to have a disinfestation day tomorrow, at Treptow."

❦—❦

After disembarking at Treptow 's station, we lined up, company by company, at a shed where an open-topped tank filled with boiling water and disinfectant bubbled like a witch's cauldron. We threw in our clothes.

"Burst damn parasites," I said with a sneer of vengeance in my voice.

"I bet there will be some with hard skin," Martin said, throwing in his one remaining garment.

Naked and cold, we entered the shed in which showers had been set up. We soaped every inch of our skins, relishing the sensation of being clean again.

"Guys! Look at Mignon, he really has phenomenal biceps," Gosse whispered.

"And the pectorals…and the abdominals," Martin added with admiration.

"The soap bar disappears between his muscles," I pointed out.

"Too bad he has an empty big head," said Gosse.

"Eh, Gosse, to each his own," Jean said.

"Want a laugh?" said Gosse.

Jean stopped soaping his buttocks to look at Gosse. "What are you plotting now, Gosse?"

"You'll see Jean," he said, leaving the showers with a smirk on his face. He came back almost immediately with a paper bag in his hands. "Sssst!" he cautioned, emptying little, intensely red pills from the bag into the palm of his hand. "I happened to see them on the table, when we came in."

"What do you have in mind?"

"Sssst…keep your voice down…watch." Gosse crumbled the pills between his palms by rubbing them together then edged up from the rear, to Mignon, who was humming out of tune. Gosse jumped to empty the powder in his hand onto the top of the giant's head and retreated, nonchalantly whistling a jaunty tune.

The unsuspecting Mignon closed his eyes and rubbed his soap bar in his thick hair. The soap soon formed a vivid-red froth which ran down Mignon's neck and shoulders and onto his chest and back.

"Hei! Mignon. You're bleeding," Jean shouted.

In the hot mist of the showers, Mignon rubbed the soap from his face and looked down at the red puddle at his feet. He stood still for an instant and then gave a feeble cry. His eyes rolled in their sockets as he half-turned on himself before collapsing to the floor.

"Damn!" We ran up to the enormous, prone body.

"Get him out of the showers." There was panic in Gosse's voice.

The three of us worked together to drag Mignon out of the wet area and were soon assisted by some of the other fellows from our company. Soon there was a crowd of onlookers staring at the naked body of the giant Mignon.

"He's bleeding," said a voice in the crowd, "He needs a medic."

"It's nothing. Only red dye," I said.

"It's a joke," Gosse added, dismissing the curious bystanders with a hand gesture. He looked at me. "What should I do?"

"Slap him in his face till he comes round," I said. "Then run."

Gosse's already pale face turned a shade or two paler. "Who, me?" he said in pained incredulity. "Not on your life!"

Farewell to Greifenberg

Shortly before Martin and Gosse were due to be transferred to Wildflecken, Gosse had somehow found out that the key for the food store was the same as the key for the clinic and that was left in the guardhouse by civilian workers when they left the base each day. Armed with this knowledge, Gosse had kept himself well-fed and was now passing this secret on to me one freezing night when we were on guard duty in the courtyard. Perhaps it was hunger that drove Jean and I to raid the food store, but I also remember the sheer terror I felt on that little foray which, if we had been caught, would certainly have led us in front of a firing squad. The departure of Gosse and Martin, who had enticed me into risky escapades on several other occasions, therefore came as something of a relief for me though I was sad to see them go.

After the departure of the likeable rogues Gosse and Martin, there were not many of us left in the base at Greifenberg in February 1945 when *Standartenführer* Zimmermann and *Obersturmbannführer* Hersche reviewed the troops in the courtyard. We stood rigidly at attention with our mess tins, gas-mask canisters, and full ammunition pouches attached to our harnesses. A few of us carried the *Panzerfaust* anti-tank weapon. Everything contributed to suggesting we were ready for deployment.

Standartenführer Zimmermann shouted at the top of his voice from the center of the courtyard, so that everybody could hear him perfectly: "Our faithfulness to Germany and to Europe calls on us to throw back the Soviet invader. The army of the 'New Europe' is ready for battle; it is ready to make the supreme sacrifice for victory... *Heil* Hitler!"

"*Sieg Heil! Sieg Heil! Sieg Heil!*" we responded in unison.

In the dormitory that evening, a sombre mood prevailed as we prepared for our inevitable transfer to the front line. Jean and I had still some leftovers from the packets of food we pilfered from the food store in Building A, and these we added to the three-day ration issued in the afternoon.

"Better get some sleep," Jean said, pulling his blankets over his head.

Within a few minutes Jean was snoring but sleep came less easily to me and I found myself thinking of the time I had spent with Heidi who, because of the permanent state of alert, I had only managed to meet on a few occasions. And the more I thought of her, the more I wished she was there, beside me, so that I could hold her close for what might be the last time. Then, as my mind hovered between sleep and wakefulness, I imagined her lips kissing my forehead in exactly the same way my mother had done when I was hiding in bed, frightened by the detonations of the cannons on the Maginot Line at the outbreak of war…

❦—❦

"*Achtung! Achtung!*" *Unterscharführer* Tron howled, opening wide the dormitory door, slamming it against the wall. "Move, move. To the muster!"

"Here we go!" Jean said, jumping down from his cot.

It was still dark. I rubbed my eyes. The cold, crisp air in the dormitory pinched at my cheeks, wakening me completely.

In the courtyard, soft snowflakes soon covered our helmets and shoulders with a delicate, white layer as we stood at attention. An *Unterscharführer* marched up to an officer standing besides Hersche to report: "*Hauptsturmführer,* the 33rd *Waffen Grenadier Division der SS Marsch Bataillion* is at your command."

"Prepare to march, by fours, in total silence!"

"*Jawohl Hauptsturmführer*!" Then, turning to the assembled soldiers, he repeated the *Hauptsturmführer's* orders.

Soon, it was our section's turn to join the column leaving the base. *Unterscharführer* Tron, his chest swelling with pride, yelled, "1st Company, in column by fours, forward march!"

We crossed the town, in the direction of the station, the rhythmical thud of our boots on the snow waking many inhabitants who came to clap their hands, to encourage us, their last defense line. They lined both sides of the street and some even accompanied us as far as the station. Girls hugged soldiers as they passed but I shunned their attention, my eyes searching the faces in the crowds, looking in vain for Heidi. At that moment, although surrounded by comrades I had grown to regard almost as brothers, a cold draught of loneliness tempered my enthusiasm for the coming adventure.

At the station, I removed the tricolour epaulette that identified me as French from my left shoulder and put it in my pocket. We were obliged to wear them sewn on but the guard section and the 1st Company rejected them on the grounds that they might incite trouble when walking out on evening leave. We at the guardhouse attached them by means of pins so that they were readily removed when guard duty was over.

❧—❧

The train left Greifenberg, running across flat, snow-covered fields. I sat near Jean, on the floor, in a corner of a packed wagon, away from the cold draughts cutting in through gaps around the sliding doors and, fatigued by boredom, eventually fell into a dreamy doze but the noise of wagons tugging at each other wakened me.

Jean was smiling at me when I opened my eyes. "What's so amusing," he asked.

"Oh, I was thinking of these jokers, Gosse and Martin. "I miss their pranks already," I said with a sigh.

"I wonder where they are now. With them leaving, our good laughs ended," said Jean.

"In combat somewhere…they're in an 80mm mortar section too."

After a moment's thought, Jean asked, "You believe they'll send us into the first line?"

"First or second, what's the difference, in times like these."

The train jolted to a halt and, minutes later, the sliding doors opened allowing the light and cold air to flood into the wagon's interior. An officer ordered us to jump out, to allow a machine-gun to be installed, a process that was repeated in nearly every wagon. Chilled to the core, we climbed back into the wagon and gathered straw from the floor for insulation.

The train backtracked several times, a ploy to confuse Russian spies, then took a different direction, into the frigid luminescence of the open countryside. I sank into the straw's embrace and, lulled by the rhythmical movement of the wagon, dozed. These innumerable diversions and seemingly interminable stops and stretches when the train moved at barely walking pace lasted three days. Boredom and hunger were rife among us. I was down to my last biscuit and was left with only a couple of cigarettes. I gave one to Jean and we smoked them together during a stop lasting several hours in open country when we leapt from the wagon to stretch our legs, pacing back and forth so that we were ready to clamber back into the wagon in case the train started moving again.

"At Greifenberg," Jean reminisced, "we had packs of these cigarettes."

"I remember that *Rottenführer*, that thief in our dormitory at Sennheim." One of our comrades, hidden under a cot, had surprised him while he was gathering dirty clothes to wash, and not only clothes: he pocketed a bunch of cigarettes left by us in plain view, just to tempt him. He had lifted several previously, arousing our suspicions. We were annoyed, not so much at the miserly amount of cigarettes we lost, but by the order forbidding us to secure our lockers. At Sennheim there were no thieves; according to regulations they didn't exist. We were therefore obliged to deal with the thief ourselves.

Jean let go a ring of smoke from his mouth, stretched in a mute letter 'o'. "I wonder if he still carries the marks of the studs of our belts on his back," he mused.

The locomotive blew its whistle.

"He was in the infirmary long enough," I said, lifting up my collar against the cold.

"Well! He had at least the good sense to stop wearing the *Waffen SS* uniform," Jean said, flicking his cigarette butt into the snow.

The wagon moved forward one step, its buffers clunking against those of the wagon in front as we clambered aboard.

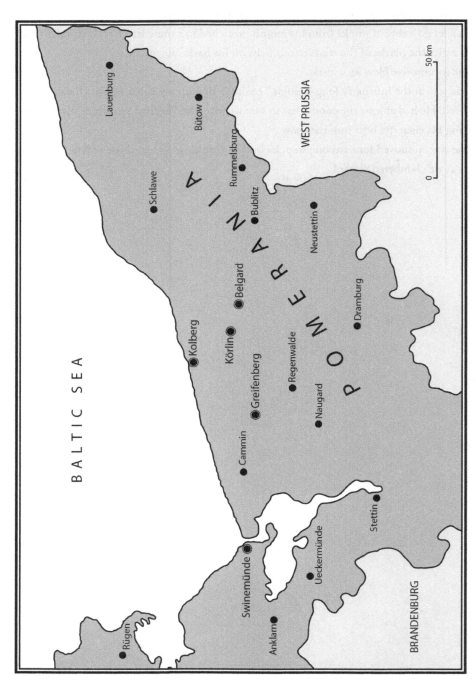

Pomerania

3

The Battle of Körlin

To War at Last

The train stopped in vicinity of Körlin. Along its length, wagon doors slid open and the troops inside jumped to the ground in haste but in good order. We, the half-starved men of the three companies of the *Greifenberg Marsch Bataillon*, formed ranks on the snow-covered ground. As we stood at attention waiting for further instructions, the seeping cold added to our discomfort by biting at our toes while our empty stomachs groaned for food. After a while — it might have been two hours — *Unterscharführer* Tron let us break ranks and gave permission to eat but we had already consumed most of the meagre rations issued in Greifenberg. Jean and I joined some comrades to undertake a hopeful search for the *roulante*, our mobile kitchen, dreaming of mess tins filled with hot soup, but were interrupted by the order for muster which forced us to run back to our wagon.

As we waited in silence for the order to board the train, the ominous, distant rumble of cannonades and echoes of explosions rolled across the grey, snow-laden sky. An *Obersturmführer* arrived carrying a briefcase; he spoke with an officer, an *Oberscharführer*, who then came towards us and promptly stopped our group from boarding the train. The *Obersturmführer* then approached and, bending forward to shelter the contents of his briefcase from the icy breeze, he took out a few sheets of paper and in a loud voice called out the names of those from our group who were to gather on his left; this included Jean, Mignon and some others, who were now under the command of *Unterscharführer* Tron. Starting with my name — that is my mother's German family name which I declared at the time of recruiting — the officer began to read a list of those who were to assemble to his right. I stepped forward to stand at attention beside the officer as he read the remaining names. When the division of the troop was complete, the officer turned to us and rasped out the duty of each of us in the newly formed mortar crew. "*Waffen SS* Papis, *Richtschütze*; *Sturmmann SS* Bournique, *Truppführer*; *Waffen SS* La Journisse, *Munitionsschütze*." I was appointed *Ladeschütze* — my task was to drop the projectiles (or charges as we called them) into the mortar tube but, I wondered, would I be able to repeat those mechanical movements with the coolness I had learned during training?

"Mortar section, three steps forward," ordered the *Obersturmführer*. He turned to the non-commissioned officer accompanying him: "*Oberscharführer* De Ville, you have the command of this section."

"*Jawohl Obersturmführer!*"

"*Oberscharführer* De Ville, you now have a four mortar crews under your command, a total of twenty-five soldiers plus two non-commissioned officers. Wait for the arrival of your weapons," said the officer as he handed a wallet of documents to the *Oberscharführer*. "These are the General Staff's maps with your route marked in black, study them well, the general direction is that way," he specified, raising his arm to indicate a point north of Körlin. He then left in a hurry to assign tasks to the other troops in the company.

"Mortar section…mark time! Right turn…forward!" ordered our new commander, who then led us across the snow towards Körlin. We marched for about twenty minutes until we reached the first buildings where *Oberscharführer* De Ville stopped and raised his right hand, "Section halt! At ease! Dismissed, boys…we sleep here tonight."

I looked at what was soon to be our billet; a shabby-looking structure made of crudely nailed-on timber slats that would do little to fend off the deepening frost. The cold, damp atmosphere inside did nothing to dispel my feeling of gloominess. I searched for a corner to lie down and gnaw at my last *Knäckebrot* (ration biscuit). Too tired to think, I closed my eyelids and fell immediately into a deep sleep. Minutes later, for so it seemed, I was wakened by distant but ominous thuds and explosions that made the ground tremble beneath my body. The light from flares falling on their parachutes cut through the gaps in the timber walls like dazzling blades, like flashes of lightening. All around, there was the sound of battle but nevertheless, after a while, I fell asleep.

At dawn on Sunday 4 March 1945, hungry and cold, we left the frigid billet to wait for the arrival of our heavy armaments. There was a thin layer of fresh snow at our feet and a sharp frost aggravated our desire for food. At last, a team of horses pulling a wagon arrived with our 80mm mortars and other weapons; a mule pulling a cart loaded with ammunitions followed close behind. *Oberscharführer* De Ville talked with the horse-handlers to make sure that the area assigned to us corresponded with what they knew since they had been there, on that location, the previous day when bringing supplies to soldiers already in position. De Ville immediately made preparations for us to move out, to follow the carts carrying the mortars and ammunition.

Just outside of Körlin, we encountered another wagon, pulled by two horses.

"Ohé, stop. Halt!" one of the drivers shouted; the other gave a wave of his hand in our column's direction.

"Look…that's two L.V.F. veterans," I exclaimed. I had come across them in Greifenberg and recognized them from a distance.

"And that's a roulante they're dragging behind them," exclaimed Jean, who was only a few steps from me.

"Our field kitchen!" somebody in our group shouted, his voice bursting with undisguised joy.

We ran to meet the L.V.F cooks, gathered around the faint but welcome warmth radiating from the device while they distributed the hot soup.

"By Jupiter…we looked for you everywhere people," the first cook said.

"True…what an effort…where the hell were you?" the second said, handing out packs of cigarettes.

I reached out my mess tin which the cook filled with a single scoop of his ladle; a trickle of the precious hot soup trickled down my hand which I licked up before it had time to cool. We ate in haste and in silence, gulping down our long-awaited breakfast, savouring its taste and warmth as it descended deliciously from our throats to our stomachs. Then, like the others, I too lit up a cigarette, inhaling its smoke with satisfaction. I could feel the exhaustion leave my body and my half-frozen facial muscles loosening up.

The hot food in my stomach restored my enthusiasm for the onward march. I joined my comrades in thanking the cooks and gave them a hearty wave before heading across the exposed fields where the wind whipped up swirls of ice crystals that stung our eyes. By the time we came to the Persante River, the bitter cold had again seeped through our greatcoats to make its home in our bones. Here, the drivers of the wagons transporting our equipment pulled on the reins of their horses, bringing them to a halt close to the slow-flowing river. At the right side of the narrow river, in foxholes, soldiers manned the defense lines with their MG 42s while upstream from us advance units had taken up position.

"It is an ideal place for our mortars," *Oberscharführer* De Ville said, observing a short incline sparsely covered with young pine trees two meters tall, or less. "Let's get to work with the shovels," he ordered, "that'll soon warm us up."

The location of every mortar emplacement was traced on the snow, spaced at equal intervals one from the other. Each was dug out; a circular pit that would offer protection for the mortar crew and their equipment.

"The ground is good," Bournique, the crew leader declared after clearing a patch of ice-crusted snow.

"Yes…clay and sand…you can cut it like a layer of coffee grounds," I answered. I knew him by sight from the 1st Company at Greifenberg; he was in his thirties, married and had children. He had been recruited originally by the *Kriegsmarine* but had been transferred, like most of the men in our ranks, to the *Waffen SS*. "What did you do before enlisting?" I asked, as I leaned on my shovel, catching my breath.

Bournique, who was stockly built but slightly shorter than average height, looked at me with his small, round eyes. "I didn't enlist! I was forced to wear this uniform."

"Eh?" Because I was a volunteer, Bournique's words surprised me.

"Leaving German Lorena and crossing into France with my wife, sons and thirty kilos of baggage didn't seem like an attractive option. I preferred to be German, even though the *Boches* were not exactly to my liking.

"What did you do for a living?"

"I was a farmer...dig with a spade I did, like now, mixing dirt...like this." With a blow of his shovel, he launched a clod of earth and snow high into the air. *Sturmmann* Bournique liked to talk about his family and his work on the fields.

Papis, the mortar gunner and a good comrade of mine, was younger, in his twenties. We had often laughed together at Gosse's quips and jokes. In some ways, Papis resembled Gosse, but had a smaller face and short, blond hair and moustache and he was a more reserved character. He often hung around with us at the base in Greifenberg and joined us on our jaunts into town. *Richtschütze* Papis and I dug like we had learned during training, with ardor, well almost. The result was a circular hole a little more than two meters across into which we lowered our mortar which we secured to the ground. To complete the installation, we dug a sloping channel in each side, ending at a right angle, and there Papis and I arranged the ammunition — about forty projectiles in all — sufficient for a limited exchange of fire had the Russians attacked in those moments.

The tanned face of La Journisse popped up from a short trench next to the mortar pit with his spade in his hand. "The mole comes out the tunnel," he said in his southern, Nice accent. He was very young too, not yet eighteen, and in his intensely dark eyes, the glint of the Mediterranean sun seemed to linger — but now there was also a hint of fear. As *Munitionschütze*, La Journisse prepared the charges before passing them to me, the *Ladeschütze*.

When the mortar pits were complete, I joined *Oberscharführer* De Ville on his inspection tour. He was very satisfied with our work and he seemed to me to be a good man with an almost paternal concern for his men. I took to him readily and from then on he always addressed me by my first name. He had taken part in the Carpathian battles and that experience had given him the confidence needed by a leader. He always spoke calmly in conversation, which was in accord with his good-natured attitude to life. It was another matter altogether when it came to issuing orders; those he conveyed loudly and without any hesitation, demanding total obedience. His authoritarian expression, the scowl on his ample face and the thick, short neck planted over two massive shoulders commanded respect, if not fear. To me, his presence inspired a certain feeling of safety; I trusted him and would have carried out any order he gave, without hesitation.

Lucky Sunday

Papis, La Journisse and I, having permission from *Sturmmann* Bournique, headed towards a cluster of houses that seemed to have been abandoned. They were graceful, surrounded by trees and complete with garden and courtyard in front and a henhouse at the back where I saw a turkey busy pecking around in the muddy snow. I picked up a stone and threw it with force, hitting the bird which began to screech and scream, flapping its wings and ruffling its feathers. I chased it, hopping here and there, accompanied by the laughter of my comrades, until I knocked it out with the butt of my rifle. "At least we'll have something to scare our hunger away," I said, satisfied, "I can barely remember having eaten that soup this morning."

"This will calm down the *Oberscharführer's* stomach too," Papis added.

"Not to mention the whole battery, don't you see how fat it is?" La Journisse observed.

Encouraged by my lucky find, I proposed searching the remaining houses. In the cellar of the first, we found shelves loaded with salami and sausages and chunks of pork meat and bands of lard hung from the ceiling. And there were still more treasures; on the shelves, a row of jars of marmalade and preserve was placed in good order. I released the lid of one of those jars and dipped in a finger, "Strawberry jam!"

"Ham…I found a slab of ham," Papis exclaimed, coming downstairs. "I found it under some dirty clothes."

"They must have left yesterday or the day before," La Journisse said, popping up with a garland of garlic bulbs and another of onions around his neck, which left his hands free to carry a basket laden with bread.

Elated by our good fortune, we laughed together, hugging each other as we jumped for joy…until the distant rumble of cannon barrage imposed its stark reality.

"Come!" I suggested. "Let's go check the other houses."

"You think they'll be full like this one?" Papis asked, swallowing his saliva.

"You can count on it," La Journisse answered.

Our good luck was still with us; we found two ducks and a pigeon and chickens — all recently plucked — in the cellar of one house and in the next, a round of cheese, a pudding and several bottles of Riesling and Schnapps.

"There's enough food for whole section," I said.

"Wrap everything in this tablecloth, it'll be easier to carry," Papis suggested.

"Wait…we're missing something," said La Journisse. He went into the kitchen and returned with several settings of silver knives and forks, "Now we can eat like civilized people," he said, placing the cutlery with the food on the tablecloth.

"Watch the pudding! Don't reduce it to a mush," warned Papis as we gathered the corners of the tablecloth together, ready to lift it.

"Don't worry… it's well-protected already…I've wrapped the sausages around it," Jean assured everyone.

"It will be a lunch fit for a king!" I said.

"And eaten with a princely service of cutlery," La Journisse added.

Back at our mortar emplacement, when we showed *Oberscharführer* De Ville our finds, he swayed on his feet, his mouth open, unable to say a word. The grenadiers from other mortar pieces soon learned of our bounty of fine foods and huddled around, looking as if they were about to attack the food spread out on the tablecloth.

"By turn, squad by squad!" *Unterscharführer* Tron ordered, "There's enough for everyone."

And so our 'banquet' began.

"Rather light, but good," *Truppführer* Bournique said looking at the label on the bottle of Riesling in his hand before passing it on. Soon the alcohol played its magic and lifted the mood of the entire crew, the bitter cold becoming only a small inconvenience.

"Hei! Save a bottle also for tomorrow's lunch. You'll see how I can cook the turkey and the ducks!" La Journisse promised. He took off his helmet and put a white handkerchief on his head then grabbed a fork to mimic a *chef d'hotel*.

"What will you call it…Turkey Popov?" Papis asked. He stood, folded his arms and began to kick his legs in movements that were supposed to imitate a Russian folk dance but with steps that would not look out of place in a fairy dance.

Everybody laughed, barely retaining the food stuffed inside their puffed cheeks.

Jean tapped me on the shoulder. "La Journisse…he worked as a chef before enlisting. He knows his trade."

Loss of Face

Early in the afternoon, happy and relaxed, we were sitting in our mortar emplacement still pecking at the food we had found in the abandoned houses, telling jokes and exchanging tales when…tch-tch-tch-tch…WHOOAM! The blast startled us. Mud and snow spattered our tablecloth, spoiling the remaining food. Nearby, there was a large smoking crater, the first blow of the Russian artillery.

"To the pieces, quick!" *Oberscharführer* De Ville screamed.

We dropped the food and bottles in our hands and sprang to the mortar. Still chewing the remnants of some delicious morsel, we were ready to shoot. We had fixed them towards the east, expecting an attack from Köslin. De Ville scanned the nearby fields with his binoculars then gave the order to turn the mortars in the direction of the river — a maneuver that took less than a minute to complete. While Papis, our *Richtschütze,* corrected the firing line and range setting on the mortar, I hurried to shift as many projectiles as possible, ready for loading.

Unterscharführer Tron shouted from the neighbouring emplacement, "They're coming!"

"Fire at my order!" De Ville said in his booming, commander's voice.

With the help of two *Munitionschützen* – crew members responsible for unpacking and arming the charges — I finished rearranging the munitions. I picked up a projectile and prepared to drop it down the mortar tube.

In the distance I saw the Russians advance across the snowy field, spreading out in a fan-like formation like black ants on a white sheet. Another cannonade screamed over our heads, exploding behind us with a succession of terrifying thuds and prolonged roars. The ground trembled at my feet. I looked at Bournique, an 80mm grenade in my hands, ready to be dropped into the mortar tube.

"Not yet," De Ville bellowed.

The Russian artillery continued to hammer us. With our heads down, lying flat at the bottom of our hole, we endured explosions, smoke and dirt raining down on us, and shrapnel sizzling as it hit the snow at the rim of our mortar pit. I reached out to a sausage on the tablecloth and took a bite, offering the remainder to Bournique — this was, I must admit, not really an offer of food but a device calculated to demonstrate my calmness under fire to my *Truppführer.*

Bournique looked at me in astonishment, then with fury etched on his face growled, "What in the hole of deepest hell are you thinking of? Don't be stupid."

"What's going on here?" Papis asked, turning towards us.

I passed him the piece of meat and, calmly, he started to chew on it.

The artillery fire ceased. A surreal silence fell over what had just become a battlefield. I raised my head over the rim of the mortar pit and was alarmed to see Russian infantry closing on our position. *Oberscharführer* De Ville lowered his binoculars, waited for some more seconds, and then bawled: "Now! Damn bordello! Fire! Fire!"

I inserted the first charge, then the second…and waited.

"Too short," Bournique shouted to Papis, our gunner.

Papis' hand worked one of the two hand wheels on the mortar's aiming apparatus. "Ready!"

"Fire!"

I inserted one projectile after another. I counted eight of them still airborne before the first burst on the ground. Grenades from our four mortars exploded amongst the Russians. Many fell to the snow for protection and lay there, motionless. After our initial barrage, those who had survived rose up to resume the attack but in the vicinity of the craters blasted out from the icy ground by the exploding grenades, lay countless bodies mown down by the hellish storm of shrapnel.

"They're closing in!" roared De Ville.

Bournique shouted to Papis. "Elevate the tube…more!"

"Ready!" Papis screamed.

"Fire!"

A second shower of deadly grenades hit the advancing Russians…thud…thud…an almost continuous series of detonations again brought the Russian attack to a standstill. During a pause in the firing, Bournique scrutinized the pulverized terrain. Black craters peppered the white expanse of the field. Russian soldiers sprawled on ground. Bravely, the dwindling band of survivors staggered to their feet to persist in their attack only to be cut down by the machine-gun fire from our right. In the distance, I saw the dark profiles of a squadron of T34 tanks, but they kept their position and seemed content to lob off a few shells in our direction from time to time.

Papis called for more charges.

"Here they come…would you like another sausage?"

"Hah, hah! Ready…fire!" He too was having fun, real fun.

The Russian soldiers continued to advance despite having lost many comrades. Then the T34s began their thundering, prolonged barrage.

"We should have a pair of MGs too," La Journisse shouted amidst that din, that bedlam of explosions, gusts of hot gas and acrid fumes that stuck in our throats.

"*Ja!* And *Panzerfäuste* to deal with the tanks," I said.

"If only we had them!" Bournique shouted, bending towards the bottom of our mortar pit as a shell whistled over our heads.

Our gunner, Papis, now relied on approximation to find his target because the Russians were too close and he didn't have time to adjust the elevation of the tube. "In a while we'll see their faces, those Popovs!" he warned. In the tone of his voice, although still bold, I thought I now detected a certain urgency, perhaps fear.

A sudden and shocking boom startled us, temporarily deafening everybody. I found myself slammed to the bottom of the pit, together with Bournique, both of us on top of La Journisse and the other *Munitionschützen* while pieces of metal and dirt fell on our helmets and shoulders.

When the bombardment stopped, Bournique took a peek over the edge of the mortar pit. "Shit…they took a direct hit!"

A comrade from the next mortar emplacement staggered on the snow, holding his hands to his face. Papis and I climbed out of our pit and ran towards the stricken emplacement and our wounded comrade. We could see now that blood poured down the sleeves of his coat, pooled red on the pure-white snow at his feet. A strange, gurgling scream came from his throat as he lowered his hands. I gazed at him, transfixed by the horror of the scene, by the absence of the face that was now in his hands. In the mortar emplacement, there was a tangle of twisted steel strips beside which lay the *Richtschütze* and *Munitionschütze* who were both still breathing. We screamed for the medics who arrived quickly to evacuate the wounded.

Papis, a look of foreboding darkening his face, stared at the remains of the mortar tube. "Bournique was wrong about the direct hit — the grenade exploded before it left the tube."

Stubborn Mules

Shortly after Papis and I returned to our mortar emplacement, the Russian soldiers resumed their advance. We fired off our last grenades while the backup *Munitionschützen* grabbed their rifles. Suddenly, the Russian artillery ceased shooting almost completely, directing, with reduced intensity, their main line of fire towards Körlin. The advance units to our left drew back a hundred meters or so.

"They're short of ammunition," *Sturmmann* Bournique reckoned.

De Ville, who had observed events through his binoculars, reported that the advance units were dismantling some of their emplacements. He let his binoculars hang around his neck on their cord, raised his helmet to the back of his head and wiped the sweat from his brow with the rough sleeve of his coat, his squinting eyes betraying his apprehension.

"Paul!" Jean called from his emplacement. He pointed towards the cluster of houses near the bank of the river where we had found the stash of food. I caught a glimpse of a Russian soldier before he disappeared behind a clump of young pine trees on the opposite bank of the river and indicated the spot to De Ville who peered at them through his binoculars. Then movements around the garden walls of some houses directly ahead caught my attention. To my right, in a trench that lay between our emplacement and the next, a skinny L.V.F. veteran aimed his rifle at the suspicious activity but did not fire. I knew him by sight, a veteran of the battles in the Carpathians. He had drooping lips and a pock-marked face, souvenirs left by the shrapnel from a Russian hand grenade that made him look like a victim of smallpox. He focused on his task with an exemplary devotion to duty, his bony hands glued to his Mauser. As I watched him, a wave of pity touched my soul for he was a man who had already proved his bravery and should have been sent home to his family. What state was our army in that it needed to return such men to the front line?

A crescendo of high-pitched whistles warned of a furious barrage that poured down on our emplacements. The shockwaves from the exploding shells beat against my chest and eardrums. Rocks and roots shot upwards, mixed in with plumes of snow and earth. Bournique gave the order to fire.

"We're short on pills," I answered.

"How many left?"

"Two boxes."

"The Devil!"

Oberscharführer De Ville piled into our mortar pit. He bent forward towards our ears to make himself heard above the noise of battle. "Ammo is on the way, keep firing…it will be here soon."

No sooner had De Ville uttered his welcome words when above the pandemonium of battle, I heard the broken-winded bray of a mule. When I turned to look for the animal, I saw only its pricked-up ears rising above a bank of drifting battle-smoke.

"Back-up ammo," yelled the handler. The smoke cleared to reveal the man tugging at the mule's reins. "She's too scared to move. I'll need help."

La Journisse and I left the mortar pit and went to the back of the ammunition cart where I counted only twenty boxes each containing three grenades. We heaved against it with our shoulders while the handler continued to yank on the reins but the wheels of the cart were stuck in deep mud and the mule had clearly decided it wanted no further part in this battle.

"It's useless," La Journisse exclaimed, "it's really stubborn this bastard."

"Coward of a mule…just a few steps more, eh?" the handler yelled, but still the mule stood its ground. The harsh edge left the handler's voice. "Just one more favor…one more you ugly beast." In desperation the handler unsheathed his bayonet to prick the mule's rump but still she refused to move.

Unterscharführer Tron and a handful of his troop arrived. "Take a case each and get back to your pieces." De Ville ordered.

As we carried the boxes across the snow towards the mortar emplacements, an ominous hissing in the air warned of an incoming barrage. We hit the ground just before the Russian shells exploded one after the other with a hellish racket. The mule went crazy. As it took off towards the river pulling the cart, which bounced and clattered over the craters in the snowy field, it was hit spot-on by a bomb and disappeared in a blinding, purple flash. Amid that chaos, the skinny L.V.F. veteran moved from one trench to another, calm and cool-headed, as if he didn't have anything to do with that corner of hell.

We distributed the twenty boxes of grenades among the three mortars still active in our battery which now had only around seventy projectiles in all. *Oberscharführer* De Ville accordingly gave the order only to fire on his command. Then he addressed me directly, "Paul! I need you to carry out a reconnaissance of those houses…you know them, no?"

"*Jawohl* Chief, but…alone?"

"Yes, alone. The others are needed here. Are you up to it?"

"What is it I have to do?"

De Ville nodded. "Good! I want to know if the Russians have already forded the Persante. Go over to that mound beside the houses…count how many Russians you see, but watch out, understand?" With his index finger, he signalled me to step towards him then he secured a white camouflage cassock on my shoulders and said, "Don't be seen… and come back quickly!"

The *Oberscharführer* was treating me like a kid but I was desperate to prove my courage. I left the mortar pit during a pause in the shelling, covered by the rifles of the skinny L.V.F legionnaire and other comrades, and made my way towards the slope of the knoll. My heart was pumping fast and hard; it was my first mission. I reached the base of that mound running, zigzagging, keeping to the cover offered by the undulations in the terrain. Then the Russian artillery played an encore, the 105mm shells smashing onto the opposite side of the mound that provided me with cover. On the right bank of the river, plumes of water, snow and mud shot high into the air. In an interlude in the firing, I ran full pace across an open strip of land toward the sloping ground of the mound. At the top, I dived for cover behind a young pine tree and I looked around, holding my breath.

There were Russian soldiers spread along the left bank of the river, covered by low bushes and young trees. My heart hammered against my ribs as I turned my attention to our side of the riverbank where the young pine trees, protected by the sloping ground close to the river, remained intact. They would provide a good cover for the Russians, once they waded across the river.

To my astonishment, I saw a group of young pine trees move forwards towards the top of the riverbank on our side of the river, straight towards my vantage point. *Oberscharführer* De Ville had feared the worst, and the worst was happening right in front of me: the Russians were advancing using the foliage as cover and had already forded the river. I tried to count them…ten…twenty…I lost count. We were in grave danger — I was in grave danger — they were heading straight for my vantage point on the mound. It was time to make my way back to our lines to report to De Ville. I retraced my steps, crouching low like a hunted hare; easy prey for any Russian soldier occupying the summit of the mound. As I retreated, I cast a quick glance toward the houses and, through a thin fog mixed with the smoke from the recent explosions I made out the shapes of more enemy soldiers. I plunged under the low branches of a pine tree, into the fresh scent of its resin, and stood there observing the enemy's movement, counting them as they crawled among the house fronts and gardens. There was no time to waste; I had to get back to warn my comrades before it was too late. With a racing heart and skin glistening with frozen sweat I leapt from my hiding place and, bent forward, ran like hell.

Snow had started to fall when *Oberscharführer* De Ville reached out to grab my rifle with one hand and pulled me down into the mortar pit with the other. "Where are the Russians?"

"On the riverbank," I panted, "...and between the houses...fifty...perhaps sixty of them."

"Which side?

"Ours."

Oberscharführer De Ville slapped me on the shoulder. "Well done kid!" he said. He left the emplacement with a wry smile on his face to give orders to reinforce our left flank.

I was still catching my breath when I heard *Unterscharführer* Tron yell, "Only two men at each tube...everyone else with me!"

Sturmmann Bournique nodded towards Papis who climbed out of the pit to join *Unterscharführer* Tron's troop then, looking at me with his tired eyes and a gloomy expression said: "We're surrounded Paul...but don't worry, De Ville knows what to do...he'll pull us out of these damned pits, you'll see." His words of consolation were, I thought, spoken more for himself than for me.

De Ville in the meantime kept a close eye on his men, moving between the mortar emplacements and trenches to verify our positions, his head continually turning on his thick neck as he scanned the terrain through his binoculars. When he reached our pit he looked down and asked how many grenades we had left.

Bournique looked up from our pit. "Just a few, *Oberscharführer*."

Oberscharführer De Ville scratched his chin, as if thinking, then said: "Bournique, your mortar is the best placed, we'll use only this one from now on. Paul! See that all charges are brought here from the other emplacements."

"*Jawohl Oberscharführer*." I crawled out from the emplacement and seeing a *Munitionschütze* from another mortar crew coming toward me, ordered him to help me with the task. Bournique, evidently surprised by the tone of my curt order, turned to look. I could hardly restrain a smile as I spread out my arms and said: "*Noblesse oblige.*" The *Munitionschütze* obeyed willingly — the news of my dangerous and successful sortie had spread among my comrades earning their esteem — but our scavenging of the other emplacements yielded only a few mortar grenades which we delivered to Bournique who remarked on the ominous silence that had fallen across the snow-white landscape.

Gunshots and hand grenade explosions sounded from our left flank — *Unterscharführer* Tron's men were already engaged in a fight to the death with the invaders I had seen on my reconnaissance sortie. Then a blood chilling cry rose up: *"Hourré Stalin, hourré!"* Russian soldiers broke from the cover of the young pines on the opposite side of the river. They charged, bayonets fixed, towards the Persante, a black, sinuous band cutting through the whiteness of the snow.

Bournique's hands formed a trumpet around his mouth, "Alarm! Alarm!"

De Ville lowered his binoculars. "Fire!"

The machine guns from the sector at our right crackled. Russian soldiers splashing through the Perante's icy water slumped into the slow, dark current. Our men in the trenches added to the merciless storm of bullets by firing their Mausers.

"To the right, Bournique," De Ville screamed, pointing to a group of Russians already on our side of the river.

I dropped the last charge into the tube; the projectile left with the usual muffled hiss and fell close to the riverbank, delaying a group of Russians who had begun to cross. I looked at De Ville, signalling with my arms spread that we were now out of ammunition.

Oberscharführer De Ville jumped into our mortar pit. "Use your rifles! Make every round count."

"They are like ants!" Bournique yelled, his face contorted in terror as the Russians advanced on us in closed ranks.

"Don't waste time aiming — you can hit them with your eyes closed," De Ville shouted.

"They must be mad," I said.

"Hourré!" yelled the first ones to reach the clearing in front of our emplacement. We fired at will. I saw them fall by the dozen, and yet they kept coming at us.

"Hei Chief," Bournique cried out, "I don't hear our machine guns!"

"They are out of ammo...they're pulling back," De Ville informed us, his binoculars glued to his eyes.

"Oberscharführer," I'm on my last few rounds too," I said.

"I have two back-up cases at the tents," De Ville replied.

"Keep your heads down...they're coming at us again!" Bournique yelled.

Shells screamed over our heads, exploding behind our lines with increasing intensity, a ploy to impede both our retreat and resupply of munitions. Tears of impotent rage trickled down *Oberscharführer* De Ville's rugged face.

A Russian soldier managed to get within a few meters of our emplacement. *"Hourré! Hourré... Stal..."* The bullet of a Mauser smacked into his forehead, lifting his beret into the air as it left the back of his head.

"Pull back!" *Oberscharführer* De Ville ordered.

"Out! *Alé!*" shouted Bournique, discharging his last shots against the sea of infantry men that were about to surround us. Covered by the bursts from De Ville's sub-machine gun, we sprang like gazelles from the mortar pit and ran towards the tents where the ammunition boxes were stored. "Quick! Quick!" he urged.

I inserted a clip of bullets onto my rifle's magazine, pressed the bullets into the loading chamber. Around me, the others were stuffing their coat pockets with the precious ammunition and I followed their example. With heavy, bulging pockets we resumed our retreat. Around us the ground trembled and the air, pummelled by explosions, seemed to push us here and there as we ran. Heat and the fumes from the exploding shell stung our nostrils, our lungs. A high-pitched buzz rang in my head but it disappeared when I saw Jean and Papis with some of the comrades who had latched on to *Unterscharführer* Tron.

"I don't see La Journisse," I said, my eyes scanning the battle-blackened faces of my comrades.

"He'll be further ahead," Papis said.

"And the L.V.F. veteran?" Jean asked.

I shook my head. "Didn't see him!"

"Holy…if he's been left behind he's done for," said Jean.

Rockets flew over our heads, tearing the air with their sinister hisses: one exploded nearby with a deafening blast, the shock wave throwing us to the ground.

"Stalin's organ's pipes," Jean shouted.

Unscathed by the rocket's blast, we got to our feet to continue our escape. Bursts from our sub-machine guns and shots from our Mausers seemed to come from every direction. Bullets whistled through the air, crossing each other's paths with a barely audible metallic vibration. The whirlwind of wayward lead made me nervous — that damned fear of a bullet catching me from behind sent a cold shiver coursing through my body. Ahead was an embankment. I hit the ground behind it, digging a niche in the snow, oblivious to the numbing cold invading my fingers. Trembling with fear, I pressed my face, my whole body, deeper into the snow.

As I breathed, I sucked in ice crystals. But the firing had almost stopped. I got onto one knee and took off my helmet to wipe away the sweat and snow from my forehead. My comrades were in the distance; they had kept on running. I was alone but at least the terror of being hit in the back was gone. I got up, put on my helmet and I began to wander in the direction of my comrades. Before long, I came across an officer on horseback. He was forcing his mount to caracole to the right and left to contain our fleeing soldiers, forming groups, seeking to instill some sort of order in our ranks. "Halt! There are no Russians! Look behind yourselves, look!" he said in German. A familiar, southern voice called out as I joined the group.

"Hei Paul!"

It was La Journisse. We embraced, patted each other's shoulders, happy to be reunited. "You're wounded," I said, noticing a sleeve of his coat torn and soaked in blood.

"I don't know how it happened, it must have been shrapnel," he said without concern.

"But you're still bleeding, let me see!"

La Journisse lifted his wounded arm a little. "It's nothing…only a scrape…it doesn't hurt."

Without answering, I ripped open the damaged sleeve and tied a handkerchief as best as I could around his wound. "At least it will cut down the blood loss," I said. Instinctively, I grabbed him and dragged him to the ground. The Russian artillery was again finding its range with fresh volleys of shells.

Some of our comrades tried to scatter but the officer on horseback drove into them, screaming out encouragement. "They're nothing but a bunch of ragamuffins full of lice! Where are Rokossovski's divisions…and those of Zhukov? Surrounded…not at all! Give a good look around you…where do you see Russians? Let's go, soldiers. Fix bayonets…and to the attack! Forward…at the double!"

And so he forced us to counterattack.

La Journisse had an uneasy look about him. "Are we going in?"

"Let's go!" I answered with confidence. "There's still some chicken left at our emplacement. I don't like the idea of those Popovs devouring everything."

I slid my bayonet from its sheath and clipped it to my Mauser. La Journisse remained motionless beside me, ignoring my example. "Why are you waiting…your bayonet?"

"Mine? Oh…" He unsheathed it, looked at it as if he had seen it for the first time and touched the blade with the tip of his index finger. There was a lost expression in his eyes as he shook his head. "It's too sharp…it can do a lot of damage!" He placed it back in its sheath with a mechanical movement.

I was extremely surprised by La Journisse's bizarre behaviour, perhaps he was still in a state of shock after being hit. Then the officer on horseback spotted us.

"Come soldiers, there's no time to waste! Let's throw back those ragamuffins! To the attack!"

We ran against Russian fusillades, towards our mortar emplacements.

La Journisse was laughing now. "They'll have their underwear wet, those Popovs."

"Aaugh!" I pulled up in a step, bent in half by pain.

La Journisse, who was a few paces ahead, stopped and came back to hold me up. "Caught in the stomach?"

"Huh…no…it's my guts…diarrhoea."

"It's too dangerous here…up, up Paul. Let's reach that pile of snow!"

"What kind of cook are you? Did you put poison in…"

"Hah! First in the marmalade, then that entire God-given lot," La Journisse joked. "Now move."

"I can't…you go on."

La Journisse ran to join in the counterattack and disappeared from sight. I headed towards a tree near a frozen creek, with the intention of expelling the unbearable burden inside my belly. I just had time to throw down my rifle and pull down my pants when a bullet zoomed past my left ear. *Damned sharpshooter,* I thought, grinding my teeth, *show me some consideration…can't you see I have my pants at my ankles?* Finishing the job was a matter of principle — and necessity. I cleaned my rear end with a handful of snow, pulled up my pants, buckled up my cartridge belt and grabbed my rifle before taking shelter behind the tree. A second bullet smacked into the tree trunk, scenting the air with a cloud of atomised pine resin. Then I spotted him for a brief instant, that devil of a Russian dressed in a white camouflage suit, as he moved to a better position. I picked up my rifle, took in a deep breath and waited. A faint glint of reflected light from the lens of the Russian's binoculars betrayed his position. I fired, breaking the deadly silence of the woods. There was the muffled grunt of a man hit in the chest by a bullet. I saw him clearly now as dropped his weapon and staggered against a tree. A surge of elation coursed through my body, a moment of pure joy. I had come face to face with death and had emerged triumphant.

After my close call with messy pants — and the Russian sharpshooter — I followed the sound of battle and soon caught up with *Oberscharführer* De Ville, Bournique and the rest of my mortar crew, just in time to join the counterattack. *Unterscharführer* Tron was close by with his troop which included Mignon, Jean and a dozen others. Their task was to cover the left flank while we recaptured the mortar emplacements.

De Ville bravely led the way and we followed, catching the Russians by surprise with a volley of shots from our rifles to which they replied with only isolated shots. Firing at will, we pushed forward until we reached and retook our mortar emplacements. With a sudden loss of nerve, the Russians retreated. I reloaded my Mauser and, together with other comrades, I scrambled from the mortar pit to pursue the Russians all the way to the river which they stumbled across in the gathering dusk. We loosed off a few rounds before returning to our emplacements at the call of De Ville, who was controlling the situation with the aid of his binoculars.

"Well! At least they didn't damage it," Bournique said, caressing the barrel of our mortar.

La Journisse was less happy when he discovered the Russians had raided our store of food rescued from the houses earlier that day. "*Fils de salop*! They didn't leave even a drumstick of our poultry, not a drop of wine."

"I hope they choke on the bones," I said.

"You'll pay for this," La Journisse shouted, raising a fist at the Russians on the opposite riverbank.

De Ville ordered each team to post a man on watch duty, each round to last an hour. I was the first from our crew to stand duty and took the opportunity to look for the L.V.F. veteran. I went towards his trench fearing the worst. In it, a coat covered a crouched body. From the edge of the trench, I prodded the body with the bayonet on my rifle and jumped back at its sudden movement.

"Cretin!" yelled a voice in French. "Let me be!"

"But... but where have you been?"

The veteran, who had stubbornly stayed in his foxhole, pulled his coat from his face to expose his puffy eyes. "I was always here, I was."

"Were you holed up here the whole afternoon?"

"Sure! Where else do you think I went with that hell going on over my head...and me without ammunition?"

"You didn't notice the Russians!"

"Burn in hell the Russians," said the veteran before retreating under the collar of his coat.

De Ville, who was doing his rounds of the watches, saw me looking into the veteran's trench. "What is it, Paul?"

"The legionnaire," I said.

"Is he dead?"

"He's asleep *Oberscharführer*, but he's out of ammunition."

De Ville chuckled. "Well fetch him some and then let him be."

❦—❦

At dusk a general silence descended, broken only by distant explosions. The hours went by dreadfully slowly; tiny icicles were forming in the course down under my chin. Little by little, the notion of time lost meaning. It seemed to me that a soldier's chief virtue was his patience; his ability to endure long stops on transport trains or holed up in the cold ground like hares, waiting for an attack.

Skirmish at the Station

The order to pull back arrived shortly before midnight. Obediently, we pulled ourselves from the mortar pits into the glacial wind that swept across the snowfields. Our long coats, soaked with melted snow during the day, were now stiff with ice and crackled when we moved. Ahead of us lay the task of carrying our heavy mortars — impotent lumps of steel without ammunition — in the eerie, blue light thrown up from the frozen fields.

After two exhausting kilometers we came, staggering from tiredness, to a farmhouse set at the rear of a courtyard. We heard voices from within, French voices. After the usual precautions, we pushed open a door and found a large kitchen where the oppressive odour of fried grease lingered above bodies sprawled on beds of straw. The air rattled with the snores of sleeping men. Next to the fire burning in the hearth, two legionnaire veterans were tending to chunks of pork cooking in the embers. They appeared lazy rather than tired, shabby in their uniforms, resigned. Their faces betrayed very little willingness to fight or to defend themselves from the advancing Russians.

Oberscharführer De Ville shook his head in disbelief. "We won't mix with this lot."

"But Chief, there is something to eat here," said La Journisse, smacking his lips.

Sturmmann Bournique stepped between us and the ex-legionnaires, siding with De Ville.

"We're leaving," De Ville said.

A sigh of resistance came from my exhausted comrades who, like me, were desperate to grab a few moments rest and respite from the biting cold.

The impending stand-off was defused by the sudden slamming-open of the kitchen door. A cold blast of air and the appearance of two officers brought instant silence to the room. Four of their men stood guard outside the door. De Ville and Bournique, standing at attention in front of the two officers, saluted.

"I need volunteers to stand watch at two advance posts," one of the officers announced.

A choir of insults and profanities rose from the 'soldiers' slouched on the floor; some, woken up by the entry of the officers, went back to snoring. The officers, their faces livid with anger and momentarily stunned by the general indifference to their presence, regained their composure. "No volunteers...then I will choose a pair," he said dryly. He cast a disdainful glance at those on the floor in the kitchen then came up to me, scrutinizing my appearance from head to toe. "You," he said, then turned to point to a comrade, "and you."

"*Jawohl,*" we answered in unison, taking a step forward.

"Good," said the second officer, "you will report the movements of Russian infantry, during the night."

"*Untersturmführer,* if you would allow me to..." interposed De Ville.

The officer looked at De Ville down his long aristocratic nose.

"If you allow me," De Ville repeated, "I would like to point out that we have just arrived from our emplacements after fighting all afternoon, my men have had no time to rest and..."

"Duty is duty, *Oberscharführer*. The Russians are certainly not resting," the officer interrupted. He threw a scathing glance towards the ex-legionnaires in the kitchen. "Demoralizing, aren't they?" he said with a sneer on his face.

My fellow 'volunteer' and I were issued with additional ammunition and a pair of hand grenades each and were then escorted towards two low buildings. Going closer, I realized they were simple stalls facing in the direction of the Persante River. My comrade took up his post in the first primitive building while my escort took me to another before melting into the night. I stepped over the stone threshold and into the unmistakable stench of pigs although there were none present — perhaps the unfortunate inhabitant was roasting in the kitchen I had just left. There was a single, small window set only a meter from the ground and I crouched in there, with my rifle resting against the sill. *Look at me*, I thought, *alone in a pig stall in the middle of nowhere...waiting*. From time to time the silence was interrupted by far-away cries and by some distant explosions.

After a time that seemed to me an eternity, a row of glimmering, faint lights appeared in the direction of our abandoned emplacements but it was impossible to judge their distance. Was it a troop of Russians with their cigarettes lit up? I beat my arms against my chest to shake up a bit of warmth and then I picked up my rifle. Suddenly, the tiny lights seemed to be dancing in front of me. My nose picked up the scent of burning cigarettes on the breeze. *Majorka*, I thought, recalling the name of that unique tobacco. Russian soldiers, obviously confident they would not encounter Germans, had carelessly indulged in the luxury of smoking. My heart was pounding as I aimed at the first red glow. I calculated that they would be so alarmed when I fired, they would run like hares. I squeezed the trigger...and then again.

Nothing!

The firing pin was frozen. I unsheathed my bayonet and, with my pistol in the other hand, leaned against the wall near the door...waiting. Boots crunched on the snow not twenty meters from the stall, they seemed to circle my little refuge then stop, the sound replaced by whispering voices. Then again the frosty covering on the snow crackled, but this time the sound was receding into the darkness.

I never did get the opportunity to report my encounter with the Russians; a comrade from the mortar section arrived not long after to tell me that we had orders to pull back. My coat was stiff, covered in tiny needles of ice which made it difficult to keep pace with him as we hurried to catch up with the rest of our mortar section. Not far from the farm building, we passed a ditch in which I recognized our abandoned mortars. Further on, where the trail ran alongside a bend in the river, we caught up on the rearguard of our retreating column where I came across La Journisse who told me that the rest of our mortar section was towards the front of the column. I hurried to catch up with them and found Jean and Papis among them.

"You look like a specter," Papis said.

"Look in a mirror," I replied. "Where are we heading?"

"North…towards Kolberg," said Jean.

It was still dark when we came to a crossroad. The ex-legionnaires in our column turned towards the east while our *Waffen SS* unit which consisted of fifteen men, including a few stragglers, continued travelling northwards over a less well-beaten trail through a valley. Suddenly, De Ville signalled us to lie down prone on the snow. A beam of light cut through the trees in front of us, flashed across our helmets, then settled on a team of Russian engineers repairing a narrow bridge over the river. On the opposite bank of the river, a Russian T34 tank lurked menacingly.

"Popovs," whispered Papis.

"Silence," Bournique hissed.

Oberscharführer De Ville observed the Russian activity for several minutes then waved for us to approach. We crawled like seals across the snow until our faces were close to his.

"The water in the river is too high to cross," said De Ville, "we have to use that bridge. Listen carefully…we'll go across in groups of three or four. Those of us left on this side will provide cover. Keep to the shadows so they don't see the colour of our uniforms…their eyes will be too used to the light. In case you get separated or lost on the other side, follow the Persante River…you'll reach Kolberg sooner or later…we'll regroup there. The password is 'pomalo'."

Sturmmann Bournique volunteered to lead the first three which included La Journisse. "Raise your collars above the rim of your helmets so they don't recognise them as German and keep your composure."

"Go!" whispered De Ville.

While two Russian soldiers directed the beam from their huge lamp according to the instructions given by the engineers, Bournique's group passed over without difficulty.

Jean, Papis and I were the last group to cross with DeVille. "Careful!" De Ville said looking into our eyes, "there's nobody left to cover us now. Paul and I will hang back a few meters…we'll shoot out the lamp if there's trouble."

"Understood," Jean and Papis whispered in unison.

As Jean and Papis stepped on the bridge's deck, the Russian soldiers manning the lamp spoke to them. I saw Papis slip his thumb between his shoulder and the strap of his rifle.

De Ville, rushing to catch Jean and Papis, pushed them onwards shouting, *"Davai! Davai!"*

A voice below the bridge called to the lamp crew who swung their beam to illuminate a different section of the bridge. We took our chance and marched past the unsuspecting Russians and, at about fifty meters from the tank on the opposite bank, regrouped to continue our trek to Kolberg, oblivious for a few precious moments to the cold and tiredness that dwelt in our bones.

As we drew closer to Kolberg, De Ville raised his right hand. We stopped behind him to listen to an exchange of fire rise then fade. Somewhere not too far away, in our line of travel, a skirmish had been played out. We resumed our march and came to a cemetery where I counted several bodies of Russian and German soldiers amongst the battle-scarred tombstones.

Oberscharführer De Ville ordered a search of the cemetery. "Two with me, two with *Sturmmann* Bournique to check the perimeter walls…the rest in the middle," he ordered.

As we searched the cemetery, turning over the bodies of the dead and dying, *Oberscharführer* De Ville rejoined us and said the words we longed to hear: "We'll stop here for the night."

As *Sturmmann* Bournique arranged a watch rota, I heard someone call the password, 'pomalo'. It was the rearguard and some stragglers arriving.

Sheltering behind a tombstone offered little protection from the cold. I moved close to somebody I assumed was La Journisse, who had, I thought, immediately fallen into a deep sleep. I pulled up the collar of my coat, ignoring the sound of skirmishes that came and went like a cloud on the wind.

It was still dark stingingly cold when I was wakened by a rough hand.

"It's our turn, Paul!" La Journisse said, indicating the walls.

My joints were stiff with the cold and, barely conscious, I used my rifle for support as I got to my feet. I looked at my sleeping companion, puzzled, and said to La Journisse, "But… if you are here, how can you be…"

"You've been sleeping with a corpse," he said.

Just before dawn, we resumed our march, following De Ville in a frost-induced silence, instinctively stepping into the imprints left in the deep snow by the boots of those ahead, to save a little energy. In the first glimmer of grey daylight, we joined forces with a squad of ten *Waffen SS* men from a different unit on a rail track leading to a station where some wagons were parked, about a kilometer ahead. From time to time, the sound of firing drifted on the air, the muffled crack from rifles and the rattle of machine guns.

De Ville, who was still the most senior rank present, gave the order to advance on the station. When we were close enough to hear the ricochets from metallic surfaces and the screams of soldiers engaged in close-quarter combat, *Sturmmann* Bournique made a gesture for us to seek cover. The Russians were in the station building, firing from windows towards a goods depot and the parked wagons.

Oberscharführer De Ville examined the situation with his binoculars pressed against his eyes and said, almost as if talking to himself: "German soldiers are returning fire from behind and underneath those wagons. They're covering their comrades as they try to across the tracks to the depot buildings."

"I see, I see." said *Sturmmann* Bournique, "and we're at the Russians' backs."

"They've no idea we're here."

"What do we do?" Bournique asked.

Oberscharführer De Ville, without hesitation, declared, "Our comrades are pinned down…they need our help."

"We attack from here?" Bournique asked.

"No! We'll advance a bit more. Take three others, run to the protection of those walls, then cover us while we cross to join our besieged comrades."

After advancing twenty meters on our stomachs, Jean and I were left at our position to form a cross-fire with the group that had taken up position behind the walls. Nearby we noticed a points-lever housed in a metal box large enough to offer cover.

Sturmmann Bournique and the three men he chose sprang to their feet and raced to the wall. Once secured there, they gave a signal to De Ville who led his group in a crazy charge across the rail tracks towards the wagons, shooting at the windows as they ran. The Russians responded with a hail of fire from a machine gun located at a window on the upper floor, hitting two of our mortar squad who fell among the bodies already on the tracks. Two or three of the *SS* men who joined us earlier fell near the wagons. Jean and I tried to keep the machine-gunners' heads down by aiming at the window but without much success. Bournique crossed in turn, leaving another companion on the ground, hit in the back, in spite of the covering fire from De Ville's men who had reached the wagons.

"Hei Jean!" I said, "I have an idea." I pointed to a narrow steel footbridge crossing the tracks just a handful of meters away.

Jean immediately saw my plan. "We'll get a better shot at the window but we'll be exposed to their fire."

"What do you think?"

"We can try. I'll lead the way." Jean courageously leapt to his feet and sprang forwards. In four mighty leaps he scaled the steps to reach the gangway. I followed on close behind and together we fired at the muzzle flashes of the machine gun at the window. In the brief moments of bewilderment among the Russian gunners, who quickly adjusted their fire in our direction, De Ville took full advantage of our diversionary action to lead his men to the relative safety of the goods depot. A few moments later, they opened up with everything they had to provide Jean and me with covering fire. Amidst a hail of machine-gun bullets, I somehow managed to leap safely to the ground on the far side of the bridge and took cover behind the body of a dead Russian. Despite bullets whizzing about my ears, I was determined to take the red star from the dead man's cap as war booty — perhaps he was a commissar. Machine gun bullets pinged and sparked as they hit the metal steps which sung with different notes at each impact. They were aiming at Jean who was now crouching on the stairs a few meters behind me and the dead Russian. I fired my last two rounds at the machine gunners as Jean clattered down the metal steps.

"Run," he screamed as he rushed past.

I sprang straight up and followed him to the depot, avoiding another burst from the machine gun.

De Ville patted our shoulders in welcome at our safe arrival at the depot. Still trembling with excitement, I looked at Jean who wore an expression that somehow combined joy with terror, and said, simply: "We made it again." His answer was a little smile of relief.

The Cheeky Prisoner

"Start marching, boys, we're out of here!" The order from *Oberscharführer* De Ville was welcomed by every man in the depot, which we were happy to leave to the Russians. At a safe distance from the station, we stopped under the cover of a copse of conifers to assess our situation. Two of our mortar section and several of the stragglers and *SS* men had been killed. But there was still no sign of *Unterscharführer* Tron, Mignon and the others from our section. The last we had seen of them was during the counterattack to retake the mortar emplacements.

His face made haggard by fatigue and the burden of responsibility, *Oberscharführer* De Ville led our mixed group past a row of trees and scrub woodland, away from the banks of the Persante River. After trudging across snow-covered countryside for several hours we chanced upon a labour camp in which French prisoners were waiting for the war to end. There was a malicious expression in their eyes, openly hostile. In an almost daring posture, one of the prisoners, bony and short, walked alongside, parodying my movements. I stepped in front of him and marched on.

"Go, go to Kolberg too," he snarled from behind, in French, "the Russians are waiting for you there, for the great final stroll."

I turned on the prisoner and in French said: "You...big mouth...come here!"

The prisoner stood motionless, ignoring me except for a sardonic grin on his face.

"You heard the order, no?" added Jean, who's eyes had narrowed to angry slits.

"I... I..." the prisoner stuttered, his Adam's apple working up and down behind the tight, thin skin of his throat. His fingers trembled, his face paled to a ghostly white. The other prisoners remained at a prudent distance.

"What did you say about the Russians?" I said in a threatening voice.

"I, I..."

His throat clamped by fear, the prisoner was unable to talk. He had not expected to encounter *Waffen SS* soldiers who spoke perfect French. With his ruffled brown hair typical of people from the Midi, with his dark eyes, now pleading, he obeyed the order.

"Speak up," I insisted.

"It...it was for a laugh...I meant you no harm, you see," mumbled the poor soul. "And then... among Frenchmen," he had the rashness to add, "we don't cause each other evil... for heaven's sake!"

"Watch your skin, low life!" La Journisse warned.

I pointed my Mauser at the prisoner's snivelling face and, containing a rising swell of anger, said in a low voice, "I, between Frenchmen...for a laugh...will plant a bullet in your head!"

"For heaven's sake, please..." he whined. Shivers of fear coursed through his emaciated body. He crumpled to his knees.

"Move! *Alé,* let's go!" *Oberscharführer* De Ville cut in. He slowly raised the barrel of my rifle with one hand and with the other on my shoulder urged me forward. I took a few steps, still looking over my shoulder at the impudent prisoner.

The Russians are Coming!

We resumed our march, stopping frequently at farms for provisions and to quench our thirst with wine we found in the cellars. In one of these farms, under the stable's portico, there were mattresses leaning against some old furniture and kids running around, cackling. A woman tried to quieten them, scolding them with a gruff voice while an old man smoking a pipe sat on a stool with a dog at his feet. A French prisoner — at that time many of the family farms in Prussia and Pomerania had a French prisoner to help with the work — on hearing us converse in his native language approached us. "Do you know where the Russians are?"

"Not far away," Jean said.

I pulled out the red star I had taken from the dead Russian to show him.

"But then it is a serious matter," he exclaimed, disconsolate, scratching his head, passing his hands through his dark hair. "I must prepare the wagon for the family but first let me show you where I left the milk and cream from this morning's milking." We followed our countryman to the stables where he gestured with a wave of his arm. "Help yourselves, take anything you wish, you look like you need it."

After bloating ourselves with milk and other dairy products we redistributed our remaining ammunition — after the battle at the station we had only a few rounds each left, if any — and made ready to continue our trek to Kolberg. We assembled at the gate of the farmyard where *Oberscharführer* De Ville scanned the fields with his binoculars; he seemed eager to move on. "We must reach Kolberg as soon as possible." He declared.

"How far is it, *Oberscharführer?*" La Journisse asked.

"Fifteen kilometers or so…we should get there by late evening, it'll be dark then."

At sunset, we came within sight of a small village with houses roofed by clay tiles that glowed red in the low, golden sunlight. De Ville, who was constantly scanning the place with his binoculars, saw the burgomaster coming towards us holding high a banner with his village's emblem. "Eyes open! It might be a trap," warned De Ville. "Bournique…take Papis and see what the old guy has to say for himself. The rest of you spread out, keep your heads down."

Bournique and Papis talked with the burgomaster for a few seconds and then came back to report. "The Russians are not here yet…just women and kids in the village."

De Ville led us forward, to meet the burgomaster.

"Welcome soldiers! Finally…thank goodness…we were waiting for you," said the burgomaster, taking off his hat with a sweeping movement and bowing deeply. "Follow me, please."

At the village square, he stopped. "Our sons, husbands and fathers are all at the front," he informed us, "I will point out the houses where you can lodge in numbers suitable to the accommodation they have to offer…follow me, soldiers."

I ended up in a small house inhabited by a skinny, pale woman, with a ten-year-old boy and a girl of six. I entered, following her, and without waiting further, asked for hot water. She gestured to her kids who immediately put a pot on the stove while she led me to a small room where I could take off my boots and undress. She took my clothes and spread them over the chairs around the stove to dry them and then left. A few minutes later, she returned with a large washbowl brimming with steaming hot water, soap, a clean bath towel and a cloth. I stripped and dipped the cloth into the hot water then rubbed it on the soap, repeating the procedure as I soothed each part of my tired, aching body. Invigorated by the sensation of being at last clean again, I went to the kitchen, wrapped in the towel. I joined the two children sitting at the table while the woman worked at the stove. The walls were bare, except for a painting of a pastoral scene and a print of a saint hanging on a nail high over the door. On a credenza, the only other furniture in the room apart from the table and chairs, was a framed photograph of a man in uniform. "Thank you for the hot water, it was most welcome after spending nights out in the snow," I said, smiling.

"May I grease your boots?" the boy asked.

"But of course, go ahead."

His mother turned to us. A brief smile of approval passed over her lips but her eyes were tortured and moist.

"My father has boots just like this," said the boy.

I ruffled the boy's hair as he passed. His mother tightened her lips and bent again over the stove, hiding the tears gathering on her lower eyelids. She came back to the table bringing bowls of hot soup, then bread and margarine. I devoured the soup in a few moments but I refrained from asking for a second portion although it was the most delicious soup I had ever tasted up to that moment.

"The Russians…are they still far?" she asked, half-closing her large, pale blue eyes. A lock of her blond hair fell on her forehead presenting her with the opportunity to wipe away her tears.

I shook my head slowly.

"They will come here too?"

"You can never say," I forced myself to answer. I would have preferred encouraging her with other words but the situation was what it was.

"I don't have news from my husband… Eastern front… They are young," she said, repressing her sobs, alluding to the boy and girl, "what will come of them? Tell me soldier, the Russians won't hurt them, right?"

"No! They won't do anything bad." I pronounced those words in haste, to hide the fear that I felt for her and her children. I knew very well what the Russians were capable of — the L.V.F. survivors of combat in the Carpathians and Galicia had told us of the atrocities and savagery of the Russian Army.

"Would you like something else, soldier?" she then asked me.

"No, I thank you with all my heart, but I think I'll lie down now." I was really beaten by the lack of sleep and the persistent fatigue of that day. She led me into a small bedroom that smelled good, scented and fresh, and there I fell into an intensely deep sleep.

"Panzeralarm!... Panzeralarm!"

The woman's cries snatched me from my precious sleep. Half-dazed, my hand automatically sought my rifle which I thought was by my side but wasn't. I opened my eyes fully and was surprised to find myself wrapped in pure-white sheets. Then I recalled where I was.

"Panzeralarm!" The woman was beating on the door with the palms of her hands. Outside, in the street, women were wailing and screaming.

"What time is it," I asked as I yanked on my uniform trousers.

"Not yet four. You must hurry."

I found her and my rifle in the kitchen — I had been too exhausted to remember always to have it at my side. She was dressing her daughter; her son had already opened the door to the outside, allowing the sound of the mad, chaotic trampling of people running to spill into the room.

The young mother clasped her cheeks between the palms of her hands. "The Russians are already coming...what do we do now?"

I tried to calm her by speaking in a steady voice. "Stay together...the important thing is not to lose sight of each other."

We stepped from the house, into the panic-stricken hustle. Our mortar section was regrouping in the square while the burgomaster, assisted by some women from the *Volksgemeinschaft*, a German civil organization, was directing the crowd out of the village. "In good order...obey the authorities! With calm. The soldiers will protect us," they called.

"We have to flee but... where to?" the mother asked me.

"Look out for each other! Follow the column. I must join my section. Good luck," I said as she turned to leave.

Now the creak and squeak of tanks moving in the distance could be heard above the hubbub. That metallic screeching would make anybody's blood run cold, including my own; they would enter the village in a few minutes. The streets were choked with women and children, old folks walking, some were on bicycles and others, panting, pulled overladen hand carts — all were abandoning their homes.

At a distance of twenty paces from one another, our motley mix of combatants provided an escort to that sad procession which echoed my own experience as a refugee in France, in 1940. Along the way more civilians, *Luftwaffe* men, sailors from the *Kriegsmarine* and old men wearing *Volkssturm* armbands joined the fleeing column. I went to the head of the column, with my comrades, for new orders. De Ville was talking with some graduates, trying to take stock of the situation, exchanging news gathered here and there.

"The White Russian Front troops have broken our resistance around Köslin, they will soon be in Kolberg," explained a non-commissioned officer of the *Wehrmacht's Pommern Division*.

Others added to the deluge of bad news:

"The T34s of the 1st Guards Tank Army are already at Kolberg," someone added.

"Then we are surrounded."

"We are going straight into Zhukov's trap."

"And the 10th *Panzer* is not yet in sight," a graduate veteran sighed.

"Their T34s roam everywhere unopposed, hunting for isolated units."

"They swoop on columns of civilians and simply crush them under their tracks."

"They're spreading panic everywhere."

"And then there are the Polish partisans."

"We have to force our way to Kolberg," proposed a fellow from the *Kriegsmarine*. There for sure our destroyers will be at sea…they'll pound the T34s with their 150mm cannons."

There was a dark, gloomy look on *Oberscharführer* De Ville's face when he ordered us to return to our escort duties. A shudder of fear one could almost see ran through the whole column when, from time to time, someone lost their nerve and screamed: "The Russians are on us!"

Everywhere, it seemed, we came across apocalyptical scenes: there was an airfield on which planes, their ammunition igniting as flames engulfed them, hurled white-hot fragments high into the air; a little farther on we passed brand new *Panzers*, motionless, waiting in vain for the fuel that was burning at the *Luftwaffe* depot. But still we kept on marching, escorting the civilians in whom the last sparkle of hope had been all but extinguished. From the information exchanged among the non-commissioned officers I came to know that *Division 'Charlemagne'* was now part of *Korpsgruppe Tettau* but still under the command of *Heeresgruppe Weichsel*.

As we pushed on in darkness, I caught up with an old man with a bad limp. "Help me, good soldier, please…I don't have strength anymore." I supported him for a while and then, because we were losing ground, I lifted the old man up, carrying him on my shoulders like a fire-fighter, and caught up with a cart driven by two youngsters who promised not to leave him behind. After that effort my feet hurt. I stopped at the roadside in order to pull off my boots and discovered that the soles were almost reduced to shreds. The cries, the sobbing, the dull trampling of horseshoes on snow and the sharp squeaks from rusty handcart wheels were shrinking into the distance, into the darkness. I lingered for a while longer, rubbing warmth into my numb toes, reluctant to pull my boots back onto my bleeding feet. I hobbled over to sit at the base of a tree intending to ease the boots onto my sore feet and to regain my breath after carrying the old man. I closed my eyes for an instant and fell immediately into a sound sleep.

4

The Siege of Kolberg

Arrival in Kolberg

The sun, a cold, white disc hovered in the morning mist. My stomach had transformed itself into a hard ball, grumbling for food with such persistence that it wakened me. I was quite alone and therefore vulnerable. I took a deep breath and bit my lips as I pulled my wrecked boots onto my ice-cold feet then followed a trail on which several small groups of three or four soldiers were marching, all heading towards Kolberg. As my feet warmed the pain returned making it impossible for me to keep up with them and so I stopped at a farm where I asked a French prisoner — the only person present — how far it was to Kolberg; he told me two hours, more or less, if I had been able to walk at a normal pace. At another farm, rifle at the ready, I was searching for fresh milk when a French prisoner leapt out in front of me, speaking German: "Get rid of your rifle! Put on civilian clothes while you still can, the war is finished. The Russians are at Kolberg." I declined his offer. We spoke as I sipped the milk he gave me but I was careful always to keep my rifle pointing at him. There was something about the way he looked at me that made me regard him with contempt. I asked him if it troubled him that I wore an *SS* uniform.

"It's not my business," the prisoner said, lowering his gaze.

"Exactly," I replied. His attitude reminded me of a French soldier in 1940 that my mother urged to avoid captivity but he refused, preferring instead to give himself up as a prisoner. I would never surrender, not to the Russians. As long as I had ammunition to defend myself, and my bayonet, I would resist until the end. I left that farm after having bathed and bandaged my feet as best I could. By now Kolberg was not too far away.

The sudden roar of an airplane startled me. Instinctively, I started to run, zigzagging to avoid machine-guns bullets that lifted clods of frozen earth around me. I took to the nearby conifer forest, cursing the pilot and rebuking myself for having been caught in the open and immediately hid under a fallen trunk. The Russian fighter plane flew extremely low, brushing the tree tops, strafing again at random. Branches torn off by the rain of bullets fell around me, rustling. I waited for several minutes, until the buzz of the plane's engine's faded into the distance before resuming my march, keeping near the edge of the forest but still under the cover of the trees. It soon became apparent that this was slowing my progress; the ground underfoot was thick with roots and boulders which made walking on my damaged feet a slow business. To speed up my progress I took once more to the open road — a serious mistake because I soon found myself dodging a spray of bullets fired by the machine gun of a Russian tank which was charging in my direction having just negotiated the roadside ditch.

"*Maudit…*I'm done for!" I was helpless against that armoured beast and took cover once more in the forest, pushing past saplings to penetrate deeper into the thicker tree cover until the clanking tank lost interest in its meagre prey. When I felt safe again, I took to the road once more but had the disquieting impression that I might be walking into another trap; perhaps this time a Russian infantry unit on patrol. I continued, half-crouching, with my feet trampling the bottom of the roadside ditch to present as little of my profile as possible and continually looking around to check for T34 tanks. The sound of grating gears in the distance brought me to a standstill, but they too soon faded into the oblivion of the blue sky.

There were two wrecked trucks and shapes, lying on the road ahead. I unslung my rifle, ready to fire but there was no movement so I continued to walk towards them. As I drew closer, the horror of the scene gradually unfolded. The snow and water in the ditch were red with blood. The larger shapes were the body parts of horses, still warm, that had been blown to pieces and amongst these were the dismembered bodies of humans. Soldiers lay side by side on the edge of the ditch, comrades to the end. Children, their bodies torn by machine-gun fire, in death, held onto their mother's necks with their tiny arms; a last embrace. The limbs of children protruded from under the bodies of some of the women — they had sacrificed their lives in a pitiful attempt to save them. That scene was familiar to me: it brought to mind the massacres of refugees I had witnessed as a child in France. *Wars,* I thought, *are all the same in the end—an orgy of death and fear.* In the churned, dirty snow, around the scene of horror there were tank tracks and footprints heading towards the woods. Oh, how I prayed that those who had sought safety among the trees had escaped that merciless slaughter. I cursed the pilot of the plane that had strafed me; he had probably radioed the T34s to tell them of the presence of their victims. At that moment I heard the rumbling engine noise of a truck, struggling on the road, getting closer. I took to the cover of the trees and waited with my Mauser ready. When I saw that it was a German truck, I left my cover to greet the driver.

Unable to drive past the wrecked two vehicles, the truck stopped just a few paces from me and from it emerged a lieutenant from the *Luftwaffe* who looked upon the carnage with an expression of sheer disgust that seemed to engage his whole body. "Poor bastards…look at them…women and children…the Russians really are the slime of the earth."

I answered him by nodding.

"Give me a hand! I want to move these two wrecks out of the way."

In the box of the first truck we found a pile of new boots and socks. We didn't waste time looking for a pair to suit but simply grabbed the first pair that came to hand. I froze for a moment as I dug my hand into a pile of socks; the buzz of the Russian reconnaissance airplane was coming closer. I sprang away from the truck to the cover of the ditch, holding my body clear of the bloodied water by perching on my outstretched hands and the tips of my toes. A spray of bullets whizzed through the trees and smacked from the road. I remained suspended over the dirty water, my arms and legs shaking, as the plane lifted its nose to rise into the sky. After a graceful turn, it dived to strafe the lieutenant's truck again before leaving.

"*Maudit...*that assassin!" I shouted, looking for the lieutenant. He didn't answer. I saw him lying against the truck's running board, riddled in the back with bullets from the first sweep of the plane.

I considered taking the truck but decided it would be far too risky and so continued by foot. Exhausted almost to the point hallucination, I arrived at Kolberg in the first hours of the afternoon. Sentries at a control post in the proximity of the first houses directed me past thick tree trunks lying across the street; behind these nestled MG42 and *Panzerfäuste* emplacements. That day was 6 March, so the sentries told me — I had completely lost the notion of time because of constant hunger and lack of sleep. To take the weight off my weary legs for a moment, I leaned my elbow on the side-board of a small, horse-drawn cart that was covered with a tarpaulin but it slipped over the edge and made contact with the lumpy contents of the cart. Curious to learn what this could be, I lifted up the edge of the tarpaulin. As if propelled by an invisible force, I recoiled backwards, horrified by the sight before my eyes. The cart was filled with the bodies of soldiers in German uniforms, broken bodies with faces that bore a thunderstruck expression, their skin a pale, translucent grey.

Dangerous Candles and New Duties

Soldiers in a *Panzerfaust* emplacement told me that a platoon that spoke French had arrived in Kolberg several hours before and directed me to the town center. Close to the main square, I heard my name called from a side street. La Journisse was coming from a first-aid post with a new bandage on his arm. "Where in the hell did you hide this time?"

"My feet hurt like hell so I fell behind. Did everyone make it through?"

"Yes...you're the last one of our section to arrive...the Chief is worried about you."

I took advantage of the first-aid post to have my feet seen to before La Journisse led me to the accommodation temporarily assigned to us. Bournique welcomed me with unrestrained enthusiasm. "So, you're back to the fold, you devil of a devil...you fooled them Russians again, eh?"

Papis welcomed me with a pat on my shoulder. Jean passed a mess tin with hot coffee into my hand. I sat down, savouring it sip by sip, my mind at last free of the tensions that had gripped me throughout my trek.

De Ville congratulated me. "Tell us what happened to you."

My comrades gathered round to hear my story of the slaughter of the civilians.

De Ville, facing me with a sympathetic look on his face, laid a hand on my shoulder and said softly, "I know, I know kid. Don't think about it. Try to get some rest now."

In the evening, after a meagre supper of bread and margarine, we received the order to move to the Tivoli where *Volkssturm* conscripts, *SS* soldiers and stragglers from other units contributed to the great confusion in that hotel. Bournique assigned us to the main hall, on the *rez-de-chaussée*, the hall at ground level, where we searched for a tranquil spot to sleep amongst some battle-hardened veterans and officers.

As darkness encroached, the order was passed round not to switch on lights, so somebody had the bright idea to use a pair of candles instead. This upset an officer who bellowed for them to be extinguished but was met with whistles and insults ferocious enough to make him return to his seat.

"Another one that doesn't give a damn," whispered Jean, referring to the madman with the candles.

"Such indiscipline…in what kind of bordello does he think he is?" De Ville muttered under his breath. "Just try to get some sleep, tomorrow we'll think about our situation." De Ville said, yawning.

Cold draughts swept across the floor of the hall from the boarded-up windows and, on the opposite side of the hall, soldiers laughed loudly, preventing me from sleeping. Then, as I lay looking at the ceiling, a great force shook the room. The whole building shook under a terrible barrage from the cannon of a T34.

When the dust settled, an officer staggered to his feet shouting, "If I catch the imbecile with the candles I'll blow out his brain — if he has any!" The dry click of his pistol's safety catch being released pierced the silence that followed.

A soldier, coughing in the veil of plaster dust still falling from the ceiling, began to rave like a lunatic. "Gentlemen…all of you gentlemen…please listen to me…don't be like children… we depend on each other…" Somebody pulled him down but he continued to mumble.

De Ville was sitting with his hands to his face, shaking his head.

It was late in the morning of 7 March when we mustered on the street in front of the Tivoli hotel. We were aligned in two rows, the dozen remaining from our mortar section plus six or seven selected by *Oberscharführer* De Ville from other units. After making his inspection he launched into an unusual speech: "Keep your chest up and a proud look on your face, show steel in your eyes! We have nothing in common with those slow thinkers in last night's bordello. Together *we* have fought a brutal enemy. I ask you to be sharp and to obey my orders by jumping like springs."

"Jawohl *Oberscharführer*." we shouted in unison.

Then he told us to dust ourselves down, to shave and wash so that we were perfectly clean before reassembling in ten minutes. Now, for *Oberscharführer* De Ville, this was somewhat out of character. Judging by the short period he had spent with us, he didn't seem like a discipline or drill-them-into-the ground maniac. He expected obedience and respect for his authority, yes, but it was the first time we heard him talking about a proud look on our face and chest up.

Jean was suspicious. "What do you think he has in mind?"

"Whatever it is, it will be a very well-thought-out plan," I said.

After ablutions, we returned to our place on the street to await — with great curiosity — *Oberscharführer* De Ville's orders.

As he made his inspection, he looked every one of us in the eyes in a proud, fatherly sort of way then gave the order to march behind him. When we reached the municipal casino, fronting the square, we saw an officer from the General Staff waiting with a black leather folder under his arm.

"Section halt! Face right, right! Mark time! Close ranks! Section halt! Stand at ease!" The officer looked on with a serious look on his face as De Ville gave the sequence of commands in a dry, impersonal voice. De Ville turned and took two steps towards the officer to salute with an outstretched arm. He then turned back to face us. "Section, attention!" he shouted before taking up a stance beside the first row. "The 33rd Grenadier Division, Greifenberg March Battalion, 1st Company, Mortar Section, is awaiting orders *Obersturmführer!*"

"Very well! *Oberscharführer*," the officer said. He took a deep breath before beginning his address. "You are soldiers of valour; the sort of men we need in these difficult times. As you have seen, there are elements that have the potential to create disorder. This is an inevitable fact of life that occurs when troops are redeployed. This is nothing of consequence but it requires great effort and a special attention to contain. From now on you will assist the General Staff in that aim. You can be trusted, as you have shown, to carry out the duties necessary for maintaining good order and tracking down and punishing traitors, rebels, spies and all other undesirables. From this moment, this section is attached to the *SS* Police Section." He turned to De Ville, handing him the black folder. "*Oberscharführer,* you have the power to fulfil your new tasks. The new depositions are in this folder. You and your men will receive your badges as soon as possible. Dismissed!"

"*Jawohl Oberst!*" De Ville answered, saluting again. Then turning to us, he shouted, "*SS* Police Section! Face left, left! About face! Forward march!"

With impeccable, precise marching we left the square and turned into a side street where De Ville dismissed our squad. We gathered around him, pestering him to tell us about our new tasks. De Ville could not keep a smile from touching his face and said: "We'll regroup in the orderly room at our new headquarters on top floor of the casino in half an hour to discuss our service orders."

❦—❦

Oberscharführer De Ville selected Jean to read to us the list of services to organize and implement. He began: "Surveillance duties — Russian prisoners employed in different departments; punished soldiers assigned to corvée and maintenance and, finally, the *Luftwaffe* provisions depots."

At that moment my thoughts turned to the wealth of food piled up in those depots — boxes of chocolate, biscuits, preserves, cigarettes, liquors, clothing; the possibilities were endless. The rest of the list was relatively uninteresting but I caught the words 'discipline', 'communal' and 'security'.

When Jean finished reading, De Ville got up from his seat at an old desk to speak. "Now this will be our work," he said, "and I demand absolute devotion. You will be assigned a cot in the dormitory — with first quality mattresses and sheets. You will each be issued with a *Sturmgewehr* and ammunition. The service order you have just heard will be attached to the door as soon as it is ready. Now, you are free for half an hour at the end of which you must report back to this room."

Jean and I used the half-hour break to take a stroll down to the harbour.

"So, what do you think?" Jean asked.

"It doesn't get any better...we are lodged on our own, we are armed up to our teeth *and* we can go in and out of the *Luftwaffe* depots as we please."

"I can see what you're thinking Paul."

"And why not?"

"And if we're caught?"

"We...the police...get caught...hardly!"

Jean was not convinced. "I don't want to risk it," he said, "we'll have good food at the mess, luxury rations."

Changing the subject, I asked him what he thought of the city.

"It reminds me of Nice," he said.

"Maybe so…if you take away the war and the snow."

At the harbour, we looked out to the Baltic Sea, to the distant profiles of two *Kriegsmarine* vessels which I learned later were the *Lützow* and *Admiral Scheer.*

Explosions on the edge of town triggered a general alarm. Jean and I ran from the harbour to the casino where there was a small plaza behind which was a bomb shelter protected by bags of sand and tree trunks. At the entrance stairway, a group of women were bickering and clawing at each other like cats. Two shots into the air from my pistol established order but there was a young woman who, clasping a small child to her breast, continued to sob uncontrollably. When I went over to her to assure her that she would be safe inside the shelter, I noticed the unmistakeable pallor of death on the child's face. No words of mine could possibly have brought her consolation. I stood there, looking dumbly at the pitiful sight.

"She can't bring a dead child into the shelter," one of the other women said.

Jean stepped in. "*Meine Damen*, go down in good order, immediately."

The mother pressed the child more firmly against her body and as she descended the stairs, turned her head. Her eyes and mine met and in that glance I saw that she was thanking me, thanking me for that tiny, pathetic moment of comfort that was all I could offer. It is a moment I shall never forget.

At the orderly room we found a further service order: since the Russians had just succeeded in surrounding Kolberg, and the only escape from the city was now by sea, our newly formed police unit was now to oversee the protection of civilians during the planned evacuation. Precedence was given to pregnant women, wounded or sick citizens, children and older people. We were to escort them to the harbour, protect them until they boarded evacuation ships. To accomplish this, our *SS* Police unit was expanded by some tens of soldiers chosen from among the best.

De Ville was worried about the competence of the new recruits. "At least for a couple of days," he said, "I want one of our section on the patrol rounds, then we'll leave this task to the new recruits. We have other matters to attend to."

De Ville chose Jean and me to accompany three of the recruits that evening. As we went to pick up our *Sturmgewehren* Jean remarked, "Now we are responsible for saving lives."

"It's a noble principle, no?" I answered him.

"Sure, especially in these days…and in this city, given the way the wind blows."

"You think we could defend it after its citizens have been evacuated?"

"Mah! They'll keep us here to resist till the last moment…it will be our utmost defense, behind us there is only the sea."

"And don't forget the *Kriegsmarine* battleships."

"We'll resist, Paul."

"Until the last breath! I will never give myself up to the Russians!"

Angels in the Basement

The *Ostarbeiter*, Russian prisoners working for the Germans, were free to come and go as they pleased. They could easily have escaped Kolberg to return to their own lines but since our arrival in the city, none had taken this opportunity.

It was our first night on patrol. As we were passing a large building, a Russian prisoner appeared at the foot of the entrance stairway, panting. He informed us that he was one of a group of Russians that slept in a large room on the top floor and that they had heard a shot fired in the attic. We rushed up the stairs to find several *Ostarbeiter* standing on the landing and ordered four of them to lift me by the legs so that I could push open a trapdoor in the ceiling and pull myself into the attic by grasping on of the roof timbers. I switched on my flashlight, illuminating every corner; the place was cluttered with old boxes that offered a good hiding place for anyone up there. Holding tight my pistol with the other hand, I ventured deeper into the darkness.

Jean yelled up from the landing. "Paul! Forget it…come down!"

I swung the beam of light around once more, saw nothing unusual, and returned to the trapdoor to lower myself into the arms of the four Russians. As I brushed the dust from my uniform I gave them an enquiring stare. The Russians, with their meek eyes, spread their arms as a mute sign of their non-involvement.

I turned to Jean saying, "There's something fishy going on here. We'll leave two of the new fellows on guard while we inform De Ville."

Our chief was just back from an inspection of a block of buildings where the veterans in charge had lost control; their French soldiers refused to maintain themselves or change the straw where they slept, increasing the risk of spreading contagious diseases. *Oberscharführer* De Ville ordered us to go to the block and ensure that the rooms were disinfected, then to frisk everybody present and confiscate all the firearms we found in their possession.

To collect the confiscated firearms, two *Ostarbeiter* held open a sack at the checkpoint we set up near the entrance of the soldiers' dormitory. Demoralized, drained and dejected they were a pitiful sight; it was hard to believe that many of them were veterans from combat in Galicia and the Carpathians. But now they were non-combatants and would be sent to work at the fortifications. I disliked depriving them of their handguns which could come in handy in case of an emergency but I had to carry out the orders. A veteran soldier from the militia with the rank of adjutant stopped at the sack, holding a pistol in the palms of both hands, as if it were a precious relic. "Please understand," he said, "I respect your orders but I would like to point out in a few words the story of this friend of mine, the Beretta my father gave me. It is a family heirloom, you see. It has gone through the First World War and because of this I would like to ask you for the authorization to keep it, if that is possible."

I was surprised by his polite demeanour and by his deferential words but said reluctantly, "Orders are..."

"Orders are orders, I know." The veteran laid his pistol inside the sac and left, his head bowed in resigned melancholy at his loss.

Towards midday, a group of *Pioniere* who were passing told us of the sad end of one of their comrades. Their latrines, a bench with holes cut out at intervals propped above a ditch, were located in a place away from the beaten path. A 120mm bomb exploded not far away. The poor devil, while was sitting on the board, was dismembered by the blast. His legs and one arm, all that was left of him, fell into the latrine. *What a grim way to end one's life*, I thought.

Since my arrival in Kolberg, the Russian artillery was an increasing and constant threat which we countered with our own artillery. To confuse the Russian spotters, our artillery pieces were transferred to different locations overnight and on the morning of my third day in Kolberg, I discovered a 105mm cannon set up in the square not far from our dormitory. Somehow the Russians seemed to know in advance the new location of this piece and began to lob shells dangerously close to our cannon's position, with serious consequences for the artillery men who were completely exposed to the shrapnel.

Just before supper, at the command post in our section, our entire *SS* police squad listened with *Oberscharführer* De Ville to the words of a General Staff officer.

"We must solve this problem immediately," said the officer. "Every time we shift our howitzers and the flak during darkness, the Russian artillery's line of fire is corrected — they seem to be able to anticipate our moves."

"And we see the disastrous results in the morning," added De Ville.

The officer continued, "Precisely...but not only that...the Russian command also predicts our patrol movements and the position of our reinforcements sent to the front line. In fact, both reconnaissance squad and platoon movements are invariably opposed by a superior number of Russian infantry men who they encounter at night in crucial areas."

"This cannot be coincidence," De Ville dared say.

"Absolutely not!" the officer retorted. "Unfortunately we have arrived at the conclusion that there are spies among us." The officer looked sternly at De Ville. "*Oberscharführer,* it is your duty to flush out the cowards or traitors responsible for this betrayal, those who transmit our movements to the enemy." With his briefing complete, the officer saluted before turning on his heels to march out of the room.

"Bordello of a bordello!" De Ville exclaimed, scratching his head. "Paul, Jean, Papis, La Journisse, take two additional men and bring me the spies…we'll treat them as they deserve!"

Immediately our little troop of six men held a meeting with De Ville and Bournique around a table in our orderly room to decide a plan of action.

"We must lie in wait and continually observe the *Ostarbeiter,*" La Journisse proposed.

"We have to shadow *all* suspicious types, follow *all* possible clues…but how can we do this with just six of us?" I added.

"We restrict our net to the suspected areas," said Papis.

Jean smiled in agreement. "We'll check the documents of all we encounter around the command posts…prisoners and soldiers alike."

"Yes…but with discretion so that we do not attract attention…otherwise we spook the spies and then goodbye…nothing to show," said Papis.

At that moment a messenger from our own division stormed into the orderly room. "Russians," he panted, "they got close to the shelters, I heard them talking."

"Bournique jumped up from his seat and yelled at the top of his voice, "Alarm…alarm!"

Oberscharführer De Ville put his hand on Bournique's arm. "Calmness…stay calm Bournique." Then he asked the soldier where he had heard the voices.

"In the basement of a building…beside the one housing the *Ostarbeiter,*" the soldier answered, still gasping for breath.

"Are you sure they were not simply *Ostarbeiter?*"

"*Oberscharführer…*the Russian workers are restricted to the ground floor… those I heard were in the basement."

De Ville now looked as worried as Bournique. We grabbed our weapons and followed the messenger to the *Ostarbeiter* quarters where we descended to the dank basement tunnels with our torches to light the way. De Ville signalled for maximum silence as the soldier led us to a massive wooden door over which planks had been nailed. De Ville leaned forward, intending to press an ear against the door, but instantly recoiled at the sudden burst of laughter coming from the other side.

"Hear that?" said the messenger in a whisper.

"You are right…that sounds like Russian in that bordello," De Ville said in a low voice.

"What do we do?" Bournique asked.

"We shoot through the door," said La Journisse.

De Ville thought for a moment. "No, not that...does anyone here speak Russian?"

One of our team stepped forward. "A few words," he said.

De Ville ushered the Russian speaker closer to the door and whispered, "Tell them to come out with their hands on their heads."

Our Russian speaker began a conversation with those on the other side of the door. I understood a few of the words such as *'pa russki'* and *'russki jazik'*, meaning 'in Russian' and 'in the Russian language' and then from the other side of the door...*Da*...the Russian word for 'yes'. Then he turned to De Ville and nodded.

De Ville signalled us to withdraw from the door saying, "Take cover...be ready to fire! Keep one lamp on, so we see their faces, these Popovs!"

The door opened slowly from the inside to reveal the silhouette of four tall soldiers, each with their hands on their head. My finger hovered close to the trigger of my pistol.

De Ville yelled, "Don't shoot...they're Latvian *Waffen SS* men attached to *Korpsgruppe Tettau.*"

We checked the *Soldbuch* of each of the Latvians, who still looked shocked. One of them said: "And we thought you were the Russians."

"Well they might have been Popovs," sighed Papis, disappointed that we had not found the Russian spies.

❦—❦

The following morning, Jean and I remained in the vicinity of the casino to continue our mission to find the Russian spies while the remainder of our unit left to reinforce a counterattack near the cemetery. We stopped some suspicious-looking characters who turned out to be bewildered refugees looking for food and shelter. We shadowed civilians strolling around without a specific purpose, stopping them to check their documents. The day passed quickly but still we failed to uncover a single clue as to the identity of the spies. I was frustrated and disappointed. Meanwhile, the roar of battle continued unabated.

"Let's forget about the spies," Jean suggested.

I knew this kind of work was testing his patience. He would much rather have been at the front line. "Don't let the chief here you say that," I said forcefully. "This mission has absolute priority... and don't forget about my guard duty at the clinic later today."

❦—❦

The director of a clinic in the city had asked for police surveillance because she had decided to leave; she was worried about the precious surgical instruments she would leave behind and demanded their protection, at least until someone able to use them could be found. In exchange, we would have the use of the kitchen, bathrooms and bedrooms and also have access to the food supplies. A comrade and I were chosen for the first stint of guard duty and so could no longer participate in the hunt for the spies — or spy — responsible for passing information to the Russians.

The whole city trembled under the continuous thud of heavy caliber shells. Inside the clinic, flakes of plaster from the walls fell to the floor, doors squeaked on their hinges and glass rattled in the window frames. Attracted by the aroma of hot soup, we went downstairs and found two officers in the kitchen, preparing a meal, apparently unaware of the battle raging nearby. They were perfectly shaven and impeccable in their grey uniforms.

We saluted them but they ignored us completely. *Strange*, I thought, *very strange*. A dream-like atmosphere permeated the place and I had the urge to pinch myself. Attracted by the increasingly loud sounds of battle from the outside, my comrade went to the only window in the kitchen. "*Panzeralarm!*" he called but the officers remained unperturbed by the warning and continued to prepare their meal.

I went over to look out the window and saw a T34 tank, motionless in the middle of the narrow street. I lifted my *Sturmgewehr*, ready to let go a few rounds if a careless commander stuck his head above the cupola.

"Don't be foolish soldier," one of the officers snarled as he hurled himself at me. "Do not seek direct confrontation! Listen to me soldier policeman...do not provoke them!" He stepped back a pace or two then ventured into an incoherent speech about non-violence.

My comrade spoke in French. "They're crazy. I'm going to fill them with lead!"

"No," I answered, "they're holed up here waiting for the war to end. We'll see what De Ville has to say about this."

We left the clinic no closer to discovering the identity of the spies.

❧—❦

At the morning briefing — I think it might have been 10 March by this time — De Ville sat at his makeshift desk in a foul mood. So far, our mission to find the spies had been a complete failure; they were still quietly active, transmitting crucial information with disastrous consequences and De Ville was unable to demonstrate to the General Staff officers even a crumb of progress.

After learning about the odd behaviour of the two officers we had come across in the clinic, he instructed Jean and me to return there that evening with a *Panzerfaust* in case a tank showed up again. I was to stay the night to monitor Russian movements and 'keep an eye on the two officers'. Jean was to return to our headquarters at ten o'clock to report to De Ville then rejoin the search for the spy.

Papis, Jean, La Journisse and I left the briefing feeling that we had let our *Oberscharführer* down.

"We must change out tactics or we are not going to solve anything," Jean said.

"We have tried everything, what's left to do?" said La Journisse.

"I have an idea," I said. My comrades stared at me with the look of a drowning swimmer who had seen a rock to cling to. "Let's start from the casino in two groups working in opposite directions. We systematically search, house by house and building by building, widening our net. It will take time but in the end we'll discover these bastards."

"We swoop in and comb the basements and below the stairs," La Journisse proposed enthusiastically.

I laid out my plan. "Papis and I will go with one group and you two with the other… that way one of us will always lead each group just as De Ville instructed."

La Journisse's enthusiasm was almost at boiling point. "Let's start right the way," he insisted.

We continued searching until supper time, without result. De Ville, who we briefed about our plan, encouraged us to persist.

⁂

That evening at the clinic, Jean and I examined the surgical instruments store in a first floor room then searched a dressing room where we found fine civilian clothes of the sort worn by the bourgeoisie…and two German officer uniforms dangling from the coat hangers. Downstairs, in the basement kitchen, the two officers were again practising their culinary arts. We saluted them according to the regulations and this time they returned the courtesy. Then, to our astonishment, they offered us roast chicken and wine. They exuded a relaxed, nonchalant demeanour — all they lacked was cigars to complete the scene. It was a surreal situation.

As we continued our search of the clinic Jean said in French, "Not everyone goes to war to fight."

"And then they survive without even a shot fired," I answered, lost in bitter thoughts. After warning me not to fire at the Russian tank the previous day, I wondered what the officers would think of the *Panzerfaust* I had left ready to use, under a window on the first floor.

"I don't think so my friend…they risk losing their skin or being captured like the rest of us," Jean said.

I shuddered at the thought of being captured. "Sure! Then Popov's will put a bullet in our heads."

Jean helped choose a strategic spot from which I would have the widest view onto the street. A dormer was ideal; from there I could see the clinic's little garden and the staircase leading to the massive timber door at the main entrance. I had an ample shooting view. Before leaving to return to report to De Ville at ten o'clock, Jean made a last tour of the clinic and returned to my position at the dormer to wish me luck and to tell me the two odd officers were sleeping in the basement "like two cute angels".

From my vantage point at the open dormer window, I observed every movement in the dark street below, listened for the faintest sound. Then I heard the mechanical clanking of an approaching tank, brought to my ears as an echo from the walls of the narrow street before I could hear the growl of its engine. As the tank drew closer, grinding fallen roof tiles and paving stones under its tracks, I felt my pulse quicken. The steel monster stopped at the same spot as on the previous night, filling the air with oily exhaust fumes. The glass in the window of the dormer reverberated to the note of the tank's engine, as if trembling in fear. I gazed upon it with a certain awe. My heart skipped a beat when I saw a squad of Russian soldiers on the opposite flank of the tank, their backs protected by the windowless wall of a large building. My heart was now pumping furiously; I had already subconsciously made the decision to use the *Panzerfaust*. With the primeval instinct of a cat stalking its prey, I crept downstairs with the anti-tank weapon in my hands and my *Sturmgewehr* strap across my shoulder. When I reached the exit door to the garden, I slung the *Sturmgewehr* to the doorsill and, protected by the dark shadow of the clinic, crept across the open ground to within forty meters of the tank. "Stay calm," I forced myself to whisper, "don't let this chance slip away."

Another ten meters, I thought, *that would make sure I would hit the beast*. I crawled on my stomach to the edge of the garden where a line of shrubs offered a little cover but allowed a good view of the tank and then paused to calm my jangling nerves. I closed my eyes as I lowered my forehead to the ground, steeling myself for my next move, breathing in the light, damp scent of a patch of moss and thinking how sweet it smelled. If I missed the target I was done for. But I had faced a tank before, at training in Sennheim, in a test of nerve. I swallowed hard before rising to my right knee, positioning the tube of the *Panzerfaust* under my armpit and tried to stay calm as I followed the simple firing procedure. I squeezed the trigger with my thumb. A cloud of white smoke enveloped me and an instant later, I heard the dull smack of the warhead as it struck the tank, then a loud bang. A rocket of flame shot from inside the tank lighting up the whole street. Hot fragments of metal rained down around me. I jumped backwards, letting go of the now useless *Panzerfaust* launching tube. As I ran up the steps of the clinic, I grabbed my *Sturmgewehr* from the doorsill and, screaming like a man gone crazy, fired a burst against the burning turret and the stunned infantrymen who had survived the blast.

My whole body tingled as if being pricked by a million points of electrically charged needles as I made my way back to our headquarters. A triumphant scream of victory gave vent to the tension of the encounter with the tank; and I had achieved this alone — a fifteen-year-old David against a metal Goliath. I wanted, needed, to tell my comrades, to share my victory with them so that they would cheer with me. I broke into a run, skipping over the debris of war that littered the streets, stopping at every crossroads to laugh like a maniac. At last, I passed the casino and ran up the stairs leading to our headquarters, still smelling of the smoke from the black powder propellant of the *Panzerfaust*.

※—※

Desperate to tell my comrades of my success, I barged into the orderly room only to find it empty except for a policeman on guard duty who told me that *Oberscharführer* De Ville was asleep in a nearby room and that he had given orders that he was not to be wakened under any circumstances. Unable to contain my excitement, I briefly told the policeman about my encounter with the Russian tank, to which he listened with great interest before offering his congratulations. Unfortunately, I had done this in too loud a voice. De Ville opened the door of his room a little and looked at me with sleepy eyes.

"*Oberscharführer*, I destroyed a T34 beside the clinic!"

"Alone?"

"*Jawohl Oberscharführer.*"

"You did well, I will make sure you get a citation for valour, a medal…but tackling the tank alone was a mistake."

"*Oberscharführer*, I couldn't call for back up. This time there was a squad following the tank and…"

De Ville suddenly seemed more awake. "How many?"

"Seven…eight…maybe ten. But only two or three of them escaped."

"It was just a probing action then…they're still too hesitant to attack *en masse*. And your two officers…is there news of them?"

"Still there, eating and sleeping. They don't move a finger!"

He drawled his words yawning, but still clearly irritated by his untimely wakening. "Well, we cannot ignore such a situation…we are the police after all."

"What shall I do about them *Oberscharführer*?"

De Ville clenched his eyes. "Let me think," he said, opening the door completely. "Take two men from the guardhouse with you to collect these officers…we'll see what they have to say for themselves in the morning…and the next time you wake me up it had better be to tell me about a thousand Russians!"

At the makeshift guardhouse I commandeered a pair of comrades who were not at all enthusiastic about the possibility of bumping into a Russian patrol at night. I led them through the rubble, telling them to keep low and to hug the walls at any glimmer of light reaching the streets. Once in the vicinity of the clinic, I made sure there were no Russians around and pointed out the smoking silhouette of the T34 I had blown up half an hour earlier. After checking the Russian soldiers strewn around — they were all dead — I ventured into the garden to pick up the tube of the *Panzerfaust* and left it near the door of the clinic. With my reluctant comrades in tow, I switched on my flashlight and entered the clinic, *Sturmgewehr* at the ready in case of trouble, and headed downstairs into the basement.

"*Kameraden… Kameraden!*" the two officers shouted at our approach.

"Watch out," I warned my comrades, "they think we're Russians. I kicked the door open and stormed into their room and found them, suitcases at their feet, preparing to leave. I nodded curtly to my two escorts. "Search them."

"But…" one of the officers began.

"I have my orders," I said, raising my *Sturmgewehr*, "you are to come with us." When my two helpers completed their search, we marched the officers a little way ahead of us, out of the clinic. At the exit, I picked up the empty tube of my *Panzerfaust* as a souvenir of my exploit. The two officers stared at the wrecked T34 and the dead Russian soldiers in the street then turned to look at me, their mouths hanging open in disbelief.

I observed my police comrades as they encouraged the two officers to move with gentle prods from the barrels of their sub-machine guns. *Surely they hadn't gone through training at Sankt Andreas camp*, I thought, *otherwise they would have acted much more firmly during that arrest*. At the guardhouse, the *Sturmmann* on duty took responsibility for the two officers and locked them in a windowless room for the night.

Interrogations

Well-rested, I woke shortly after mid-day and, after lunch, joined with my comrades allocated to the unit responsible for hunting down the spies. They welcomed me with smiles and pats on the shoulders — a reward for my elimination of the Russian tank. But there was still work to be done; we were no closer to discovering the whereabouts of the spies and so we resumed the task of combing the district for anything suspicious. Towards evening, half a kilometer from the casino, our four-man unit entered a building on a side street. We checked the rooms at the ground floor level and, in the corridor, stopped a tall and athletic-looking man around forty years old and dressed in civilian clothes. He spoke German and his documents were in order but something about his bearing raised my suspicion. I ordered the two new additions to our unit to guard the man while Jean and I searched the basement.

After rummaging in every corner, we could find nothing but dust and cobwebs and were about to go back upstairs when we looked under the central heating system and saw a dark-coloured, leather suitcase. We kneeled on the floor to drag it from its hiding place; it was heavy, but surprisingly clean given its location. A smile cut across Jean's face as he opened the suitcase. I looked inside…we shook hands, got up on our feet, barely hushing our cries of joy as we performed little hops of elation.

Jean said: "Just look at this gear…transmitter…earphones…antennae."

"De Ville will jump for joy too."

We returned the suitcase to its hiding place and went upstairs as if nothing had happened. I told one of the two new arrivals to inform Papis and La Journisse of our find and the other to relay the good news to De Ville. Jean in the meantime had begun to interrogate the tall civilian. "From your papers I see that you live in a different building…then why are you here?" The civilian didn't answer.

De Ville was out on business when we arrived at the headquarters so we locked the tall suspect in a room near that of the two officers from the clinic. Bournique immediately placed himself on guard in front of the door for good measure.

La Journisse and Papis joined Jean and me to pick up the suitcase with the radio and bring it back to the headquarters where we set it on the bench that doubled as De Ville's desk. "Very well done, my young hounds," he exclaimed with a wide smile on his face, which had suddenly become less tense. "I will interrogate him this evening, in your presence."

We dragged the tall civilian in front of *Oberscharführer* De Ville who, sitting at his desk, directed the suspect to sit in the chair opposite. We withdrew into the background, some sitting, some standing.

"Well, well, let's see," De Ville began in a very calm tone of voice. He examined the prisoner's documents. After flicking through the pages, he declared, "Everything seems to be in order," before clearing his throat. "So, tell me, what were you doing in that building?"

"Keeping an eye on the radio."

"This suitcase, with the equipment it contains, is it yours?"

"I don't deny it. It belongs to me. I will explain if I may. I've had the radio since before the war. I am a technician, you see, and have a passion for transmitting…it was my hobby."

Silence, tight as a bowstring, met his plausible, open answer. "Hmm…a passion for transmitting," said De Ville thoughtfully, "but what and to whom?" De Ville's voice grew suddenly more aggressive. "Was it information to the Russians?"

"Absolutely not," the suspect defended himself in a firm voice.

"You were arrested in a building you don't live in…explain that."

"True, but I have already explained why I was there. And I wasn't surprised while transmitting, in fact I've not used the radio since the war began so I have done nothing illegal."

De Ville drew a deep breath. The interrogation seemed to be stalling.

"Hear how well our spy talks," exclaimed La Journisse, not in the least convinced of the prisoner's claim of innocence. "All spies have the gift of the gab. Do you remember the Marseillais at Greifenberg's guardhouse, Paul?"

"Of course I remember him! He came to a bad end," I said menacingly.

"We are experts with traitors, spies and secret agents," added La Journisse, accompanying his words with a cutting gesture of his hand across his throat.

De Ville cut our growing swell of frustration with a barked order. "Silence!" Then he turned his attention once more to the suspect. "And why didn't you keep the suitcase with you, in the building where you live?"

"As you can see from my papers, I live on the edge of town. I hid my equipment to prevent the Russians getting their hands on it…exactly where your men found it."

"And you didn't let anybody know about the new hiding place?"

"One cannot trust anybody in these times, and then, that radio equipment was very expensive, you understand."

"True, true!" said De Ville, apparently conceding ground to the accused.

Growing in confidence, the civilian continued, "If there is an accusation, surely I have a right to defend myself."

"Under normal circumstances that is true," said De Ville. "However, we are at war and don't have time for trials. You know what I mean?"

The civilian's face suddenly turned ashen grey; he ran a trembling hand over his dark, grizzled hair.

"Military Justice will take care of you. If you are guilty you will be shot by a firing squad." De Ville, staring the prisoner in the eye said: "Bournique! Inform the artillery commander that it would be advisable to move every battery where it is possible to do so." Still staring into the eyes of the prisoner, De Ville continued, "If the Russian artillery doesn't shift its aim towards the new emplacements you will find yourself with twelve holes in your skin. I will send you to prison under strict surveillance anyway, until your case is completely cleared up. Afterwards, you still run the risk of being shot for the simple reason of having been found in possession of the radio."

The civilian's dark eyes became glassy, as if fixed on a distant object; his face turned grey and he slumped on the chair as if he had suddenly lost his spinal column, his curled body giving the impression of a giant mollusc.

De Ville ordered two of the squad to take the prisoner away and said to Papis and me, "I'm in the mood for interrogations, bring me your two officers."

Somebody had already thought of adding another chair in front of *Oberscharführer* De Ville's Spartan desk before the two officers were brought before him. "Well! Let's begin," De Ville announced.

"I would like to remind you, *Oberscharführer*," said the more talkative of the two officers, "that you have no right whatsoever to…."

"Save your breath for answering the questions," De Ville cut in, annoyed by the snobbish tone of voice from his superior.

"As you wish, *Oberscharführer*."

De Ville opened a file on his desk. "I notice that you have already filled out the procedural forms…company, regiment, etcetera…but I don't see an explanation for your presence at the clinic."

"*Oberscharführer*, we simply lost contact with the General Staff during our last redeployment and, as you might know, after a reasonable waiting period we were free to act as we wish, in the best interest of the *Reich* of course."

"Yes…but why the clinic?"

"Doesn't it seem to you an ideal refuge while waiting to re-establish contact?"

"I don't doubt it. What I don't understand is why you didn't present yourselves to the General Staff in charge of this city's defense, particularly after your first encounter with my military policemen."

"There is an answer also to this question of yours, *Oberscharführer*. You see, we were on a special mission and waiting to re-establish contact with our direct superiors."

"Ah…a special mission." De Ville turned his attention to the other, more taciturn, officer. "Do you wish to comment?"

With the same haughtiness shown by his colleague, the second officer replied, "Even though I would be inclined to propose a confidential conversation, away from these indiscrete ears," he said, indicating with a slight turn of his head the rest of us in the room, "I do not think I will feel obliged to reveal the nature of our mission. After all, it is none of your business."

"And the suitcases in your possession, were they part of your mission?" De Ville made a signal to two policemen near the door who went immediately downstairs.

"Certainly! But you would not understand…"

"I understand this: you were holed up in that clinic eating and drinking without moving a finger against the Russians and without the least intention of making yourselves available for the defense. What were you waiting for, the end of the war?"

"Certainly not…only the most propitious moment to carry out our mission."

De Ville shook his head. "I call your behaviour desertion." At that moment, the two policemen returned with the suitcases and placed them on the desk, under the officers' noses. "You have the keys, no?" De Ville pressed. "Unlock them!"

"If you continue in this manner, I will be compelled to make a report to your superior," the taciturn officer said threateningly.

Deville looked up to the policemen who brought the suitcases. "Open them," he said, and watched as they executed his order with the points of their bayonets.

"Ah," said *Oberscharführer* De Ville, his hands searching amongst the contents of the suitcases, "Gold jewellery…lots of gold…silver bracelets…and the very best quality watches…somebody write up a list of all this and attach it to the report."

❋—❋

Most of the remaining inhabitants were holed up in shelters, basements and cellars, awaiting their fate as the Russians poured heavy, unrelenting fire upon Kolberg. I was returning from a patrol with two other soldiers when the ground shuddered — a Russian shell had made a direct hit on an ammunition depot which erupted with an infernal racket. Thousands of rounds of ammunition of all sorts shot into the night sky leaving colourful trails before lighting up the city as they fell. Rockets burst one after another creating a fantastic display of light and colour. Other bombs exploded after short, horizontal trajectories, some very close to the casino where several officers had paused on the staircase to witness the incredible nocturnal display. Unfortunately, a blast of shrapnel hit one of them, knocking him backwards. As I ran towards a shelter with my comrades, I saw a myriad of dark red patches spread rapidly, soaking his uniform.

When the frenzy of blasts, lights and colours ceased, we ventured out of the shelter and into a scene of terrible devastation. From amongst the rubble came the groaning of many wounded. Others leaned against what was left of a wall, begging for help. Kolberg was a smoking ruin with streets cluttered by fallen masonry and the charred and torn bodies of the dead.

As well as being pummeled by an enemy with numerically superior manpower, tanks and heavy weaponry, there was a crucial weak point in our defenses — spies and saboteurs. It was for this reason that we policemen stopped everybody we encountered at night; those who failed to explain their presence on the streets or whose documents were not in order, were treated as spies and brought to our headquarters for interrogation. In these desperate times, we didn't have time to ask too many questions and, consequently, suspects were treated in the way they deserved to be.

Anything for a Drink

The following morning, which was probably 12 March, while enjoying a rest period, I learned from the three policemen from our section who made up the firing squad, that the two officers I had arrested were shot on the beach. One of them lost his calm, shouting that he didn't want to die but the taciturn one fell bravely, riddled by bullets. I also found out that De Ville's stratagem had been successful: the Russian artillery, after the arrest of our spy with the radio, failed to pinpoint the positions of our artillery pieces with the accuracy shown during the previous days and nights. In the afternoon I shuttled between the city center and the harbour with my squad, protecting civilians as they made their way to the landing stage where they queued for a place on patrol boats or barges that would ferry them to ships waiting offshore. On the way, I came across an old woman sitting on a suitcase in the loggia of a villa with fine, white stone balconies. She told me she felt too dizzy to go any further. Her skin was shrivelled and her lips stuck together at the corners. I recognised the signs of dehydration, an increasing problem, particularly for the very young and the elderly, because the Russians had cut off Kolberg's water supplies. She presented such a pitiful sight that I told her to sit where she was until I returned.

With Jeans' help, I set up a corvée with the purpose of fetching water from the river. The three man team left with bins tied to the flanks of a horse but came back with the bin riddled by bullet-holes and without the horse. When they saw me about to leave with a jug in my hands, they asked if I was mad. "He will do it and come back with water... which won't wet *your* throats," Jean told them. I knew that with just a five-litre jug I could do very little, but to me it was a question of principle. I took to the road, which was cluttered with all sort of debris, towards our front lines of defense — holes dug to the depth of a man's shoulder in which *Wehrmacht* soldiers, armed with MG42s and *Panzerfäuste*, countered the enemy's overwhelming firing power. These brave soldiers were for the most part around fifty years old with thick stubble on their faces some of whom were prostrated by dysentery, thirst and lack of sleep. As soon as they saw me, they signalled for me to keep low, out of sight. I piled into one of the foxholes. "Where do you think you are going?" the occupants asked.

"To draw water at the Persante."

"Our hero! For days we've seen it flowing past without being able to get close enough to drink from it. Sometimes we could at night but not anymore."

"One acting alone might get through unnoticed," I replied, offering them cigarettes.

"Be careful on that open stretch," one of the *Wehrmacht* men warned, "before the shell hole with the plank across it. The Russians get a kick out of sweeping away whoever tries to cross it. You must get there in four big leaps, otherwise they will nail you."

I took a deep breath, as they taught me at Sennheim, and I sprang forwards. Bullets hit the ground around me kicking up clumps of frozen soil. At two meters from the hole I dived into it, onto the back of a soldier who fell under my weight. He got up on his feet, cursing. "*Du meine Fresse!* What do you think you're doing?" The fire from the Russian machine gun came to an abrupt halt.

"I'm here for water!"

The old *Wehrmacht* soldier indicated towards the river with a nod of his head. He spoke slowly, with a dreamy glance, as if meditating about what he was going to say. "You see there…at about ten meters…the three cadavers…they wanted water too."

"*Scheisse!*" I gaped at the fallen soldiers who were piled up, one on top of the other.

"Haven't had a drop to drink for two days myself," said the old *Wehrmacht* soldier.

"In a while you will drink," I promised. I laid my *Sturmgewehr*, ammunition belt and pistol beside the old soldier's MG42. "Where exactly are the Russians?" I asked.

He answered with a vague gesture from his arm, indicating 'everywhere'.

"Just the sharpshooters."

"There…behind those boxes…near the mattresses on the left."

"Cover me!" I jumped into the open, dodged the three corpses and under the cover of shrubs, slid down the riverbank to dip the jug into the ice-cold Persante. With the jug full, I scrambled back up the riverbank and into the open. A burst of machine-gun fire whizzed above my head just as I slithered into the shell hole. The old soldier took hold of the jug with both hands and raised it to his mouth, gulping down the water.

"Watch you don't spill it. Your comrades are waiting for it too."

The old soldier wiped his mouth with a sleeve. I took the jug from him. "Keep me covered, I'll be back."

"Thanks…and don't worry…I'll keep you covered."

Again I ran across the open ground, from foxhole to foxhole, keeping the jug upright and serving water to quench the thirst of the grateful soldiers. And when the jug was empty, I returned to the river to fill it — I still had a mission to complete; to bring water to the old woman. Holding the full jug in both hands, I made my way back to the villa. At first I didn't recognize the building where I had told her to wait; it had been hit by a shell. I stumbled among the rubble hoping that someone had already helped her and that she had moved on but my hopes were dashed when I saw a wad of grey hair soaked in blood under a fallen lintel.

On my return to the casino, Jean and Papis welcomed the water with cries of delight while the three men of the corvée looked at me as if I were a ghost. Jean fetched a coffee pot into which he emptied a packet of sugar mixed with coffee that he had 'acquired' from the *Luftwaffe* depot and we poured a cup of the precious drink to present to De Ville who savoured it without asking where it came from.

Joy before Sadness

The morning of 13 March started, as usual, with an earnest shelling of our positions and the surrounding houses, but with a greater ferocity than any we had previously endured. Every kind of projectile in the Russian arsenal rained down on the city, forcing me to make for a shelter already occupied by civilians. When suddenly calm returned, as usually happened after such barrages, I emerged from the shelter and, taking the same route as a group of Latvian *Waffen SS* from the 15th Division, arrived at a little square where they had tied their horses to trees and lamp posts at the beginning of the barrage. Faint neighs and death rattles came from the poor animals felled by shrapnel or covered by stones and debris from the explosions. They were lying, one on top of the next, some still kicking feebly as they suffered an agonising death. The luckier ones had been dismembered in an instant. For a young man who had worked with, and grown to love horses at Sennheim, this was a heartbreaking sight. Old and young, one of whom was a boy with a cut to his head, gathered around to offer support for the grim task I was about to perform. I lifted my *Sturmgewehr* and hesitated. Then with single shots and tears in my eyes, I systematically finished off each wounded animal. When the deed was complete, the old folks left shaking their heads but a few young kids remained to watch as, with the Latvians' help, I untied and removed the bridles of the few lucky horses that had survived the massacre. I came to a magnificent sorrel, still frightened, which I caressed, patiently trying to calm him. Still in a state of fear, he was tugging at his reins. I leaned my *Sturmgewehr* against a tree and, helped by the kids around me, searched for oats on the side sacks of the dead horses. While the sorrel munched on them, I soothed him, rubbing his neck, talking with a soft, slow, singsong-voice until I was able to reach his bridle. I untied his reins and waited a moment before sliding my foot into a stirrup to mount him. Immediately he got frisky and, veering to one side, narrowly avoided debris and dead horses on the ground. He kicked then ran, dodging ripped-up paving stones and smashed carts. I pressed my knees to his shoulders, pulled hard on his reins then slackened…pulled hard then slackened…until I was able to bring him to a trot. When the sorrel, snorting and vibrating his nostrils, calmed down, I led him towards the tree where I had left my *Sturmgewehr* and there, a smiling boy — the one with the cut to his head — clapped his hands in applause. Beside him, younger children jumped for joy, a moment of happiness amongst the ruins of war.

With only few thousand soldiers left in Kolberg to cover the last sea transports that were part of the evacuation effort *Operation Hannibal*, those of us assigned to the port area had our hands full. Tens of thousands of refugees were arriving at the harbour with sacks and suitcases containing items essential for a few days survival. In the harbour, patrol boats ferried terrified civilians from the landing stage to the ships offshore. Our task was to maintain order among the refugees waiting for their moment to board the ferries. Every face wore a look of utter dejection; the inhabitants were fleeing their homes, exhausted in body and soul, to board ships that would brave the ice-cold Baltic Sea in which the *Gustloff* had already been mercilessly sunk by torpedoes with the loss of nearly 10,000 lives of wounded soldiers, women and children.

By this time, the Russians had crushed our defense lines along the Persante River and were very close to our emplacements at the port. *Oberscharführer* De Ville informed us that our police squad was being reassigned with immediate effect to the protection of civilians gathering at the harbour. "The enemy is in every house," De Ville said, thumping his desk with a clenched fist. "The moment to show what we are capable of has arrived…*gran bordello!* Our job here is finished, now we must spit fire and blood."

Our defending forces, exhausted by the lack of sleep, were engaged in house to house combat just a few blocks from the harbour and fighting with astounding vigour against tanks, Pak, flamethrowers and a numerically superior enemy infantry force. Although they succeeded in pushing the enemy back at several points temporarily, for example at Adolf Hitler Platz (which opened the way for the escape of many civilians), it was inevitable that our troops would lose ground.

The invitations in French from Russian loudspeakers to give up our arms were rejected by the commander of Kolberg, Fritz Fullriede. As a consequence, the Russian assaults increased in both ferocity and intensity. Many members of our police unit fell in combat and our defense lines, hour by hour, were becoming increasingly exposed.

When it seemed that the authorities had completed the civil evacuation of Kolberg, at the last moment a new wave of civilian refugees poured onto the beach every one of whom claimed the right to evacuation. The authorities, although caught off guard, were somehow able to ship them to safety, despite a heavy sea-swell that prevented the patrol boats from reaching the beach. Instead they moored at the end of a long footbridge at the head of the pier. It was there that I ordered two Russian prisoners to take care of an old *Volkssturm* soldier who had slipped into the water. Dripping and cold and in the grip of a diarrhoea attack, the soldier had soiled himself. As the two prisoners wrapped him in a blanket, a woman around fifty years old, bejewelled and almost hidden by a luxurious fur coat approached me. In her arms she was carrying a Pomeranian poodle. In a voice heavy with melancholy she said: "I beg you, put down this dear friend of mine but without making him suffer. I don't want him to fall into Russian hands."

"As you wish, Madame," I answered, looking at her and her dog, surprised and uncertain about what to do. I let the dog down on the beach, aimed and shot once. The dog fell, sat on his flank contorting himself on the sand, barking and howling sorely.

"No...not like this," the woman called, bursting into tears.

I let go another shot; the dog fell still. I picked him up in order to give him back to the woman who was sobbing quietly. She hugged him, squeezing him in a tight grip, careless about the blood stains smearing her expensive fur coat. At that instant, shots from the Russian artillery reached the beach. Everyone dived to the ground, seeking cover, except the woman.

"Keep your head down!" I shouted, fearing she was certain to be hit.

"I want to bury him here," I heard her say. I had seen bizarre moments during recent bombings but that scene was astounding. The woman wandered back and forth, in search of a nice spot on the foreshore. I shook my head in disbelief and, after the round of explosions, returned to take care of the old *Volkssturm* soldier who was busy scolding the two Russian prisoners because they were energetically rubbing him, trying to warm him up. "Imbeciles, stumps! You'll break my ribs if you continue like this," he roared.

I ordered the three of them to return to the casino but decided to accompany them to keep the soldier under control because he was by now hopping mad and railing at the prisoners on account of the rough treatment he received. He shut up, though, at the sight of the sorrel lying on the ground at the square with a hole in his head: a piece of shrapnel had gone straight through it.

"Poor animal," I muttered in a faint voice, overcome by a deep sadness.

"A great looking horse," echoed the old soldier, dark of face and sincerely sorrowful.

I caressed the sorrel for the last time, untying him from the tree.

The Fall of Kolberg

For security reasons we, that is the effectives from the police section, had been sleeping at the municipal casino. The morning of 16 March started, as usual, with heavy shelling. I got up from bed with a sore neck because I had been using a small suitcase as a pillow and let everyone know about it. Papis on the other hand wakened up without complaint; he had rested his head on a small leather sack. We had planned for the days to come and packed in addition to our personal underwear, cigarettes, cigarette lighters, cigarette papers, shaving blades, soap and brilliantine and some other small but useful items we had patiently accumulated since the first days of our arrival in Kolberg. I stored my meagre treasure collection in the small suitcase while Papis kept his in the sack. For good measure we slept on them and, before leaving the casino, we hid them under a pile of discarded, almost shredded clothes.

"You two…with me to relieve De Ville," Bournique said while Papis and I were going downstairs. "Where are Jean and La Journisse?" he asked.

"Still at the pier, they took our place when it was their turn for duty."

Bournique waved his arm to hurry us along. "There's no time to waste…the Russians are already in the houses nearby."

"And the ammunition?" inquired Papis.

"Plenty…also hand grenades."

"Where are we heading?" I asked.

"Where they shoot! Beast of a devil!" our *Sturmmann* answered, evidently rather annoyed by my silly question.

Our defense line was reduced to a couple of blocks in front of the casino and, behind a pile of rubble, we reached our comrades. The sound of cannonades and discharges from rifles and machine guns came from the direction of the Persante Estuary and from the vicinity of the train station. Papis and I took up position behind a thick wall, one of the few still standing, which offered good protection from bullets and a good position from which we could take a run-up to launch our hand grenades. Fortunately, we had a good supply of these, some still sealed in their boxes. We fired from each end of the wall through gaps in the ripped and chipped bricks, but with caution; Russian soldiers were in every floor of the houses in front of us and kept us under constant fire. At every round from us, they returned a whole host of whistling bullets in our direction, in a quantity disproportionate to the size of the enemy force they faced.

"Bulls eye again!" I shouted at Papis, after he hurled his umpteenth hand grenade which, through the broken glass of a window, exploded inside the first floor of a house. I let go a brief burst from my *Sturmgewehr* in the same direction, then ducked for cover. Our shoulders were aching with the repeated effort of flinging hand grenades at the Russian positions so we took turns to launch them. I was able to hurl a few through those windows but after every blast, each of which was followed by a brief pause, the volume of Russian fire quickly returned to its previous level.

"There are hundreds of them in there!" said Papis.

"Like ants…just like at Körlin."

"One falls and five replace him!"

"You mean ten!" I said.

"If we don't flush them out we'll be glued behind these walls for who knows how many days!"

"Just like in the trenches!"

"You two! Save your breath!" Bournique rebuked us. "Keep them under pressure!" His face was red; his veins a network of throbbing blue lines on his temples.

We didn't need Bournique's incitement; we continued to return the Russian fire without respite. Since the eruption of the artillery barrage in the morning we had been locked in a close-quarter battle, exchanging fire from rifles and sub-machine guns and tossing hand grenades at each other but we were still there, behind the walls, thwarting the Russian's progress.

Toward evening, Jean and La Journisse came to take our place at the wall while Papis and I, after a hasty supper, returned to the pier. The civilian evacuation should have already been accomplished but when they saw us, groups of old people and women with wailing children rushed towards us, seeking assistance in getting aboard a boat.

"Give them precedence! Get them on board right away," an officer ordered but we knew already that evacuating civilians had been given the highest priority.

When the last of the civilian refugees — which included railway workers and *Organization Todt* operatives — had been taken to the waiting ships, the fighting units received the order to start pulling back. First came the turn of the *Pioniere* that slept in the casino. We from the police section, since it was our task to attempt to maintain good order throughout the evacuation, were the last to withdraw and it was at this time that I learned that the Russians had transmitted an ultimatum in which they dictated the conditions for our surrender on 14 March. The General Staff officers evidently ignored this, probably because they were pressed by the more immediate problem of evacuating some thousands of refugees and wounded soldiers and time was short — the Russians had been systematically reducing the city to burning rubble and were preparing for the final assault.

The Siege of Kolberg was reaching its final, bitter conclusion and now we were fighting not only the Russians but also units of the 3rd, 4th and 6th Polish infantry divisions. The Russian prisoners, the *Ostarbeiter*, fearing reprisals from their countrymen, pleaded with our officers to let them board the evacuation ships but their appeals were refused — the ships were already overladen.

I was amongst the last to leave. With other comrades, I spent the night at the harbour directing the flow of unarmed soldiers and survivors from the fighting units who had just received the order to leave their emplacements.

On 17 March, under a dawn sky that trembled with the continuous thunder of the barrage of Russian ordnance of every description, Papis and I returned to the casino with the intention of picking up my small suitcase and his sack containing the treasures we had accumulated. We soon realized the precariousness of the situation: we glimpsed Russian soldiers as they darted across the streets that opened onto the square in front of us. We had very little time left to fulfill our own, personal little mission. We entered the casino to find it was empty — except for a *Luftwaffe* colonel who was playing the piano in a hall near the entrance. Enraptured by the melodies, he was oblivious to the shouts, shots and explosions taking place in the nearby streets. We ran upstairs to our dormitory to find our stash of valuables, grabbed them from their hiding place and rushed back downstairs. It was then that I noticed that his music, the last expression of human culture in Kolberg, had stopped. I opened the door to the hall and saw him, slumped on the keyboard, his legs bent and half-crossed under the piano stool. When I went to see what had happened to him, I noticed the bright red blood on the white keys of the piano. There was a bullet-hole in his temple. At that moment a tremendous blast shook the floor.

"Out of here! Quick!" I shouted at Papis.

"Too late, Paul!"

"Popovs?"

"On the square, I see them!"

We ran to the entrance where the door was still wide open. A storm of bullets ricocheted from the stonework around the entrance and we dived to the floor to return fire with a few rounds from our *Sturmgewehre* and then crawled towards the back door. With no Russian berets in sight, we left the casino for the last time.

"Bastards! A few more seconds and they were going to nail us," Papis said as we made our escape.

"That colonel," I said, "he played good music."

"*Ja*, he used to play whenever he had the chance."

"One evening he asked me if I knew how to play."

Papis, his lips drawn tight, shook his head then said: "A congenial fellow...but look at how he ended up."

We ran through rubble-strewn streets, a landscape of devastation littered with burning trucks, smashed wooden carts, carcasses of dead and half-charred horses and the corpses of civilians and soldiers. Where they had fallen, they stayed — the living were too concerned with saving themselves to care about the dead.

At the railway station, *Oberscharführer* De Ville received us with a grunt. He was in a very angry mood because several of our comrades were missing and two were seriously wounded. Papis, Jean, La Journisse and I, the youngest in our unit, had all survived so far, as had Bournique, De Ville and five or six policemen — that was all that was left of our section.

"Paul! Papis! Take care of the wounded. Get then onto an evacuation ship."

"Certainly *Oberscharführer*," I answered smartly. I felt sorry for him; his sad eyes were drooping and his shoulders were hunched giving him the appearance of a much older man.

"It will be done, *Oberscharführer*," said Papis who, I was sure, shared my sentiments.

"The remainder of you will stay here, with me," said De Ville. He turned to Bournique, "Put up a barricade...use anything to hand then get the men under cover. We must resist at all costs."

We left the station carrying the wounded on stretchers with the help of Russian prisoners, wondering what fate had in store for our well-respected *Oberscharführer*. By this time the beach area to the east of the Persante was under constant fire from Russian tanks and Pak but we avoided that barrage and came safely to the harbour. The weather was fine despite the cold air and wrinkled bands of white clouds but the sea was choppy with tall waves capped with brilliant-white foam. At the pier there was a small gathering of civilians mixed with soldiers of all ranks waiting for the patrol boats. As a precaution, I held my pistol at the ready but finally we were able to lift the stretchers with the wounded onto the patrol boats that would transport them to the ships farther out. I sent the Russian prisoners to their fate and remained on the beach with Papis, me sitting on my little suitcase and he on his sack of treasures. What was once Kolberg lay to the south, flames and smoke rising from the remnants of the once attractive city — hundreds of years of history wiped out in a few days.

"What do you intend to do?" Papis asked me.

"I'll keep clear of *them*," I answered, nodding at the unarmed folk in the waiting crowd.

"We dig a hole?"

"In the sand?"

"And where else?" said Papis.

"Good idea!" I agreed. Using a helmet we found on the beach, we scooped out a hole in the sand, almost reaching the water underneath, forming a shallow depression just deep enough to offer us a little cover but not big enough to accommodate either my little suitcase or Papis' sack containing the items we once thought precious but now seemed trivial. I laid my *Sturmgewehr* to the side — Papis had left his at the station but was grasping his pistol — to reach under my coat for my canteen. I twisted open the cap to release the sweet smell of the rum I had filled it with during my last surveillance duty at the *Luftwaffe* depot. I took a sip, offered it to Papis who, glued to the spout like a lamprey, swallowed a long gulp. After a few minutes, the alcohol lifted his melancholy and he started to sing at the top of his lungs: "*Les bateaux des îles, les bateaux des amoreaux...*" (*The Boat of the Islands*, *The Boat of Love* was a hit song by Tino Rossi). In that instant a series of bombs landed around us, throwing up gigantic plumes of wet sand.

"*Katyushas,*" I shouted, pressing myself as deep as possible into the shallow pit.

"*Les organs à Staline!*" he replied, in French.

The crowd on the pier panicked. Some ran for their lives, yelling in fear. Others hid as best they could or threw themselves to the ground behind abandoned wooden boxes. At that moment a *Luftwaffe* officer rushed to our entrenchment from behind, panting. There was terror in his eyes, his helmet was askew and his cape open at the neck. He asked to join us in our hole.

"Disappear!" I told him, pointing my 7.65 pistol under his nose.

As the shells and rockets screamed and whistled, he bent over us, leaning his hands on the edge of the hole so that it began to collapse. "Comrades...the duty...to help in combat..." he stuttered.

"*Raus! Sofort!*" Papis threatened him with his pistol too.

"*Ach,*" he exclaimed, getting up, cursing as he left.

"He could have dug his own hole...he had all the time he needed, no?" I said, putting my pistol back in the holster then grabbing my *Sturmgewehr*.

"Maybe the *Luftwaffe Ausbildung* was different from that in our home-base, in Sennheim," Papis shouted above the thunder of the big guns on the *Kriegsmarine* ships offshore and the 105mm cannon, located at the harbour. The blast of a mortar grenade showered us with heavy, wet sand. The enemy mortar crews were finding their range. Our entrenchment protected us from shrapnel and bullets but, being in the open, we were vulnerable to these almost vertically falling projectiles.

The Final Redoubt

In the harbour, Russian shells sought out the evacuation vessels. Great plumes of seawater rushed into the air, held there for a moment, and then fell like cascading waterfalls. Two patrol boats were moored at the jetty, their light cannons firing off in a pathetic response to the continual bombardment by the enemy's heavy calibre cannons. Those waiting to board were mainly soldiers now — only luck was saving them from obliteration. Near the first houses overlooking the harbour, German *SS* soldiers were defending a street from the shelter of a line of rubble with maniacal determination to prevent the enemy infantry storming the harbour and slaughtering everyone they came across. Papis and I looked each other in the eyes.

"Are you ready?" I asked. Papis nodded, and then started to turn and rise as if to make for the jetty. I grabbed his arm. "Not that way!"

"Which way, then?"

"There's nothing we can do to help at the jetty." I pointed to the violent skirmish taking place near the first houses. "We can help these *SS* men." There was, though, about two-hundred meters of open ground to cross. Mortar grenades whistled through the air — one landed close, too close, showering us once more with damp sand, which we slapped from our coats.

"Are you mad Paul...you want to be slammed full of lead right now?"

"Listen to me, Papis...not one bomb fell between here and the street."

"But it's as flat as a billiard table. There's no cover apart from that burning truck and the *Kübelwagen* just beyond it."

"I see that...but there's nobody there for the Russians to shoot at. They're aiming at the landing stage." I talked swiftly; my nerves were jangling at the thought of what we were about to attempt. "We'll make it back to the pier later," I assured Papis.

"I don't want to miss the last ride," Papis replied. He took his helmet off, passed a hand through his blondish hair, inhaled a deep breath and sat his helmet back on his head.

"Remember your sack," I said.

We leapt from our hole in the sand and launched ourselves forward, in a lame run, impeded by the hand grenades stuck into our belts and our reserves of ammunition in our pockets and ammo pouches. Things didn't quite work out the way I thought they would. When we were ten meters from the wrecked truck, the zip-zip of bullets passing close to our heads made us dive instinctively for cover behind the truck. I let go a series of short bursts from my *Sturmgewehr* in response. Tears streamed from my eyes, a reaction to the acrid vapours from the burning truck tyres. I took a deep breath and moved towards the cab to get a better view of the field of battle and saw in the cab, on the passenger seat, four magazines for my *Sturmgewehr*. I snatched the welcome find up and took cover behind a front wheel. Bullets pattered into the truck's metal skin and ricocheted from the fender.

Papis threw me a dirty look.

"I know…they've spotted us," I said, answering his silent rebuke. We returned fire with a rapid discharge, aiming at the windows of the houses in front of us, on both sides of the street. The enemy infantry had occupied them but they were also outside, at the corner of a wall of one of the buildings, and from these vantage points, they had the truck under crossfire. A hail of bullets smacked into the vehicle for a good half-minute, some of them passing straight through; the supressing fire was clearly intended to prevent us reinforcing the *SS* men at the wall. We kept under cover, behind the wheels, until there was a pause in the firing.

"They don't like us," Papis remarked ironically.

Now you have it, your personal battle, your small war, just as you wished, I thought. I understood then what it feels like to be the prey, without a way out. It was a strange, surreal feeling to realize that my young life could end at any second. Surrender was not an option; even if we tried, we would have been filled with lead in an instant, judging by the immense volume of fire laid down by the enemy. "Never!" I shouted against them, firing another few rounds.

Papis looked sideways at me. "What did you say?"

"I was thinking aloud."

Then Papis yelled, "Now think about getting us out of here. We must move!"

"To the overturned *Kübelwagen*?"

"Let's go!"

When ran the first twenty meters without attracting the Russians' attention and the next twenty through two bursts of machine-gun fire. At the *Kübelwagen*, we flung ourselves down again, wondering how we had survived. At that point the German *SS* soldiers noticed us and realized what our intentions were, so they sprayed windows of the houses with machine-gun fire which gave Papis and me the opportunity to complete the run to the *SS* mens' defense line.

A *Sturmman* looked at my suitcase and Papis' sack with a quizzical eye. "Going on leave, you two?"

"Ammo for our pistols," I answered — a half-truth.

"Take up position wherever you can," said the *Sturmmann* ."There are Russians on the right of us and Poles at the left — and they're even more furious than the Russians."

One of the soldiers flung a *Sturmgewehr* to Papis who, grabbing it in mid-air, put it to immediate use. I followed his example, countering the enemy fire which was increasing in intensity. From the harbour, our 105mm piece returned fire at regular intervals and then was silent for long minutes during which we heard only the hiss of Russian projectiles, some of which overshot their target and splashed into the sea.

"The 105's short of shells," Papis observed.

"They're saving them for the T34s," the *Sturmmann* said. But the Russian tanks weren't showing themselves yet; perhaps they feared the 150mm cannons on the *Kriegsmarine* ships which were still sitting offshore.

We repelled two efforts, one Russian and the other Polish, to force a passage towards the pier. The enemy retreated to his starting point, leaving many soldiers dead or wounded on the ground. During those assaults they came at us in the open and it was easy to stop them although they sometimes managed to get so close that we used hand grenades to repel the attacks but, for the most part, the enemy assaulted us with an intense hail of machine-gun and rifle fire that gradually chipped away the edges of the wall providing us with cover. Mortar grenades blasted around us, throwing up stones and debris, smothering us with clouds of choking plaster dust, but we had grown used to it and didn't budge one millimeter.

At every new docking at the pier, our patrol boats answered the enemy with the howl of their on-board light guns and in those minutes, not a single Russian nose could be seen sticking out from the houses at the edge of the harbour area. However, in the late afternoon while the patrol boats were disgorging their passengers onto the ships offshore, the Poles seized the moment to mount a strenuous attack. In the close quarter fighting, we resisted by firing off a series of machine-gun bursts and throwing most of our remaining hand grenades. During this attack, two of the German *SS* men were wounded, compelling them to withdraw from the fighting and sit in the protection of the walls. But the Poles withdrew, leaving piles of dead and wounded in the street separating us from the houses. Having failed to dislodge us with infantry assaults and mortars, the enemy then targeted us with accurate artillery fire; instead of small shrapnel and stones, the explosions hurled bricks and debris in all directions. Now it was impossible to defend the wall and the approach to the pier so the *Sturmmann* signalled us to pull back. Papis and I made for the overturned *Kübelwagen* which was now in flames. We returned fire with our *Sturmgewehre*. In that temporary shelter, at the moment of reloading, I realized that Papis didn't have his sack nor I my little suitcase. Our carefully saved little treasures were lost. I tapped Papis on the shoulder. "We've forgotten our stuff."

A rain of bullets peppered the chassis of the *Kübelwagen*; we both lowered our head until the firing stopped then sprang to our feet, shooting at anything moving. Four or five careless Russian soldiers fell under our fire, forty meters from us, caught in the open in their effort to flush us out.

"So, our stuff?" I asked again, ducking down behind the *Kübelwagen*.

"It doesn't matter, Paul! Let it go."

"After all the time we spent gathering ..."

"Paul, think about those damned Russians. The sack, the suitcase, they don't matter now."

There was a pause in the fighting; I'd made up my mind. "I'm going to get them."

"You're mad."

"Cover me."

I back ran to the wall we'd left a few minutes before. My suitcase was easy to find but it took longer to locate Papis' sack, which was half-buried in debris and dust. I grabbed it and zig-zagged back to the burning *Kübelwagen* where I flung Papis' sack at his chest as I ran past. "Make for the truck first!" Papis followed.

As we ran towards the truck, bullets ricocheted at our feet making almost musical whirrs and whines but we continued onwards until we reached the relative safety of the smouldering vehicle. When we looked back, we saw the Russians closing on us; they were already past the *Kübelwagen*.

"You see them?" Papis said, puffing and panting. "They're coming at us...in the open!"

"Stupid...courageous," I added.

"We should've followed the others...to the pier."

There was a sudden crackle of submachine-gun fire from our right.

"It's De Ville with the rest of our section," I exclaimed with joy.

The German *SS* men from the defense line at the wall, having reached the pier, also joined the skirmish, creating a protective cross-fire for Papis and me. We seized the moment of confusion amongst the Russians to make a dash towards the pier. "Head for those wooden crates," I screamed. Suddenly, Papis fell. His helmet rolled away from his head then settled on the ground, rocking from side to side. I staggered to a standstill and turned, fearing the worst, but saw Papis rise to his feet with a dazed look on his face. I picked up his helmet — now dented at the side — and planted it back onto his head. "Hurry...we're showing them our backs."

"Oh my poor head," Papis whined, breaking into a run.

We reached the wooden crates, which were about a hundred meters from the pier, and sheltered behind one. Papis gathered the still-full magazines from the weapons left behind by the departing soldiers while I opened the crate to see if it contained anything useful — it was filled with hand grenades which we made ready for use by inserting the fuses. We piled up the bundles left behind by civilians on top of my suitcase and Papis' sack then dragged together some of the smaller crates containing metal components for ships to form a makeshift defense post as stragglers continued to arrive at the pier.

As the daylight faded, our 105mm cannon and anti-aircraft pieces around the harbour thundered defiantly as Russian shells whistled in with their terrifying crescendos; the ground vibrated under our feet as if the end of the world was near. De Ville however, with the remains of our police section and other units, had been able to push the Russians beyond the first houses fronting the beach, and had occupied them. Papis, Jean, La Journisse and I, our way lit by the white light of Russian magnesium flares, carried boxes of hand grenades and ammunition we had gathered in the area of the pier to the houses occupied by De Ville's men.

When we arrived there, De Ville was running around organizing things. "You and Papis, take the grenades upstairs, you'll get a better throw from there." He seemed exhausted from the relentless fighting; his eyes, the skin below them circled blue, drooped at outside corners; his face, caked in dried mud, seemed suddenly thinner than I remembered. Only a glimmer of energy kept him going. He smiled at me briefly, laying a hand on my shoulder, and then repeated the gesture with Papis before moving on to the other emplacements.

As instructed by our *Oberscharführer,* Papis and I set up shop in a room upstairs from which we could dominate a substantial proportion of the ground in front of the house. Flashing tongues of fire from Russians and Polish machine guns and rifles in the building opposite lit the street with their flickering yellow light. For an hour, maybe more, we sporadically returned fire, oblivious to the continual thud of the Russian bombardment until it stopped suddenly. There was movement in the darkness, opposite our window. Suddenly, the air was ringing to the cries of the Russian soldiers... *Hourré... Hourré.*

Papis and I went into full action, hurling hand grenades.

"These chestnuts are for you!" Papis yelled.

We flung one grenade after the other, perhaps a dozen each, amongst the dark shapes rushing in the street below. De Ville's men fired on them from ground level. Their cries of war turned to screams of panic as the enemy soldiers, surprised by the ferocity of our defense, stumbled over their wounded and dead comrades in a headlong retreat. Bursts of fire from De Ville's men helped them on their way to the cover of the buildings on the opposite side of the street from which they were content to fire on us with rifles and sub-machine guns for a while. We returned the favor but other enemy soldiers rushed over from where the railway tracks crossed each other, to our left, and so we resumed our grenade lobbing.

"This reminds me of when I was kid playing soldiers," I shouted between blasts. "I lived near the Maginot Line...when we found old bombs from the last war, my friend Dodek and I exploded them."

"Help yourself," Papis said, passing me a box of hand grenades.

"After you," I replied nonchalantly. I was having fun, great fun.

This time the Russians continued their attack on our stronghold, despite their grave losses — they were desperate to reach the pier. We of course continued to drop grenades among them until Papis opened the last box and announced that we had only eight left. At that moment, Bournique shouted up the stairwell to tell us to pull back.

"But we still have grenades," I replied.

"Throw them and come down! Make it quick! You're the last ones here."

We flung the remaining grenades in rapid succession at the houses on the opposite side of the street then clattered down the stairs. Once outside, we ran headlong in the direction of our barricade made of crates; there we had left magazines and back-up weapons, ready to fire. This time it was our turn to be chased by machine-gun bullets but the bursts flew harmlessly over our helmets. At the harbour, the light cannons on the moored patrol boat came alive as it prepared to leave the landing stage.

"Hei! It won't be the last ferry I hope," Papis exclaimed.

"They'll tell us when it's our turn to embark, you'll see," I reassured him.

There were about a hundred soldiers still waiting, bent down on the gangway leading to the landing stage. From our barricade, we continued to return the fire from the houses facing the harbour, the same ones we had occupied a short while before, supported by our isolated defense posts on the beach. Our 105mm cannon and the anti-aircraft pieces were silent now, their work complete; only the light cannons on the last patrol boat returning to the pier howled in our defense.

"I don't like it," Papis yelled above the noise of combat.

I grabbed Papis' hand. "We must make a run for the jetty, otherwise it's good bye."

Papis nodded. "All right, we'll run when we see the last ten at the jetty."

"Sooner," I insisted.

It must have been past midnight when we recovered my suitcase and Papis' sack hidden beneath the pile of discarded civilian bundles. We ducked low as we ran towards the landing stage and the gangway to the boat. At the moment of laying foot on the deck I turned for a last look: a squad of German soldiers from various units had reached our barricade and a handfull of *SS* soldiers were firing from their posts on the beach, the last dozen or so men left onshore. Papis and I slid through a hatch, descending on an iron ladder into the hull of the patrol boat. We were the last *Waffen SS* from the 'Charlemagne' to leave Kolberg.

Passage to Swinemünde

My *Sturmgewehr* was still hot as I squeezed past the soldiers crammed inside the hull of the patrol boat. To make my passage through the dimly lit interior easier, I held my little suitcase over the heads of the other escaping soldiers. Papis, in front of me, took his flashlight from his pocket; the beam of light shone over the pale faces of a number of wounded who bore their pain in silence. The boat's engine revved harder and I felt it slip from the jetty. Its cannons fell silent and the machine guns on deck fired their last volleys as the vessel began to pitch and roll so that all who were standing swayed from side to side as if they were drunk. Every face wore a look of anxiety for there was still the danger that a Russian shell might blow us out of the water. As the boat moved further into the Baltic Sea, the waves gained in force and amplitude, buffeting against the boat's hull and bringing moans and laments of pain from the wounded soldiers. The engine opened at full throttle, roaring under the effort of ploughing through the rough sea, and soon we were offshore, out of shooting range and, we thought, almost safe.

An alarm sounded and the patrol boat's engine fell silent. "Submarine" I heard a *Matrose* say through the open deck hatch. Each violent slap of a wave against the drifting boat brought a fresh chorus of agony from the wounded, the only sounds as we contemplated this new and deadly threat. I pushed my way to the ladder, where Papis was already standing, and grabbed a rung to steady myself. We were both contemplating the worst — if a torpedo hit, panic would assail everybody and the only way out was up the narrow iron ladder. There would be a rush towards it — pushing, elbowing, a suffocating scrum. *Better to stay attached to the rungs*, I thought. And once on the deck, what would I do then? I would have to find something that floats. It was a habit of mine, to think about a way out when I was hemmed in by a crowd.

Someone started blazing with anger, shouting and swearing; one of the wounded perhaps, whose fever had made him delirious. There was an intensifying sense of nervous tension, a hint of panic. I looked Papis in his eyes and we understood each other immediately — we two were armed *SS* policemen and it was our duty to maintain order, even in these extreme circumstances.

The hull vibrated when the engine restarted suddenly, then the engine's roar became a continuous purr as the patrol boat slowed and bumped gently against a larger, more solid structure. A light shining through the open hatch appeared and disappeared according to the swell of the waves.

Papis and I directed the exit of the wounded, who had to be lifted by hand, and maintained order as the remainder climbed the ladder. We were the last to scramble onto the bobbing deck of the patrol boat, into the fresh and briny air, as it moored alongside the merchant ship *Kolberg*.

Through a hand-held megaphone, an officer yelled orders to lower a gangway and to illuminate it with the ship's floodlights; after a couple of attempts it was hooked to our patrol boat. The two vessels rose and dipped alternatively, following the swell, making the transfer of evacuees difficult. Then a particularly powerful wave lifted the patrol boat and lapped the gangway, soaking those still crossing with ice-cold seawater. They cried out as they stumbled and made to grasp the handrail as the wave receded, dragging the patrol boat and the end of the gangway into its dark trough. The boat began to rise again on another wave which flooded the gangway sweeping away all those still hanging on. There was nothing that could be done for them; they sank instantly, sucked in by the surging sea.

After the shocking loss of the soldiers from the gangway, crossing to the *Kolberg* was only permitted in fits and starts — during the moments when the gangway happened to be in a more or less horizontal position. Papis was able to cross, jumping onboard the ship with his sack in his hand. A second later, though, the patrol boat suffered a strong and deep rolling that caused everybody on deck to lose balance. The gangway screeched and creaked as those few of us still onboard boat waited patiently for it to get back into a favorable position but, as I was about to step onto the gangway, the seamen aboard the *Kolberg* pulled it away. I couldn't believe my eyes and I was unable to understand the orders the officer yelled on the megaphone. I looked across at Papis who stared at me from the deck of the *Kolberg*, his eyes as round as cartwheels.

"There will be another ship," a voice on the deck of the *Kolberg* assured us.

I shouted towards the soldiers still on the deck of the patrol boat, "They can't leave us here. There might not be another ship!" But they just stood there, speechless and incapable of lending me their support. I didn't think for an instant to stay aboard that patrol boat in those conditions, waiting for another ship that might not come. My only chance was disappearing from under my nose. I had to do something. The two ships almost touched each other at times as they rose and fell on the sea. I was desperate to be reunited with Papis and decided to jump at the next opportunity. I stood near the edge of the patrol boat, at the gap in handrail where the gangway had been, waiting for the right moment to jump. On the *Kolberg* Papis, sensing my plan, stood poised to grab me. I threw my suitcase first and then my *Sturmgewehr* to him. The two vessels parted, heaved, and then rolled towards each other. I took in a deep breath. A wave lifted the patrol boat a little above the deck of the *Kolberg*. I sprang across the gap just as the *Kolberg* fell away from me so I fell roughly on the deck. Papis grabbed my arm to help me to my feet, showing his white and perfect teeth in a wide smile. I was happy to be reunited with my comrade but felt sorry for those left behind on the patrol boat which had already been absorbed by the darkness. Despite listing slightly, the *Kolberg* seemed to gain speed quickly, as if it too was anxious to reach the open sea.

Fatigue and lack of sleep caught up with us suddenly so Papis and I went below deck to look for somewhere to rest. We sat with our backs against the warmth of the engine room bulkhead, among the last women and children to escape the depraved intentions of the Russian soldiers. I let go a long sigh and said to Papis, "I wonder where De Ville and the others are."

"On this ship, for sure," Papis answered.

"Then we'll find them."

"We'll find them," Papis said.

The *Kolberg* cruised into the port of Swinemünde the following afternoon, past a shore pummeled by bombs and strewn with the rubble of buildings. We drifted slowly past capsized ships and boats, half-submerged in the harbour; others had turned turtle, their keels exposed to the sky.

During our disembarkation there was a general air of confusion — the only semblance of order on the quayside was the rows of stretchers which had been laid out for the wounded. Above the hubbub, a hoarse voice called "Police section! Mortar section!"

"That's De Ville," I said to Papis.

"He's calling the muster."

We shouldered our way through the crowd, "We're here, *Oberscharführer*." I yelled.

"Out of the way…we're coming through!" Papis told anyone blocking our way.

When we reached the gathering spot, De Ville looked at my little suitcase and at Papis' sack and declared, "*Gran* bordello! Have you become tourists, now?" He was smiling, happy to see us safe and sound. I began to explain about our 'luggage' but the chief was already moving on to some other business. But there, standing before our eyes, were Jean and La Journisse.

"Still with your skin on, eh?" said La Journisse, laughing.

"*Ja*, we were the last two from our section to get out of that hell," I said.

"Bournique and three others are missing," said Jean sadly.

"It seems we and the chief are all that's left of our mortar section," La Journisse observed.

Little by little, *SS* soldiers from various units gathered around. Stragglers, they had lost contact with their companies but they were still armed, and prepared to fight on, and asked De Ville if they could join us. The chief, impressed by their devotion to duty and fighting spirit, willingly accepted them. Now we were about twenty in all.

De Ville raised his voice. "Listen everyone! Our orders are as follows: we must keep going towards Carpin and then reach Neustrelitz. From there we go to the camp at Wildflecken."

We joined a long column of soldiers forming at the quayside, beside refugees still waiting at the pier. Their faces were downcast, their eyes tired and dull. Some stared into the distance, looking at nothing; children clung to their mothers' coats. And then there were the harrowing groans of the wounded. It was a scene of utter misery, of dejection and lost dreams.

We marched out of what was left of Swinemünde, a port that only a week or so earlier had suffered a devastating bombing raid by the Americans in which more than 20,000 civilians had died in the fires and tumbling rubble. De Ville led our little band away from the main column; this, he said, gave him freedom of action. "In a while we should reach a village, we'll stay there for the night," he told us in a voice made hoarse by shouting during the last days in Kolberg. He too was all burned out from hunger and a lack of sleep.

Tunisia. Sports team. Paul is second from right.

Paul Martelli, July 1945. Unfortunately no photos survive for Paul's Eastern Front service.

Tunisia. Sports team. Paul in foreground, squatting.

Demonstration on the boat.

At the Peripheral Quarter.

Hanoi. Towards the Doumer Bridge.

En route towards
Gia Lam.

During 'Operation Delta'.

Sub-sector of Phu Lo. Viet Minh prisoners laying foundations.

Sub-sector of Phu Lo. Fortifications from Paul's project.

Sub-sector of Phu Lo. Vietnamese partisans, pro-French. Paul at right.

Sub-sector of Phu Lo. Advanced emplacement #6. Paul with 'cail's' aide.

Sub-sector of Phu Lo. Block house near Song Ca Lo River.

Paul with 'cail' (village chief) To Van Phuc.

Sub-sector of Phu Lo. Advanced emplacement #6 along Song Ca Lo River.

Sub-sector of Phu Lo. Surveying fortifications.

Paul at Phu Lo village.

Sub-sector of Phu Lo. Working on fortifications under Paul's control.

Peripheral
Quarter.
Back from a
mission.

Advance base of Dac Tai.

Dac Tai.
Fortifications.

Dac Tai. Paul at the start of a patrol.

Paul, at right, with a
friend who would end
up at Poulo Condor's
prison.

Dac Tai. Paul's combat emplacement. 57mm cannon on turret.

Back from a patrol - note the bullet-hole in the windshield. Photo taken at the Peripheral Quarter.

Radio tower at Phu Lo.

Paul's friend, Super TD tank driver 'Souché'.

Small daytime-only
control post. Paul at right.

Sub-sector of Phu Lo. 37mm cannon on turret.

Gymnastics at Hanoi.

Paul on motorbike duty.

Paul on motorbike duty.

5

Escape to the West

Farewell to Swinemünde

Without losing sight of the main column, De Ville led us alongside a rail track with Jean scouting ahead. Before long Jean came back, running. "There are wagons on the track but the locomotive is missing," he reported.

De Ville was suspicious. "Paul...La Journisse...take the other side of the track. Keep your eyes peeled...everyone else with me...fire only at my order."

We advanced towards the train without a locomotive. La Journisse and I reached the first car ahead of the others and found the bodies of German soldiers slumped over machine guns. On the floor of the car, some lay on their backs with their arms dangling over the edge of the doorway and beside the track, on the grey stone metalling were strewn the bullet-riddled bodies of a dozen others. Nothing moved. La Journisse waved 'come forward' to De Ville.

De Ville checked one of the bodies. "At most two days ago, they also used hand grenades. Check the wagons and cars for survivors."

A search revealed that all those present were dead but we found a pile of wooden boxes in one of the wagons. De Ville cracked one of them open with his boot.

Papis staggered back in amazement. "I've never seen so much money."

"Bank notes, stacks of banknotes," La Journisse cried out. He began to hop around like a madman, laughing and cackling.

"Brand new, just minted, but not like ours," Jean observed.

"But are they good?" I asked, still not believing my eyes.

"Russian bordello! Where did they come from?" De Ville said to himself, picking up a wad of banknotes.

"It doesn't matter, we're rich!" La Journisse declared.

"I wouldn't be so sure," De Ville said. "But check the other wagons and cars."

"Equal parts, eh?" La Journisse said, pocketing bunches of notes sealed by paper ribbons. We didn't waste time. We filled our pockets with money. My hands trembled with greed as I stuffed my small suitcase so full I could hardly close the lid. In the other two wagons we found more of the same type of banknotes which we started to stuff into our tunics.

De Ville interrupted our joy. "Forget the money…if they're counterfeits we'll be shot as traitors if we are caught with them and if they are real we'll be shot as thieves."

"What a misery! I'll never be rich," La Journisse complained, throwing his money in the air, an act that we all imitated, laughing at our naïveté.

"Let's get out of this damn bordello!" De Ville cut short.

Toward evening, we arrived at a temporary *Kriegsmarine* camp. Many of us took advantage of the pause to delouse ourselves by washing our personal items and our evening rations — a bowl of soup and a piece of old, hard bread — kept our hunger at bay.

Morning muster was held at a village near the *Kriegsmarine* camp. There, we were assigned a spacious granary where *Oberscharführer* De Ville made sure that each of us found a comfortable spot to sleep later. During the following two days, we felled several trees and piled the trunks along the bank of a creek and planted pointed stakes in the ground, 'Frisian Horses' as we called them, which served as anti-tank barriers. The hard work in the forests was enough to relax the nervous tension accumulated during the siege of Kolberg. Away from the thunder of cannons, these tasks reinvigorated our spirits and, pleasantly tired and sleepy, we simply stretched out on our straw beds without the preoccupation of guard duty, inspections and patrols playing on our minds. In short, we were living an almost normal life until, on the last evening, shortly before Jean and I went downstairs for rations, a loud, whooshing draft brushed past us, not even a meter away. A projectile passed through a pile of straw and smashed through the timber-clad wall. Stunned, we looked at each other.

"A rocket…am I still in one piece?" Jean said in a faint voice.

"Thank heavens it didn't explode," I said, open mouthed.

We ran downstairs to see what had happened, wondering if we were under attack from the Russians, and discovered an ex-L.V.F. soldier from our division in the courtyard, beside a collection of *Panzerfäuste*. By this time a small crowd of his comrades had gathered around him.

"Hei you! You know where your missile ended up?" I asked the soldier, barely able to contain my rising anger.

"*Eh là*! It was a mistake…the charge went off when I was cleaning one of these trombones," he said, referring to the shape of the anti-tank warhead.

His laid-back attitude inflamed my wrath. "I'll play that 'trombone' on your head!"

"Hei! Just a moment! It was an accident…I didn't try to kill anyone."

"Strange that it didn't explode," Jean said, scratching his head, "but now we need somebody to disarm it."

Papis arrived on the scene and was listening to the drama unfold. "A good task for that rat."

"No, no…you cannot do this to me…it was an accident," whined the ex-L.V.F. soldier.

I pulled my pistol from its holster and planted the tip of the barrel on the culprit's forehead. "If I see you around here again I'll shoot a hole in your head you stupid bastard."

The unfortunate soldier staggered backwards a few paces before turning to run.

"Forget it Paul, he's only an L.V.F. soldier," La Journisse remarked with disdain; a statement that brought frowns to the faces of the onlookers.

"Forget it? Not on your life! We could have ended up roasted because of that idiot," I said, venting my frustration.

"It would have been a stupid end," Jean agreed, "but my friend, we are still alive and well." He put his arm around my shoulder and, together with La Journiss and Papis, we headed for the mess for evening rations.

As we ate super Papis told me that, soon after our arrival, he had lent my spare pair of boots to an L.V.F. non-commissioned officer for a few days so that he didn't have to see him going around barefoot and that he was still waiting for them to be returned. I was, to put it mildly, annoyed that the L.V.F. soldier had not bothered to try to find his own boots — particularly having been nearly killed by one of his men. I was keeping them as a backup in my suitcase and since the ones I was wearing were beginning to fall apart, I was keen to be reunited with my reserve pair.

I woke up the following morning still in the grip of an irrational rage. To shake it off, I kept myself busy sawing and nailing new boards to repair the granary wall. I also built some supports to improve the structure of the latrines and a washbasin that nobody used, not even to rinse their hands. Nevertheless, I discovered that I was a passable carpenter.

In the afternoon, still feeling the need 'to settle the score', I decided to track down the non-commissioned officer who was wearing my boots and found him in his barrack. I pointed at his feet and snapped, "Boots please!"

He muttered something about making a poor showing at the muster as he pulled them off his feet.

"So, how did it go?" Papis asked when I returned to the granary with my boots.

"Another idiot!"

"Paul, you have to agree they're not all like that."

"You're right. There are very good officers and heroes among the ex-L.V.F. men — but not that one. If he wasn't such an idiot he wouldn't have had his boots stolen, and if he did, he should have looked for a new pair. A true *Waffen SS* man wouldn't have come begging."

At morning muster, the non-commissioned officer showed up wearing a pair of shoes that were too large and too low at the sides to be of practical use to a soldier. Papis and I smiled at each other, shaking our heads, showing our contempt.

�֍—֎

A few days later, at morning muster, a *Hauptsturmführer* appeared. He gave a brief, general outline of the war situation in our area before ordering all those fit for combat to present themselves.

Without hesitation, *Oberscharführer* De Ville shouted. "Police section! Two steps forward!" Other squads and individual soldiers followed our example. Those who had refrained from presenting themselves were attached to free-worker squads responsible for carrying out emergency work and repairs.

That evening at the granary, as we made ready to leave, I said to Papis, "I'll leave my suitcase here, it's almost empty. Our days as tourists are done."

Papis nodded thoughtfully, "I'll ditch my sack too."

✖—✗

Our initial posting was to a prisoner of war camp holding, among other inmates, the aircrew of American and British airplanes that had been shot down. They spent their time idling and smoking, or resting inside their barracks in good order.

During an evening, while on guard, an English pilot approached me to offer me a cigarette. I read in his eyes his intentions: he was looking for favors, possibly the company of a beautiful woman. "Cigarette?" he repeated, presenting the pack towards me.

"I never smoke while on service," I answered, "and I don't accept anything from a prisoner and furthermore, I can confiscate the entire packet, if I feel like it."

"*Bonne soir!*" the pilot wished me, walking away.

Right thing to do, Englishman, I thought. *Who knows how many cigarettes you've distributed to other guards before me, but you don't buy me with a smoke, not at all, mister.*

Good Horse, Crazy Horse

Our spell as POW guards did not last long. We were moved south to an area halfway between Swinemünde and Berlin, in which there are many lakes. After completing a cold spell of night-time sentry duty, I was making my way back to our new barracks when I saw a horse standing unattended. As I drew near to the animal, I tripped over a Latvian soldier sprawled on the ground, and almost staggered against the horse. At first I thought the man had been thrown and was injured but, when I kneeled to examine him, the strong smell of stale alcohol made me retch. He was, I discovered looking at his collar insignia, an *Obersturmführer*. I dragged him into the barracks, onto a pile of straw before returning to take care of his horse.

I took hold of the bridle, making sure everything was in order, rubbed his nose and talked to him sweetly — he was a fine animal with a beautiful ebony coat. I put my foot in a stirrup and swung my leg over his back. He was as docile as a lamb, responding to every command, so I took him for a trot around the barracks until I came to a path I knew well and stopped. Lit by the moon, the pale, silvery, sandy trail stretched out towards the dark forest. The temptation was too strong to resist; I took a deep breath and spurred him into a gallop. The cold, nocturnal air caressed my face. Overcome by the sensation of freedom, I spurred him into a still-faster gallop, yelling and laughing like a crazed maniac as we sped along the track. I thought about *Obersturmbannführer* Hersche and his famous night rides. A sense of infinite satisfaction filled my soul. Inebriated with joy, I slowed the magnificent beast to a trot, caressing his throat from time to time. I gave him a name — *Torello*, little bull — because I had felt his strength and power under the saddle. Ah! Now I completely understood Hersche's passion for night rides.

Torello gave a sudden swerve. Somehow I was able to stay firmly in the saddle. A vapour trail, gleaming white-blue in the moonlight, was left by something big swishing overhead. I had heard about the existence of special rocket launch-ramps erected not far away but this was the first time I saw one of those missiles cutting through the sky, straight and majestic.

I rode *Torello* to the barracks, returning at around five in the morning. I groomed him well, rubbing his sweaty coat with dry straw and then I covered his back with a large blanket, leaving him tied to a tree nearby. When I took to my bed, I closed my eyes and relived that glorious ride until exhaustion overwhelmed my dreams.

At muster, *Oberscharführer* De Ville made an important announcement: we were to return to our duties as a mortar section by relieving a nearby German unit in the vicinity of Fürstensee, taking over their weapons. A short march at a brisk pace late in the evening was all it took to reach the German mortar men's emplacements. As soon as they saw us arrive, they all jumped out to welcome us, happy at our presence and even more so at the prospect of a well-deserved pause when they could finally sleep under a roof.

"The heck...they're all rather old," I observed, looking at the faces of the first soldiers.

"*Franzozen...gute Soldaten*," they said, receiving us with smiles, many of which lacked a few teeth. Most of them were in their fifties; some had silver hair and were certainly at least sixty years old.

"Go see if you find my grandpa among them!" Papis suggested to Jean, in French, as he returned their smiles.

Oberscharführer De Ville intervened. "Jean...take over this emplacement, you'll be the new *Truppführer*. Paul! I want you to find out the exact number of charges available...and get the Germans to brief you before they disappear."

I managed to intercept the German *Truppführer* before he skedaddled into the encroaching night but the information he gave was at best fragmentary. "There...the Russians are over there," was all he told me before he too rushed off.

"Anyone would think the plague had struck" La Journisse observed, straining his eyes as they followed the receding Germans.

"They're in a damned haste to leave," Jean added.

The cold night induced us to hole up near the mortars wrapped in our *Zeltbahnen*. I thought of Heidi and her warm embrace and wondered where she was. I thought too about Martin and Gosse and their endless schemes to pilfer anything they could. And then I wondered why I had swapped a bed of perfumed, clean sheets at home for one of straw bales or the hard soil at the bottom of this pit. I gazed at the stars, so faint and distant, detached from our earth-bound miseries...from this war. I shivered, turned onto my side, searching in vain for a more comfortable position but nevertheless slipped inexorably into a heavy sleep.

❧—❧

It was dawn. *Oberscharführer* De Ville called us with a touch of impatience in his voice, "Paul and Papis...it's your turn on patrol...search for food."

"*Jawohl Oberscharführer,*" we answered.

De Ville looked around, before coming closer then spoke almost in a whisper, "It's important to stick to the rules... remember the regulations regarding the acquisition of food from German homes...clear?"

"Leave it to us," said Papis.

Moving around the minefields that surrounded the 'Frisian Horses' and other anti-tank barriers, we reached the road and headed towards a nearby village. Freshly dug dirt at the road's edges alerted us to the insidious traps left by the platoon of wily mortar men: holes had been dug at regular intervals, each containing a mine covered by a thin wooden board over which a layer of soil and snow was laid.

We came in the vicinity of some houses on one side of the road; on the other side, and two hundred meters from us, a thick forest stood. In that open space many soldiers were preparing for combat by reinforcing weak points, checking their *Panzerfäuste* and shifting ammunition boxes. Then I noticed a horse tethered to a tree, snorting and wheezing noisily from his dilated nostrils. Nearby, a squad of young soldiers were on a break.

"Poor animal," I remarked in passing.

The horse started kicking furiously in the air. "He's crazy! He's been like that for two days...every time somebody goes near him," one of the soldiers said.

As I paused to observe the animal, Papis looked at me. "Hei Paul, you won't..." He grasped my elbow as if to lead me onwards.

"He's only spooked," I said, pulling my elbow free. "Somebody needs to calm him down."

Papis looked on with the soldiers as, sitting on a branch of the tree, I worked my way above the horse. When I was above the animal, I tried to lower myself to his back but he kicked as soon as my boot touched his coat and I dropped to the ground. Undaunted, I climbed the tree again and this time, when I was above the horse, told Papis to turn him and hold onto the bridle.

"Oh! My misery," Papis wailed. "You and your rodeos!"

I dropped onto the horse's back at the right moment, grabbed his mane and gripped him between my legs. Papis let go the reins and leapt backwards to avoid being trampled. "Bravo!" somebody yelled as I grabbed the reins.

The horse stopped for an instant, then let out a peevish neigh as he reared. He swerved from the tree, pounding his hooves to the ground, sprang forward and then lowered his neck almost to the snow. My audience cheered my efforts — other soldiers left their work to rush over to the show.

"Here's to the rider! Bravo! Hurra!" they shouted, clapping their hands.

The horse arched his back and bucked, then sprang into the air with all four legs leaving the ground. But I remained anchored to him, yelling for happiness, adding my voice to the chorus of cheers. He pawed the snow, raised up his muzzle and started shuffling backwards.

"Long live our cowboy," they shouted.

And like a rodeo rider I raised up an arm amid the enthusiastic applause. I kicked the horse's flanks with my heels but he ignored me and continued to track backwards. The applause stopped suddenly as the onlookers dived for cover.

"The ditch — anti-tank mines!" somebody screamed.

Papis screamed, "Jump Paul!"

At a few meters from the mines I kicked his flanks for the last time but he continued to ignore me. I jumped down and aimed a hefty blow at his rump that sent him galloping towards the forest, and away from the mines.

Papis shook his head. "To hell with you and that crazy horse!"

Tough Measures

Our mission to find food, and the sound of German voices, drew us into a large, old house on the outskirts of the village. Inside, we found what might have been the tail end of a wild party. In the ground floor rooms, soldiers from a variety of German units idled about drinking, eating, laughing and arguing loudly. Upstairs, others lay motionless on beds and on the floor, snoring. "It's not worth wasting time here," I said to Papis.

As we left the house, on the road in front of the courtyard, we saw that a tank had stopped. From its open turret the youthful commander was saluting a *Hauptsturmführer* who had just arrived in a *Kübelwagen*. The officer rushed to the waiting tank. "What happened?" he yelled with in an ill-tempered tone of voice. "Why didn't you take up position?"

"*Hauptsturmführer*, this house is in the middle of our field of fire," said the tank commander.

The *Hauptsturmführer* left the tank and brushed Papis and me aside before barging into the house to bellow, "You have ten minutes to clear out!" His order was met with much cursing from those inside. "Ten minutes exactly," repeated the *Hauptsturmführer*. He turned on his heels, returned to the waiting *Kübelwagen* and tinkered with a radio, causing it to crackle and screech.

"We'll stay a while," I said to Papis, "I'm really curious to see how this ends."

Soon the courtyard was filled with the mumbles of the soldiers who had gathered in front of the house but upstairs, near a window, one stood shaving in front of a mirror, oblivious to the order to clear the building. They were, from the disheartened nature of their conversations, tired of fighting and simply waiting for the end of the war. Discipline to them was nonsensical: just a few more days and then everything would come to an end.

The ten minutes went by. The young tank commander waited, impassively looking out from the turret of his tank. The *Hauptsturmführer* went to the tank to talk to the commander, pointed to the house and said: "Knock it down."

The tank commander lowered himself inside, closing the hatch behind him. A moment later the turret moved half a turn to point towards the tank's rear and its engine revved hard before it sprang towards the house. The crash against the façade and the entry door was tremendous: the ground vibrated, plaster and bricks flew down, almost burying the tank which then backtracked about ten meters, dragging and scattering debris everywhere. The soldiers still trapped inside the house dashed out, some jumped from the windows. Papis and I watched open-mouthed, stunned. The tank then lurched towards a corner of the building, made contact and kept pushing. A slab of the external wall disintegrated. The last of the soldiers ran into the open, whitened with dust, some hobbling on legs wounded in combat. Above the roar of the tank's engine I could hear the screams and cries of the wounded still inside the house, then the tank screeched on its treads, charging towards the other corner. The wall collapsed; great wooden beams were laid bare like ribs stripped of flesh. Another charge demolished the front wall, sending up clouds of dust that forced those watching from the courtyard to fall back. The façade now looked like a toothless, cavernous mouth. A last push reverberated through the building causing the back wall to fall outwards, pulling down roof and floors. In a short time, the house was reduced to a pile of ruins. The tank completed half a turn, its body vibrating as if to shake itself free from the dust and debris. In the meantime, two further tanks had arrived almost unnoticed by the crowd. They waited, one behind the other on the road until joined by the first tank. The *Hauptsturmführer* gazed into the distance with his binoculars.

"A job well done," I said to Papis.

"Yes...but the wounded?"

"Those lazy bones," I snapped, "they deserved it!""

There was regret in Papis' voice. "I still wish the *Hauptsturmführer* had forced them to evacuate,"

"Papis! You *know* they would've ignored him!"

Papis thought for a moment before answering, "You might be right Paul, but still..."

Food for Thought

The approach to the village was littered with burned out trucks, abandoned ammunition, bullet casings, worn out boots, twisted bicycles and, most pitiful of all, items of civilian clothing from burst suitcases that had been scattered everywhere. Walking by a farm, we saw a crossroads not far ahead with a store on a corner. Papis and I hurried onwards deciding to search the farm later. Inside the store, a woman sitting on a stool in a corner was crying. With her was an older man who was doing his best to calm her down. And there were boxes filled with packets of margarine and tins of preserves piled near the door, as if waiting to be uplifted.

"There is something fishy going on here," I said in a low voice.

"We should leave our weapons on the counter," Papis suggested. "It might look suspicious if we take food at gunpoint."

My eyes settled on a loaf of bread at the far end of the counter. "I'm sure nobody will complain," I said cutting two slices and spreading a thick layer of margarine on both and then sprinkling them with sugar I found in a can. As we neared the end of our simple but delicious snack, a truck pulled up in front of the store. Papis and I stuffed the last crusts into our mouths and picked up our weapons. The door of the truck slammed and moments later a *Wehrmacht* soldier around thirty years old breezed into the store. I noticed a Walther P38 pistol on his belt. He seemed to know the place very well but stopped on the spot on seeing us.

"Who let them in?" he asked the old man and woman.

The old man answered with a shrug.

Papis let out a tremendous cough; his crust had stuck in his throat. Entering houses occupied by civilians was not permitted unless it was to follow a specific order so his question unnerved us.

"You two can bugger off now," the *Wehrmacht* soldier said.

"Our *Oberscharführer* sent us to look for food," I protested, to let him know he was not dealing with two deserters or plunderers. "We intend to commandeer these boxes."

The soldier suddenly became rather irate. "That is theft!"

I let my hand slide slowly down to my pistol holster and the P08 inside it; Papis followed my example. "Theft, is that so? And what would you do with this food?"

"Everybody's hungry these days," said the soldier.

I realized then he had no more authority over the food than Papis and I. "So you're swiping everything using the truck, eh?" I drew my 08 in a smooth movement and aimed it at his face. The old man and woman in the corner disappeared through a door behind the counter, into the back shop, to safety.

"Take it easy with that thing," said the *Wehrmacht* soldier, "or you'll find yourselves in front of a firing squad."

"Are you're looking for trouble?" Papis snorted threateningly.

With a sideways jerk of my head, I indicated the door to the back shop. Bloated with bile, and clenching his teeth, the *Wehrmacht* soldier did as he was told.

A familiar voice shouted from the entrance to the store. "Hei! We found you at last." It was La Journisse, with Jean standing just behind. "The chief was worried...you were supposed to be back at the camp by now."

Papis and I showed our comrades the boxes and jars.

Jean opened one. "You have a good nose Paul, eh?"

"And good luck...there's a truck outside you can load then into," I said, feeling rather smug. "And tell the chief that Papis and I still have to complete the patrol...there's a farm we still need to check."

There was a bull and cows and a heifer grazing between patches of snow at the farm we had passed on our way to the store. Papis and I checked the farmhouse and found that the owners had already fled, taking with them every morsel of food. Close to the farmhouse, there were stables and a large brick-built shed which contained marvelous machines and polished copper tanks big enough to swim in. Everything had been cleaned to the highest standard.

"They're set up for dairy products," Papis said. "It's probably the collection center for the milk from neighbouring farms."

A wondrous sight awaited us in an adjoining room. Slatted wooden shelves filled the entire room and stacked on them were hundreds of wheels of cheese in various stages of maturation.

"It's enough to feed a regiment," Papis said.

"Let's go out, I've got a better idea." I led Papis into the courtyard and pointed to the cattle grazing in the field.

Papis looked at me askance. "Don't tell me you want to break-in the bull."

"The heifer, Papis."

"You want to ride that miniature cow?"

I leaned on a fence post to admire the heifer. "Doesn't she seem tender and fat?" I asked, dreaming of a succulent steak.

Papis recoiled. "Oh no, I know what you're thinking and I don't like the idea of being stood in front of a firing squad."

"Everything will go smoothly, you'll see," I reassured my comrade. "First we catch her, then we lead her back to camp through the woods…nobody will see us…then we eat her."

"And what do you think the chief will say?"

"Nothing…he's hungry too, just like the rest of us."

Papis shook his head as he stared at the ground. "It's a hare-brained idea."

I approached the heifer from behind with the intention of driving it in front of us, but she had different plans: she ran here and there, keeping just far enough ahead to elude capture. "Papis! Give me a hand!" I shouted. Reluctantly, he joined the chase. The heifer trotted between the bull and the cows, arousing only some weak mooing, then led us towards a stable.

"We'll catch her now," I assured Papis.

At that moment a fellow soldier from 'Charlemagne' was passing in front of the field. Amused by our clumsy efforts he guessed our intention and intercepted us at the entrance of the stable to offer his assistance.

"Of course! This beast is giving us a sweat," Papis answered.

I found a halter on a hook on the wall and, arms out-stretched, the three of us danced around the heifer in an attempt to corner her. As the heifer dodged and ducked, she pushed our helper into a drainage channel the contents of which were deep enough to overflow into his boots. "Devil of a shitty cow!" he cursed. Papis and I laughed but finally we were able to stop that lively heifer just long enough for me to slip the halter over her head.

"If she doesn't walk, I'll kick her," our helper offered as he emptied his boots.

We led the heifer to the edge of the woods where we invited our now smelly helper to join us later for dinner. He accepted our offer and promised to bring along several bottles of wine before we parted company.

Leading the heifer through the woods turned out to be much more difficult than I imagined. She jibbed frequently, refusing to follow; slid on the snow patches and bumped against trees and sank her hooves in every hole she found.

"We'll never make it," Papis complained.

"Yes we will...even if we have to carry her in our arms." I said, tugging the halter.

"I'll take care of her now," Papis declared, unsheathing his dagger. He hit her on the rump near her tail with the side of the blade. The trick seemed to work because the heifer moved without any further resistance. I pulled harder on the halter and she started to trot. "So now she likes you, she's following you everywhere," Papis laughed.

"I hope she arrives at the camp without losing weight," I answered, happy that my friend's mood had improved.

Oberscharführer De Ville saw us popping out from the forest with the heifer. He stopped dead in his tracks, his eyes wide open and an expression of utter horror on his face. "Bordello of...of...have your brains gone soft?"

"Her steaks will be as tender as margarine," I said.

"They've put soldiers to the wall for much less than this," De Ville blustered. Then, being a very prudent man, he calmed himself before glancing around. "Are you certain nobody saw you?"

"Nobody!" I confirmed. "There wasn't a soul at the farm."

"Now hear me well, you fools," De Ville said, "up to now we've been lucky to come out of this war without a scrape. We are the only survivors from our original section and I intend to keep it that way. For God's sake hide her somewhere in the woods before a firing squad fills our bellies with lead."

※—※

"So," De Ville said after summoning our squad later that afternoon at the edge of the woods, close to where the heifer was tethered, "I want a quick and clean job. Who's going to kill her?"

"I was a butcher but without my knife it will be difficult not to mess around," said one soldier, excluding himself from the gruesome task.

"I worked in an abattoir; we need chains and ropes to hang the carcass..." said another.

There was an air of excitement, everybody chattering at the same moment. I left them and headed to the woods. I couldn't understand why all the discussion was needed. When I reached the heifer, I looked for the last time into her big, brown eyes and then pulled out my P08. I put the tip of the barrel at her temple and fired. The heifer remained standing for a brief instant, as if paralyzed, before falling to the side.

And then I noticed that De Ville and my comrades had followed me to the woods — but they were looking in silence at De Ville's foot and not the heifer. My shot had passed through the heifer's head and onwards for about thirty meters. I rushed over to De Ville, fearing I had wounded him. De Ville stood stalk still, apparently unable to move until I was just a few paces from him before turning to walk away without a word.

"You were lucky," said Jean. "The bullet polished the chief's boot...no blood."

The butchers prepared the meat, demonstrating their skill in cutting it according to its quality while La Journisse sprang into action at the spit. Everybody happily gathered round, watching like a pack of famished wolves ready to pounce on their prey at the earliest possible moment while I mulled over the careless shot that might have caused serious injury to our beloved chief.

"Don't think about it, Paul. He'll forget everything pretty soon," Papis consoled me.

"I'm a damned idiot! And this after his survival speech...another centimeter and then..."

"It's done! You can't change the past," Jean interrupted. "Such accidents can happen to anybody."

"But it always seems to happen to me."

Oberscharführer De Ville approached me before that unusual evening meal and took me aside.

"I can't explain the..." I started.

"Pay attention, *bebè*," he cut short, "you're the youngest here...and you are a good and skilled soldier." He gave a loud guffaw. "Next time you intend to slaughter an animal, wait till I leave first, clear?"

"Clear, Chief. It won't happen again."

"Very well, let's eat," the non-commissioned officer said with a hearty grin. We reached the others who already were sinking their teeth into the large and tender meat portions, soaked with margarine, as only La Journisse could prepare. The meaty fragrance from the spit was an irresistible invitation for all those soldiers camped around, among them the 'Charlemagne' comrade we met at the farm who arrived with comrades 'armed' with bottles of wine as promised. The sense of guilt and remorse that had plagued me since my near miss with De Ville gradually lifted under the influence of the wine and the good company of my fellow soldiers. Together, we celebrated until the 'wee sma' hours, enjoying a meal fit for a king.

The Green Devil

The order to move to Neustrelitz, which we received in the morning, found us still heavy with the desire to sleep after our binge on heifer's meat and drinking fine wine. After all the work done to reinforce the anti-tank barriers near Grammerthin, we abandoned our emplacements without firing a shot and left to stem a Russian break-through in another zone. We were by then in the first days of April.

At Neustrelitz, in the evening, we lost time in a banal confrontation that could have cost us dearly: we had been assigned to the barracks of the *Kriegsmarine* and, to convince the soldiers already there to move their prostitutes and share some straw with us — solely for the purposes of sleep of course — we didn't hesitate a second in showing them the muzzles of our *Sturmgewehren*. After some very tense moments they relented, and we set ourselves up for the night.

The next day, marching on again because of new orders, we came to several German tanks idle on the road for lack of fuel. Further ahead we reached a long column of refugees mixed up with soldiers from various units. After half an hour the distant buzz of Russian airplanes threw the civilians — mainly women and children — into a blind panic. Amid the chaos, a baby in swaddling clothes was abandoned in the middle of the road, near a crying girl separated from her mother. I grabbed the infant and stretched my hand to the girl as the diving airplanes screamed a terrifying crescendo. The girl grabbed my hand; I dragged her to the roadside ditch and flung her to the ground while still grasping the baby. Machine guns rattled. The planes were so low, the bullets whizzed almost horizontally above the road surface. Splinters of timber exploded into the air as bullets ripped into wooden carts; atomized blood formed a haze around horses and people hit by the hurricane of bullets. The aircraft passed overhead leaving behind a swirling gust of wind and it seemed I could almost reach out to touch the red stars on the underside of their wings. As the planes wheeled into the clear sky, the scream of their engines faded to a sinister buzz above which the groans of agony from the wounded could now be heard. I was reluctant to leave the ditch, not because of the chance of another strafing, but simply because I knew that a scene of utter horror awaited my eyes.

"My girl, my poor beautiful girl," wailed a woman, moving on all fours amid the bloodied dead and dying as she searched for her daughter. Another woman walked as if blinded, fumbling, with her hands stretched forwards. As I returned the girl I had dragged into the ditch to her mother, who received her with tears in her eyes and a fierce embrace, a man grabbed the infant from my arms with almost aggressive force. I ran from that scene of horror, of tragedy, over the blood-stained snow in a mad dash to search for my section but saw only Papis. We sat together, waiting for our comrades, on an abandoned cart which had skidded into the ditch with two old horses still at the shaft.

Gradually our section gathered at the cart and someone put forward the idea of using it to save our boot leather. After examining the horses thoroughly and finding them miraculously unscathed, we pulled the cart back onto the road. I took the reins while my comrades lowered the tailgate and climbed into the box. La Journisse rummaged inside the wooden crates he found there, chanting out the names of the items as he pulled them out. "Clothing… pots…two trumpets…tea pots…"

"Trumpets?" a comrade asked, with an enthusiastic lilt to his voice.

"Hei! I play too," another said.

"They are all yours," La Journisse answered.

And so, I gave the reins a flick and the two horses obediently pulled the cart behind the two comrades walking ahead to shift the corpses cluttering the road while the trumpet players blew musical notes to each other to establish their tuning. A chorus of cheers greeted La Journisse when he waved a large sausage in the air and the two trumpeters at that moment burst into *Grüne Teufel*, a tune very familiar to us: *Wo wir sind da ist immer vorne…Und der Teufel, der lacht noch dazu ha,ha,ha…(Where we are it's always forwards…And the Devil he laughs like this ha, ha ,ha…)* It would be difficult to image a more incongruous scene. The civilians who survived the strafing stared at us with bewildered eyes, as if they thought we had fallen into the grip of a madness brought on by the horrors we had witnessed. How were they to know that this was our way of dissipating the frustration we felt at being unable to confront an enemy that was now forcing its way towards Berlin?

More soldiers jumped onto the cart to join the chorus. De Ville ordered me to turn onto a trail through the forest; perhaps he wanted to avoid the many objects abandoned on the road or to move more quickly but the trail was bumpy and before too long a rear wheel cracked over a protruding rock, tilting the cart. The horses stopped suddenly, the trumpeters ceased blowing and the singing came to a stuttering end. Papis jumped from the cart to assess the damage and discovered that the axel had given way. As he unhitched the horses to let them run free, he let go a sorrowful sigh and said: "Well, that's the fun over."

Oberscharführer De Ville seemed uncertain about the direction to take during the following days although we marched briskly for long hours, resting and sleeping at night in abandoned houses. Occasionally we heard the chatter of machine-gun fire in the distance but we never made contact with the Russians. We proceeded always with caution, spread out, ready to fire our weapons at the faintest inkling of an ambush. In this way, one morning we came to the edge of a quarry which was around 15m deep and 150m long. Inside the quarry were two pylons and, half-embedded in the ground, four barracks. De Ville was on his knees, looking into the excavation. "It has all the appearance of a radio station," he said.

"The gate's been left wide open...it looks as if it has been abandoned," said Papis.

"I can see that," De Ville replied calmly. "This bordello of a place...I don't like it at all." After a moment's thought, he formulated a plan. "We're going down to investigate. Watch out for Russians but fire only at my order."

We descended towards the quarry with great caution. La Journisse, Papis, Jean and I checked the four buildings — one each — from the outside while our remaining comrades waited with De Ville close to the open area near the gate.

A voice seemed to call, God-like, from the sky. "Stop where you are! One move and it will be your last!"

De Ville, and everyone else in our group, looked up to the rim of the quarry to see six soldiers in *Luftwaffe* uniform pointing their sub-machine guns at us — we were surrounded.

"Sit down slowly," ordered a *Luftwaffe* officer as he came through the open entrance gate. He signalled to the four of us reconnoitring the barracks to re-join our platoon. De Ville looked nervous, unsure of how to respond. His nostrils twitched as if he could barely contain the paroxysms of rage coursing through his bulging veins. He whispered to us as we lowered ourselves to sit, "No bright ideas...just do as he says."

"The first one to move goes straight to hell," the *Luftwaffe* officer said, coming closer, still overlooked by his six soldiers at the rim of the quarry.

"What do we do?" whispered Jean.

"We mow them down!" La Journisse proposed, gnashing his teeth.

"You two stop it!" De Ville snapped angrily.

"Lay your arms down...slowly," the *Luftwaffe* officer ordered.

"I would like an explanation..." De Ville started.

"Silence!" The officer's order stopped De Ville mid-sentence. "*Soldbücher!*" At the officer's gesture one of us gathered in our identity books and passed them to the officer for examination.

"We are the survivors of an 80mm mortar section," De Ville dared say while the officer continued his scrutiny of our *Soldbücher*. "*First Company 33rd Waffen Grenadier Division der SS* recently in combat at Körlin and at Kolberg, headed to..."

"Charlemagne eh?" the officer interrupted, raising his eyes from the *Soldbücher* in his hands. A little upward nod told De Ville to stand. "You can go but on one condition. You must leave your weapons where they are," the officer said bluntly. He returned our *Soldbücher* to De Ville's care and turned slightly to check the position of his soldiers at the quarry's edge.

"Damned pestilence," La Journisse mumbled under his breath, as dumbfounded as the rest of us by the strange proceedings.

"How can we go on without weapons?" De Ville protested.

The officer's eyes remained cool, inexpressive. "You can go," he said again.

Slowly, we got to our feet leaving our weapons on the ground and made our way to the exit gate. I still had my P08 and the officer didn't requisition De Ville's P38 — it was still in his holster. Papis signalled that he had his pistol too. Once through the gate we walked away in haste from the quarry and within a few minutes were again in open country.

"Infamous bordello!" De Ville was remorseful, and angry at himself for his lack of foresight. "I should have posted guards around the quarry's edge before we went in. And now...what do we do without arms?"

"We're sitting ducks for the Popovs, that's what we are," Papis said glumly.

"Let's keep to the cover of the trees as much as we can," De Ville said. He shook his head, still perplexed by what had just happened. We tramped on in silence, our morale depleted to almost zero.

Time to Ponder

"Alarm!" somebody shouted.

Only a fleeting shadow warned of the Russian plane's attack. It swooped on our little marching column from behind, gliding silently, catching us by surprise. Then its engine coughed back into life and its machine guns flashed; ricochets danced around our feet. Papis and I threw our bodies behind a tree stump, pressing ourselves to the ground as if trying to sink under its roots. The plane climbed steeply, veering with its engine under stress and then plummeted towards us on a second strafing run. My back was exposed but the powerful burst of fire from the plane missed by several meters. As the plane's engine noise faded I said to Papis, "That planes damned guns uses double charges!"

"It seems like it," he replied. "Here it comes again!"

I braced myself, pressed my body harder against the hard gnarled roots of the tree thinking about those bullets that were easily capable of opening up the rump of a horse. I held my breath. *It's the end*, I thought. *This time I'll catch one in my back.* A primordial scream left my throat as the plane swooped low overhead. Something whipped against my shoulder. My arm and neck felt cold and wet. I remained motionless for some seconds, choking a cry of terror in my throat. "Damned bastard," I mumbled, wincing with pain and pressing a hand to my shoulder.

Papis helped me struggle to my feet. "Two more spans and it would have nailed us, that damn Popov," he said.

"*Ja*, two more spans," I repeated mechanically, using the terminology of horse measurement.

Papis examined my shoulder. "There's no blood...it was probably a stone thrown up by a bullet that hit you."

"It hurts like hell...I can imagine now what taking a bullet might feel like."

At the next village, a civilian official welcomed our arrival. "Finally!" he said, "finally we have reinforcements." He was a man that carried himself boldly, short and chubby, around sixty years old and wearing a camouflage uniform adorned with the badges of a general which gave him something of a comical appearance. While *Oberscharführer* De Ville talked to him we stayed at a distance, trying to hold back our laughter. De Ville, however, managed to keep his composure as the man began: "I will accompany you to our defense positions. We have adapted them to..."

"Take it easy!" De Ville interrupted.

"You will defend us?" continued the 'general'.

"We have no weapons!"

"*Ach so!* I can help you with that problem," he said emphatically. "I will show you where we keep them."

"For all of us?"

"Sure! For all of you. We have lots of armaments at our depot, follow me!" the 'general' urged with an authoritative voice. And off he strode with the brisk pace of a man in a hurry.

De Ville turned to us, signalling to proceed. "Keep your eyes open," he warned. But by now we were ready for anything; nothing could surprise us, not even a civilian with the badges of a general. We followed on behind still bemused by the pompous military bearing of the fat little man.

"There! That barn with steel grates on the windows!" he said. There was a sentry at the door whom the 'general' greeted with an arm stretched forward in salute while still walking. "Take everything you need and then join me at my headquarters right away where we will organize our defense to perfection." With that, he clicked his heels and left us to help ourselves to the arms stash.

Our gaze followed the little 'general' until he disappeared into the village. De Ville shook his head theatrically and we exploded into a chorus of raucous laughter. Inside the small, narrow building serving as a depot, we found a rack stacked with sub-machine guns and, on the floor, several ammunition boxes piled up in good order against a wall. I took a sub-machine gun, an MP38, from the rack, stripped it down and then reassembled it in an instant under the civilian sentry's astonished eyes. I marched past him with it to the outside where I fired a short burst against the trunk of a tree. Rearmed to the teeth, we saluted the sentry and headed towards the village square but, after the first houses, De Ville took to a side street, leading us away from the village.

"We can't defend every small village we come across," De Ville announced. " These are not our orders. Anyway, if we were to stay, we would be an invitation for an attack from the air and without our mortars and *Panzefäuste* what could we do against a Russian ground attack? Maybe these people will get away without having their houses destroyed if we leave." De Ville concluded his exposition on military tactics saying, "We should leave quietly and keep to the cover of the forest whenever possible."

We marched for several days through forests and bombed-out or abandoned villages, sleeping in stables on beds of straw, eating what we could find, pursued by the machine guns of Russian fighter planes as soon as we put our nose into open country. In the larger centers of population chaos prevailed, the authorities having lost control over discipline and public order.

One evening, during a moment of relative tranquillity while eating dry bread as we sat on a low wall at the entrance of a village, I asked Jean how he thought the war would end.

"For us or the Third *Reich*?" he asked after a brief silence.

"For our idea...the 'New Europe'."

"Paul! The front doesn't exist anymore. The Russians will enter Berlin...if the Americans don't beat them to it."

"Then it was all in vain?"

"I don't know," Jean said. "But at least we fought for an ideal."

"I'd be curious to know what the brains at our Division Command think," I said, running a finger along the barrel of my MP38.

"Who...*Brigadeführer* Krukenberg?"

"Him, or Zimmermann, or Puaud. Do you remember their speeches before our departure?"

Jean let go a long sigh. "Ah, the 'New Europe'; the young, united Europe."

"It's for this that we enlisted, no?"

Jean gave an ironic little laugh. "It seemed like a good idea...last year."

"It's still a good idea," I insisted, "a strong, rich, peaceful Europe, without the communists and their lice to get rid of."

"Unfortunately, now everything is different. It's a lost dream Paul."

"These damned Popovs," I hissed angrily, "you hear them bombing, shooting and you don't see them for days. It was better at Körlin or at Kolberg when they were in front of us. Now it's as if they were invisible."

"It's the civilians who are suffering the most," Jean said. "The war has entered their hearths and homes and we cannot help them. The Russians are too many. What they did at Kolberg, they will do here too…a question of days, I think."

"And so the Third *Reich* is finished. Who will ever chase away these Russians, if not us?"

"Certainly not the Americans," Jean said.

"What kind of Europe will we see…a Europe without ideals?"

"It will be worse, for sure, Paul…a disaster, perhaps," Jean sighed.

"And what about us?"

"What else? Resist and attack like we've done until now."

"It's the only thing we know how to do," I said, realizing quite suddenly that my youth had been spent fighting on the side of a foreign country. "It's better that than surrender," I said, only half-convinced by my own words. "But after?"

"After what?"

"What happens if we are able to save our skins?"

Jean shook his head pensively. "Things will be difficult…especially for us of the *Waffen SS*."

Hope Fades

It was almost impossible to move by day without attracting the attention of the Russian fighter pilots. In one of these frequent aerial attacks, I slipped on all fours into a narrow tunnel dug under a secondary road. Russian aircraft zoomed overhead; bullets smacked against the road surface or ricocheted from stones and the metal parts of trucks and cars. This was supplemented by a brief but intense barrage from the enemy's artillery. I stayed holed up to await the end of that hammering, plugging my ears as best as I could, my back pressed along the vault, my body shored up by my feet and elbows in a futile attempt to avoid the ten-centimeter-deep water in the bottom of the tunnel. I stared down at the black, oily surface, dreading the appearance of the streaks of red that might flow into my refuge at any moment.

The bombing ceased but the cries and the death rattles of the wounded lying on the road continued, incessant and heart-rending. I pressed my hands against my ears to block out those harrowing screams, to keep them from entering my brain where they might take up residence. On the road above my head I knew there were broken bodies, scorched faces. The wounded would be writhing in agony, pleading for help when there was none. The contents of my stomach pushed their way up to my throat, acidic and burning. Using all my remaining strength, I remained in that position, propped up on aching limbs, on the verge of unconsciousness. I was desperate to breathe clean, fresh air but knew that by now the road surface would be spattered with the torn organs of those caught in the open, that the air would reek with the sickly-sweet, vaguely metallic taste of blood.

My muscles quivered, exhausted by the long-held and awkward pose I had adopted within the tunnel. If I stayed there, in that tunnel, I would soon collapse into the cold and muddy water. Crawling like some underground insect unable to move backwards, I made my way to the opening at the other end of the tunnel and then into the roadside ditch, into the light. On the road, the survivors, dazed and with limbs still shaking with fear, were forming a new but ragged column. Some were tending the wounded, vainly trying to stem the flow of blood from horrific wounds. I went back and forth, my eyes darting from person to person, hoping to catch sight of someone from my section but there were none to be found. A group had already made some progress down the road ahead. I hurried after them, closing the gap, searching for familiar uniforms and faces but unable to find my comrades from the mortar section. Damn! I'd lost them. In frustration I kicked a helmet at the edge of the road, thinking of *Oberscharführer* De Ville's words, which I had heard many times: *I don't tolerate laggards.* There seemed nothing better to do than to continue tagging along with the dishevelled column until, at a distance, I recognised the uniform and then the shambling stride of a comrade I had known from my time at Sennheim. "Hei Tyrol!" I shouted.

His lean face broke into a smile. "Paul...is it really you...where are the others?"

"I am looking for them."

"They'll be further ahead," he said. Tyrol was four fingers taller than me but skinnier and wore a short, unkempt beard in which some of the hairs shone like golden threads in the spring sunshine. Older than me, Tyrol was around twenty five. We exchanged information, hoping to find out something more than we already knew about the war situation but with scarce results. However, through a conversation with refugees fleeing the Russians, we learned that Neustrelitz had fallen into enemy hands and that Russian advance troops had entered Neubrandenburg a couple of nights earlier, between 27 and 28 April. None of the refugees knew with certainty where they were headed, only that they hoped to find a road that would lead them to Schwerin. But still, Tyrol and I were unable to find our comrades although we were both certain that we had not seen any of them killed or injured by the strafing. "Don't you worry Paul," Tyrol assured me with his customary confidence, "we'll find them again, sooner or later."

Walking had made me thirsty. I had already finished the water from my canteen but my throat and mouth were still dry so I suggested to Tyrol that we should visit a farm sitting a short distance from the road where a mother with a daughter at her hand stood at the threshold of the farmhouse door. Her expressionless eyes stared into the distance, beyond the horizon; her long and uncombed hair hung loose on her shoulders. The girl looked up at me, her eyes sad and timid. With a barely perceptible nod, the woman invited us in. Before stepping into the house, I turned to check the situation in the barnyard and saw two prisoners assigned to manual work crossing furtively towards the stables.

"Polish?" I asked her.

She answered with a disinterested nod and without looking at me.

"Did you see them, the Poles?" I said, addressing Tyrol in French.

"They're like vultures, waiting for the end and then…"

"Then they'll vent their hate on her."

"It's only a matter of time," Tyrol said, hopelessly.

The woman pointed to two chairs in the kitchen and mechanically, as some locks of her hair fell across her beautiful cheekbones, she poured milk into two bowls already on the table. I was worried about the Polish prisoners in the stables, about what they had in mind for this woman and her daughter when the opportunity came their way.

"Paul…forget them," Tyrol said, looking me in the face, "leave the door ajar if you want to keep an eye on them."

"Scoundrels! They're partisans, for sure. We have to be all ears," I warned my comrade. The woman finally looked at us but her expression remained detached, as if we were harmless ghosts that would visit only once. We sipped the milk without losing sight of the barnyard.

"Better move on," Tyrol said, getting up after emptying the last of the milk into his mouth.

I hesitated to rise from the table. "Do you think that…" I looked again at the girl's meek and fearful eyes, "there's anything we can do for them?"

"Nothing. Their fate is marked. Fill those two in the stables with lead and another two will take their place. It's only a matter of time."

I thanked the woman and reached out a hand to stroke the girl's blond hair. At first she shied away. I smiled at her and she accepted my caress. Those eyes, I shall never forget them, I see them when I dream, those big, innocent, tearful eyes, staring at me. Was she sad that we were leaving?

In the barnyard, Tyrol went straight towards the stables with his weapon ready to fire. With a kick he slammed the door open but he stopped on the threshold. "They've disappeared," he said, turning toward me. But, I wondered, who would be her next visitors.

A column of civilian refugees and troops snaked along the countryside road, growing longer as more and more joined the exodus. When a convoy of *Wehrmacht* trucks full of soldiers approached from a side road, the column opened up like the Red Sea, then closed again. From time to time, armoured vehicles also passed by, overflowing with fully armed combatants. "The Russians!" they shouted from the last vehicle — a warning of impending danger.

We were coming close to a copse where German soldiers lay motionless on the ground. They were all in khaki uniform. Once among them, judging from their smooth skin, I saw that they were probably younger than I was.

"*Standartenoberjunkers,*" remarked Tyrol.

"Strange," I said, taking a closer look at one of the young aspiring officers, "there's something that doesn't quite fit."

"Sure! They're all dead," said Tyrol.

"But I can't see any wounds," I said going towards one propped against the base of a tree trunk. When I was closer to the youth, I saw a dark-red, ragged, coagulated trickle of blood on his face.

"They all have a hole at their temples or in the back of their head," Tyrol observed.

"Judging from the distribution of the bodies and the clean uniforms, they didn't die in combat," I said.

"It's an absurd ending."

"Better to die in combat."

"Much better," Tyrol agreed.

Our chapped skin turned a beautiful shade of pink in the light of a low sun. Golden rays broke through the clouds, now deep-red against the intense blue of the evening sky. But still, neither Tyrol nor I had heard news of our units and we decided to continue our search for them.

An open truck approached, breaking and accelerating as it avoided obstacles in its path. Tyrol and I stood back, to the edge of the road. As it passed, the soldiers crammed in the back of the truck called to us, "*Kameraden,* save yourselves…quick, quick. The Russians are already in Berlin!" The truck continued without stopping, leaving a cloud of dust suspended in the red light of the sinking sun. Tyrol and I resumed walking, searching for a place to spend the night.

During the night the mayhem intensified. The beams of vehicle headlights crossed each other out in the open countryside. Drivers who had become disoriented ended up driving in circles, and some backtracked towards Schwerin.

During the following days we went back and forth, asking if anybody had seen our units. The traffic had died down but the trucks and other transport vehicles, when they did pass by, were so overloaded with soldiers it would have been impossible for us to hitch a ride. Still, that was of no great consequence to us; we felt safer walking because of the risk of attack by planes. And as we walked, we talked, talked about what we would do if we came face to face with the Russians.

"Surrender to the Russians...never!"

"Me neither! Never!" said Tyrol. "If we must go, we'll take down as many of them with us as possible."

Tyrol has a Plan

By dawn, the road was almost deserted and things seemed suddenly calmer despite the abandoned objects that hindered the way...until the thump and thud of shells exploding, some near, others more distant, broke the peace. I picked up an MP38, fully loaded and in perfect condition, from the edge of the road as we walked.

"Paul, why do you need another one?"

"We are *Waffen SS*," I answered. "I might need it."

"Everyone else gets rid of their weapons and here we are...the last heroes."

"We will carry out our duty Tyrol, you and I."

"The front is crushed," said Tyrol, "the Russians have run over it. They're already in Berlin. Didn't you hear it?"

"Maybe that's only communist propaganda, as usual," I said, almost convincing myself.

Tyrol stopped to point to the debris on the road ahead and behind, "This doesn't look like we're pulling back to regroup. This is defeat."

❧—❧

Tiredness had taken up residence in our bones and our legs could manage nothing better than plodding, heavy steps. On my feet, I had my second and last pair of boots which, after the marching of the preceding days, were on the verge of disintegration — as were those worn by Tyrol. We lost not only our bearings but also our sense of the passage of time but I think it must have been 3 May.

Tyrol shuffled to a standstill. "Remind me why we're going to Schwerin."

"Everybody's heading there," I answered. I could think of no better reason.

"If we want to annoy the Russians, we're going in the wrong direction."

"We'll never be able to re-join our comrades," I said, "so one way is as good as another."

Tyrol's eyes were closing as he spoke. "The Russians…we'll wait for them here."

And he was right — we were too exhausted in body and in spirit to carry on walking. In preparation for our last stand we gathered a good number of abandoned magazines for our weapons and took to the cover of a copse near the edge of a forest from which we could keep aim on a crossroads with a secondary road. Our intention was to take to the shelter of the forest to our rear when we ran short of ammunition. We were both good fighters and I could think of nobody I would rather make a last stand with than Tyrol who, after the battle at Körlin, was able to cross the River Oder with a small squad to reach Neustrelitz. All we had to do now was to wait for the Russians to show.

By late afternoon we had consumed the little reserve of food we had, but our canteens of water were still half-full. Tyrol stood up to get a better look beyond the crossroads. He tapped my shoulder. "Look Paul! Do they seem like soldiers to you?"

I got to my feet and saw in the distance a column heading towards us at a pace too slow to be soldiers. We observed them for the cover of the copse until Tyrol exclaimed, "Women…women SS. They're guarding a column of women prisoners. How many guards do you see?"

I shielded my eyes with a hand. "Two ahead and six alongside, they've got rifles."

We left the copse to take up position at the crossroads, to wait for the arrival of the column. The two women SS leading the column carried carbines on their shoulders. They saluted us as they passed. Behind them, in ranks of four, female prisoners dragged themselves lethargically along, some carrying small sacks on their shoulders, some a little bundle in their hands. They were of shabby appearance, pushed along by the presence of an old *Volkssturm* soldier at the rear with his rifle held ready to fire.

"Paul!" Tyrol whispered. "I've got an idea!"

"Spit it out."

"We stop them and hand them to the Russians."

"You're mad," I answered, looking Tyrol straight in the eyes.

"Think about it, Baby!"

"Don't call me Baby!" I hated the nickname that I had been lumbered with as the youngest soldier at Sennheim.

"Reason it out Paul! We free them, we tell the Russians that the two of us are French prisoners and they will hand us over to…"

"Prisoner to the Russians…never!" I snorted.

"You're not listening Paul…I said *French* prisoners…of the Germans…we use the Russians to go back to France."

"It's far too risky. They'll never believe us."

"With those women as proof, maybe they will."

I laughed in Tyrol's face. "You're crazy. Those women will betray us at the first opportunity."

"Not if we free them," said Tyrol.

"It's a moronic plan! It will never work," I answered.

"You have a better one?"

"Fight till the end!"

"Agreed! But against the Russians that don't show up?"

"Sooner or later they will stick their nose out…"

"Yes, after the war's ended, maybe. And so we'll be arrested for breaking the Conventions of… of…oh, whatever it was… and then they hang us if they don't fill us with lead first."

"And how do you intend to proceed?

"We'll take two or three rows from the column…"

"What about the guards?"

Tyrol laughed. "That old timer…what can he do to us?"

"If he starts trouble we'll have to take him down and then we'll have the entire column to…"

Tyrol persisted with his plan. "Paul, it's risky, I know! But we have to try. This is our only way out alive."

The last of the column passed with only the old *Volkssturm* guard at the rear.

"Choose the younger ones," Tyrol said. A moment later we caught up with the middle section of the column and, with his MP38 pointed forwards, Tyrol signalled two rows of four to step out to the roadside ditch where I was waiting. I motioned the women to sit down and they obeyed me promptly. By now the guard at the rear was coming close. Tyrol diverted another four while I guarded those already squatting in the ditch. The women in column showed complete disinterest in the fate of their companions and continued to walk without glancing or speaking to the ones we had removed.

The *Volkssturm* old-timer stopped when he drew level with us. He raised the muzzle of his rifle and grunted, "What's happening here?"

"A search…continue…we'll catch up!" Tyrol explained.

"We'll take care of them," I assured the *Volkssturm* man. He muttered some insults, cursing the prisoners but resumed his march without turning to look back. We led the women to the cover of the copse and waited until the column was out of sight.

Tyrol gathered the women together in front of him and in a grave tone said: "Where you were going, there is death!"

"We won't hurt you," I added. The women stared at us without understanding, speechless and apathetic. They were half-starved with gaunt faces inhabited by resigned look and bluish circles under their eyes. "Do any of you speak German?" I asked. Two of the women raised a hand.

"Follow us, we cannot stay here," I explained as Tyrol gathered our arms and ammunition. I pointed to the forest. A look of sheer terror came to every one of their faces.

"We are French," Tyrol said, attempting to reassure them.

"From the '*Charlemagne*' Division," I specified to one that was staring at my uniform.

"We are going to escort you until we find the first Russians," Tyrol promised.

"Then you will be free!" I added.

After a long pause for thought, one of the young women who could speak German said: "I believe you." She came up to me with the ghost of a smile on her lips then bowed to kiss my hands.

The second German speaker, with a strong Russian accent, addressed the remainder of the group who, after chattering amongst themselves in low voices, gave assenting nods. "We will follow you," said the woman.

I led the women along a forest track while Tyrol followed at the rear. Once at a clearing that I judged far enough from the road, I raised my arm. We stopped there, protected by the densely planted trees. The women slumped to the ground holding their bundles, exhausted.

"Food?" Tyrol asked. They shook their heads. He passed his canteen to the women who gratefully quenched their thirst. I followed his worthy example.

"We have to provide them with food for tomorrow," I warned Tyrol.

"And clothing," he added, "it would be better not to attract attention with their prisoners' uniforms."

One of the German speakers was a young woman called Mirka. She was twenty years old and Polish. The Russian woman, Irina, was over thirty and she was the oldest of the group — the others, Polish and Ukrainians, ranged from twenty-three to twenty-seven years old. None were willing to tell us their personal stories but they explained that they had worked in factories as weavers, assembled bombs or repaired shoes. They came from Schwarzenforst, Mirow and Malchow and from other villages where they had been transferred during the last few days and where the column was swelled by other arrivals. At nightfall all twelve of them curled close to each other, at the side of a fallen tree, covering themselves with rags pulled from their bundles. I looked at them, wondering if they were grateful and trusting enough to allow us to dupe the Russians when we finally met them.

"Well…up to now it was smooth sailing," Tyrol said, confident that his plan was working.

In the morning, I left Tyrol with the women while I returned to a village through which we had walked the previous night hoping to find a shop or store that had not already been stripped bare. At a junction near the village, I approached a soldier directing the traffic. "The Americans?" I asked. He signalled with his chin the opposite direction. I felt reassured by this news, perhaps we would end up surrendering to them. In the village, I found a clothes store which was still intact. I looked around and, without hesitation, went in with my pistol drawn and ready to fire. There was nobody inside so I hastily gathered as much as I could; shirts, skirts, jackets, bras, handkerchiefs, pants and socks which I squeezed into a cardboard box, tying it with a string. As a precaution I went out through the back door that led to a yard out of sight from the road. Carrying the box on my shoulder, I was going to make my way back to Tyrol and the women waiting in the woods, hoping that no one would challenge me about its contents — after all, looting was punished with a shot in the back of the head so I had to be very careful.

"*Soldat!*"

I stopped in my tracks. My heart raced, skipped beats, and then seemed to stop. I turned very slowly to face the direction from which the voice had come. Then I let go a huge sigh of relief — it was only a kid from the Hitler Youth with short pants and brown shirt, and a dagger at his side. He was probably ten or eleven years old.

"What are you doing here?" I asked him.

"*Soldat*, take me with you," he implored.

"Where are your parents?"

"I don't know. Take me with you."

"Tell me something," I asked him, "do you know where I can find a bicycle or a small cart…any means of transport?"

The kid's big, clear eyes brightened up, and then he took my hand. "Come with me!" he said full of hope. I followed him into the portico of a large house, where I laid the box on the floor. The kid's blond mane disappeared behind some boxes and sacks under a stair just inside.

"Look," he said, as he lifted a blanket to reveal the handlebar of a motorcycle, a BMW.

"Is this possible?" I let my words escape from my mouth, quite surprised. The kid's smile widened, almost touching his earlobes. As we pulled the motorcycle from under the stair, the boy asked again, "You'll take me with you?"

"Sure, Sure! But we need gasoline first," I explained, bending over the tank to check the fuel gauge, "it's almost empty."

"Wait here," he said, disappearing behind a corner of a house nearby. Meanwhile, I mounted the seat — it was a really nice motorcycle. The kid was probably looking after it for someone he knew very well and now he was handing it over to me, in the hope that I would take him with me.

"Here, this is full," the boy said dragging a twenty-litre container that was too heavy for him to carry. He began to open the spout.

"What's your name?"

"Karl, and yours?"

"Paul." I filled up the motorcycle's tank and started the engine at the second push on the pedal. "Listen, I have to deliver this box, first, and then I'll come to get you."

"Make it quick," he answered, his eyes now veiled with tears. He stepped in front of the motorcycle and grabbed the handlebar in both hands. "I will wait for you here."

"Don't worry, I'll come back soon to take you with me." I retracted the kickstand, put the motorbike in gear and left. On the road the traffic had increased but, dodging the debris and slipping between vehicles, I was soon at the crossroads. I slowed and turned onto the trail leading into the forest. When I reached the clearing, I shut off the engine. I was alone. Of Tyrol and the women there was not a trace.

Loyalty and Trust

With my pistol in hand, I crouched behind the motorcycle. My eyes darted from side to side, looking for signs of movement amongst the trees and bushes. I listened to the sounds of the forest, the birds, the rustling of the leaves. But there was nothing unusual or threating to be seen or heard. As I cautiously left the cover of the motorcycle, the lower branches of a pine tree rustled and I swung my pistol to point in that direction.

"Paul?"

"Tyrol?" I answered, lowering my weapon. He lowered his sub-machine gun while the women gathered around.

"The *Feldgendarme*…the reprisals…I thought of many things when I saw the motorcycle," Tyrol explained. "I never imagined seeing you on that motorcycle… I could have sprinkled you with…"

"I am an idiot! I didn't think about it," I said, apologizing. "It's all right, Tyrol." We hugged, patting our hands on each other's shoulders, under the intrigued gaze of the women.

Little squeals of delight came from the women as they searched through the items of clothing in the cardboard box. They flattened out jumpers on the grass to admire them and little squabbles broke which were soon resolved without our intervention. Without shame, they undressed completely, before putting on new pants, skirts and blouses. When they were satisfied with their new clothes, they hid their old uniforms under the roots of trees and covered them with soil. Dressed up, their appearance improved considerably.

"Now we have to think about food," Tyrol said.

"There are stores in the village but…if I am caught…good bye!"

Tyrol shook his head vehemently. "You're not going alone Paul."

"And the women?"

"We leave them here. They won't try to ran away, trust me," promised Tyrol.

We returned to the forest in the afternoon carrying water and food, mainly canned sardines, biscuits and things we could transport easily. From the driver of the last truck in a convoy we came to know that the Russians were by now everywhere and that resistance would be futile. After sharing the rations in equal parts, we decided to remain safely at the camp amongst the trees for the night. The traffic noise from the road continued late into the night and sometimes faint flashes from headlights cut past the trees into the forest, up to our emplacement where we were half-asleep with our weapons close at hand.

In the morning I guided, with Tyrol sitting on the back of the motorcycle, that small cortege of women out of the forest. We stopped at the village clothing store to search for items that I overlooked on my first visit, such as shoes. While the women were free to rummage on the ground floor, Tyrol and I went upstairs to choose new civilian clothes. This was the beginning of the second part of Tyrol's plan except that, for both of us, it was too heartbreaking to leave behind the SS shirts we wore and so we kept them, wearing them under the new civilian shirts.

When I looked down from a window towards the crossroads nearby, I saw that the soldier directing the traffic had gone. Then I went to the rear of the building to look onto the yard where I had left Karl, but he too was gone. My conscience troubled me — I had not kept my promise to the boy — so I hurried to the yard to look for the youngster. Events, as they happened, had prevented me from returning earlier but I had not forgotten him and now I felt so desperately sorry. *What will happen to him?* I thought. *And what does he think of me — a Waffen SS soldier who wears the uniform of his country and yet betrayed his innocent trust? What happened to the principles of integrity, respect and loyalty I had learned of during training at Sennheim?* This was no passing moment of regret; it was a matter that would weigh on my heart forever.

When I returned to the store I found the women in a good mood; they appeared transformed, some of them even pretty, especially Mirka. As she tied a large handkerchief around her head, in the manner of a Polish farming girl, she looked at me, smiling, turning with a graceful swirl that lifted her skirt.

Toys, shoes, suitcases, everyday objects of all sorts, lay scattered on the road outside the store, flattened by traffic. A flag of the Third *Reich* had been trampled like a rag into the mud and nearby, a black *SS* standard had been subjected to the same treatment. Sharp shards of glass were scattered everywhere. As before, I led the way driving the motorcycle with Tyrol sitting behind me with his MP38 at the ready, while the women followed on foot.

I felt Tyrol lean against my back to speak in my ear. "Paul, I have a new plan," he said in French. "Now that we have civilian clothing and a motorcycle, it might be better if we left the women to look after themselves."

I stopped the motorcycle and twisted my head to look at him. "You want to abandon them here, on the road?"

Tyrol dismounted to talk to me face to face. I shut off the engine. "Think, Paul...they can give us trouble, as you said. We'll have some hassles, for sure..."

I had failed to keep my promise to Karl and was not disposed to betraying these women; my anger simmered at my companion's suggestion. "But they trust us."

"Paul! We have a full tank. We can reach the border, you and I. We'll make it out of here, both of us. We've already done plenty for them. They'll manage fine."

"Never...never again," I said, talking more to myself than to him. The women gathered around wondering, looking at us, uncertainty etched on their faces. I restarted the engine, determined to continue with or without Tyrol. He cast a glance at me, a sneer, as if decrying my decision to remain with the women before he remounted the motorcycle's rear seat. I drove onwards, my conscience lighter than before and certain that I had taken the right decision.

Late in the afternoon, I turned into a trail across the fields with the intention to put up for the night as far away from the road as possible. Mirka hurried to walk at my side. She kept her gaze fixed forwards, except during those brief moments when she looked at me with a trusting smile. I was grateful for her unspoken gesture of faith that pushed all thoughts of Tyrol's dumb derision to the back of my mind. I stole a couple of glances at her too: she was pretty, her features delicate despite the pallor brought on by short rations and months of forced labour indoors.

The farmers we encountered had become more diffident, even mean, when they saw that we were still armed. Only with great reluctance did one old farmer agreed to allow us to rest in his barn. At the door of his house, where a large number of people sheltered, he kept a white sheet ready to wave at the sight of the first Russian. After refreshing ourselves at the water pump, we were about to eat when, along a wall inside the barn, almost hidden by a pile of firewood, we discovered a black Mercedes.

"Nice car," I exclaimed.

Tyrol, reading my thoughts it seemed, rebuked me. "Paul! He's no fool...he knows it's easy to notice this Mercedes. Besides, he doesn't like us being here...I think he'll try something...betray us to the Russians maybe. I have a nose for these things!"

"You're right Tyrol. We better..." A tug on my sleeve distracted me. It was Irina. She pointed a small window through which we could see the farmer's house. We moved closer to look out and saw that, in plain sight behind a window of the farmhouse, the old farmer stood with a gun in his hand, observing the barn.

"We'll have to get out without being noticed," Tyrol said.

Mirka, who like the rest of the women had grown to trust Tyrol and me, pointed to a door almost hidden behind timber boards which had been stored vertically on the side of the barn facing away from the house. We removed them one by one and found that it opened onto a field. I pushed the B.M.W. through the door to avoid attracting the suspicions of the vigilant farmer and continued to push the machine across the fields until we came across a hut where we nibbled on biscuits before falling asleep.

When I wakened, Mirka was lying beside me, her breathing light and rhythmical, her face serene and beautiful in the emerging light of dawn. I wanted to reach out to her, to touch her short, brown hair but something held me back and I remained there, looking at her. Her eyelids quivered a little, then she turned, stretching her limbs while still under the spell of a deep sleep. On my other side, Tyrol was snoring beside Irina. Her hair was dry and faded except for flecks the colour of copper; her face was ashen, grey, her eyes deep set. This was the face of a woman who had suffered greatly yet one could still detect, beneath the mask left by hardship, a feminine beauty.

From the distance came the intermittent sound of detonations; somewhere not too far away the battle was still raging, men dying for no further purpose. I thought of the day ahead. Up till now everything had gone to plan and even the quarrel I had with Tyrol about not leaving the women behind had somehow been resolved. He understood that we had to take decisions together, in common agreement.

We decided to keep away from the main roads and continue on the tracks across the farmland, a decision that slowed our progress mainly because the women became readily fatigued. We spent the following night inside a large tool shed, after sinking our teeth into old potatoes and drinking milk we came across at a farm. By this time we were worried that the women were weakening so Tyrol and I decided to return to travelling on the main road in the hope of finally encountering the Russians. And so we resumed our march with our minds focused on the impending encounter with the enemy. To ease the women's fatigue, I took four at a time — one on the tank, one on the seat behind and one each side — shuttling back and forth over stretches of several hundred meters. Along the main road, a farm attracted our attention because of the unusual number of prisoners at work, all busy around a corral and, closer to us, a barnyard.

"On guard, Paul!" Tyrol warned, "I smell those lice-bags!"

"Let's send forward Irina and Mirka," I suggested, "we'll cover them from that pile of firewood at the entrance."

"Ask the prisoners where the Russians are," Tyrol instructed the two women, "and don't be afraid," he added, patting his sub-machine gun. We took up position behind the pile of firewood while the other women waited on the driveway leading to the barnyard. Near the corral, it was Irina who spoke. Two prisoners left their group to speak with her and then, so it seemed from their gestures, they invited them and the rest of the women to come to the house. Irina turned, coming back towards us with Mirka at her side. At first, the two prisoners hesitated but then they began to follow the two women.

"They're up to no good," I said to Tyrol. "I'll take the one on the left."

The two prisoners were about twenty paces away and just about to flank Irina and Mirka when we left our cover behind the woodpile, weapons in hands. As soon as they saw us the prisoners stopped, turned quickly and left in great strides.

"So?" Tyrol asked Irina.

"Russian soldiers are nearby, about one kilometer. Officers are in castle with large park," she reported, indicating then the direction to take in order to turn onto a secondary road ahead.

"And the prisoners with whom you talked?" I asked her.

"Russians."

"Why are they still working here?"

"They don't want to go with soldiers."

Tyrol exclaimed, "They don't trust their countrymen!"

"They have no desire to fight," I said with an ironic chuckle.

We headed towards the castle but, out of sight from the farm, stopped behind a small, abandoned house. We hid the motorcycle inside, covering it with rags, and then prepared for the encounter with the enemy. Near a small stream, on a little fire that Tyrol had started, we burned our *Soldbücher* and a pair of pictures that I kept in my pocket and which I looked at for the last time. Then we wrapped our MP38s and the ammunition with our military shirts and dug a hole to bury them in, trampling the freshly excavated soil with our new shoes, to bring an end to that sad event.

"There is still something to see to," Tyrol said. "The women have to explain the details of their imprisonment to us and we have to decide on our story...everything we tell the Russians must match."

Having understood our intentions, the women freely disclosed the details of their imprisonment: where they came from, where the guard towers in the prison were located, whether there was barbed wire and if it was electrified or not, what work was done and where the camp for male prisoners was located — details that the Russians might ask when we encountered them.

"Paul, once there, the less we talk the better it is," Tyrol said.

"I hope the women think so too," I replied. "Without weapons we depend entirely on their help."

"Trust them, Paul! They like us. They won't betray us."

Tyrol's Toast

As we approached the park in front of the castle, the Russian soldiers on guard duty, well-armed, advanced towards us. They appeared different from those I had known at the Maginot Line: these men were the victors, audacious and bold. They informed Irina that Hitler had died on 30 April and that Berlin had fallen.

"It's really ended, Paul!" Tyrol whispered in my ear.

"Less babbling," I answered him with anguish in my voice. "You know what communist propaganda is like."

"Baby! Don't think about it anymore!" he said to me, putting his arm around my shoulders.

❧—❦

On the large stone stairway, at the main entrance of the castle, we climbed the steps slowly, with Irina, subliminally postponing our inevitable encounter with the enemy. At the top of the stairway, two soldiers stood behind a Russian officer whose jacket was adorned with conspicuous red epaulettes and shining, aluminum buttons embossed with the hammer and sickle insignia. His knickerbockers were tight at the knees – *a beautiful uniform*, I thought, *cavalry probably*. A middle-aged man of robust appearance, he was clean shaven and smoked a cigarette, his hand going to his mouth in slow, relaxed movements. I began to feel more at ease. The soldiers signalled us to stop on a landing, halfway up the stairway while Irina continued to the top. There, after exchanging a few words with the officer, she turned to signal Tyrol and me to join them. The officer inhaled another lungful of smoke that he expelled slowly in a cloud that hung around his pale and puffy face. He said something to Irina without even looking at her, his eyes fixed on Tyrol and me and there was a serious expression on his face. He stubbed his cigarette butt on the soil of one of the ornate flower vases either side of the door then asked in French how we were. I swallowed hard, surprised and alarmed by his unexpected welcome. "The woman called Irina told me everything. You helped them escape…bravo. You can stay here. You will lodge in the servants' rooms, at the granary. I'm sorry I can't offer you better accommodation."

"It will be a great pleasure for us, many thanks," I was able to mutter. He saluted us with a nod, gave an order in Russian and disappeared inside.

We followed the two soldiers and Irina to the foot of the stairwell where she joined her eleven companions to walk in the opposite direction while we followed the soldiers to our accommodation. Once inside our little room, I took my precious Luger from inside my shirt.

Tyrol's face suddenly paled. "Idiot that you are! And if they had frisked us?"

I shrugged my shoulders. "We're in the clear, no?"

"From now on we must watch what we say," said Tyrol. "That officer understands French very well. He's a literary man or a poet, I have good nose for these people."

At the dinner table, there was no sign of the women we had freed. Tyrol and I sat side by side, opposite the officer who had welcomed us on the stairway. Beside him sat three others wearing similar uniforms. An old woman caretaker performed the duties of a waitress. I had noticed her on our arrival, at the doorstep of a small house in the park. The officers conversed among themselves in an excited manner as they ate. Surprisingly, their table manners were rather refined; they wiped their mouths with napkins before and after drinking and used the cutlery without making a sound on the plates. Tyrol on the other hand slurped his broth and I felt compelled to draw this to his attention by prodding his ribs with my elbow.

"Well, from which side of France do you come from?" the officer asked us, introducing himself as a captain — from his epaulettes, I had reckoned he was at least a major.

"Marseille," I answered "And so too is my companion," I added, looking at Tyrol who, with his mouth stuffed full, nodded.

"I was in Paris years ago," said the captain, smiling. "Ah, pretty women in Paris, very elegant. I'd like to go back there one day, maybe I come with you. You'll go back to France, now that we have freed you, right?"

"Thanks to you," I said while Tyrol nodded enthusiastically.

"I like the Eiffel Tower, your symbol, and the Champs Elysees. And Montmartre is such a joyous district." He leaned conspiratorially across the table, towards us and said: "I like French people."

We smiled at him, somewhat awkwardly, and then I took the risk of raising a glass to him.

"Fascist?" the officer sitting beside me said.

"No!" I answered automatically, returning his hard stare.

"Nazi?" he continued, raising his tone of voice. He pointed his index finger under my chin, as if to force me to spit the truth. My blood ran cold in my veins. I glanced at Tyrol, he too was speechless, his face pale.

"Nazi?" repeated the officer, rising from the chair. I felt drops of cold sweat form on my temple. "*Heil* Hitler!" he bellowed, saluting with his arm outstretched. He brought the index finger of his left hand under his nose, mimicking the *Führer's* mustache and his companions burst into resounding laughter. We joined in too…after a few seconds.

"Hitler *kaput*," added another officer, still laughing.

"*Oui! Oui!*" the captain echoed, talking through his laughter until regaining his composure.

I looked again at Tyrol who was heartily laughing, probably at the sight of those ridiculous clowns. I laughed sincerely too, but more in the hope of relaxing my nerves than for joy.

"Vodka?" the captain asked, pouring the liquor into my glass. I stopped him courteously when the glass was half-full. Tyrol let him fill his to the rim.

"*À votre santé*," I proposed.

"*À la votre*," the captain answered, fully at ease, amused by our company. Tyrol gulped the liquor while I limited myself to sipping it slowly, savouring the vigour that flowed back into my stomach, which until that point in time had been knotted by fear into a fist-tight ball.

The officers, their glasses overflowing with vodka, then raised another toast. They stood up to attention as the most senior of them said: "To Stalin!"

We got up too, noisily pushing our chairs backward.

"To Rokossovski," said one of the other officers.

"To Zhukov," said another.

"To Mother Russia!" the captain said.

"To France," I proposed.

"To the *Führer*!" blurted out Tyrol, unable to restrain himself. The Russians froze holding their glasses in mid-air. A frigid silence descended on the room. Every Russian eye was on us. I felt my head swoon.

"The *Führer*, hah hah hah!" the officer at my side laughed, mocking him once more. His elbow hit me in the ribs. I spilled half the vodka from my glass. Everyone joined the chorus of guffaws, uproariously, except for Tyrol who coughed because his vodka had gone down the wrong pipe.

As we staggered back to the granary, I grabbed Tyrol by the collar. "You're the idiot this time!" I said, hissing in his face.

"It was a joke, Paul! They laughed, no?"

I promised myself then and there to avoid strong drink and to restrain Tyrol, who had demonstrated a weakness for vodka. I recalled the advice I received during my instruction at Greifenberg — resist and deny everything, even during the most insidious of interrogations, the psychological ones. I didn't have the least intention of giving myself away but as for Tyrol…well, I would have to keep him away from the vodka. The captain had all the time he needed to cajole the truth from us and if he found out that we were not French prisoners, we were doomed.

Complications

I had tried to meet up with Mirka the following day but the news that Germany had surrendered to the Allies the day before created great confusion at the castle. The soldiers danced and drank to celebrate the end of the war while the officers were attached to their telephones or otherwise kept busy. But toward evening, I saw the women at the celebratory feast. A soldier played Russian tunes on an accordion accompanied by several musical instruments played by his comrades. The bedlam continued, fuelled by drink and food brought from the kitchen, until very late at night but I was relieved that I would not have to bear the officers' inquisitive glances and questions at dinner — who knows how many toasts they would have drunk to celebrate such a famous victory? Of course I wasn't in the mood to celebrate anything, for me the fall of the *Reich* was the end of a dream.

Between dances with Russian soldiers, when she caught my eye, I had the impression that Mirka wanted to tell me something but couldn't find the right moment. Then, when the music grew in intensity and every hand clapped to the rhythm, she left the circle of dancers to come looking for me. When we met, she looked over her shoulder several times to make sure no one was watching then led me towards the little house in the park where I had seen the lady caretaker. Under a dilapidated brick arch, Mirka squeezed my arm, bringing me to a standstill.

"It's a furious dance," I remarked.

"Paul," she said in a warm, seductive voice, "perhaps we don't have much time to talk but there is something I wish to tell you. My father is a well-respected businessman. There will be much to do in his factory now that the war is over and, if you wish…well, he would receive you with open arms."

I was astonished by her offer. "But I fought with the Germans."

"The Poles hate the Russians more than the Germans. Besides, you are French."

I looked into her sweet eyes and, as I caressed her face, caught the scent of perfume.

"I would like you to come with me, to Poland."

It was a tempting offer. She was a beautiful girl. "I would like it too, sure! But we're in a very messy situation these days," I said.

"I understand, Paul. You don't have to decide now. Take your time."

I let my arms slip around her waist and pulled her towards me. "You are very pretty," I told her. She rested a hand on my shoulder and stood on her tiptoes to kiss my lips.

※—※

In my bedroom in the granary, I told Tyrol about the conversation with Mirka. I suppose I was seeking his opinion because he was older and more experienced in such matters. "What would you do in my shoes?" I asked him.

"Whatever you want but from my point of view, you'll find yourself acting as a slave sooner or later."

"I will have a secure job…whatever I want!"

"Reason it out Baby! They are rich, you are nothing…sorry…you *have* nothing. What are you going there for? It will be a golden cage. You'll die of boredom. It's an idea that doesn't square out. The war is over, we are about to go back to France…and you want to get stuck in Poland. Does it make sense? And there are girls that are just as pretty in France."

"But I like her, seriously."

"Then bring her with you. Her father's money won't disappear." Tyrol yawned. "Remember my advice, Baby. I know what I'm talking about."

※—※

Life was very pleasant at the castle, which was to my mind more like an old manor house or country mansion. I wouldn't have minded staying there: the meals were good, with a home-cooked taste to them; the weather had turned warm and the bouts of dancing were just what was needed to lift everyone's spirits. The Slavic women knew how to fend off the uninvited advances of the soldiers so their behaviour was exemplary. And talking of dances, those Russian soldiers seemed to take every pretext to continue with their music;

they celebrated Germany's surrender to Stalin again with another feast and so the war for them came to end twice in two days.

At the house in the park where the old caretaker lady lived, I encountered a blond girl about twenty years old. I had smiled at her when we first met. But on this occasion she was accompanied by her sister, a younger girl about my age. I was smitten at once by her natural elegance, so much so that in the evening I invited her to take a spin with me in the circle of dancers, Russian celebration or not, and she accepted. Her name was Erika. With a clear complexion, blue eyes and shining, blond hair — and a dazzling smile — she had the purity and beauty of a fresh flower. Her graceful manners and clear, gentle voice fascinated me. Mirka passed close by a few times during the dance, locking eyes with me, giving a glance of admiration without any shadow of jealousy. I had mulled over her proposal and had made my decision — she was the type of girl I liked but, for the moment, I preferred Erika's company.

"Watch out Paul," Tyrol warned later, in the safety of our bedroom, before falling asleep. "It's Slavic love. Mirka has respect for you and would follow you to the end of the world even if you have other women...provided you go back to her in the end. They love you until they feel you belong to them but as soon as they realize you don't they are capable of anything. Listen to me Baby, you're playing with fire!"

The following evening, I was reflecting on Tyrol's warning as I leaned on a fence waiting for Erika when a rustling from behind attracted my attention.

"Cigarette?" the captain asked. He had offered me one at our every encounter but we didn't really have time to talk because his officers were coming and going at any moment with reports and messages for him. But now we were alone.

"Thanks," I answered. As I put the cigarette to my lips, he lit it with his cigarette lighter. There was something about his manner that made me feel at ease, a sense of paternal protection. But he was also capable of swamping me with questions to which I had to pay the utmost attention.

"The sky is magnificent, full of stars, bright stars," he said in French.

I repeated his sentence with the correct pronunciation since I knew he wished to improve his diction but nevertheless I felt trapped by that implicit agreement. Did he want to put me to a test or perhaps lead the conversation to a matter more interesting to him?

"Stars, stars, marvellous, mysterious sparkles...were they like this also at the camp?" he asked point blank.

"Yes, sometimes."

"When?"

"During punishments; kneeling down, in the open, in the cold the whole night long."

"Are you happy to be free?"

"Immensely! Again thanks to you."

"And your prison companions, where did they go?"

"I don't know. During the escape everyone thought for himself."

"How many escaped with you?"

I was beginning to feel a little nervous. "About ten I guess. It's hard to be more precise because everyone was on his own or by twos, like me with Tyrol."

"And when did it happen?"

"During the last days while on a transfer march."

"Ah!" he exclaimed, inhaling the smoke from his cigarette, his eyes fixed on a distant point as if he were reciting my story in his mind before abruptly wishing me goodnight and leaving.

After a brief dinner with two of the Russian officers the following evening, Tyrol, as usual, went directly to join the Russians' celebrations while I went for a stroll in the park and, almost without realizing it, headed towards the little house where Erika stayed. I was thinking about my apparently friendly encounter with the captain the previous night and why he had not questioned Tyrol — and that troubled me. Was he allowing Tyrol enough rope to hang himself?

"Paul!" Erika's call dispelled my gloomy thoughts. She was smiling as she left the little house, illuminated for a moment by the light from inside as she closed the door behind her.

"Erika!" I hurried to meet her. I took her hand in mine and together we strolled towards the courtyard where the Russians were feverishly dancing. I felt calmer now, happy to be close to her.

Erika squeezed my hand. "You haven't yet told me where you come from."

"From a labour camp."

"And before that?"

"First deported...then a prisoner."

"Oh!" she said, as if disappointed by my answer.

As I led her towards a large oak tree on the grass to the side of the path, in search of some privacy she stopped and looked at me with her large compassionate eyes. "You know," she said, "I don't believe a word of what you told me."

I was dumbstruck. Somehow she knew I was lying.

"You have nothing of the prisoner about you," she continued, "you don't act or look like someone who has been deprived of freedom for a long time."

I quickly regained my composure; maybe I still had some hope of convincing her. "You know how to invent things," I answered, smiling.

"Paul, your attitude toward me, a German girl, is surprising. It's certainly not that of a prisoner who has just been set free."

"You mean that I should hate you?"

"My brother was fighting at the front but we haven't heard from him yet. He is with the *SS Panzerjäger* and in a strange way you remind me of him, the way you walk and hold yourself. Now, look into my eyes and tell me the truth."

"*SS*, just like me." I felt as if a heavy weight had been lifted from my chest.

"I knew it!" she said, suffocating a squeal of joy. She hugged me, covered my face with kisses.

"*Waffen SS*, 33rd Division 'Charlemagne', 1st Company, 80mm mortar section and ex-police section," I revealed.

"I wasn't mistaken then. I had this impression and I couldn't get it out of my mind. Where did you fight?"

"At Körlin and Kolberg."

"Oh my precious hero," she said tenderly. She laid her warm lips on mine and we exchanged our first, true kiss before we joined the Russians who were having another drunken party in the courtyard.

As I escorted Erika back to the little house just before midnight, I regretted having confided in her. Deny always, until the end, until they get tired asking the same questions — it was a lesson I had stupidly ignored. How could I be sure that she wouldn't talk? And what if she was a spy or a Russian collaborator? With her deep, sincere eyes, with her open and pleasant character, with her generous heart, I could hardly believe that she would betray me. And her brother, he too was *Waffen SS*. But the doubts lingered like a bad taste in my mouth; I had known her for just a few days and had told her everything. To make the situation worse, Mirka had made a point of manoeuvering her partner close to us while dancing, her eyes burning with undisguised hostility as she realized I had already rejected her in favor of Erika. She too knew my secret and could easily denounce me and Tyrol to the Russians. My comrade and I were now in a *very* precarious situation of my own making.

The Russian soldiers were crouched on the floor in front of the officers who sat on a couch further back from the wall that was about to serve as a movie screen. Someone had come across a projector and reels of films a few days earlier in a storeroom and, because I knew how to loop the film onto the spools, I volunteered to act as the projectionist. I turned off the lights to show a grainy film featuring a female ice-skater. As she performed a fast spin, a soldier pushed up from the floor towards the monochrome image and, with his arms raised as if holding a woman, followed the movements of the skater. Two companions, irritated by his interruption of the show, sprang up to grab him and throw him to the floor amid general laughter.

Later in our servant's room in the granary, Tyrol said: "If you are useful you are untouchable but, when they don't need you anymore, they cut your throat." The constant vigilance we were forced to maintain, and which I had broken, was wearing on his nerves too.

❧—❦

I was walking in the park the following afternoon, hoping to encounter Erika. As I passed the brick arch near the little house where she stayed, I heard a voice call, "Cigarette, Paul?" It was the captain.

"Thanks," I answered. After all, I was in no position to refuse.

"The climate is nice here," the captain said. He handed me the cigarette and when I brought it to my lips he used the one he was already smoking to start mine instead of his lighter. *That natural gesture*, I thought, *could have been a well-thought-out ruse to give the impression that I had nothing to fear, a false expression of friendship*. As we spoke, I paid close attention to even the minutest, the most apparently insignificant, details we discussed. That each gesture or word of the captain might hide a trap made me restless.

"Yes it is," I answered in monosyllabic words — the less I said the better.

"But in France it is much nicer, as you know, compared with this region. Did you travel much, in Pomerania?"

"Not much, we never left the *Lager* once we arrived there," I replied. *Shit*, I thought. I had blurted out the German word for camp — *Lager*.

"How long were you in the *Lager*?" he asked casually, exhaling a puff of smoke without looking at me.

"I don't know exactly…almost a year perhaps."

"Hmm…a long time then." He glanced over my shoulders, his round, dark eyes staring at a distant point. "Young people withstand things better…those conditions," he said.

"Indeed," I answered, hoping he would change the topic of our conversation. I took some deep puffs from my cigarette in an attempt to stem my rising unease.

A pout of sympathetic disapproval passed across his face. "These Nazi's…why would they send a young fellow like you to the *Lager*?"

"A question of women!" I answered promptly, reassured by my own inventiveness.

"Hah, hah, bravo my young man…you are the typical French womanizer. *L'amour! Ah, l'amour!*" His manner suddenly became more serious, reminding me of a priest about to receive the secrets of a sinner. He brought his face close to my cheek and whispered, "Was she French?"

"No, German. Her boyfriend was at war, at the front. The Gestapo caught us one night."

"Did they interrogate you?"

"Sure! They fabricated a story that they forced us to sign and the rest you know."

"So where did you find that nice girl?"

"In a small German village, just across the border from where I lived…they sent us to work for the *Todt Organization*, like in Marseille." I surprised myself by the ease with which I told that heap of lies.

"And how old were you?"

The captain was probing relentlessly. "Almost fifteen," I lied, adding on a year to my age at the time.

"Have you ever heard of the French Volunteers Legion?"

"I don't care about politics," I said in response.

"Exactly so! You are right not to. Politicians say one thing and do another," he said, flicking away his cigarette butt with some style. "And Tyrol, how did he come to the *Lager*?" He kept on poking on that word, that irritating little wound.

"I found him there, we escaped together."

"Interesting. Very interesting," he muttered. "Well, it's almost movie time, too bad we don't have better films. I'll see you in the main room," he added, leaving at a pace that was unusually brisk for a chubby man.

"Sure!" I answered, suppressing a sigh of relief. *I came out of the encounter quite well*, I thought. But now there was a new problem — Mirka.

We sat on the doorstep of the little house in the park, talking about our problems. By now I knew Erika well and my doubts about her had vanished. She had kept my secret safe and had not told even her sister Anna that I was a member of the *Waffen SS*. I felt reassured and happy in her company but it was getting late. We kissed before I left with a promise to meet her in the park in the morning.

I retraced my steps after watching her close the door, waving a last farewell for the night. When I returned to the hall in the castle, I found Tyrol, as usual, sitting with the Russian soldiers and the women we had freed from the column of prisoners. The captain was talking with Irina, separated by a short distance from the other revellers. The Russian soldiers grabbed me as I passed their table, forcing me to sit with them and Tyrol. They poured vodka into a large glass they had launched at me and which I had caught in mid-air. They were to put it mildly, rather tipsy, as was Tyrol. I raised my arm to their shouts of incitement to drink the vodka in a single gulp but to avoid drinking all of it, I 'accidentally' spilled half a glassful. Tyrol meanwhile gulped his vodka without stopping for breath and then held out his glass for a refill.

"*Krashivaia dievoutschka!*" shouted the soldier, pouring the liquor into Tyrol's glass. He then grabbed my comrade's chin, forcing him to face Irina.

"What did you say, you bag of fleas?" Tyrol slurred.

"Tyrol!" I cautioned. He didn't even look at me. The soldier said something else and then clapped his hands in time to the frenetic rhythm of the accordion that had started a new tune in the background.

"You, stinking Mongols!" Tyrol shouted, struggling to get up to join the dancers, much to the amusement of the watching soldiers who, laughing wildly, showed the gaps between their teeth.

"Tyrol!" I shouted above the clamour.

"You," said Tyrol, his arm describing an arc to include the Russian soldiers, "are a cess-pool of true…hic…imbeciles."

I handed Tyrol another glass of vodka to shut him up. Meanwhile, the captain still seemed engrossed in conversation with Irina. Tyrol, now red-faced with drink, spluttered and coughed. The soldiers were laughing at him, unaware that he had just insulted them in French. I cast a quick glance to the captain who evidently hadn't heard Tyrol amidst the racket. When the last of the women, fending off amorous hugs, slipped away into the darkness I grabbed Tyrol's sleeve, pulling him further from the captain and telling him to come back with me to our room. He pulled himself free. "I'm telling you all…you communists are full of lice!" he shouted, keeping his glass high.

"*Hurrè*," the Russian soldiers replied, raising their glasses to what they believed was Tyrol's last toast.

"You are all cutthroats of…"

"*Hurrè!*"

The cheers encouraged Tyrol's alcohol-induced bravado. "You shit your pants because of…of…you fear of us."

"*Hurrè!*" The Russians were still amused by Tyrol's speech.

"I saw you…at the front…coward rabbits!"

"Tyrol!" I said, springing up. He ignored me.

"Yes, I, *oui, oui, moi! Ja! Waffen SS*…Grenadier der…der…" he yelled beating his chest and stretching out his arm in salute. I stuck three of my fingers in his mouth, causing him to lose balance and crash backwards amid the uncontainable laughter. They didn't take him seriously but I was wondered if the captain had followed the entire incident; a stolen glance in his direction confirmed my fears. I lifted my companion onto my shoulders, jesting to all, trying to explain that he was too drunk as I headed towards the granary door. The captain kept his eyes fixed on us, continuing to smoke.

I was furious with Tyrol. "It's the end for us…damn! That captain doesn't even bother to follow us. You'll see tomorrow what the fuss is about!" Tyrol replied with a snort, moaned and then went limp. With Tyrol draped across my shoulders, I made my way towards the little house.

Bitter Farewells

I propped Tyrol against the wall and, holding him steady with one hand, knocked on the door. Erika's sister, Anna, opened it. She looked at Tyrol. "What happened to him?"

"He's drunk!"

At that moment, Erika appeared. "This way, into the bedroom," she said.

I dumped Tyrol on top of the blankets. Anna brought a jug of water and a small porcelain washbowl. She mopped Tyrol's forehead with a dampened cloth. Tyrol gradually regained consciousness, babbled something, tried to stand but succeeded only in knocking over the water jug with his big, clumsy feet.

"Why did you bring him here?" Anna was confused by the hassle.

"He drank too much and spilled the beans."

"They're *Waffen SS*, like our brother," Erika explained to her sister.

A fist hammered on the door. I instinctively slipped my hand inside my shirt to grab my pistol but then recalled that I had hidden it earlier. I felt lost without it.

"Silence," Anna whispered.

"Don't move," I breathed to her, after another hammering on the door. I went to the lamp on the dresser and fiddled with the wick to turn it off.

"*Soldaten…Ruski!*" they shouted from outside. We waited in silence, except for Tyrol's snoring. At last they left, their curses fading as they crossed the park.

Anna continued to talk in whispers, fearful someone was still at the door. Erika came to me and I held her close; her whole body was shaking.

"It's unforgiveable of me to put you in danger. We'll go before dawn," I promised.

When she was certain that there was no one at the door, Erika took me by the hand and we followed Anna upstairs. The two women lay down on the double bed and pulled the blankets over themselves. I waited for a moment, wondering if I should go downstairs to keep an eye on Tyrol but Erika patted the bed. I lay down on top of the covers but was too worried by the events of that evening to even close my eyes. Erika touched my cheek with her fingertips. "Get some rest at least, you will need it for tomorrow," she said. She got up to sit, freeing her hair over her shoulders. I looked at her, bewitched by the harmony of her movements and by her bright, clear eyes. I hugged her tenderly, touched her lips with a light kiss.

"Paul, do you think my brother will come back?" she asked, wrinkling her perfect brow.

"He'll come back, you'll see," I answered, wishing with all my heart that he was still alive.

"I really hope so, we love him so much." Tears ran in little rivulets down her cheeks wetting both our faces. "It's difficult, Paul. Our thoughts are always on him. Anna misses him very much. My aunt cannot find peace unless he comes back to us."

I broke away from her. "Erika, I'm sure he will come back," I repeated. "I would willingly take his place if I could, if it would make you happy.

"You are very kind to think in this way," she said, wiping the tears from her face. "What will you do?"

"If I'm able to escape from here I will try to return to France. And you? You won't stay with this soldiery they…"

Erika pulled me close. "Shsst," she whispered, "don't think about it."

❧—❧

As dawn broke, I went downstairs to see what sort of condition Tyrol was in. I was not at all surprised to find him in a deep sleep. I shook him, just a little at first but this had no effect and I resorted to shaking him with both hands.

"Oh! My head!" he moaned.

The smell of sour alcohol made me retch. "Wake up, ass!"

"Where are we?" he asked, forcing his eyelids to part.

"In a cesspool…that's where we are! The shit is up to our throats if you don't get up quickly."

"I want to sleep, let me be," he whined like a little kid.

"I'll leave you here, sure…and in ten minutes they'll cut your damn throat!"

"Why?" A deep seated cough rattled his chest.

"Don't you remember, you drunken oaf? Move! We must go!"

Tyrol struggled to his feet. "No, no," he mumbled, holding his head with both hands.

"I'll explain once we're on the road," I rasped angrily.

Anna and Erika appeared from upstairs. I embraced Anna briefly and then Erika, kissing her for the last time before looking from the doorway to check if the way was clear: the few sentries dotted around the grounds were sleeping at their posts, as drunk as Tyrol. They didn't need to care about their safety anymore since German stragglers were shot on the spot or deported to prison camps. Not a leaf rustled in the park. Tyrol and I slipped outside and I turned to wave goodbye to Erika, my heart aching.

In the open fields away from the castle Tyrol, wobbling on his feet behind me, dared to break my stony silence. "And the Slavic women? We didn't say goodbye to them."

"Ass!" I answered, barely holding my rage at bay. "Because of you and the alcohol in your head we are fugitives."

"Oh," he said.

"Because of you I don't have my pistol, nor the motorcycle, nor the MP38, and the captain, when he learns we're missing, will hunt us down because *he* is *not* an idiot."

"Baby! I can't forgive myself. I am older than you but also an imbecile." He rummaged in a pocket. "Here, slash my throat open, I deserve it," he said, holding his penknife towards me.

"A saber would be better!"

"Paul...from this moment on, you give the orders and I will obey."

"Shut your beak. Forget about it," I answered curtly. At least I felt free and relieved that I wasn't tormented by the presence of the captain anymore. Perhaps one of the women had already informed on us and I was being overly harsh with my comrade. I took a deep breath and lengthened my stride — we had to put as much a distance as possible between us and the castle before sunrise.

"How long will it take to reach France on foot?" Tyrol asked after a long silence.

"If everything goes smoothly...two weeks."

"*If* everything goes smoothly," Tyrol repeated, but as a question.

"I wouldn't want to come across the captain."

"Then we must avoid the road," said Tyrol. "The less Russians we encounter the better."

We immediately took the first trail across the fields, heading towards an isolated farmhouse in the distance.

It was already daylight when we knocked on the door. There was no answer but after a few moments we heard the desperate crying of an infant. The door was unlocked so I pushed it open and left it like that as a precaution for a speedy exit. In the spacious kitchen stood a tall, skinny woman who gave the impression that she was waiting for someone. Her son burst into tears and hid behind her skirt when he saw us while a little girl, sucking her thumb, hugged her leg. The woman's face was devoid of emotion and her dispirited eyes, lost in an absent glance, ignored our presence. She had a dazed, almost crazy look about her. A large, blood-filled swelling below her cheek bone rendered half her face purple and blue, in stark contrast with the paleness of her skin.

"We won't hurt you," I said gently.

She immediately burst into tears and then through sobs said: "You speak German... thank God you're not...not Russians." Her long, unkempt, blond hair fell in front of her shoulders as she looked down to button her torn shirt and straighten her rumpled skirt; she ran a hand through her hair to sweep it from her face.

"What happened? Did they hurt you?" Tyrol asked.

The woman's tears flowed anew; she nodded then took a deep breath. "Every evening … for days…four or five of them…they gave bread to my kids and then they…"

I couldn't bear to hear what I already knew. I asked about the bruise to her face.

"This is nothing, nothing," she said with her eyes fixed towards a bare wall, "not compared to what happened. If I could die, I…I would avoid this shame. My son, he understands what happened to me, everything." She caressed her son's head. "And he suffers more than I," she said, containing a moan.

"The war is ended, you'll see, everything will be all right," Tyrol said in an upbeat tone. But his attempt to infuse her with at least a glimmer of hope passed unheard.

"I lost everything… only the pain remains. What else can they do to me?"

Tyrol, his face contorted with hate, snarled, "They're like ants these bastards, they get everywhere."

The woman's story tore open my heart, filled it with a hopeless yearning for revenge against those who had molested her. It would have been easier to bear if I had found her dead, maimed by a bomb or squashed under rubble. I had seen such sights many times… but to listen to that dreadful tale of suffering…to witness the veil of pain that inhabited her face was more than I could stomach.

"I cannot offer you anything… I have nothing left," she said forlornly.

"Nor do we have anything to give you," I said taking her arm in my hand. "We are trying to escape captivity and have no weapons to defend ourselves."

"We must go," Tyrol cut in, "if they find us here it will be the end for you too."

"I understand," she said, lowering her head.

We ruffled the kids' hair and told her she would survive if she kept her spirits high and that it was important for her to do that for the sake of her children. Standing at the door, she wished us good luck and added, "Thank you soldiers, for your kind words, they have helped me see what I must do."

We turned away and left in silence.

"It's terrible to see her like this," Tyrol said after a while, shaking his head.

"I saw it in Kolberg…women killed their children and then themselves rather than give in to the Russian soldiers' perversions. If she was dead, she wouldn't have to suffer," I answered.

"Her ordeal is not even finished."

"Who knows for how long it will last."

Sunset surprised us while we marched along a secondary road. We had tried to avoid the Russians but now we found ourselves in the middle of one of their detachments. A number of carts with horses still at the shafts were standing along the sides of the road while, in small groups, Russian soldiers danced around fires. The growing darkness carried the merry notes of an accordion and the clinking of bottles of liquor.

"Damnation!"

"Into the cesspool once again," Tyrol hissed.

"No chance to backtrack, they've seen us," I said, alluding to a soldier coming to offer us a sip.

"They're *all* drunk!" Tyrol observed.

"Mouth shut and eyes open," I warned him. We headed nonchalantly to the center of the gathering, accepting a couple of sips so as not to offend them. On the carts they had piled up furniture and tables together with boxes full of dishes and silverware.

"They're celebrating, *again*," Tyrol said with disdain.

"*And* they'll continue for days," I said in the same tone.

Shattered bottles lay strewn across the courtyard; the stench of alcohol contaminated the sweet-scented spring air. At the epicenter of the celebrations a German woman about forty years old was being passed from group to group like a limp puppet. Further ahead, on a clearing near a shed, were horses tethered to poles planted in the ground and from there we heard a commotion that aroused our attention. Amid the shuffling hooves of the unsettled horses, we glimpsed a Russian soldier on all fours, crazy drunk, attempting to escape being trampled. Suddenly he screamed out in pain as he was caught under a caracoling horse. As we pulled him to safety he screamed like a madman and I noticed that his leg was twisted at a peculiar angle. His comrades were too engaged in their own pursuits to pay him any attention and at first ignored the wails of agony. When at last a jabbering soldier did come to investigate, he put the bottle he carried to the lips of the wounded man. Tyrol, unable to contain his fury, kicked the Russian hard, sending him tumbling into a ditch. The drunken Russian, unable to extricate himself, cursed and swayed on his feet but soon fell into an alcohol-induced stupor.

I pointed to the wailing Russian with the broken leg. "What will we do with him?"

"What can we do? They don't even have a doctor in their units, these savages."

We dragged the Russian to the shed where good fortune awaited us — inside we found plundered cartons packed with tins of sardines. We opened a can each and devoured the oily fish with relish while the man with the broken leg writhed at our feet. His wails had given way to grunts and sighs and then snores and we decided to rest there for a while confident that the Russians would remain unaware of our presence. We tried to sleep but found it impossible to ignore the screams of the German woman. Without seeing what was happening, images of her torture flooded my brain – she was being raped, her pleas that she had had enough brutally ignored as they took their sadistic revenge, one after the other, on an innocent woman amid a bedlam of demented laughter.

At dawn, having hardly slept, we left the shed and the laments of the crippled Russian behind to find the soldiers sleeping in the most unlikely places and poses. Taking care not to stumble on or disturb their slumbers, we pocketed a few cans of preserved food before leaving. Later, as we marched along a road, we came across squads of Russian soldiers repairing telephone lines while trucks overloaded with goods plundered from houses, all roughly piled up, drove past in a continuous coming and going. The doors of every house in every village we passed were bolted up. The civilians still at home didn't dare stick their noses out for fear of the Russian cavalry which, it seemed, had a propensity for raids, plunder and rape. They were a slovenly bunch; we had seen them in action at close quarters, they had no compassion and were out of control when drunk and their uniforms, contrary to those of the other Russian troops, were adapted to their personal choices.

In a small village we passed through, there was a sentry at the entrance to a house commandeered as a Russian command post. He sprawled on a bench with a sub-machine gun on his knees. Two of his comrades — one with a German helmet on his head, the second with ceremonial silver tassels round his neck and a bayonet in his hand — mocked every German that passed them. On the village square, a pile of bicycles, radios, hunting guns and other articles of value awaited uplift. Further on, a young soldier asked us to show him how to ride a motorcycle and, after we demonstrated the use of clutch and accelerator, he drove away like a rocket, laughing at the thrill before colliding with another soldier riding a bicycle.

In another, larger village, where there was a factory that produced accordions and harmonicas, we ventured into a store hoping to find something to eat and came across a number of browsing Russian soldiers. Some big fellows were in front of mirrors, stretching themselves in the most unusual positions, surprised by the reflected images which they touched, laughing as if this was the first time they had seen their own reflection. Another soldier was gobbling one tube of tooth paste after another, squeezing them directly into his mouth; we looked at him, amused. He then moved to the gargle bottles, gulping down their contents.

"They're crazy!" Tyrol exclaimed.

"Crazy savages, and that's worse, much worse," I replied.

As we left the store, a soldier approached us pointing to his wrist, checking by sign language if we were wearing watches. When he saw that we didn't, he lifted his sleeves showing a dozen of them, all taken from French prisoners he had encountered. On the road a muscular, tall soldier slammed a bicycle to the ground when he found that he was incapable of disentangling the chain which was jammed between a pedal and the main gear. A few steps farther on we reached a group of men who had just come out from the same store, all without watches on their wrists so I guessed, correctly, that they were French. "Tell us something," I asked, "do you know how my friend and I might reach the French border...in a hurry, I mean?"

"If you want to go back to France, jump on a truck until you find the *gendarmes*," one of them explained.

"Or get a hitch from the Americans, they have big GMC trucks, the Americans!" another said.

"American trucks?" said Tyrol.

"Are you deaf, my friend?" a third asked. He came alongside Tyrol so that Tyrol could look along his straight arm. "There, go in that direction and you will be in the American zone. They're always coming around searching for French prisoners and refugees who want to go back home."

6

Trials and Tribulations

Safe at Last

Acoloured banner under a small archway, which looked as if had been hastily set up, carried the words: 'US Army' and 'Welcome'. It was not with complete confidence that we approached the first building where a French junior officer received us politely and directed us to the de-infestation unit. We looked at each other, without saying a word and I sensed that Tyrol was wary; his eyes betrayed his fear that we were just about to make a big mistake but I kept the thought to myself.

After delousing, we were issued with a box of rations that included, among other items, powdered milk and cigarettes. Our situation seemed to be improving and Tyrol appeared more relaxed after smoking a cigarette. Another junior officer sent us towards a group of soldiers one of whom held a clipboard and pen. "Give your name so you can receive rations and transport coupons," he explained. An American sergeant then came to collect the completed list.

Several thousand people hung around in that assembly camp waiting to be processed. Finally, a loudspeaker announcement instructed the newly arrived groups to muster. Tyrol and I aligned ourselves promptly as if we still were at our base in Greifenberg. I waited patiently with Tyrol at my side, thinking about the events in those last days. I closed my eyes, listening to the names as they were called, recognizing some that were members of 'Charlemagne'. "*Heil!*" a few ex-comrades-in-arms answered loudly, "*ici!*" was the answer from all the others. We had learned to attest our presence clearly, with pride in our voice, but when my turn came I replied, as a cautious measure, with a faint "*ici*" which Tyrol imitated. The American administrative machine was in motion and there was nothing we could do to step away from it.

"Do not lose your coupons, you can't get on the trucks without them. Keep with your group. Obey the man in charge," the loudspeaker reminded us. It seemed to me a well-organized undertaking.

In the evening, at our barracks, we inquired about the composition of our group and found that they were all French prisoners of war.

"There's something wrong," Tyrol whispered as we lay on our bunks.

"What's troubling you…it's perfect here," I replied.

"Our tattoos…if they get the idea of checking us, they'll know where we come from, no?"

"I don't have one…there was confusion at the infirmary and I didn't get it done. Don't think about it, everything will go all right. We'll be home in a few days," I assured my friend.

❦—❦

After a long and exhausting journey, the following day trucks took us to another camp where a sergeant with a copy of the list of names received us. This camp, we soon discovered, was in the French occupation zone and its proximity to the French border lifted our spirits. Tyrol's misgivings seemed to have evaporated and he too wore a broad smile. Once more we were obliged to submit to disinfestation by a dusting of DDT and then we waited for a long time behind a row of low panels that divided the assembly area into sections. Before allowing us into the barracks, the camp guards added us to a long line that crawled forwards but we couldn't see what was happening and had no idea what the purpose of this queue was. Then, we shuffled forwards, I noticed that from time to time MPs escorted certain individuals from the head of the queue to an isolated barracks surrounded by a tall tangle of barbed wire. Doubt surfaced in my mind. Tyrol touched my arm, he placed himself in front of me to get a better view when the line advanced a few paces. Our eyes followed another MP, accompanying a bare-chested man towards the isolated barracks.

Tyrol turned to me with a look of desolation on his bearded face. "Paul," he said in a calm voice, "my mother still lives in that village I told you about. You must promise me…"

I didn't let Tyrol complete the sentence. Resting my hand on his shoulder I told him, "As you wish my friend, I understand."

The line advanced; we were close to the exit. The five or six ahead of us were told to remove their shirts. Two American MPs were at each side with their weapons in their hands, another carried out the check for *SS* tattoos. It was impossible to escape.

"Paul! Go to my mother. Tell her I always think of her…" he choked up, then forced himself to swallow. "Baby, make your best effort to see her. You'll go there eh, Baby?"

"I will Tyrol," I said, as he removed his shirt.

Tyrol raised his arms in front of the MP with the checklist who nodded to his fellows when he saw the *SS* tattoo. Tyrol turned to look into my eyes with an imploring glance. He walked away without turning again, with hunched shoulders, in front of one of the armed MPs.

"Hoho!" the others in the line shouted.

"Did you see that Nazi?"

"He was hiding among us!"

"Look at him! He is not at all skinny, that butcher!"

Tyrol continued walking, impassive, until inside the isolated barracks. I peeked from behind my raised left arm, waiting for the MP to finish jotting his findings on the checklist. My head started to spin and my strength abandoned me.

"Are you OK?" the MP asked, holding me up by the arm. He helped me to my feet and, walking slowly, I joined the other ex-prisoners waiting in front of the barracks.

"But you were with him," one said.

"You were talking to him."

"You knew him!"

"They're everywhere these Nazis!"

"They are like lice," an ex-prisoner said in a southwestern French accent, "they're hard to get rid of."

I forced myself not to choke-up, thinking about Tyrol and our ups and downs with the Russians and relived the moment at the infirmary at Greifenberg when, with Jean, I took to the exit without having the tattoo and thanked my good fortune for having done so.

Other formalities followed in the coming days — questionnaires to fill out and forms to sign — but, finally, I found myself sitting in one of the English trucks that were to carry us to France with a group of fifteen ex-prisoners from the southwest. Before leaving, I recognized the voice of a Belgian non-commissioned officer from the 1st Company at Greifenberg who was issuing instruction to those about to depart for France. He too had escaped detection as an *SS* man and I smiled at that.

It took another day of travel along a dirt track to arrive at a location within easy striking distance of the French border where a squad of deportees were washing boots and mess tins, drawing water from a pump half-buried by debris and filth. Nearby, American soldiers chattered to each other or called out orders in French. *Here I am,* I thought, *safe at last.*

An Unfortunate Coincidence

At the assembly center there was indescribable confusion; nobody knew what to do, where to go, what orders to follow, in fact we were left to fend for ourselves. My attempts to find out what would happen next were met with indifference and sometimes hostility: that's your problem, I was told several times. Like everyone else, being held there I could only wait for the authorities to take action and with the only highlight of the days being mealtimes, I was dying of boredom. To avoid the long queues that formed at the pump in the mornings, I got up early to wash. On one such morning, after giving the pump lever several energetic strokes, I bent forward to catch the water in my cupped palms and splashed it onto my face and neck. When I opened my eyes, I saw the legs and boots of someone standing behind the pump.

"*Bonjour*...how are you?"

I instantly recognized the voice but took my time to dry myself with a handkerchief. This was the greatest of all unfortunate coincidences that I could have imagined. I straightened to look into the face of the man who had spoken. His skin was more tanned than I recollected but there was no mistaking the features. It was the Marseillais, the spy we had mistreated at the guardhouse at the Greifenberg base, the traitor who passed our names to the *Maquis*.

He took a cigarette from his lips. "I work for the Second Bureau," he said through a sarcastic smile.

"You're still alive," I remarked.

"I have seven lives, rest assured of it," he said, throwing the butt to the ground then grinding it into the dirt with the sole of his boot. Then he turned to leave without another word.

I was shocked to find the Marseillais still in one piece; usually, when we caught a spy they were executed. Now the situation was reversed, I was the one at risk. I mingled with the others in the camp, trying to disappear into the crowd but was soon confronted by a young French soldier whose chin almost pressed up against my face. "Follow me!" he ordered in a harsh, aloof voice. He drew an American pistol from the holster on his belt and took me inside one of the barrack buildings, into a room that was completely empty.

I began to speak, "I would..."

"Silence! Take your shirt off and keep your arms high!" he interrupted.

"But..."

"Don't be a smart ass," he warned, pointing his pistol between my eyes.

I pulled off my shirt thinking with bitterness at that welcome from the French Army.

When he failed to find the *SS* tattoo, the young soldier turned angry. "Put your shirt on and come with me," he ordered.

He led me to another room which was this time furnished with a table, a bench, two straw cots and bars on the window. I recognized a companion from the 1st Company at Greifenberg but I refrained from throwing my arms around his neck. He looked up from his cot as I entered but showed no sign of having recognised me. In a casual way, I moved closer to him, asking his name in a loud voice. "René," he said, "and you?"

"Alain."

In a low whisper, hiding his lip movements with a hand, my companion said: "Paul, they got you too?"

"*Ja!* That traitor, the Marseillais, he must have betrayed me," I answered in like manner.

"Me too…he gave us away in exchange for favors, I know it. There's no way out…and after all the effort to get this far."

"I'll slash the scoundrel's throat if I get the chance," I whispered.

The door opened suddenly. A soldier pointed to me. "You…with me!"

For a brief instant, I locked eyes with my companion in a mutual wish of good luck before I left: it seemed absurd that things should have gone so wrong when I was so close to freedom.

In an office with bare walls, a slim lieutenant with bulging eyes was sitting, his elbows propped on a desk. At a bench to the side, a soldier wearing spectacles sat at a typewriter, his fingers hovering over the keys.

"I don't have time to waste. I want the truth," the lieutenant warned without preamble. He got up from his seat and walked around the desk to sit on it, directly in front of me. "I already know everything about you. All I need is a simple acknowledgment from you. So?"

"So nothing. What do I have to say?" I didn't lose my coolness. I remembered the training at Sennheim about how to behave at interrogation and didn't bat an eyelid. What could he know? I had given false names; they were clearly typed on my accompanying papers.

"I demand you tell your entire story!" he said, slamming a fist in the palm of the other hand.

I noticed that he was losing his patience and so, after a long silence, I decided to tell him a tale, since he desired one so much. "I was working for the *Todt Organization* in Marseille," I began, providing places and dates. Up to this point it was all true.

"Tell me something else," he said, folding his arms.

"One day, they sent us to a large base on the Atlantic Coast and then, after a long journey — three days perhaps — on a train loaded with material stripped from the base, I found myself in Germany."

"To do what?"

"To clean up the ports after the bombings."

"Where?"

"Hamburg, then Stettin. We were in continuous movement, following the path of destruction to repair roads and railways." The typist caught up with my story then handed a copy to the lieutenant who put it on the desk. "Sign it," he said, "it's your deposition."

I read every detail before signing it with my false name, knowing they would check my story even though it might seem plausible to them.

"Cigarette?"

"Thanks!" I accepted the lieutenant's offer, maintaining my composure and withholding any sign of relief.

"Be available at all times… you leave on the next train," he said, lighting up my cigarette. "However, you have worked for the enemy…but this is not necessarily so bad," he said before leaving abruptly.

On leaving the interrogation room, I passed in front of some companions aligned in the corridor, with their arms raised — one of them forced to hold a brick in each hand — guarded by an armed soldier. They returned my glance with eyes that spoke of abject resignation.

After dinner I was able to scrounge a cigarette which I smoked avidly but still I kept thinking about Tyrol. We had become like brothers, bonded by hardship and danger. His last, heartfelt words about his mother kept coming back to me, insistently. There was nothing we could have done to prevent his capture; we had fallen into an inescapable trap. I only hoped that he wouldn't be shot by firing squad, as happened to so many of us from the *Waffen SS*.

❦—❦

An officer with three stripes on his sleeves came to speak with me in barracks where I was detained. "They placed you under my responsibility," he told me with a good-natured smile.

"Very well, *mon capitaine*," I answered, heartened to have a middle-aged man rather than an arrogant novice in front me.

"I have the task to accompany you to Lille where you will appear before a military investigation," he explained.

"At your command, mon *capitaine*!" I answered, straightening up automatically to attention but mulling over the words I had just heard in order to evaluate their exact meaning.

"Ah! I should mention that a Marseillais is coming with us, and three other former prisoners," he added nonchalantly as we wandered over to the door of the barracks.

My brain flew into overdrive trying to think of all the possible reason that would make it necessary for that despicable traitor to accompany us.

"Life was really hard for us French war prisoners," the captain continued. "I am happy it's all over."

❦—❦

At the station we climbed aboard a carriage and settled into a neat compartment furnished with polished wood and shining, metal strips. I sat in front of the captain, near the window, and opposite the Marseillais, who pretended to fall asleep when the train started rolling.

In the few instances when our eyes met, he turned his head away from me to gaze at the scenery or lowered his eyes to look at the floor.

After several hours, the captain was served breakfast and was kind enough to offer me some of his food but I politely refused. I was beginning to form the impression that he had taken a liking to me. "How come you let them catch you?" he asked after his tasting the first morsel of a slice of toast. With a sideways movement of my eyes I indicated towards the sleeping Marseillais. As the captain continued with his breakfast I looked at him closely, trying to discern the nature of his character. His face, I concluded, showed him to be a good-natured man; his eyes reflected wit and intelligence while his respectful and sensible demeanour reminded me of the officers I had encountered when I was a boy playing at the Maginot Line. "You can beat the crap out of him if you want to! I certainly won't be the one to restrain you," the captain told me when he finished eating.

"Throw him out!" the nearest of the three former prisoners who were travelling with us said with a sneer.

"I'll give you a hand," one of the others offered.

"Who would know?" the third added, shrugging his shoulders.

I was surprised by their attitude to the Marseillais. Maybe they were desperate to vent their frustration by indulging in a fistfight — or maybe they too hated traitors, irrespective of the side they belonged to. As the captain looked out of the window, the Marseillais continued his pretence of sleeping and it seemed to me that he was trembling a little, as if he was anticipating trouble from the four of us. "He's a worm and he'll stay that way, clobbering him won't change a thing!" I said, making sure the Marseillais heard my words.

"It's not worth dirtying our hands on that lurid being," agreed the nearest ex-prisoner, who had calmed down after hearing my reaction to their tempting offer. Meanwhile, the Marseillais kept his eyes tight shut and the captain smiled.

The train slowed as we approached a small Belgian station close to the French border and, even before it stopped, I heard the *Marseillaise* played by a band on the sidewalk beside the tracks. Everybody leaned out the windows to clap and sing along enthusiastically, impatient to participate in the musical celebration and demonstrate their love for the Motherland. The Marseillais remained 'asleep' and I remained seated, impassively looking out of the window.

The captain, standing at an open window of the carriage to get a better look at the revelry turned to say, "Isn't it beautiful? The *Marseillaise*...our homeland?" As I gave him a little nod of acknowledgement, I noticed that his eyes were moist with tears. He returned to his stance at the window, leaning out and waving with both arms.

"Eh, I understand," he said, having taken his seat again after the last notes of the national anthem, "it is not the same for you…I know how it feels to be a prisoner. It is a given fact…at the end of a war there are always victors and losers."

I nodded.

"But cheer up! Let us drink, let us all celebrate!" he proposed, pulling a bottle of red wine from his haversack.

"Thanks," I answered, accepting first sip — I needed it.

"I prefer to have a toast with a Nazi like you instead of sharing the spout with that double face," asserted the ex-prisoner sitting beside me, alluding at the Marseillais who remained still, always with his eyes closed. "You seem a decent guy, although your ideas are different from ours."

"You just chose the wrong side *mon ami*," one of the others said.

By the time the train reached Lille, they managed to lighten my mood a little. It seemed that I had ended up in a large sorting center: some ex-prisoners were directed to buses, others to trains on secondary railways that would take them to their villages. Groups of volunteers distributed food and money while the wounded were received by the Red Cross.

The captain accompanied the other three former prisoners and me to the office of the military police and, after taking care of all necessary formalities, he said goodbye, shaking hands with each of us. "Do not worry," he said to me, "you will be released soon."

"Good luck!" the three demobilized former prisoners wished me, patting my shoulders as if they were friends before leaving. The playing of the *Marseillaise* hadn't raised a shadow of emotion in me, but at those two words, and their sincerity, I swallowed the tears that were threatening to roll from my eyes as an officer directed me to a tiny, dark cell with a barred window.

Freedom

Hours of boredom passed before the key of the gloomy cell turned in the lock and the door opened. The officer who led me there had returned with a folder containing typed papers. "So, let's review your testimony," he said in an impersonal tone of voice. He motioned with the folder for me to follow him to an office that was, in contrast to the cell, bright and sunny. There I confirmed word for word what I had told the lieutenant at the previous camp but I had to wait another half-hour before the officer led me into another, more spacious room where an elderly man in civilian clothing was sitting on a massive carved-timber chair behind an imposing desk. Close to the desk, there was a bench with a type-writer and typist and, farther back, a tricolour hung limply on a polished-metal pole. Two other officers arrived to take seats next to the officer who had brought me to the elegant room. *This was more than another interview*, I thought, as I stood in front of the massive, polished desk. A shiver ran down my back.

One of the officers whispered in the ear of the elderly civilian who nodded in response. The officer then cleared his throat. "I think you have understood, young man, that we do not believe a word of your deposition. This is your opportunity to reveal the truth."

For an instant I felt lost but I regained my coolness and, as usual, didn't show any reaction.

"Your signature is false…the family name you gave is false, isn't it?"

"What I have said is the pure truth. I have nothing to add," I said curtly.

"Come, young fellow," the elderly civilian interjected, "why do you want to make matters more difficult than they are? Your lies will come to haunt you."

"We know, with absolute certainty, that you were a member, up to a month ago, of a *Waffen SS* Regiment at Greifenberg. You cannot deny this fact. We have circumstantial evidence," affirmed the officer.

"Come now! The sooner we end this session the better it will be for you," the elderly civilian said.

I remained silent as I looked into the eyes of the officers — they were neither hard nor hostile. The atmosphere was one of conciliation, unlike that which I encountered during previous questionings. And the elderly civilian, he was treating me almost as a father might treat a son who had made a forgivable mistake. They were unarmed and it seemed to me that their purpose was simply to establish the truth.

One of the officers broke the silence. "We are preoccupied only with obtaining a sincere confession and to validate it. There is no advantage in perpetuating a falsehood."

"So be it," I said, relaxing, "as you wish."

An officer moved a chair, placing it near the typist, and invited me to sit. He returned to his place at the desk and sat there with the others, folding his arms as he waited patiently for me to begin my confession. I started with the propaganda poster, inducing me to enlist in the *Waffen SS* and continued cautiously, describing life at the bases. I noticed in the officers' attitude to me a certain tacit complicity as I told my story. I had the impression they would treat me as a rascal who had played a mischievous trick and that a simple confession would be enough to obtain their forgiveness. I explained to them how the combat at Körlin and the defense at Kolberg took place and how I was able to escape from the Russians. They didn't miss a word of what I said and the typist stopped only when the elderly civilian started talking.

"Very well, young fellow, very well! What is past is in the dust, forgotten. Not forgiven, understand me well, because there is a deep difference between the two terms. Let's forget then the past: that is erased, expunged. Now you have to think about your future. I don't know what you intend to do once you are free but there is something you have to keep in mind," he said raising his glance to look deep into my eyes.

"I'll do everything it takes, your honour!" I was revived at the word 'free' and I realized that my future was hanging on his lips.

"You are aware of the fact that at this moment you are in debt to your country. There exists a noble possibility to redeem the tremendous mistake you have made, influenced as you were by the impulses of youth. You owe it to your compatriots and to the soldiers who fell for freedom."

Freedom...it seemed that everyone was using that word.

"So it is about a very simple matter," he continued. "You have had the sort of experience that France now needs desperately. You have therefore a simple question to answer...would you be inclined to enlist to fight on the right side this time, for a just cause, against the Japanese?"

"Yes, yes!" I answered without hesitation, caught off-guard by that strange proposal.

"Well, young fellow, very well!" the elderly civilian — who I now knew was a judge — said, looking at a paper in his hands. "You are free, my dear fellow, you can go."

Dumfounded, I stood there, stunned at that declaration.

"Give him a travel allowance and a train coupon," the judge concluded, instructing the officer accompanying me as we left the hearing.

I waited in a side room for the officer to return with a ration box and a train ticket. "I suggest you take a couple of weeks rest with your family and then show up at the nearest recruiting office. Good luck!"

I thanked the officer and then, feeling that my troubles were over for the time being, jumped on the first available train to travel home, at last. Still, I wasn't suffering too many illusions about my future. That proposal — to fight the Japanese — seemed to me extremely bizarre and the more I thought about it, the less convinced I was that I had made the correct decision. But I had given my word and intended to keep it.

❊—❊

At Villerupte-Cantebonne, I discovered that my aunt had moved to Nancy and that she had had problems with the authorities because she met an Englishman on a special mission during the war who had assumed the identity of her deceased first husband. Fortunately my mother had intervened and testified in her favor in front of a judge. My close family had, I was also told, moved to a place in the *Midi* and Dodek, my Polish friend from childhood who had chosen to fight with the Resistance, had been killed. One old neighbour said Dodek had been riddled by bullets from MP38s fired by German officers as they retreated. Another offered a different version: the *Maquis* frequently attacked isolated groups of *SS* soldiers heading north, setting up ambushes in order to disarm them. Dodek had stopped a solitary soldier on a main road, but was surprised by the arrival of a car carrying those officers. A stone recalling his heroic act was erected in his memory with the engraved words: *Assassinated by the Nazi hordes, he died for France.* It was news that left me stunned and saddened.

At Nancy my aunt received me warmly. After dinner she showed me pictures of English and French military parades and then began to lecture me about my part in the war. I listened to her for a short while but got bored and made to leave.

"But say something, at least," she scolded with a bitter voice. "If you had enlisted on the free side, or the French or English ones, today you would savour the taste of victory." She stared at me as if I were a criminal.

"I was among the losers. Too bad for me!" I answered curtly before slamming the door on my way out.

Pursued by the Past

Life returned to almost normal. I met a girl and after a few dates she asked me to visit her home to meet her parents. I knocked on the door of her house and listened to her dainty steps approaching from inside. She opened the door just enough to look around its edge. "Wait here, I'll tell my parents you're here," she said in her alluringly feminine voice.

I waited for her return recalling the scent she wore when I kissed her neck during a dance. She was the sort of girl that possessed an innate enthusiasm for life, a *joie de vivre* that helped me overcome a constant sadness that seemed to have taken root in my psyche.

"Come, Paul," she called from the corridor, leaning from a side door.

After three or four hesitant steps I was at the door of the living room which was elegant and well-furnished. A big man, with shirtsleeves rolled up to his elbows, stood next to a piano. He came towards me, stretching his muscled arm and strong hand in welcome, introducing himself in a cordial voice. "*Monsieur* Victor, communist and member of a cell of the *Maquis*, in Saint Étienne."

I muttered my name and then didn't know what else to say — after all I was shooting at the communists a couple of months earlier.

"I know, I know, young fellow," continued *monsieur* Victor, inviting me to sit down, "my daughter has already talked about you, she told me a lot of things."

I remained stunned. I had taken a good deal of care not to reveal anything concerning my past except that I had mentioned to her that I had fought in Pomerania.

"Would you like a glass of wine, or do you prefer some liquor?"

"Wine, if it's no trouble *monsieur*," I answered timidly.

"Ah! Between you and me, I really don't like the word *monsieur*, I would much prefer that you called me Victor."

"Father, please, don't start with your politics," the girl interjected, "he's not interested in any of that stuff. Come Paul, I want you to meet my mother."

I followed her into the kitchen, where her mother was busy preparing some finger food.

"You have to forgive my husband, Paul, he talks too much, especially about politics. He hates the Nazis to death," she warned before bending forward to plant a welcoming kiss on my cheek.

When I returned to the living room, Victor asked, "Your parents, do they live near here?"

"Yes, for the time being. My father is just about to finish building a house and I help him. My mother gives us a hand, when she can."

"Ah! The genuine communist spirit! Roll up our sleeves, we must rebuild, advance hand in hand, make progress by working together — only in this way we can eliminate the mischief makers — those outlaws of fascists and Nazis — that undermine our communitarian ideals and our unique internationalism.

I stood there, listening to him, unflappable. He dished out the history of the communist party since its beginning, almost without stopping to breathe. I was never as well-learned in politics as during that evening and I must say that I admired the oratory skill of that man.

The girl looked into the living room. "Father, enough of your stories...come to the dining table."

"Ah! Now the best is yet to come," Victor said with a conspiratorial tone in his voice. He went to a cabinet and returned holding in his hands an old, dusty bottle, treating it as if it were a precious relic. "You will taste how fine end exquisite this wine is. I saved this very bottle to celebrate the victory. It is a wine very well-aged, and from this region," he explained, pouring me a glassful.

I took a polite sip. "Good...very good," I affirmed.

"Eh, eh! The *Boches* didn't find this one." He raised his glass. "To victory!"

I too raised my glass but without answering. My thoughts went to Körlin; over the rough sea at Kolberg; to the dead civilians and soldiers scattered on the roads, mixed with mud; to the maimed horses. Even Karl's face — the kid from the Hitler Youth — popped up in front of my eyes. Was he still waiting for me? A hard lump choked my throat when I thought of Tyrol standing bare-chested with his arm raised saying, "You'll go to see my mother, eh baby?"

"The table is ready," the girl said.

All of a sudden my head started to spin, I felt the floor under my feet disappear, I crashed over a nearby chair though I was still conscious.

"The salts, quick! Let him breathe the salts," shouted Victor.

"You and your wine, Victor!" I heard the mother say, "you've given him too much to drink."

"It is certainly not the wine's fault," Victor assured his wife.

The girl arrived from the kitchen with two pills and a glass of cold water. "Take these Paul. Are you ill?"

"It's nothing," I assured her.

That was the last time I saw the girl or her parents. The meeting with Victor stirred too many unpleasant memories. I inhabited a world where nothing made sense and took refuge in a deep bout of melancholy.

❧—❦

One morning, towards the end of June, two *gendarmes* were standing at the door when I answered their knock. "You are Paul Martelli?" one asked.

"I am."

"Then you are under arrest." The *gendarme* patted the holster on his belt. "Do not try to escape."

The second *gendarme* held handcuffs towards me, his stern look demanding that I should present my hands to them. He squeezed the ratchets tight on my wrists. I couldn't understand the motive for my arrest. I had shown up at the recruiting office on time and was told to go away but always to keep myself available and I had done that. The two *gendarmes* escorted me through the city, one on either side while they guided their bicycles, with one hand. Instinct told me to run but from what? I didn't know what crime I was accused of and was determined to solve this mystery once and for all.

Later that day, my mother arrived at the *gendarmerie* with a small basket containing food covered by a dishcloth. "Did they interrogate you?" she asked, her brows furrowing. "Did they mistreat you?"

"Yes, but they were kind enough."

"My son! What will happen to you now? What will they do to you?"

"Don't worry mother. Everything will be cleared up. I was dismissed as a free man by the military tribunal...they will do the same here too."

Mother put her hand on mine. "Oh Paul, I have a bad feeling about this."

Her visit was brief but she promised to return later and I soon found myself hemmed in by *gendarmes* interested to hear the story of my adventures in the *Waffen SS*. As the first night of my captivity approached, I was taken to an office where a *gendarme* handed me a paper to sign from a folder on the desk. On the paper was a typed statement which I confirmed that I didn't resist arrest and that I didn't undergo unjust coercions or ill treatments. After signing the paper, I asked the *gendarme* how he knew I was staying with my parents.

"I cannot tell you anything," he politely answered. He looked at his watch, and then, getting up, left the folder in full view on the desk. "I have to leave for a few minutes. Don't do anything stupid," he added.

I peeked over without getting up from the chair and I was able to read the heading though to me it was upside down: it was my dossier. I lifted the cover and squinted at the first lines which told me what I wanted to know. The warrant for my arrest had come from the judge of the tribunal in Nancy. Before I was transferred to prison, my mother arrived with canvas bag containing clothing and a water-proof pouch with toothpaste and soap. Thanks to the kindness of those *gendarmes* we also had a few moments to hug each other before I was taken to a cell already occupied by two inmates.

❊—❊

The lawyer representing the court was an unpleasant-looking character; his reptilian face and his bulky body wrapped in a jacket that was too large for him brought to mind a shell with a head jutting out which gave him something of the appearance of a giant turtle. I sat at a desk in the interview room, facing him, waiting for him to finish shuffling a sheaf of papers taken from his briefcase.

"Well," said the lawyer, "let's see if we are able to disentangle you from these accusations," he said slowly. "There is a note in here that emphasizes your young age," he said, stretching his fat, short neck as he looked at me. "You see, we are not yet aware of the extent to which external factors weighed on your choice to enlist with the Nazis. From what we know, it could very well have been your father who advised you on such a decision. After all your father is Italian, isn't he? You know, Mussolini…Hitler…"

Turtleface's insinuation angered me. "My father knew nothing about it."

"But still, he must have signed your enlistment document, considering your age," he insisted.

"I lied to him. He thought I was going to learn to drive trucks and, besides, he can't read German," I explained.

The lawyer leaned forward on the desk. "You see Paul, here we are not dealing with lies or half-truths…we have to determine the weight of your father's responsibility in… "

"I said, he didn't know squat!"

"So, you're telling me that a fifteen-year-old kid decides, on a whim, to enlist with the *Waffen SS* and his father is not aware of it?"

"That's what happened."

"You have to concede that it is difficult to believe such a version. And then there is still the matter of your father's signature…it will be impossible to convince the jury at the trial that he had no part to play in your decision."

"Trial?" I asked, dumbfounded. This was a surprise, a nasty one.

"Yes, you will be tried in a couple of days. It is my duty to make you aware of everything relevant to the situation."

I remained speechless, thinking about the unwelcome turn of events.

"Do not worry, Paul. It will be a simple formality if you affirm what we are talking about. You see, there are two mitigating circumstances in your case — your young age and your father's signature."

I thought about the cell I was sharing with two other inmates, the revolting cabbage soup in my mess tin, the dry bread issued once a day, the stench from the urine in the bucket and the hostility of the warders. "What happens if I do as you suggest?" I asked, with my head bowed.

"They will let you out immediately. You will be free to go this very evening," he answered promptly.

"No…I mean, to my father."

"You must understand that somebody has to answer to the jury. In short, your father could sit on the defendant's bench in your stead. It will be a more appropriate solution, believe me!" His tone of voice sounded almost friendly, even fatherly.

"So you want to slam my father in prison, to take my place?"

"I wouldn't put it quite so bluntly but he *will* stand trial and then it's up to the jury to determine the gravity of his involvement and then…"

"And then bollocks!" I interrupted. The two inmates — who faced much less serious accusations — in cells close to mine counted on 'very favorable mitigating factors'. They had been condemned to death that same morning.

"The choice rests with you. I was simply here to explain matters," the reptilian-faced lawyer said with a very impersonal tone of voice. He gave the impression of withdrawing into his shell as his fat fingers fiddled with the documents on the desk. "I hope you will take a wise and mature decision," he added before leaving.

I left the interview feeling agitated. I had spent the once-daily twenty-five minutes of exercise time listening to someone trying to persuade me to betray my father. The confinement was suffocating me. I was desperate to breathe clean, fresh air.

I couldn't sleep that night. I listened to the tapping on the walls, a code to communicate simple messages from one cell to the next.

"Hei Paul, still awake?" a cellmate asked.

I grunted.

"You know, the two condemned this morning?"

"*Ja*, so?"

"One has been pardoned but he doesn't know it yet, the other will be shot tomorrow morning. It is so not to aggravate the condemned one."

"Then they will both have a bad night."

"And another two disappeared today."

"Executed?"

"In secret…no trial."

Retribution

From inside the tribunal hall, an usher opened wide the massive timber door and called out a name. An inmate at the head of the line in the corridor followed him, escorted by a *gendarme* on guard duty. The accused prisoners advanced by one step. Those who anticipated an inevitable verdict of guilt wore a mask of dumb resignation; those in whom a sparkle of hope still flickered had it dashed by the despondency of the condemned as they left the hall.

"What are you accused of?" the young fellow preceding me asked.

"I don't know for sure. I was at the front, against the Russians, against the communists."

"*Waffen SS?*"

I nodded. "And you?"

"Gestapo…driver and mechanic…never took up arms."

"Then it should go smoothly for you," I encouraged him.

"I hope so. My lawyer told me the same thing."

The jury was very hasty in churning out judgements and had already tried about fifteen of us and it wasn't yet ten in the morning. The turn for the driver-mechanic came; he disappeared behind the big door, accompanied by the usual *gendarme*. It would soon be my turn. I thought about what the court lawyer had proposed but with contempt — I was not the kind of son who could betray his father. Sure, I had belonged to the *Waffen SS* but that didn't mark me as a criminal. The ones guilty of the massacre at Oradur-sur-Glane certainly deserved that description but not those of us 'Charlemagne'. We had risked and left our lives at Körlin and at Kolberg; we didn't kill women and children nor burned churches and houses, on the contrary, thanks to our efforts civilians were saved by the tens of thousands and I would spell this out to the jury if they couldn't understand it. I had no part in the senseless and cruel actions of the *SS* groups under orders of mad commanders who cast a shadow over all of us and had only heard these stories at the end of the war. And besides, the French were no less guilty in some cases. What happened in Bad Reichenhall was just one example — twelve *Waffen SS* were shot by firing squad on 8 May, a few hours *after* the capitulation, without trial by an army of a 'democratic' nation. My two dear friends, my comrades at Sennheim and at Greifenberg, were among those twelve. Martin and Gosse died bravely, refusing blindfolds, as did the others. They fell together, riddled in by French bullets while they shouted, I'm sure, *Vive la France*.

The door of the hall opened; the driver-mechanic came out sheepishly, his head bowed. He avoided my glance and disappeared down the corridor accompanied by a warder. One of the guards lined up along the wall caught my eye. "Capital punishment," he murmured in a low voice, shaking his head.

The usher called my name. I entered the hall and confirmed my identity. Without wasting a second, somebody rose from a bench beside the jury to read from a paper: "The defendant is accused of having fought in combat while wearing a foreign uniform against French allies in times of war."

"A serious crime," the judge remarked, gravely.

The prosecution took the floor. "Your honour, esteemed members of the jury, this case is very simple and, at the same time, very serious. Considering the young age of the defendant and the general mitigating circumstances, the prosecution proposes a sentence of fifteen years."

A grumble rose from the public benches behind my back, a buzz of disquiet.

"I give the floor to the defense!" the judge said loudly, hammering on his desk with his gavel to settle the disturbance.

My lawyer rose up. "Esteemed members of the jury, yes this case is very simple but it is also unique. Consider this fact: the defendant's grandparents, although they were German, were forced to change their nationality after The Great War but, despite this, remained good French citizens. They suffered and withstood vexations and reprisals from one side and from the other, without counting the inevitable consequences…"

I didn't listen to anymore. He could continue with his lecture, my lawyer, but if that was the strong point of my defense I had little to hope for. I thought of Martin, the little mistreated orphan, son of the Motherland, shot by firing squad; of Gosse, a brave and happy rogue shot by firing squad; of Tyrol, my faithful companion during our escape from Germany, arrested, probably shot by firing squad. Every one of them had survived the war only to be shot by firing squad and now it was my turn. I had already lost hope by the time my lawyer finished his speech. The jury retreated to its chamber to discuss my case. I looked around. The *gendarme* on guard duty was standing to attention; the judge was conversing with someone. In the first row of the public benches my mother patted her eyes with a handkerchief while my father stood, expressionless, at her side and behind them, a rabble of communist spectators waited, ready to applaud every 'guilty' verdict. The president of the jury returned with a paper in his hands as the other members silently took their places on the jurors' bench. The clerk of the court called for everyone to stand.

The president of the jury declared the verdict and sentence. "The accused is found guilty and sentenced to fifteen years imprisonment!"

I had trouble conceiving the length of such a time but knew it was far too long for me to survive being locked up in a cell.

"However," continued the president of the jury, at the end of the applause from the gleeful communists, "taking due account of the young age of the defendant, the punishment is commuted according to the following: internment in a juvenile reformatory until he reaches the age of majority."

The judge hammered again, impatient to proceed with the next case. "Guard, escort the prisoner from the room!"

I followed the *gendarme* on guard duty back to a waiting room where I was allowed a few minutes alone with my parents. Tears ran down my mother's cheeks; my father put a hand on my shoulder. I looked him straight in his eyes, proud that I was willing to take any punishment rather than betray him.

His face took on a puzzled look. "Why are you smiling Paul?"

I threw my arms around him, hugged him, as a son who had grown into a man.

Captivity

The carriage swayed with each rhythmic jolt on the rail joints. I sat between two *gendarmes*, handcuffed. It had been two days since the trial and, compared to those condemned to death, good fortune had been by my side. It would have been an ironic twist of fate to have faced a firing squad after surviving the battles at Körlin and Kolberg. Rather than facing execution by my own countrymen, I would, on reflection, have preferred to die an honourable death even if that meant at the hands of the Russians in a distant Siberian labour camp.

After a while, one of the *gendarmes* released my handcuffs. I rubbed my wrists and looked out of the window, focusing on the horizon. I felt at ease — no more bombs or strafing or stray bullets; the war really was over. I cast a last glance at my two guardian angels and then I closed my eyes.

We arrived at the Fresnes penitentiary in the depth of night. I was frisked once more and then, passed from guard to guard, led to a cell where there was already a figure asleep on a bunk. The key turned in the lock. I looked around, dejected, and then lay on the thin mattress on the floor.

The next morning, I came to know that the penitentiary was holding five times more inmates than the number allowed by the regulations and that my cell companion was a young and burly Alsatian.

The first days passed very slowly, the boredom made even more unbearable by the daily repetition of the sounds common to all prisons. At first I kept to myself while observing everything and everyone but as the days went by, I came to look forward to the meetings and collective discussions that were included in the rehabilitation programme. Despite the close contact with other inmates, I avoided the scuffles that broke out from time to time and steered clear of trouble.

Occupying a cell a little way down the corridor from mine, I recognized a familiar figure: it was Joseph Darnand, chief of the militia who had arrived one evening at Sennheim with his men. They shot him by firing squad in October. There were other important civilian and military personalities penned up at Fresnes the most famous, some might say infamous, of which occupied the cell opposite mine. This was Chief of Government at Vichy, Pierre Laval, who had signed the decree authorizing young Frenchmen to fight for the 'New Europe'. When he was taken from his cell, the warders treated him with respect. He walked ahead of them with tranquillity, wearing his black greatcoat and often with a foulard around his neck and a hat on his head. He paused often in front of the door of one cell or another, had the guards open the observation window, and then exchanged some encouraging word with the inmates. He was shot by firing squad a week after Darnand, in a prison courtyard, after having been escorted along the back of a building where all the inmates of that wing saw him. And so a rebellion rose up — prisoners at their windows shouted: "Vive Laval, to death the Beauharnais!" Others sang the *Marseillaise*. As for me, I didn't feel any emotion.

There was much gossip about Laval's execution; all were unanimous in saying that he stood bravely in front of the firing squad, shouting '*Vive la France*', but there were rumours that he had attempted to commit suicide by poison using a vial he had managed to keep hidden from his captors and was already moribund at the moment of the shooting.

After the execution of Laval, life in the prison continued as usual, except for a little problem that arose in my cell. I didn't bond very well with my cell companion, the Alsatian, and the situation worsened when I lost forty rations of bread while playing cards. To be without bread for all that time would have led me to the brink of starvation so I decided to resolve the matter with a bold strategy. When Alsatian requested his due, I hung a slice of bread on my ear and told him in a daring tone: "Come to take it if you want." I had risked my life at the Greifenberg and Sennheim bases for just a handful of rations so what did I have to lose here, in prison? At most I would register a few blows on my snout and nothing more, and this due to the fact that the Alsatian weighed over a hundred kilos. I braced myself for the Alsatian's attack. "I'll give you nothing!" I said, looking straight in his eyes. He hesitated, then turned his back and went to sit on his cot, content to eat only his own rations. I learned in that way an important lesson: courage and daring could overcome unfavorable situations.

❦—❦

Sometime later, together with other young men, I was transferred to the prison at Fontainebleau, to the rehabilitation center I.P.E.S. (Public Institution Center Supervision). Compared to Fresnes, this place was not too bad at all: it had a recreation room and a library and, when we went out for a stroll, they made us sing. It was like life at the German military bases more or less and this was probably because the director was a retired colonel. Although my stay at Fontainebleau was not as unpleasant as I had anticipated, events spiralled out of control at a ping-pong game during which I came to loggerheads with my opponent over an accusation that I had switched bats. Insults flew and then fists. I detested being ill-treated — especially if I knew I was right — and let fly a straight right followed by a left hook. The unfortunate fellow was taken by surprise and crumpled to the ground like a sack of potatoes and stayed there, unconscious. The straight right would have been sufficient, I judged in retrospect. There was of course an investigation into the incident and as a result I was called to stand before the colonel in charge. "There are two ways out of here," he said haughtily, "either with your head held high and free, or with handcuffs at your wrists and on the way back to Fresnes. The choice is yours."

"I would like you listen to my version..." I dared request.

"Silence!"

I sprang automatically to attention at the official's injunction."

"Very well! I see that you have learned something in the armed forces — at least you still have respect for discipline. Nevertheless you can expect to be punished. Your will lose your hair. Your head will be shaved. This is your punishment."

I recalled at that instant Martin and his stories about public institutions and his patient endurance of them, and the mistreatment he suffered. This was unjust treatment being meted out and I was determined not to be subjugated so easily. I felt the muscles on my face tighten with rage. "Never!"

"And why not?" he asked me, perplexed by my strong reaction.

"Because I know I'm right!"

"Ah, but in the German army they shaved off the hair of trouble makers, isn't that so?"

"Only for thieves and deserters and that before they were shot by firing squad."

The colonel looked straight into my eyes, somewhat surprised. He realized he had in front of him either a stubborn youngster or a fanatic, or both. "I authorize that your hair will be cut to three centimeters from the skull."

"Not at three, nor at anything at all," I answered, digging in my heels. I had forced his hand and I knew it.

"Before sundown I will see you with your hair shaved off. You will serve as an example for the others who think they can behave as they wish."

I escaped the same evening with another of the inmates by jumping over the perimeter wall. We headed towards Paris but we were without money and personal documents: a difficult thing to explain if we were stopped and asked for proof of identity. I said goodbye to the companion who went out from Station East and I jumped on a train for Nancy, avoiding the ticket inspectors by stepping onto the platform when the train stopped at stations to mix with the crowds then getting inside the carriage again. I got off at Longwy and arrived home at Villerupte-Cantebonne where my family had by now returned. I knocked on the door in the depth of night and it was my father who came downstairs to open it. He was dismayed when he saw me at the entrance, trembling in the cold of the night.

"I escaped," I apologized.

"Come in, quickly." He closed the door, after casting a glance to the left and right, making sure nobody had seen us. My mother came to hug me and then brought me fresh clothes and hot soup. We talked for a long time that night but in the end, there was only one way to avoid being sent to back prison: I still had uncles and paternal grandparents in a small village in the vicinity of Pescara, in Italy.

It was still dark when my mother packed a small suitcase with spare clothes and underwear. "Your Italian family will receive you well," she assured me.

"As soon as you arrive at the village ask for your grandfather, Gildo. Everybody knows him," said my father.

"Tell them only that you are the son of the Frenchman and keep everything else about you to yourself," my mother added.

I said goodbye to them before dawn and then I took the train to Marseille. By that time the war had been over for about a year.

La Dolce Vita

I arrived at Menton, a few kilometers from Ventimiglia, by bus and without delay left the town at my back and began the hike along a difficult trail that led away from the main road towards the Maritime Alps. At the border, marked by a bar with white and black stripes spanning the roadway beside a small wooden hut, nobody came forward to stop me so I stepped around it setting foot in Italy. The descent on the Ligurian slope was rather dangerous because of mine fields: warning signs with the writing *'Minen'* were scattered everywhere. At the side of the winding, downhill trail, I saw the desiccated corpse of a German soldier, still completely dressed, with his helmet, cartridge cases and bayonet. He lay there on those heights fronting the sea, his hollow eye sockets directed at the azure Italian sky.

Farther down the slope, there was a wire stretched across the path. As I straddled it, a movement several hundred meters lower down the winding path caught my eye: it was a figure in uniform, climbing up. I couldn't risk encountering a border guard so made for a rock at the side of the path but unfortunately found that my intended hiding place offered insufficient concealment from someone passing on the nearby path and it was too late to find a better one. I looked around hoping to find a solution to my predicament and saw that on the ground there were many unexploded mortar grenades. I crept towards the nearest one and tentatively picked it up to throw it towards the steep trail. It landed against a rock jutting out from the dry scrub and exploded with a roar that shook the mountain and echoed from the rock faces of the surrounding cliffs. I looked down and, amidst the smoke and the dust, caught sight of the fleeing guard, running with the speed and agility of a wild goat. I continued downhill through deep gorges hidden from the sun until the vast sweep of the sparkling Mediterranean Sea opened up in front of me.

At the first houses of Ventimiglia, I ventured into a vegetable garden to pick small green tomatoes to stave off my growing hunger as the sun beat on my head like a physical weight. I unbuttoned my shirt to allow the warm air to waft over my skin and breathed deeply, savouring the scents of flowers unknown to me, savouring too my freedom.

It took me another couple of days to travel the several hundred kilometers to the Adriatic Coast. The trains travelled very slowly and, at the stations and bridges destroyed by bombs, buses were utilized for an alternative service. From there, after another day of waiting, I managed to sneak onto a cargo train, lying on the straw of a wagon for animal transportation; it wasn't the first time I had travelled in such a way and so caused me no great discomfort, in fact I found the journey rather pleasant.

Having left Pescara, I finally arrived at the small village of my ancestors. The first person I encountered was my aunt, my father's sister. In a flash the news spread to the entire village and, after a few minutes, many inhabitants came to crowd up in front of my grandfather's house. He was a fine figure of a man, one meter and ninety centimeters tall, an ex-paramilitary policeman. He threw his arms around my neck, as did my grandmother who, showering me with kisses, seemed reluctant to let go of me. Curious villagers queued to peer through the window simply to catch a glimpse of me. "The French, the French," they said, "the Frenchman has arrived."

The villagers too welcomed me with warmth and enthusiasm, as if I were a prodigal son, and many invited me to their houses for dinner, impatient to talk to me, to know more about France. So I became everyone's friend and, in less than two months, I even learned the local dialect. In the evening, sitting in the still warm sunshine with my grandparents and relatives on the doorstep, I told them about life in Lorena and about my father. Then my grandfather lit his pipe and began to recount an incident that took place as the Germans were retreating. "They often stopped by your Uncle Francesco's workshop to repair trucks and cars," my grandfather explained. "Understand me well — he didn't help them because of his political ideas, he did it solely because it was another job, a professional duty. So, you'll know already that the shop is right in front of the train station and a that a small train is in service, going through the valleys, stopping from time to time. Well, one evening some German soldiers got off a train to drink with the stationmaster who was always arguing his wife because she complained about him lifting his elbow too often. A soldier wanted the company of a woman and the stationmaster, without worrying, pointed out his wife's bedroom. This woman, poor soul, repulsed the German and yelling at the top of her voice, escaped through a window. Enraged, the drunken soldier went downstairs, protesting and threatening the stationmaster who somehow managed to calm the soldier and drank with him until morning and then, more drunk than the soldier, pointed to your uncle's house." My grandfather took a pause to clean his pipe. "And to think that your aunt had sent her two sons, one six years old and the other fourteen, here to us earlier that morning — and she was supposed to come too."

"Francesco was already at work, busy with the forge," my grandmother said, wiping her eyes with a polka dot handkerchief.

Grandfather continued, "Your aunt was making the beds and when she saw the drunken German soldier in front of her, she screamed. Francesco went upstairs in a hurry with a long iron plier in his hands and slammed it on the soldier's head a couple of times. This soldier, furious, pushed your uncle into the kitchen and defended himself by crashing a terracotta flower vase on your uncle's head."

"Your aunt went out in the street yelling for help but nobody wanted to listen, nobody rushed over," my grandmother added, raising her hands to the sky.

"The German, once on the street, headed toward an armoured car from a convoy that was passing by at that moment. He reported to the officer that partisan rebels had attacked him. Behind the soldier, your aunt was crying, trying to explain what happened. The officer ordered a search of the house and the arrest of the partisans." My grandfather patted his pipe on the open palm of his hand.

"My poor son in the meantime got upright and, as best as he could, was able to walk fifty steps into the vineyard," my grandmother said, sighing.

My grandfather's strong hand wiped away the tears that had gathered on his lower lids. "He raised his hands high but they shot him there, on the spot, under the eyes of your aunt."

"The paramilitary policemen, German and Italian officers came but...too late," grandmother said, muffling her crying with the handkerchief at her mouth.

"They verified the facts and said they would punish the guilty soldier but that coward joined the convoy...by now he will be free, I imagine."

"And to think that my poor Francesco had gone through the Greek and Albanian campaigns and came back safe and sound, without a scratch," said my grandmother.

"He was well-liked by everybody," affirmed my grandfather, "now your aunt is widowed and her older son is running the shop."

I remained there, listening without interrupting them, respecting their pain, in spite of being hardened to atrocities by my experience of war.

At a dinner with my aunt one evening, my cousin pulled me aside. "Paul, the Germans that killed my father are guilty," he whispered at my ear, "but the guiltier one is him," he added, pointing in the direction of the train station.

⚜—⚜

Life was sweet in that small Italian village. The food was simple but all the more delicious for that simplicity with polenta, oil, olives, cheese and crispy bread. The wine, furthermore, was a specialty and I smoked *Macedonia* and *Nazionali Semplici* cigarettes. Unfortunately this *dolce vita* lasted only until the winter of 1946-1947 — the officials at the municipal hall and the paramilitary policemen couldn't hide their suspicions and, because I had no passport, I was left with no other option but to leave my idyllic lifestyle behind.

Early one morning, between tears and glasses of wine, I said good bye to my Italian relatives and took the train, paying the ticket as far as Rimini. From there on I would rely on good luck.

After Rimini, in the compartment where I had found a seat, the travellers were talking loudly, laughing and singing — until the arrival of the ticket inspector. All of them presented their stubs, except the fellow sitting next to me, who had been the most vocal, fanatical singer but was now, all of a sudden, deaf and mute.

"Your ticket! You must pay the ticket, sir. If you don't have it, I can provide one for you," the inspector said, waiting patiently but in vain for an answer. He scribbled the amount on a form and held it in front of the fake deaf-mute who now gave the appearance of having become suddenly blind. "Your ticket, sir," he then asked me, tired of waiting for a response from my fellow traveller.

I couldn't imitate the comedy the Italian traveller had masterfully demonstrated and after an instant of feigned bewilderment I said: "*Je ne comprend pas.*"

"What, what? I don't understand this language," blurted the poor inspector, on the verge of losing his patience.

"*Je ne comprend pas*," I repeated, sure of having found a brilliant cop-out. The fake deaf-mute and blind fellow gave me a glance of admiration while the others started a contest to guess my nationality once the inspector left the compartment.

The ticket inspector returned after a few minutes accompanied by a paramilitary policeman who said: "So, where is this lad that doesn't want to pay for his ticket?"

The spectators simultaneously nodded in my direction, hoping no doubt to prolong the show.

"*Bonjour!*" I said respectfully. "I don't understand Italian," I explained, talking in French.

"Ah! French!" he exclaimed jovially, with a happiness that gave his eyes a sparkle. "I was in Nice for two years during the war and can speak a bit your language." He smiled enthusiastically at the idea to be able to exchange a few words with me. "Forget about the ticket, he is a Frenchman and the French have won the war," he explained to the inspector.

He invited me to the guard's van at the rear of the train where I found three colleagues of his enjoying a snack of bread, cheese, slices *mortadella* and a bottle of wine. I was treated like a guest of honour and at the end of the meal they offered me cigarettes that I smoked with them until we reached Bologna. There, the policeman accompanied me to the train for Genoa and explained to the ticket inspector that he should treat me well because I was French and not to worry about the ticket. I thanked him and then we said goodbye as if we were two comrades-in- arms.

At Genoa, matters were more problematic, not because of the Italian authorities but because of the strictness of the French ones. There were French military personnel deployed at every exit of the Italian station. I didn't attempt to hide my nationality when they questioned me and they took me to their command post where I told another false story and they let me go. That night I slept in a depot together with several Italian immigrants who intended to return to their houses in France, which they had left in 1940 and 1941. I remained in Genoa for a couple of days, wandering along the narrow streets in the old quarters. In those alleyways the black market prospered: eight or ten years old kids sold a bit of everything including cigarettes of all brands and American and English tobacco.

Mixed up with the Italian immigrants, I headed to the border but I was stopped because of my lack of documents. The French custom officers maintained that I was Italian and the Italian authorities insisted that, without the shadow of a doubt, I was French. At every hour I was sent from one side to the other but there were always obstacles complicating my situation. In the end, the Italian officials, since I came from Pescara, took care of me, handing me coupons to use in the city and a little money for my daily needs. They told me to wait. But wait for what? I had formed in my mind a precise and malign idea about the workings of the French administration and so took the bus until Ventimiglia where I climbed again the Italian slopes, hiking in the opposite direction along the trail that I had used to enter Italy. When I came to the corpse of the German soldier, I saluted him, and descended to Menton, on the French side of the border.

I arrived back home to a dramatic welcome. "The police come in search of you almost every day," my parents informed me. After another night spent in discussions, given that I didn't want to impose my presence on my family for more than a few days, we decided that the best thing for me to do would be to reach Portugal, a country that had remained neutral throughout the war.

A Brief Visit to Spain

Once more, I took a train to Marseille and from there headed to the west, to Perpignan and then to Le Boulou, close to the Spanish border. Seeing that it was impossible to cross the border undetected on the road, I decided to hike over the Pyrenees hills into Spain but after following a line of summits, found that I had become disoriented and so was forced to spend the night under the stars, sheltered by some rocks and by my suitcase. The following day I kept going, hoping that I was already on Spanish soil. All of a sudden, after crossing a plateau, a strong gust of wind snatched the suitcase from my hand and tossed it over a cliff. And then the wind stopped as suddenly as it began, a change that was accompanied by a dramatic drop in temperature. As night fell, so too did snowflakes. Compelled to sleep in the open again, I sheltered under the overhang of a rock, piling up as much gravel as possible around me, my teeth chattering, my hands blue with cold. I was scared. For the first time in my life, I seriously feared the forces of nature.

In the morning I resumed my march, still trembling in the bitter cold, sliding continuously on the snow with shoes unsuited to the terrain. Finally, out in the distance, down in a valley, I saw the glint of sun reflected from distant slate roofs. I kept them in my sight as I trudged onwards. Dragging my wet feet, I knocked on the door of the first house, tired and hungry. An old-timer let me in and, realizing my miserable condition, pointed to the burning logs in the fireplace. While I was drying myself up he prepared a bowl of milk with a trace of coffee and a piece of bread and then he went out. When he returned, I thanked him as I was about to leave and asked for the direction to Portugal. Without ever talking, he indicated a pebbly trail. Just as I was about to pass the last of the houses of that remote village, two guards appeared on the path, apparently in the area by chance.

※—※

The Spanish prison at Figueres was small and dark. The guards made me sit on a chair with a seat made of interwoven straw, in a small room like the cell where I had just spent a couple of hours waiting. On the wall, hung a portrait of Generalissimo Franco.

"*Clandestino o bracero migratorio?*" a young officer asked, resting his jack-booted heels on a dusty table while a guard stood at his side. On a corner of the table, hand-stamps with wooden handles stood on a stack of yellowed papers.

"*Clandestino,*" I answered. *No point in lying*, I thought, *since this would simply have further aggravated my situation.*

"*El motivo?*" he asked me, calmly lighting up a cigarette, staring at the match's feeble flame before it died out.

I waited till he could take a first puff. "Political reasons."

"*Obrero?*"

"*Sì,*" I said after a moment of hesitation. Certainly, I could describe myself as a worker, a carpenter after helping my father build houses. The officer asked nothing more. I was taken to a cell to wait where the village chicken thief and two drunkards took turns to keep me company during the following days. After these inmates, I had the pleasure of the company of three men in uniform who wore shoes with triple soles and big rings on their fingers — veterans from the *Legión Azul* that had fought on the Russian front. After they returned to Spain, they had enlisted in the Police Corps but had been a bit too rough with somebody and so were in trouble. Together, we were transferred to the prison at Girona. There, at the command post of the *Guardia Civil*, things changed for the worse; the veterans' hair was shaved but, thanks to local rules, the guards didn't touch me because I was a foreigner. Besides the usual routine of form filling, they took my fingerprints. In my cell, I asked the veterans about the efficiency of the Spanish police and I was told that they were usually well-informed. At my inevitable interrogation, I decided then to dish out the truth and, besides my personal data, gave them the address of my parents. Under the line headed 'offence' they wrote: *illegal border crossing*.

Spanish language was not an obstacle for me in that prison because there were many French and German prisoners who had been condemned in absentia by their respective tribunals and had sought the protection of the last fascist bastion in Europe. In fact, I became friendly with a fellow called Franz, who was about twenty years older than me and had been an agent of the Gestapo in Marseille during the war and for this had been condemned to death *in absentia*. The Spanish inmates were mostly republicans and they talked often about friends and parents who found shelter in France, after fleeing Spain in 1938.

In prison, kitchen, infirmary, library and administration duties were reserved for the Spanish prisoners while more menial jobs were carried out by foreign prisoners. I remained indifferent to that life: they didn't do anything bad to me and besides the months spent in waiting, I couldn't complain much except that the lack of money forced me to sharpen my wits in order to get some cigarettes. After the usual maize flour, the daily fried fish and the *chusco* (a form of bread distributed every day) a good smoke was always welcome. The daily stroll in the courtyard offered a blue sky, space and the opportunity to dream.

One day Silvino, a Spanish cellmate who had committed fraud and who had relatives in Tolosa, where he had spent a brief period working, remarked, "The walls are very tall."

"*Ja*, too tall," I answered with a sigh. I liked his company. Silvino was a big youngster and a little older than I. He had a straightforward manner and was alert and athletic — the ideal type in case of need.

"I can't stand those guards on the towers," said Silvino.

"One at every corner, nothing escapes their sight, both inside and outside."

"And yet there should be a way...to escape, I mean."

I too had thought about escaping but initially dismissed this thought because I only had to wait a while longer, just the time necessary for the verifications of my statements — Spanish justice worked well but very slowly. Even the walls encircling the internal yard were very tall. Substantial dressed stones, long and short in alternation, supported the portico's vaults and the other sides of the L-shaped main building. A massive wooden door, reinforced by heavy, flat iron plates and studs, barred the exit from the internal courtyard. The entry on the other hand, was at the center of the main building and was guarded for every moment of the day. And then there was a church which a bell tower that protruded from the roof. The priest, incidentally, represented both religion and the nationalist party and as a consequence exercised authority on warders' promotions, working conditions and on the situation of all inmates, who assiduously attended Sunday mass. I detested hypocrisy and neither I nor Silvino, nor any of the German inmates, visited the church.

I got involved in a fight over a card game...again.

Franz, as we took our exercise in the courtyard, told me, "You must hold back the impulses of youth."

"That crook was cheating," I explained.

"You lose and you win, it goes like that with cards, but was it necessary to throw blows in his face? Was it a surprise to you that he called the guard for help?"

"It was a question of principle," I said, "and it won everyone's respect."

"You really think so?"

Franz had the ability to make me think beyond the obvious, like a mentor who analysed my behaviour and offered impartial judgement. "What do you think I should do?"

"Self-criticism will help you make the correct decision whatever the situation."

"It's faster using my fists," I said.

"You mean it's more difficult to use your head," said Franz.

I thought for a moment. "Maybe."

"Paul, you are young and you prefer the physical solution to problems. You have a talent for this…it bursts out of your body. One can immediately notice this in your personality and it comes in handy, doesn't it?"

"Up until now, yes."

"The only thing you lack is the concentration and self-control to keep yourself calm. Only when you master this will you be ready to break out."

I was shocked by Franz's knowledge of my plan to escape, which I had discussed only with Silvino. "How do you know about my plan?"

A faint smile came to Franz's lips. "It doesn't take much for someone like me to guess your intentions," he said, looking at me with his sky-blue eyes.

"Do you want to come with us?" I asked him.

"I don't even think about it. I'm too old for acrobatic feats, I prefer to wait," said Franz.

"Not me! I've spent eight months here and I'm sick of the sight of these walls, I recognize them stone by stone and I hate that trumpet call in the morning, it seems to make fun of us."

"It is an impertinent sound, you are right."

Keeping a certain distance from the other inmates, we walked for a few more minutes in the courtyard.

"Have you thought out your plan?" Franz asked.

"I was thinking of going over the roofs…it's the only way I can see."

"And at what point are you with the preparation?"

"The preparation?" I repeated, caught off guard.

"You don't want to escape without first having tried a dry run, I hope?"

"Dry run?"

"It's important to be sure you will not find obstacles at the last moment…have you given thought to this?"

I shook my head.

"Paul, think hard about what you have in mind. As far as I am aware, nobody has been able to escape from here. There are too many walls, and once outside, there are yet more

walls…all Girona is encircled by walls. Do you think you can pull it off? It will take not only enormous physical but also mental strength to succeed in this attempt."

The one-hour exercise period was about to expire and we marched through the door that lead into the internal courtyard to go our separate ways at the porticos, towards our cells.

The 'dry run' went smoothly with Silvino picking the lock of our cell door to gain access to the first floor corridor linking the main building with the secondary wing, enabling us to select an escape route. This was to be a window in a corner where the corridor made a turn towards the block holding the female prisoners. On the night of our escape attempt, we waited for the right moment. As soon as the beam from the searchlight passed our chosen window, I opened it and swung my legs over the sill. Then, turning my body so that my stomach was now on the sill, I searched for the narrow ledge — about a meter below — with my feet. This manoeuver had to be performed quickly, before the window was again lit by the searchlight. Two meters away was the outside corner of the building and a cast-iron downpipe connected to the gutter. Pressed flat against the wall, I ran my hands over the stonework feeling for finger holds as I edged along the ledge towards the downpipe. Silvino followed like a shadow. Clinging to the downpipe, I climbed a few meters up to the point where it joined the roof gutter. This was a critical point in our escape attempt — a missed grasp, a moment's hesitation and it would be the end. I threw myself outward, hooking my fingers over the edge of the gutter, my body dangling in the air, and then swung to and fro until I had sufficient momentum to raise a foot onto it. After a desperate heave, I found myself lying at the edge of the roof. When Silvino's leg appeared on the gutter, I grabbed his belt to help pull him up. As planned, we made for the ridge of the roof so we could easily alternate between the two slopes to avoid the beams from the searchlights on opposite sides of the prison's perimeter.

Silvino pressed on my arm. "Look…there, in the wing."

We were at the same height as a window on another block from which a political inmate was observing us. "Guards. Guards. Alarm!" the inmate shouted.

"What do we do, Paul?"

"We are almost there Silvino. Keep going, they won't catch us."

As we reached the church's bell tower, the siren began to wail.

Silvino let himself down onto a building with a lower roof. Ignoring every precaution I caught up with him, jumping from one roof to the next, losing height, until we were low enough to risk leaping down to a garden. A dog barked furiously. We climbed a chain-link fence and sprinted across a vegetable garden and then through a wooden gate leading to a side street. Silvino came to an abrupt halt after a few strides to turn back to close the gate which was squeaking on its hinges before we continued onwards to reach the cover of a retaining wall. Hearts pounding, we paused to consider our situation.

"Did you see him, Paul?"

There was a sentry at a crossroads a little way ahead. "They're already out hunting us."

The dog's insistent barking, the siren's scream, the intersecting lights from the search-lights and the shouting of orders combined to stir my instinct to run away as far as possible, but the sentry was still there, blocking our way. The bedlam lasted for about ten minutes before calm returned, broken only by distant voices.

"They're in position, now," I grumbled.

There was dismay in Silvino's voice. "We're surrounded. They'll have all the city's gates shut by now. It's impossible to go through."

"Not if we go over the walls," I said.

"If they see us they'll start a target shooting fiesta."

"That damned politico!" I exclaimed. "He sold us out."

"Bastard republican, he'll pick up a reward for sure."

"*Ja!* The devil's tail is always in our way."

"It's pure folly to keep on going, Paul."

"It was a good try," I sighed.

We hid under a timber deck in front of a house until dawn; a few precious hours of freedom and fresh air. When a guard spotted us, we crawled out immediately and raised our hands. Followed by the disapproving stares of civilian onlookers, we were led back to prison under the watchful eyes of an armed escort.

Silvino was subjected to blows on his head and kicks in his ribs from the guards. I waited for my ration of punches but they simply threw me into a small cell with a heavy door and left. I soon discovered that the cell was too short to allow me to stretch out on the floor. Although there was a skylight in the ceiling it was impossible to reach it by bracing myself between the walls to climb because they were a little too far apart. An electric lamp cast a dim yellow glow, even during daytime.

In the late afternoon, the sound of steps echoed in the corridor. The cell door opened and in walked the director of the prison and four warders. He cast a disdainful glance at me as he fluttered a copy of the town's newspaper in my face. A headline reported the news of the first successful attempt to break out from that famous prison. "What did you gain, eh? Did you think you were in a *Lager*? Were you ill-treated here? What a gratitude! What a reward for you and me," he yelled in a voice that was becoming hoarse. He kicked the cell door and left, cursing loudly. Two days later he was relieved from his post and temporarily substituted by the administrator.

A Tempting Offer

A man in his sixties, well-dressed with greatcoat, hat and black gloves, entered the office in which the warders had me waiting. He looked at me from head to toe, went around me and then, at his slight nod, the warders left, closing the door without much noise. "Take a seat," the well-dressed man said, indicating a cushioned, leather chair. I obeyed. "I come from Madrid, I am the inspector general, responsible for police and guard personnel. I want a precise description of your escape," he said, taking a seat on a couch in front of a desk.

I explained every detail, every step of my escape attempt.

"Impossible," he muttered to himself after listening with the greatest attention.

"They caught us out of the prison, no?" I said timidly.

"I have an important and confidential proposition," he said suddenly, after a brief pause.

"A proposition?" I asked, failing to conceal my surprise.

"You can speak French, German, Italian and you have made incredible progress in our language. In short, you have received an education tailored to our requirements and you are not alien to risks and the use of weapons." He paused to look into my eyes. "What would you think if you could obtain Spanish citizenship, a bright career and a good future in the service of our Generalissimo's government?"

"A career?" I was dazed by the surprizing turn of events.

"As an inspector at the port of Barcelona."

"It is…it is a very good proposition."

"Mull it over, you can give your answer to the governor of the city…he has been informed about this matter."

I was taken back to the confinement cell where I had time to ponder the unexpected opportunity. Spanish citizenship, freedom, beautiful girls, a good job, money to spend, it was almost too good to be true. I was flattered. Of course I harboured some doubts. Police inspector…hmmm…this was too good to be true. And what specifically was the job on offer?

Two days later I was returned to my normal cell and during the exercise period, I told Franz about the fabulous proposition and asked for his advice.

"Listen to me carefully and then you will have a deeper idea than you have in your head right now," he said. He cleared his throat and, giving the right emphasis to every word, began, "So you *think* it would be an interesting career, the one they are offering you…very convenient. It means a beautiful life, free to go where you want, or more precisely, to go where others cannot because of the limitations imposed by law. But think carefully about it…what type of work will it involve? Spy at the port…the underworld…searching among delinquents or assassins and all the gamut of their associates? You will never be able to free yourself from these. Once you accept this proposal it is for your entire life. And then, if one day you are not useful anymore…a simple accident will get rid of you."

"Hum!" As usual Franz was showing me the downside of the matter.

"Think well, Paul. I talk from personal experience. This type of work will absorb you more and more, and you will lose your power to decide things for yourself. This is precisely the type of work that has brought me to this prison."

"But it's different for you…you are here because of the lost war."

"Not that different Paul. Listen, your case is not that serious. You have an alternative… if you refuse the offer they will send you back to France."

"And how will I deal with the French police?"

"You will do that little time remaining from your sentence in some halfway-house and then you will be free like the wind, no more prison, no more delinquents. And you will be the master of your life. You wanted my advice…I have given it to you as if I were talking to a son. The decision is yours to make." He wandered off, enjoying the rest of the free hour.

My refusal of the offer left the Governor of Girona quite surprised. I explained to him that I simply wanted to go back home. He told me that the police enquiry had been completed and that everything they discovered about me matched my original deposition. Nothing, he said, impeded my release.

The next day, an agent from the French Consulate came to hand me a diplomatic visa that would allow me to cross the border into France. There, having left my *Guardia Civil* escort behind in Spain, I was interviewed by French journalists who were curious to know how life was in a Spanish prison — the quality of food and other little details. Desperate to begin my journey home, I answered in monosyllables, apologizing for my haste.

At home, I found that my parents looked aged, tired, and more anxious than I remembered them. Without knowing where I was, they had suffered continual visits from the *gendarmes* and so, in order to give them some tranquillity, I decided to give myself up to the police.

"You have to have a serious reason to turn yourself in. Do you have one?" the *gendarme* on duty laughed but as soon as I revealed my identity, he hurried to fill in all the necessary forms.

The Madhouse

I was immediately sent to the prison at Neufchâteau, close to Nancy, and then transferred to the isle of Belle-Île-en-Mer, off the coast of Brittany, in the Bay of Biscay, between Quiberon and Saint-Nazaire. *From there,* I thought, *every attempt to escape would have been in vain, given the fourteen kilometers of sea to swim in order to reach the nearest coast.*

When I arrived in that prison, I couldn't believe my eyes. In the courtyard, amongst the crowd, I recognized some young comrades from the base at Greifenberg. "Papis!" I called out.

"Paul!" he exclaimed, coming towards me. We flung our arms around each other's neck, laughing.

"It's a pleasure to see you alive!" I said.

"And I thought you had fallen into the Popov's hands! We have all the time we need to talk in here, eh?"

I spent every free moment in the company of my friend, exchanging information. He too knew about the shooting by firing squad of Martin and Gosse at Bad Reichenhall but knew nothing of Jean and De Ville. "There was tremendous confusion in those last days, after you lost contact with us. We were fighting an advance unit of Russian infantry. De Ville couldn't keep our section together. Some fell, hit by fire from the T34s. La Journisse and others who had been wounded and unable to walk, preferred to stay where they were, hoping for medical care. After the last aerial attack, we mixed in with a column of retreating soldiers by jumping into the backs of passing trucks, some on one, some on the next, anywhere there was room to squeeze in, and so we lost sight of each other. The rest you know — the Americans, then the French and the guilty verdict."

I told him of my adventures, which he listened to avidly together with a small group of ex-comrades who found the description of my escape from the fortress of Girona highly amusing. We worked together at Le Palais, as the building was called, canning sardines and were subjected to boring preaching from incompetent 'educators' but when we had free time, we exchanged recollections from our days of combat at Körlin and Kolberg, talking often about friends who had fallen.

"Look where we ended up…among delinquents of all sorts," I observed bitterly one day. For no apparent reason my anger had swelled to bursting point and I knocked down a colossus of a man on duty at the infirmary and then I scuffled with one from the *Kriegsmarine*, an ex-boxing champion whom I flattened with a direct right, much to the astonishment of the onlookers.

Without warning, I was transferred to another correctional institute for apprenticeship training. I chose to be a bricklayer but life among my fellow apprentices was certainly not easy; among the convicts there were murderers, thieves, burglars, crooks, mad sex-maniacs and freaks with delusions of grandeur. Gradually, our degree of freedom was increased from nil to semi-controlled but we were still treated like beasts — except by a few warders who had been prisoners of war in Germany and who understood my internal dilemma. I would rather have served twenty years in prison with my comrades from the front than suffer the constant exposure to life's riff-raff. Soon, I forgot all Franz's advice and answered provocations with my fists and prepared for this by lifting weights in the gym, boxing, playing ping-pong and tumbling on the trampoline. I was at the apex of my physical strength and in good health…all I lacked was freedom.

The place was a madhouse. To avoid work, it was not uncommon for inmates to inflict wounds on themselves. A fifteen-year-old took exception to an ex-inmate, who had returned as an instructor to the arts and trades school with the goal of helping the convicts, and cut his throat — a rash, senseless act. Sooner or later it seemed to me, everyone was driven crazy by that place.

One of the warders — an ex-prisoner of war — confided in me one day, offering me a cigarette. "Do you know, Paul, I can say that the Germans treated me better than how we must treat you here, but these are the rules, we cannot make exceptions."

Mostly, the warders were incapable of imposing their will, of giving orders and earning respect. That place was a madhouse from which I felt I had to escape to preserve my sanity, even if only for a few days. And so I came up with a plan to abscond with a fellow inmate, knowing full well that we would soon be recaptured and when that happened, we were locked up in punishment cells and beaten to a pulp. In my cell, three warders entered, each with a whip of ox sinew in his hand. With all their strength they cracked the whip on my back as I tried to protect myself in a corner, screaming at each cutting sting of leather before fainting. I stayed there for a day, on the floor, incapable of moving and bleeding from my wounds. Seething with fury, I swore to myself that I would never again tolerate such inhumane treatment and woe to anyone who dared lift a hand against me. I was ready to kill.

I survived a month in those solitary conditions: rations came once a day but sometimes only after two. Once out of confinement, after receiving certification as a bricklayer, I broke the jaw of an arrogant convict who thought he was big enough to get away with insulting me. For this I was pulled in front of the prison's director who, I sensed as he circumnavigated me in his office, was thinking of pulling me by the ear. "Touch me and I'll kill you!" I raged. He was a tough man who loved tough action but he stepped back at my warning.

"It seems that the fellow you hit has a long stay in infirmary ahead of him," the director told me, "with a tube to allow for nourishment."

"His business," I answered.

My call-up papers for the French Army arrived when I was still in the punishment cell. This was a sort of blessing, considering the circumstances, which allowed me to leave prison behind to join the French Army with the first contingent of 1949. *Better to be in military service than locked up in correctional institutes*, I thought at the moment of my release. At Marseille, during the instruction period, I felt as if I had been reborn. I was issued with a Mauser — at that time a standard issue for the French Army — and practiced firing again with German and Italian mortars, the model with the round plate at the base.

At the beginning of training, an instructor invited us to disassemble the Mauser, as he had just demonstrated. When my turn came, not only did I dismantle the butt plate, the trigger, the bolt and the chamber but other components as well, laying all the pieces neatly on the desk. As I was about to go back to my bench, the instructor asked me to reassemble the whole thing because nobody else could. Training at the Sennheim base had been immeasurably more thorough.

Instruction continued with the 80mm mortars, which to me were very familiar. Days were spent orienteering and marching. On seeing me hesitate at a jump from an embankment, a sergeant major urged me on. I performed a backward somersault, landing perfectly on my feet, leaving him agape but from that moment he detested me. To amuse my comrades, I took to the habit of performing the same jump from ground floor windows to their applause. During training I bonded well with a giant of a man called Armand, strong like a bull, a true force of nature but not at all violent. As a civilian he was a photographer and he had brought with him a case containing all the equipment needed to develop photographs. On one occasion, while he was developing photos under the cover of the blankets, a recruit fell on Armand's bed after a scuffle, ruining the entire process. Armand picked him up and threw him four cots away, having finally lost his patience. After the dull swearing-in ceremony, because we didn't have any relatives visiting, Armand and I took a stroll downtown to a bar where we discovered an Armenian kid threatening other recruits with a rifle. I disarmed the Armenian without difficulty, a feat that won Armand's admiration, even though the weapon was found to be unloaded.

I was attached to the NCO course and so the instruction became more intense but this activity was interrupted one day by a service note that had absolute priority. It was read over the loudspeaker: "...for this reason we strongly encourage every soldier. Step forward, volunteers! Go fight in Vietnam! You will receive eight days leave immediately and then you will be assigned to the Colonial Infantry at Fréjus camp." The list of benefits followed. I went to sign up and then I asked Armand if he was tempted by the offer.

"I can't, Paul, I'm not like you. I'm not too fond of combat, and then…well…you need a certain type of character for that kind of work."

We said goodbye the same evening; a sad occasion. Our captain, from Nancy, congratulated me, the only one from his company to accept that inviting offer.

A Change of Mind

At home I had ample time to consider my situation. So, I would be fighting the Indochinese, killing the Viet Minh, all according to the law. This time I hoped the politicians weren't mistaken; I had already suffered enough tribulations for being enlisted in a regular army.

The period of leave passed quickly. At Fréjus camp, training included nocturnal assaults with live ammunition, defusing of mines, firing new sub-machine guns, hand to hand combat and guerrilla tactics. The majority of junior officers and instructors had first-hand experience of the battlefield; some had followed De Gaulle with the Free French Forces, some had fought in Libya, in Germany and in Italy. I was at ease in that camp where I could breathe fresh air but was always uncomfortably hungry. Naturally, small inconveniences were not lacking; a sergeant-instructor who trained recruits to fight with blades demonstrated his skill by throwing onto the ground whoever closed in on him. Usually a recruit shows a certain respect while hitting a superior despite the order to do so, but that swashbuckler was taking advantage of the situation, humiliating everyone. So, when my turn came, I evened things up a little. I charged as I had done at Körlin against the Russians, with my anger raised almost to boiling point. The sergeant avoided my bayonet by a centimeter, but he was not fast enough to dodge the magazine of my sub-machine gun which I slammed in his face as my knee caught him in the stomach. He bent over, collapsing to the ground and, after feeling the blood on his face, got up again with a great effort, gasping pathetically. With a broken-winded and hoarse voice he pointed to me and said to recruits, "So have you seen? This is what you must learn to do." After a few minutes he suspended training for the day.

In order to quell the hatred in that sergeant's eyes I agreed to meet him one evening behind the barracks to settle the matter. At the muster the following morning he had a rounder head, puffier cheeks and a black and blue face.

As luck would have it, I badly sprained my foot in a fall during gymnastics. To recover, I was given three weeks home leave plus a supplementary one. Then I met a beautiful girl who convinced me to change my decision to volunteer to go to Indochina. Her words were, in short, more or less the following: Paul, it is all right to be a mercenary and to kill, it is your duty, but have you ever thought your enemy could do the same to you? Up till now you have been very skilled or lucky but one bullet is enough to end it all.

When I returned to Fréjus, I asked for a breach of contract, even though my name was on the list of the next to graduate and so they sent me, for disciplinary measures, to Gabes in Tunisia. There I couldn't avoid a fist fight with two African kitchen hands — at their expenses of course. As a consequence a lieutenant threatened to lock me up in a confinement cell. "I will throw you in and you will stay there until the end of your draft," he shouted in my face.

"Private I am and as such I'll come out," I answered him.

A puzzled look came over the lieutenant's face. "What do you mean by that?"

"Simply this — I'm ready to write to the president of the republic to tell him that in here we starve."

The lieutenant lost his cool. "In here, everyone gets equal rations. What the administration allocates, we divide equally."

"The army doesn't have enough food to feed me so I will ask to be sent home," I replied curtly.

The lieutenant didn't insist further; he understood that it was not worth risking exposure of the food trafficking organization he had set up with great care. He was in cahoots with a sergeant who spoke Arabic. They regularly ran the route Gabes-Medenine-Fezzan in the Libyan Desert with military trucks loaded with food originally earmarked for us. From that day on, I was treated much better at the mess.

The visit of a captain, who was the director of the military sport section in Tunis, changed my routine for the better. When I was accepted at the sports center, I jumped for joy. The company of Maltese, Italians and Tunisians, the flavour of spicy tomato sauce, the taste of grilled sausages seasoned with rare spices and the perfumes and exotic smells of the city completed the image I had of the Tunisian capital. At last, I felt perfectly at ease.

My time was spent training in various disciplines and I agreed to a boxing match with a local champion who I knocked out after a few rounds. I had many friends, including women, artists and musicians whose recitals I had the pleasure to attend. And there was a casino. But my enriched social life didn't prevent me from taking part in the military maneuvers at Kairouan and at Foum Tatahouine where I met some ex-inmates who invited me for a merry drink or two.

At the end of May 1950, I was placed first in the North African Gymnastic Championship in Tunis with a total score of sixty-three points. Life became ever more beautiful but my draft was about to end. During my last days, I was on duty with the Military Police in

Tunis and then, suddenly it seemed, I found myself as a civilian, free but confused about which path my life should follow.

Once legitimately back at Villerupte-Cantebonne, I worked for a time in a foundry and with my spare money I bought a 350cc Peugeot motorcycle and sidecar. However, after the initial excitement of speeding along the countryside roads, the usual feeling of emptiness returned to haunt me. The methodical life, the inflexible and monotonous hours at work made me think deeply about my future. Had I resigned myself to life in the foundry, day after monotonous day? Despite being paid more than my father, I became more and more restless, impatient. My broken and quickly forgotten relationships with women complicated my already unsatisfactory situation, convincing me to go back on my decision to quit the army.

7

Vietnam

A Lesson in Timekeeping

In August 1951, I enlisted again, this time as a mercenary bound to fight in Indochina, and signed a contract with the French Government for the duration of three years. I left the port of Marseille aboard the ship *Cap Tourane* and felt I was in my natural environment in the company of fellow soldiers. As I leaned my elbows on the ship's handrail, I felt the sea breeze on my face, smelt the sea air. I longed for freedom, action… adventure. The depression and melancholy that had swamped me at the foundry lifted and I began once more to savour life. I had the impression that the old, dry skin of a sedentary life was flaking from my body like the scaly veil of a snake.

When the ship moored at Singapore, policemen escorted two Foreign Legion deserters onboard, handing them over to a commander of theirs who was travelling alone. He confined them to certain areas of the ship, gave them a handful of francs and undertook a long interrogation. As soon as I had the chance, I approached the two.

"*Porca vacca!*" one exclaimed, glancing out of the security cell's porthole.

"Are you Italians?" I asked.

"And you, what do you want?" one asked cheekily.

"I'm only intrigued to know where you came from."

"Simply said…from the desert! Picture in your mind arid dunes where you die of thirst and your skin cracks with the heat. And where a passing patrol picks you up, only to throw you in the guts of a prison, waiting for a ship to come."

The man's companion burst into a tirade. "It's your entire fault, cousin! Look where you got us!"

"You should thank me, instead on moaning at me. You'd still be there, hoeing a dry little field if it weren't for me."

"Better eat soil than rot in this tub! Three years, three more years to do. I'm going mad!"

"You've already done two, what does it cost you to do three more?"

"What does it cost me? Think of what I will gain instead…mosquitoes and flies. And now I'm empty handed I am. And all because of you…you and the nice pay with the Legion here, and the Legion there… and the nice women and the adventure. Nice my butt!"

I offered them a pack of cigarettes and they reciprocated with the ones they were given from their travelling commander. I grew to like these rascals and paid them a visit each day; they reminded me of my sojourn in Italy. They were released from the security cell when we were within sight of Saigon where they disembarked all dressed up in parade uniforms, escorted by the commander who I came to know was a former *Waffen SS* officer. We parted with strong handshakes wishing each other good luck. During those days at sea, having deepened our acquaintance, they came to consider me as a brother. And I too disembarked at Saigon, with my fellow recruits.

I was perplexed when I saw the pitiful state of Camp Petrus Ky. It was, as De Ville would have said, a bordello of a bordello, an incredible bordello. I couldn't believe the confusion, the disorder and the filth that prevailed there and, to make life even more irritating, a swarm of flies decided to adopt me as their constant companion.

That evening, at bedtime, two half-drunk corporal majors arrogantly set themselves down on my cot. When I asked them politely to move they answered in a mocking tone, "Listen to this recruit, how long have you been here?" and, "how much combat experience do you have, chick?"

Their attempt to belittle me only inflamed my rage. I grabbed one of the corporals by his shirt and pulled him off my bed. When his comrade protested, I straightened the both of them out in no time at all — without the need for words. In the morning I was summoned to the service room to explain how one of the corporals acquired a fractured nose. Luckily, the sergeant major dealing with the incident recognized me and repaid a favor I had done for him in France by inviting me to pay for a round of drinks for the unfortunate victims. I accepted this punishment willingly and everything ended there.

Every morning at muster, a company adjutant forced us to stay in our ranks and at attention under the scorching sun. It was impossible to dismiss the notion that he took a certain sadistic pleasure in seeing us suffer in that way.

"Maybe he thinks he is the Sun King," I whispered to another adjutant, from Corsica, at my side.

"We should do something," he answered in a low voice.

"I'll take care of it," I replied. I had in mind a strong, tall fellow I had become acquainted with during the sea voyage who was often involved in scuffles and as soon as a bruise healed on one of his eyes it seemed to pop up on the other. He liked to get involved in free-for-all fights but he took some lumps too and was a formidable punishment taker. For a good bottle of wine he was willing to brawl anywhere in the whole of Vietnam. At the first opportunity, I took him aside for a moment. "Listen," I said, "there's a big bottle of the best red waiting for you and 200 francs want to pass from my pocket to yours."

"Done deal!" he answered with great enthusiasm, without even knowing the nature of the task at hand. I explained the plan and left only when I was certain that he had clearly understood my instructions — I wouldn't have liked to waste the Corsican adjutant's money.

The next morning the company adjutant, stiff as a ramrod and with a show of medals on his chest, kept us waiting in the shimmering sunshine as usual. Just as the first beads of sweat formed on my brow, there was a frightening roar as the brute I had hired sprang from the ranks, running and yelling towards the non-commissioned officer to launch an assault with fists and feet. They rolled to the ground and, before the dust could hide them from view, several junior officers intervened to separate them. But it was too late, the damage was done. The furious adjutant, with one of his earlobes bitten through and his face cut and bleeding, was pulled to his feet and taken to the infirmary. Serious acts of the sort, in front of 500 soldiers, occurred from time to time and were generally attributed to a temporary madness induced by sunstroke and therefore judged benevolently. The Corsican adjutant congratulated me and from that day forward the musters featured shorter speeches and no lingering under the relentless sun.

New Posting

In the orderly room, a list of new postings appeared on the notice board and I discovered that I had been attached to a *Bataillon de Marche Tirailleurs* deployed at Hanoi. I arrived there by train on a day when the sun itself seemed on the verge of melting from the sky. On a cot close to an open window in the barracks reserved for soldiers in transit, I lay waiting to be called to duty. Towards evening, a soldier appeared at the open door, a Senegalese with big, round eyes. He invited me to accompany him to the mess, handing me a dish for the ration.

A week went by but after that first invitation nobody took the trouble to acknowledge my presence and so I took the opportunity to rest and become accustomed to the climate. During this period, I had the chance to observe the comings and goings on the base and it seemed to me that it was completely lacking in camaraderie. I was attached to a company made up of Senegalese soldiers — only the captain, a Corsican adjutant in charge of the garage, a sergeant in the depot and the junior officers were European. Boredom eventually persuaded me to report directly to the captain who had not been officially notified of my arrival. He flicked through my transit papers then looked me up and down, as if evaluating my abilities. "Hmm, so you have the motorcycle permit. Report to the depot to fetch your kit and then drag your ass to the garage," he said, pointing out the direction with a disinterested, tired gesture, as if he couldn't be bothered dealing with an inexperienced recruit, as he surely thought I was and then added without looking at me, "Ah! I see here that you are deployed to the Peripheral Quarter Command."

All things considered, the general impression that I had in those first days in Vietnam was not promising at all; I felt more at ease when I was on the side of those who had lost the war in Europe.

At the depot, I had an argument with the sergeant because I insisted on trying on the equipment: I didn't like the boots and the jacket and motorcycle helmet were too large for me. Things took a turn for the worse when, the following morning, I entered the garage.

"You know how to handle a motorcycle?" the adjutant in charge asked. He spoke with a tired drawl, the sort of attitude that irritated me immediately.

"Yes," I replied, still calm.

"You have your driver's licence?" he continued, sucking in the hot, humid air through his teeth.

"Yes!"

"How long?"

I looked into his small, beady eyes which looked as if they had been stamped onto the flaccid skin of his pale, chubby face. "Two years."

"Then you must be familiar with motorcycles."

He must have noticed the twitching of my jaw muscles, sensed my growing irritation, and so led me slowly to a row of motorcycles where he straddled one and started its 500cc engine. With a pat of his hand he invited me to sit behind him. The engine revved and we took off from the garage at speed. Once we had left the city, on a straight stretch of a road almost devoid of people, he opened up the throttle to send the motorcycle charging along at 130 kilometers per hour. On the way back to the garage, I took the handle bar but he directed me to drive along a road through a crowded market, which compelled me to drive slowly. I zigzagged to avoid pedestrians, kiosks and market benches at 50 kilometers per hour. I felt his knees press against my thighs as he drew them in tight to prevent them being scraped by the fenders of the rickshaws. During our little sortie he didn't say a word but once we returned to the base he dismounted with unexpected coolness and then said: "If you drive in this manner you won't live long!" He took a handkerchief from his trouser pocket to wipe the sweat from his neck before handing the motorcycle to me, reluctantly, like a protective father giving away his precious daughter on the day of her wedding.

As soon as I checked in at the Hanoi's Peripheral Quarter, I came to blows with a Senegalese sergeant, recently degraded to the rank of corporal after having assaulted a patrol made up of Europeans. He had ideas of self-grandeur because he had studied a bit more than the others and he believed himself to be something of an intellectual. He annoyed me at our first encounter, saying without mincing his words that he didn't have any empathy for those with white skin and so I solved the matter with my strong manners, as usual. I received, inevitably, eight days confinement even though the thrashing didn't displease the officers at the command post; but he was still a corporal and the rules had to be respected. The commander, on the other hand, had been quite restrained in punishing me — he could very well have saddled me with thirty days detention. Once again, I had convinced myself that violence was the only solution for certain individuals: after the 'cure' they changed their behaviour without fail.

My first paycheque financed a trip to Hanoi where I paused in front of coffee bars and restaurants reserved for European officers. Privates like me were excluded, only good enough to face death in combat for a salary far below that of the officer class. Money flowed like a river from French pockets in that corrupt city in which the cooks in restaurants, the waiters, the prostitutes and the indefatigable pedal pushers on those rickety rickshaws had a good nose for singling out the spendthrifts. For them, only the almighty god of money mattered and, for the right payment, they were quite prepared to act as informers for our enemy, the Viet Minh.

Motorbike and Other Problems

The word going the rounds at the Peripheral Quarter was that the Viet Minh had recently changed tactics, turning to offensive actions supported by artillery in a conventional manner. However guerrilla style warfare still prevailed in many areas and here the enemy was countered by our side with great patience and at high personal risk.

Rain was gushing from the heavy sky when I undertook my first mission. As a dispatch rider, I was to make contact with a platoon that was impossible to contact by radio. The muddy road on top of an embankment peppered with potholes and puddles, crossed paddy fields in an area completely in the hands of Viet Minh and, to put it simply, I was scared enough to push my motorcycling skills to their limit to get out of that situation. I accelerated a bit more under the pelting rain but the rear wheel ended up sliding on the mud. My hands gripped the handle bars tightly but I was unable to keep the motorcycle under control and it skidded down one side of the embankment, stopping with a jolt in a rice field. When I dismounted, I felt the mud suck at my feet and soon found myself up to the knees in the murky water. I pulled on the handlebar and tried lifting the motorcycle by the saddle but its wheels seemed glued to the mud. I looked around and, amidst the roaring rain, made out the shape of three bamboo huts about fifty meters away; rural dwellings that my comrades called *caï nhas*. I climbed up to the top of the embankment, aware that I was under observation, and withdrew my 7.65 calibre pistol from its holster without great confidence in its effectiveness and wished I had my P08 or Beretta instead. And all the while I had the feeling of being spied upon.

I ran towards the first of the huts and slammed open the woven-bamboo door with a kick. The wide, scared eyes of women and children stared at me. I noticed immediately the absence of young and fit men and figured they were not missing because they had all gone fishing. I waved my pistol in the air and shouted, "Out!" But they remained clinging to each other, timorous. The children's eyes, as wide and round as saucers, followed the movement of my pistol. An infant started whining. I shot once into the roof and they immediately went out into the torrential rain.

"There, the motorcycle," I indicated to them, shooting then into the air which seemed to have the power to make them understand my intentions.

Pulling and pushing, the Vietnamese managed to return my motorcycle to the road before running back to their hut. I followed them with my eyes, perturbed by their furtive behaviour. At first, I consoled myself with the thought that they were running to get out of that damned rain — but they were already soaked, so why all the haste? My blood ran cold when I happened to glance at the other huts, barely visible among the bamboo sticks and pelting rain, a rifle pointed at me.

I turned slowly, still holding my pistol and, with my free hand grabbing the accelerator, I pushed down on the foot pedal to start up the engine. Nothing — it was choked. Fear took hold. My legs trembled and the thought of a bullet in the back terrified me. "Coward of a moto," I hissed at the inert machine. In other circumstances I would have instantly reduced it to scrap. Time was not on my side, I had to get out of that damned trap. Strangely, at that moment the BMW of Karl, the Hitler Youth kid in Pomerania, came to mind. It had started at the second try. With my heart pounding, I tried again to start the engine but was met only by an asthmatic cough and a puff of oily smoke from the exhaust. "Rotten moto! What are those bastard communists waiting for?" I yelled, losing my cool. If I were to die, I hoped it would be by a bullet to the heart so everything would end suddenly. I gave another useless stamp on the pedal. I looked right and left, almost in the throes of exasperation. I was completely in the open, an easy target for that enemy rifle. My sweat mingled with the rain at every successive kick on the pedal. I tried again and the engine coughed, took a breath and then burst into life. I engaged first gear, accelerated slowly so as not to slide, wondering why I had not been hit by a bullet. "What are you waiting for?" I shouted under the continuous downpour. My nerves were stretched to the limit; raindrops stung my face, washed the mud from my helmet and into my mouth. I couldn't take it any longer, I glanced over to the huts but they had disappeared behind a grey veil of mist raised by the intensity of the deluge. Visibility zero: I was safe!

At the Peripheral Quarter, after my report, an order was posted that forbade travel on the road in question. Furthermore, towards two in the morning, the commander decided to carry out a sortie of the area. The rain had stopped but along that embankment the *tirailleurs Sénégalais* (Senegalese infantrymen) accompanying us, still half-asleep as they walked in the sultry darkness, were sinking up to their knees in puddles of muddy water. In the vicinity of the huts, the commander deployed the *tirailleurs* along the edges of the embankment at regular intervals, while he remained with me. He accompanied me for about eighty paces and then stopped to provide covering fire as I advanced towards the huts alone, sinking on a bed of mud that covered the road and was deep enough to stop any vehicle. I worked around it and came to large trenches, more than a meter deep, running from one side of the embankment to the other and full of murky water. When I reached the first hut, I slammed the door open again, this time holding my sub-machine gun. There was not a soul inside. I checked the other huts but they too were empty. I waved to the commander to come forward. "These trenches are too big to have been dug by a handful of people in such a short time," he said, "something's going on here."

An airplane of ours flew over a village not far from the huts around mid-day, bombing it because, at our command post, the officers had good reasons to expect a massive Viet Minh presence there. Rain returned as evening approached, starting exactly when a captain, a battalion adjutant, demanded to be driven to the 2nd Company who were executing a combing operation. Although he had a jeep and a Ghanaian driver available, he preferred the back seat of my motorcycle. He had been taken prisoner in Russia in 1940 and at the end of the war was able to return to Germany by getting a passage on a Russian tank. He was no intellectual and had a marked disdain for bureaucracy. This was the type of officer I could get along with so I willingly drove him through the relentless monsoon rain.

As a dispatch rider, I had a pass with absolute priority, day and night. On returning from a mission one evening an agent of the civil administration, a *prévôtè* on road traffic duty, stopped me on the Doumer Bridge — renamed Long Biên Bridge after North Vietnam gained independence in 1954 — just before I entered Hanoi, because I was travelling against the one-way system that was in force at the time. This restriction, however, did not apply to me so I was allowed to continue my journey. I accelerated quickly but as soon as I selected second gear, I found myself bouncing along the ground with the frame of my motorcycle broken in half.

"Sabotage!" shouted the agent, rushing over to me.

"Yes, from the French manufacturers," I answered, somewhat shaken, "and to think that I was going 120 just minutes ago."

I arrived at the garage workshop by hitching a ride on a passing truck. There the adjutant in charge raised his arms in disappointment as soon as he saw me without his precious motorcycle. "What did you do? How did it happen? What a way to treat the poor motorcycle!"

Tired of his complaints, and having seen that he refused my request for another motorcycle, I went directly to the captain's office to explain what had happened to the machine. The captain listened sympathetically and wasted no time in calling the adjutant by phone. "Since when does the army's materiel belong to you?" he shouted into the receiver. Then, turning to me, he continued, "You can fetch another one."

I thanked him and, while I was going out a Senegalese came in, panting.

"What do you want?" the captain asked.

"I just killed my woman," he blurted in one breath after saluting.

"What did you do?"

The soldier answered by placing a long and bloodied knife on the captain's desk.

"Go see what happened," the captain ordered me.

I knew in which hut the Vietnamese woman lived; she was the 'companion' of several Senegalese *tirailleurs* simultaneously and pocketed a good portion of their paycheques but she had to be careful not to be caught out or surprised by one or other of them. Those *tirailleurs* involved in this unusual web of relationships knew about the situation but there seemed to exist between them a sort of tacit consensus not to interfere with each other.

The sobbing of the dead woman's relatives and neighbours led me to a small hut constructed of straw and timber boarding. As soon as I stepped over the threshold I had to suppress the desire to vomit. Spread on a mat, the woman lay half-naked in a puddle of blood. Her head had been severed from the body and had rolled away from it. Nobody dared touch it. The Senegalese was arrested and sent, some weeks later, back to Africa. He had found her in the arms of a companion, he explained.

In the Vietnamese villages making money was the major preoccupation for everyone and the easiest way for a woman to earn it was by offering a type of prostitution in which she behaved as a part-time wife. Every time I visited the depot in the city, on the streets in front of dirty stores and restaurants, I inevitably encountered a good number of women looking for clients.

When I arrived at the depot courtyard each day, I often found Senegalese soldiers surrounding my motorcycle caressing the headlamp or the handle bar, or simply gazing at the machine in admiration. A blast on the horn was enough to make them jump backwards laughing and showing their very white teeth. In general, they had great respect for Europeans and I was always happy to spend time in conversation with them. Only the Senegalese corporal — the one reduced in rank because a fracas with a patrol — displayed anti-European ideas. To show his countrymen that he too was able to ride a motorcycle, he rented one from a nearby mechanic's workshop and drove around the courtyard shouting. "You see, it's not only Europeans that can ride a 'moto', I can do it too!" He was immediately surrounded by his compatriots who cheered and clapped their hands. I was about to deliver a message to an officer so, to even things up a little, I started my bike, revving the engine hard so that the back wheel spun as I turned before slowing at the exit gate. When I came back, I was just in time to see the Senegalese corporal performing the same maneuver, but instead of slowing at the gate, he shot across the road and collided with the wall of a restaurant on the opposite side, smashing the motorcycle. The owner of the small workshop let go an ear-piercing shriek, adding to those of the waitresses as they jumped clear of the careering motorcycle. With blood streaming down his face, the Senegalese corporal was helped up by his countrymen but he kept his eyes lowered when he saw me.

Another Bordello

The visit from the Minister for Indochina, Jean Le Tourneau, was an unusual event in Hanoi. Starting at Gia Lam airport, along the ten kilometers of route leading to an area set up to receive the minister near Doumer Bridge, local police and agents of the *prévôté* imposed exceptional measures and all secondary road exits were blocked until the minister's cortège had passed. The twelve motorcyclists assigned to escort General De Linares, Commander of the French Forces in North Vietnam, having departed from his palace in Hanoi, were already at the airport but it seemed the flight was late. In the meantime, I was called urgently to the captain's office, where I received the order to leave immediately on a mission to establish contact with the commander of another company. When I reached the main road, a *prévôté* guard signalled me to stop. I explained that I was on an urgent mission and so, after a little hesitation, he let me pass with the provision that I should carry out my mission as quickly as possible.

Along the route, at fifty-meter intervals, soldiers had been placed on and beyond the bridge, as far as a crowded stand where civilian and military authorities, protected by the city police in black uniforms, awaited the arrival of the minister's cortège. As I approached the stands, after crossing the Doumer Bridge, I received the rifle salute from the guard of honour and the first notes of the *Marseillaise*. They had mistaken me for a vanguard of the cortège so I slowed down in order to fully enjoy these honours, passing in front of the stand with my chest out, my chin up and returning the salutes of the guards with firm

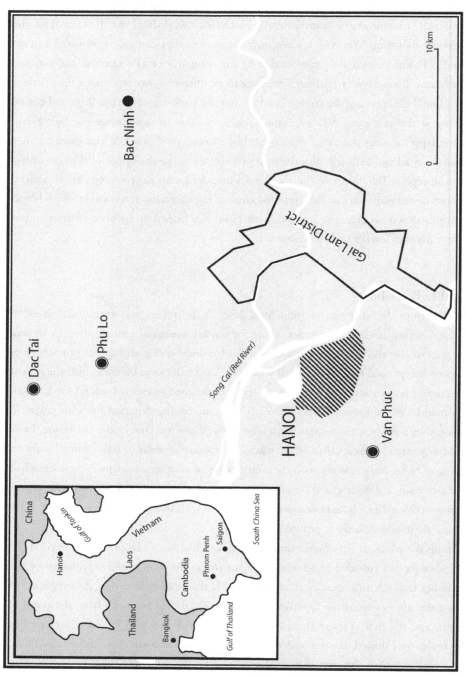

Indochina

hand. I savoured those moments of triumph with total satisfaction — who could forget such a glorious welcome? Fifteen minutes after my passing, the band repeated the national anthem when Le Tourneau finally arrived.

Soon after my triumphal parade, my notions of grandeur were replaced by pangs of guilt. As I arrived in the city, my motorcycle's back wheel skidded on a street puddle sending the machine into a wild spin. The rear wheel collided with the bicycles of two young Vietnamese that were pedalling together and knocked them to the ground. Fortunately, they bounced back onto their feet paying more attention to their bicycles than themselves. They immediately began gesturing for compensation. I saw that the wheels of their bicycles were deformed and was just about to recompense them when a local traffic policeman, who had seen the whole accident, rushed over. He saluted me and then pulled out a truncheon to pound the heads of the two cyclists as he fired a stream of invectives at them. The two youngsters left dragging their bicycles, after which the policeman saluted me again and then continued to direct the traffic as if nothing had happened. I stood there, astonished at the policeman's callous assault on the cyclists who had run off before I could make amends with them.

Some evenings later, having stopped for dinner at a small advance post, I didn't hesitate to shoot a sweep with my MAT-49 against a Vietnamese who was one of the cooks. As soon as I finished eating the tripe he had prepared, strong cramps gripped my stomach and spasms choked my breathing. I thought of poison, of death. I dragged myself to the kitchen door, aiming at the blurred shadows that still were in my sight, and continued firing until the magazine was empty. In the throes of convulsions and vomit, I was given first aid by an Italian adjutant who, having understood the situation, saved me by administering a gastric lavage. Later I learned that the cook avoided the rain of bullets by diving into a massive, steel soup-cauldron.

There was something about the stifling atmosphere of that place that tipped folk to the edge of madness and sometimes beyond. I recall that a soldier, a native from Guadeloupe, let go a sweep of his sub-machine gun at a captain who was continually vexing him and who had punished him by cutting off even his salary for a month. Besides the captain, other officers at the captain's dinner table were also wounded.

And if the heat and humidity didn't drive you mad, military justice could soon make up that deficit. Once, when I returned to the Peripheral Quarter after the tripe incident, I got news of the conviction meted out to a companion. A tribunal, composed of half from the French military and half from local civilian authorities, accused him of raping a Vietnamese girl. The punishment arrived in the most severe form: eighteen months of solitary at the disciplinary section in Poulo Condor, a penal colony on an island off the southernmost tip of Cochinchina. There the inmates were treated like beasts, worse than in any *Lager*. Some left their sanity behind when they were freed, others had broken bones, especially at the wrists and knees. The dreary infamy of that place was known by everyone.

"Paul, it's not true what they accuse me of," the companion confided in me when I visited him before he was sent away. "That prostitute…she wanted to be paid double and I didn't have enough money. She started yelling for help, crying out and tearing her dress until a policeman pointed his pistol between my eyes. What a bad luck!"

That was the last time I saw him.

At Christmas I had to share a pack of American cigarettes — a gift from the Motherland — with a companion. At Greifenberg I had received, like all my comrades, cigarettes made in Germany and an entire pack at that. At evening mess I forced myself to swallow half-cooked, hard meat before making my way to the dormitory to think but my way was blocked at the door by a German legionnaire and his drunken companions who were shouting and staggering around making a mess by spilling the contents of the bottles in their hands. I tried to reason with him but the matter soon came to punches and he dropped onto a pile of empty bottles, cutting his face in several places and bleeding profusely. I left there wondering why I had volunteered to join that aimless rabble. It was, as De Ville would have said, a bordello of a place.

Phu Lo

A few days after Christmas I was transferred to the subsector of Phu Lo, Advance Post number 6, on the embankments of the Song Ca Lo River, about 20 kilometers north of Hanoi. Captain Subreroque, a true gentleman of a commander, entrusted about forty Viet Minh prisoners to my care. To keep them focussed on the work I had planned for them, I also had two 12.7mm machine guns and eight Senegalese *tirailleurs*. My task, for which I was given a free hand, was to reinforce the existing defenses and erect new ones. There was concrete to be cast for the construction of block houses, barbed wire to stretch out, mines to place in strategic points, offices, depots, showers and washrooms to plan and build brick by brick.

Captain Subreroque, a man of a lean physique and average height, and never completely shaved, took a liking to me as soon as he discovered that I was a novice bricklayer. After a few weeks of work, I gained his complete trust and was soon looked upon as a master mason and architect. At the end of my first construction project, I received an inspection visit from a cadet officer from the Engineers School who had never lifted a brick but had a head-full of theories. He began the inspection accompanied by the captain while I walked behind them. "This wall is not thick enough, it couldn't even withstand a shot from a bazooka!" he ruled.

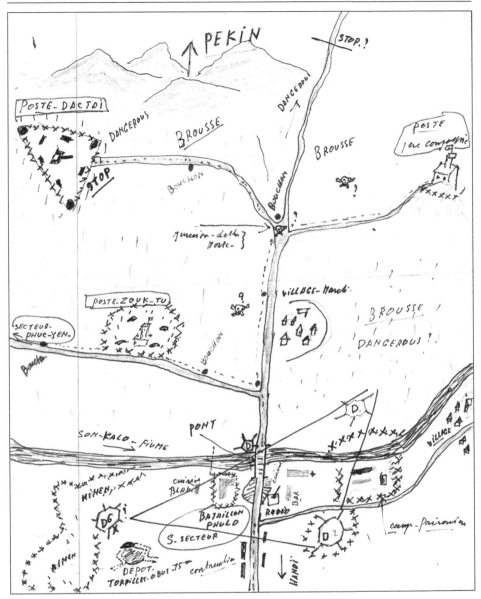

Fortification map by Paul.

"Hum," said the captain, who by then knew that I had a volatile temperament. He turned to look at me, his eyes inviting me to defend my work.

"Then you and I stay inside here," I proposed to the engineering cadet, "in the bunker, while we test the effect of two hectograms of TNT."

The captain smiled and waited for an answer from the officer who suddenly turned pale.

"Shall I order the charge?" I pressed on, "we can do it right now."

The officer cadet didn't mutter a word and became even more awkward.

The captain intervened to ease the officer's embarrassment. "Paul, we know it, the wall is resistant enough, let's go on with the inspection."

From that moment, there were no further criticisms about the fortifications I was building with the Viet Minh prisoners' help.

The Senegalese *tirailleurs*, returning from sorties or patrol rounds, made use of *bouchon*, defensive positions consisting of blockhouses large enough to host five or six soldiers. From them, they could control the road and search for mines. They also had the habit of pausing to play with the local kids, who spied on them, observing everything. A Senegalese sergeant, leading a patrol of fifteen *tirailleurs*, decided one day to leave a radio operator and another eight soldiers at the most remote *bouchon*, with the order to transmit every twenty-five minutes. After few hours, though, the contact failed and so, at the base, a company adjutant who had lived for some years in Africa and thus had the complete trust of the Senegalese, left onboard a truck 6X6 with an escort to investigate the reason for the loss of radio contact. He found the *bouchon* destroyed, the soldiers massacred, and no trace of the radio, ammunition or rations. After joining up with the rest of the *tirailleurs* from the patrol, he returned to the base. The Senegalese, two of whom had cousins among the dead, itched for revenge:

"At the nearest village," they shouted together.

"Let's burn them!"

"Let's cut off their heads!"

"Blood for blood!"

"Vengeance! Vengeance!"

The adjutant held back their anger by promising them he would find out how their comrades had been overwhelmed without any great signs of resistance and organized a patrol to the *bouchon* to investigate the matter. Accordingly, I left with a Corsican sergeant and a handful of selected *tirailleurs*. When we arrived at the *bouchon*, we discovered pits in which the Viet Minh lay in wait at the night: they had lids made of bamboo sticks and mud and at the most opportune moment, probably when the sentries had slackened their watch, they sprang to the assault, killing everyone.

The Viet Minh were a cunning and fearsome enemy; their ambushes, mines and traps had a disastrous effect not only on personnel and vehicles but especially on our morale. A few days after the assault at the *bouchon*, a truck hit a mine and exploded, killing the driver and the soldiers it carried, literally blowing them to shreds. In the same week, a *tirailleur* stepped on a sharp bamboo cane hidden in the mud; its tip had been infected with dung and other excrements and this set up an infection that turned into a large wound that refused to heal.

Unforeseeable and treacherous dangers were a constant threat. One night I was wakened by the thump of exploding mortar grenades and the distant crackling of machine guns from a defense post a dozen kilometers away. Their radio had remained silent so Captain Subreroque and the other officers feared for the safety of the men at the post. At night it was forbidden to leave the protection of the base to give assistance to outlying defense positions under enemy fire because of the risk of ambush and because the Viet Minh under cover of darkness were quite elusive. Only artillery fire support from the General Quarter could effectively dissuade the attackers — provided the gunners were given accurate fire-coordinates by radio from the defense posts in danger. In the morning, together with the soldiers of the Intervention Section, I reached the location of the battle where we found just two wounded survivors who had saved themselves by fleeing the defense post. They explained how their Vietnamese compatriots, commanded by a European corporal, had been wiped out. About thirty of them deserted at the beginning of the battle while the Viet Minh, with the help of about a hundred coolies, removed all the armaments, including the mortar. They also took the radio and a box of medical supplies.

It was very easy for Viet Minh spies to infiltrate the base and defense posts. They soon learned the location of our emplacements, the number of soldiers and pattern of troop movements. They used persuasion and threats to secure help from the local population and, in the case of the devastated outpost, the sentry betrayed everybody inside by opening the block-house door to the enemy. Those daring Viet Minh raids, prepared with the utmost care, were often depressingly successful.

Abandoned

To counterattack and limit the Viet Minh's nocturnal incursions, a force consisting of five Super TD tanks, a company of Moroccan soldiers, two companies from the Foreign Legion (coming from the area of the Seven Pagodas) and a search squad of sniffer-dogs were assembled at Phu Lo. I was happy to meet among them a soldier who I had known in France, now a tank driver.

"Are we going to dance, Paul?" he called when he saw me.

I waved at him. "Souché, you old fox! You're with us then?"

"And where else would I be?"

"With the beautiful girls we left in France," I said.

"Good times they were. Too bad we don't have them here, Paul. Instead we'll be flushing those Viets from the mud." Souché saw the stripes on my sleeve. "Hei! So they made you a corporal eh?"

"Come, I'll offer you a drop," I invited him. We made for base canteen to drink, talk and laugh, reminiscing about the good times we had shared as soldiers.

The next day, at dawn, the convoy left Phu Lo heading towards a large village. Our trucks stopped half a kilometer from the first houses. I positioned my soldiers according to the orders I had been given: eight Vietnamese and four Senegalese *tirailleurs* in a line near the huts with an MG24/29 at each end. And then we waited. A few meters behind the five tanks took up position and, to break the monotony of the wait, I asked the commander in the turret of the closest, "Tell me, *mon* lieutenant, what happens if I can't stop the Viets when they come?"

"Don't worry corporal," said the lieutenant as he caressed the barrel of the tank's 12.7mm machine gun, "you have 'Rosalia' here to protect you. If they come at you, you'll see what a present they'll get." He puffed up his chest. "In the Forties, even the *Boches* couldn't finish me off."

I went over to Souché who was also in his tank's turret. "Did you hear him?" Souché asked in a lowered voice. "If he's as valiant in action as he is with his words then we have nothing to fear, but I've never seen him in combat."

Two days dragged by, during which I heard the sniffer-dogs barking on my right and fusillades to the north of the village. From the sounds of their machine-gun bursts — I could distinguish those of the Moroccans from those of the legionnaires — it was evident that they were pushing the Viet Minh into a tightening pincer grip which would force them to flee to the south, into my enfilade fire and that of the tanks.

On the morning of the third day, the first of the Viet Minh bolted out from the village, shooting wildly and pursued by the Moroccans and legionnaires. My soldiers, well-covered, were waiting for the order to fire but the tank lieutenant requested artillery support from our 105mm cannons. The projectiles arrived promptly, hissing through the air and exploding too close to our own positions, some only a few meters from our line. Amidst the smoke, dust and panicked cries, the two Senegalese at the machine guns abandoned their positions. I promptly stopped them in their tracks by firing a sweep at their feet, screaming at them to return to their posts. But by then, the damage was already done. Their cowardice infected the Vietnamese who spontaneously left their cover to cut and run. I grabbed one of them by his shirt, forcing him to turn back to gather his abandoned ammunition. With the continuous roar of explosions and the choking shroud of smoke intensifying the chaos, I resorted to strong-arm tactics to re-establish discipline. A Senegalese fell to the ground yelling he was hit. I helped him to his feet, looked him quickly up and down then slapped his face. "You're only dirty. It's nothing, damn! Move!" I took a deep breathe to bellow an order to reform the line, threatening to shoot whoever dared disobey me. One by one, the Vietnamese went back to their initial positions but realized when I turned to check the situation at my back that the tanks had retreated. My eyes must have almost popped out of their sockets when I saw that demoralizing surprise. "Coward of a lieutenant," I roared, full of blind rage, "I'll cut your damned throat!"

The Viet Minh came at us, shooting blindly.

"Fire!" The machine gunners swept the charging Viet Minh with a storm of bullets. Some twirled as they ran before falling to the ground, others crumpled to their knees. Those that survived the crossfire from our machine guns tried to force their way through by running on the road towards our line, towards the position the tanks were supposed to cover. I stood up upright, firing at them, joined in my efforts by my soldiers who had found their courage. We continued shooting until ordered to stop while the Moroccans and legionnaires searched the village. Around our position, twenty or thirty rebels lay face down on the road or floated in the shallow water of the paddy field but, because the tank commander abandoned us, a much larger number managed to escape.

When we regrouped at the trucks, we found the tanks.

"So, Paul, do you understand now?" Souché said from his turret, "now that you've seen the lieutenant at work!"

"The coward!" I hissed through my clenched teeth, barely containing my anger.

"Don't be upset, Paul. For sure he'll have a good explanation ready, that hot-shot braggart."

"Excuses more like," I replied, "he had the firepower of five tanks and he could only think of calling in the artillery."

"At the first explosion he closed his turret and gave order to backtrack...to preserve the materiel," he said.

I was becoming increasingly annoyed with our lieutenant as I listened to Souché's account of his behaviour. "So to save his precious tanks he left us without cover and without even warning us."

"That's our hero!" Souché said, his voice full of irony.

"If he had been with the 'Charlemagne', he would have been shot, right there, for high treason," I said.

As I passed the lieutenant's tank with my soldiers, I looked up to the turret and said: "Thanks for the cover." He lowered his head and looked in the opposite direction.

※—※

Back at the Phu Lo base, I placed the soldiers for the night guard and, after the usual round to make sure everything was in order, I went to the canteen to share my frustration with Marchi, the tall and lean Italian adjutant who saved my life with the gastric lavage. "What in the hell happened?" he asked as we sat at a table together. I launched into a tirade about how my soldiers and I were left exposed in a dangerous position by the lieutenant's lack of backbone. Then I felt a light finger tap my shoulder and turned to see the lieutenant who motioned for me to stand.

"Paul, please try to abstain from these reflections, could you?"

I sprang to attention, I stared him in his eyes and I answered proudly, "Corporal Martelli at your command, *mon* lieutenant."

The lieutenant left without further comment.

Marchi passed me another glass. "Forget him, Paul. Tomorrow is another day," he said, in an effort to cheer me up.

I found Marchi again at the canteen the following evening. We understood each other well and shared the same point of view on many matters although he was at least a decade older than me. Despite his age and his sparse brown hair, Marchi had the overall appearance and demeanour of a man of action with very quick reflexes — the sort of fellow that would be an ideal companion in difficult situations. Although superior in rank, I could talk to Marchi as an equal and he listened to my concerns with the utmost attention and because of this I enjoyed his company.

At about nine thirty, while enjoying a glass of cold beer, we heard the crackle of 12.7mm machine-gun fire coming from the direction of tower number six which was located on the west point of the defense triangle — the emplacement under my command. We left our drinks standing on the table and ran across the compound to a Senegalese *tirailleur* firing bursts from the heavy machine gun. "Cease fire!" I ordered.

"The Viets, *mon caporal*...they are crossing the river by boat!" said the nervous *tirailleur*.

Marchi ordered the sentry manning the searchlight to shine it on the water, then on the embankment. My eyes followed the beam as it scanned back and forth along the river and the vegetation on the opposite side. "You see something?" I asked Marchi.

"Nothing!"

The telephone rang. It was the commandant. "We heard the machine guns...what's happening?"

"Here is Paul. False alarm, *mon* commandant."

"I'll alert everyone, just in case," said the commandant.

"I'll prepare a reconnaissance party at dawn," I promised.

At first light I emerged from my bunker, as I called my small room because its roof was at ground level. In fact, all the dormitories had been built in a deep excavation to protect them from mortar fire. I untied the boat at my disposal, the one used for transporting rocks from an old pagoda to the new fortifications, and with three Senegalese *tirailleurs* on board began to search riverbanks. After a few minutes, I noticed someone near the water's edge. With our rifles at the ready, we closed cautiously on a Moroccan soldier who was curled up in the vegetation. "What are you doing there?" I asked. He was trembling so much that he was incapable of talking so we brought him onboard with the intention of interrogating him in the calmer surroundings of an office back at the base.

"Why were you on the river at night?" I asked him, bending over the desk.

"The… market," the Moroccan slurred.

"Yes? Continue!"

"The women at the market…they invited me to go with them."

"On their junks?"

"Yes, they wanted to go back to their village."

"By crossing the river?"

"I don't know, they wanted to leave…" he droned, shivering with fright once more.

The Morrocan had every sign of being intoxicated. "You drank *choum* eh?"

"A little."

"And now, where are the women? Why did they leave you there?"

"The shooting…the junk broke in a half…they all jumped in the water…and then I cannot recall."

Strange, I thought, *very strange*. The thought came to me that the women were perhaps trying to recruit him as a traitor and spy. I found him some days later, abandoned in the mud of the rice fields with his hands tied behind his back, killed by a bullet in the back of his head.

Good Luck, Bad Luck

The base at Phu Lo was practically enclosed by a triangle of emplacements with a defensive tower at each vertex. It was cut through the middle by Colonial Road Number Three which went north from Hanoi towards China and then followed the Song Ca Lo River from west to east, starting at a bridge beside which there was a forth tower. Inside the compound, west of the road, was the tower which had been assigned to me. The barracks and other buildings were close to the tower an a little farther away lay the ammunition depot. East of the road, in the direction of a village, was a cluster of buildings housing the radio station, kitchens, canteen and infirmary and, a little detached from these was the prison camp. All emplacements were surrounded by mine fields. Going along the Colonial Road towards the north, a turn to the left led to the fortified post of Zouk Tu and, about another 20 kilometers further on, to the sector of Phuc Yen. Continuing to the north on the Colonial Road, one came to a village where a market was frequently held and beyond it lay the so-called 'crossroads of death', which marked the beginning of Viet Minh held territory. Turning right at the 'crossroads of death' led to the post of the 1st Company while a left turn led to the fortified post of Dac Tai. *Bouchons* were positioned along all roads at regular intervals. At night, between these posts, the Viet Minh reigned.

After completing the building offices and showers, I was fortunate enough to be granted three days leave which was very difficult to obtain at that period, given the unstable situation. I was obliged, however, to command the crew of a truck directed to the Military Commissariat in Hanoi to pick up supplies, since the rules required the presence of an experienced soldier —generally a European — every time a truck left the base. In the cabin, as well as the Senegalese driver, were two Viet Minh prisoners, who would help load the provisions, and their accompanying guard.

Seated comfortably and with my feet on the dashboard, I whistled a happy tune, elated, not only because of the impending leave, but also for another reason — I had fortuitously come into a substantial amount of money. This came about when I was commanding a squad on patrol during a combing operation on a suspect village. During that action, my Senegalese troops had stopped some old farmers while I continued briskly towards the opposite side of the village where I encountered a young *niaqué* (female farm worker) with two heavy baskets hanging from a yoke across her shoulders. She was moving in a hurry so I followed her without being noticed, keeping at a distance of about fifty meters. She turned a couple of times to look back, as if checking that she was not being followed, and then quickened her pace. I kept my distance until she entered the forest and then I closed in, stopping her with a burst from my MAT-49 that lifted spurts of mud around her bare feet. With terror in her eyes, she laid the baskets to the ground. I kept my MAT-49 pointed against her while I rummaged carefully amongst the rice in one of the baskets. And then my fingers detected something with the texture of paper. When I pulled my hand from the rice, it was full of new banknotes with the image of the last emperor of Vietnam, Bao Dai, printed on them. The other basket too, under a layer of rice, was stacked with yet more neatly packed banknotes. The woman, her eyes burning with hatred, held me in her gaze as if she hoped to see me struck by lightning. Those thousands of piasters, an enormous amount of money, were too much for it to have been her own and since she was running away from the village at our arrival, I figured that the notes were bound for the Viet Minh and that she was a Viet Minh rebel. I glanced around to make sure nobody was watching and prodded her away from the baskets with the muzzle of my MAT-49. With a certain calculated impudence she started to yell and to despair, hoping no doubt to attract the attention of her companions, but the deafening explosion of our grenades falling nearby drowned her crying. Two bursts from my MAT-49 at her feet persuaded her to run: she disappeared from my sight yelling with rage.

I could have killed her right there and then, and probably would have been decorated for my part in the disruption of the Viet Minh finances but I decided, instead, to fill up my pockets, my haversack, my shirt and socks with the packets of money. I didn't think twice about it although I knew the risks and the consequences if I was found out. According to the rules, all goods confiscated from the enemy belonged to the army and the French government. The mildest punishment I could expect if caught was a long sojourn at Poulo Condor.

In the privacy of my bunker I counted the banknotes: I had some tens of thousands of piasters and, unlike the devalued marks we found on the train full of the bodies of German soldiers near Neustrelitz, they were all legal tender. At that time, a piaster was valued at seventeen French francs.

The Senegalese driver was happy at the steering wheel, cheered by my good mood perhaps. *It had been a hard blow for the Viet Minh*, I was thinking, *and one they certainly wouldn't recover so easily from*. In the meantime, I was rich, much richer than the commander. Now I had the pleasant problem of thinking about how I would invest that capital after being demobilized. As an immediate treat, once at Hanoi, I intended to rent a Harley-Davidson for a round of visits to the bases, to visit my friends. And a brief stop at the various night clubs and a good drink were in order too, just to celebrate. I had to be careful though, not to give myself away. Nobody knew about this matter but what a pleasure it would have been to be able to flutter a handful of notes under the eyes of the diffident *sommeliers* as I bought the most expensive bottle of champagne in a restaurant.

We encountered a convoy of armoured vehicles passing in the opposite direction. The road at that spot became quite narrow and, although the Senegalese at the wheel drove as he learned at driving school, he couldn't avoid slamming into an armoured truck. The impact was rather violent, so much so that the guard's rifle slipped out of his hands and the two Viet Minh prisoners were flung from the back seats into the front seats. I stepped out of the truck cursing our bad luck — we had crashed into the colonel's vehicle, one of thirty in the convoy.

"Imbecile! Good for nothing! Gaol-bird! I'll throw you in punishment cell without pay for the rest of your days!" the officer barked in my face. He seemed like a wild devil, with his crème coloured beret dancing on his head. When he had vented his wrath, I gave him my personal data and resumed our trip. Before arriving at the Doumer Bridge, I asked the driver if he was all right and he returned a reassuring glance. My physical integrity had suddenly become very precious to me and I didn't wish to end up in the river, now that I had all that money at my disposal. But I didn't dare indulge in a spending spree even though I was as rich as a general. No, there was a limit to what I could spend without arousing suspicion but nevertheless, that didn't prevent me from lighting up a cigarette by burning a one hundred piaster bill under the astonished stares of a *maître d'hotel*, and this in front of my companions and the officers present. I could have used the candle on the table as everybody did, but I had something to celebrate. That bravado gave me an immense satisfaction.

Police Duties

"Paul! Paul!"

"*Oui, mon capitaine*," I answered, recognizing the alarmed voice of Captain Subreroque, even before he barged into my bunker.

"Quick! Quick! See if you can do something. He is armed and he is firing at anybody, at Sergeant Tixier too," he said, short of breath.

"Who?"

"That Senegalese drunkard, the hell! We have to act before the worst happens!"

I followed him up the stair leading to the roof, at ground level, and then ran towards the shouts.

"I'll kill everybody, the first I see I'll fill him up with holes…with lead, I mean." The Senegalese *tirailleur* let go a short burst that chipped the stones at the edge of the road. The curious onlookers, after rushing in and crowding around, jumped back to relative safety.

"Watch out!" the captain warned. He then turned in my direction with a look of expectation on his face, waiting for me to spring into action. I motioned him to help me by distracting the *tirailleur*.

"Show your face if you dare! I'll tear out your guts," the *tirailleur* was garbling.

Some of the NCOs answered in kind, insulting him so that the *tirailleur* became even more enraged but this acrimonious dialogue kept his attention from focussing on me.

"The first I see I'll slit his throat! Where's my dagger, where?"

I held back until the *tirailleur* happened to turn his back to me and was exchanging words with the captain. I crossed the ground between us silently, rapidly. The Senegalese was very surprised when I tapped my knuckles on his shoulders; he turned with a thunderstruck expression in his dark eyes. I flung a straight right at his drooling, open mouth and I let go an uppercut to his chin that left him staggering with a vacant look on his face. The MAT-49 fell from his grasp and he crashed heavily onto his back.

After turning him over, I pulled one of his arms around his back, forcing his hand to his shoulder blade. A corporal major who had been observing the action came to offer assistance, extracting the magazine of the MAT-49 before raising it to aim a blow at the Senegalese's head. I grabbed the corporal's wrist to prevent the blow telling him there was no point in him intervening now that I had the *tirailleur* already subdued. I slackened my hold on the drunken soldier and left him in the care of a Senegalese sergeant who, with the help of two of his *tirailleurs*, ensured that the drunk was deprived of all his weapons.

In the morning I called as usual into Captain Subreroque's office to discuss the ongoing construction projects but he seemed more concerned with the incident of the previous day.

"Congratulations Paul, you did well yesterday," he said.

"It's nothing, *mon capitaine*," I answered, taking a seat at the desk.

"No, no! Your quick reflexes, last night, your rapid action rendered that mad drunkard harmless."

"There was no difficulty."

Captain Subreroque looked into my eyes and he smiled. "Well!" he said, "I don't want those actions to happen again...they come up too frequently so I have thought about building a security chamber and reached the conclusion that you should start working on it immediately. Why don't you design the project and show it to me. Ah! One more thing, Paul. I want to institute a patrol, a stable picket of soldiers functioning as an internal Military Police, you know what I mean."

"Understood," I answered. This was the sort of work I had carried out in Kolberg when I was a *Waffen SS* soldier.

"Choose the three most accomplished *tirailleurs*, men capable of intervening in cases such as last night," he suggested, leaning forward with his elbows on the desk. "Instruct them, train them, and do as you think best! You have a free hand and my complete trust."

Captain Subreroque was a man of integrity, an upright soldier, forged in the hard school of military discipline. He did not tolerate disorder of any kind and he talked directly in the face of his underlings without wasting or mincing words. Our attitudes to military discipline were similar and I felt at ease with him.

For a week, relying on the experience I had gained during my days at Kolberg, I taught the three Senegalese *tirailleurs* I had selected the principles of martial art: personal defense, intervention, surprise attacks and the techniques for immobilizing prisoners without the risk of killing them and to ensure that they were not inflicted with the vice of drinking out of proportion, I investigated their backgrounds. I was pleased with my choice of personnel and they soon became perfect military policemen. They cut magnificent figures with their helmets and white webbing that stood out in contrast with their black skin.

The captain was very pleased with my efforts and issued a service note in which he warned everybody, officers included, about the authority given to the Police Patrol which was to be in constant service. Naturally that note didn't sit well with everyone and some still found the time to get drunk at the base canteen, but such events now had very limited consequences.

One day a GMC truck of the 1st Company arrived at the base from the provisions depot at the Military Commissariat in Hanoi and stopped near the radio tower. The Senegalese driver and crew, and the soldiers who had hitched a free ride, were happily received by the Senegalese *tirailleurs*, girls from the brothel and by the Vietnamese that gathered around the vehicle to receive the small purchases ordered by them and brought back by the returning soldiers.

With several other European soldiers, Marchi and I joined the small crowd but I immediately noticed, while the truck was being unloaded, that the driver was a little too euphoric and seemed rather tipsy. All of a sudden he came to blows with a French sergeant who, in order to avoid a scuffle with an unpredictable drunkard, backtracked. At that moment, as the hustle was brewing, Captain Archanbeau arrived. He grabbed the driver by the collar and tugged at him, receiving as an answer a series of rapid punches. They fell into a rough brawl against the truck, oblivious to the people around them. Captain Archanbeau, quite different in character compared to Captain Subreroque and of inferior ideas regarding underlings, began to tire and puff but nobody thought to intervene. He suffered a nasty bite to the biceps of the right arm and the two grappled with each other after falling to the dry dust of the courtyard. To me, the captain had handled the situation poorly and was now involved in a brawl that was degrading not only to him, but to the prestige of the French army.

Marchi urged me to intervene.

"I don't have the least intention of being dragged into this," I said, observing the captain's worsening predicament.

"You won't leave those two to…"

"It's Patrol Police's duty."

"They'll end up killing each other," said Marchi.

I relented, not to save that loathsome Captain Archanbeau from a beating, but to please my adjutant friend. I seized the driver by his short, curly hair, lifted his face and planted a fist on his nose, followed by a karate blow to his nape that caused him to collapse onto his back.

After struggling to his feet, his mouth slobbering, the captain said: "What are you doing here?" Then he turned on the crowd. "Go on, to your duties," he said as he shuffled towards the infirmary.

Marchi shook his head. "He didn't even realize you helped him out of that tight spot, Paul,"

"What do you expect?" I said, "there's a reason why he is so badly tolerated by everybody."

The Senegalese driver was handed over to an officer responsible for African matters who issued a fine off before sending him back to the 1st Company. Later, once briefed about my action, Captain Archanbeau summoned me to his office. "I called you here to thank you, you have done your duty; dismissed," he said without even a handshake. *Next time I'll let them demolish you completely*, I thought on my way out.

A week later, as Marchi and I sat on a blockhouse studying a project to place mines in an area near the base's entry gate, my friend pointed to a patrol just arriving.

"They're assigned to the road checks," I said without raising my head from the plans spread on the concrete.

"They are from the 1st Company, did you see who commands them?" Marchi insisted.

"Why?" I asked with my eyes still fixed on the drawings.

"Look!"

I relented. When I looked up, the patrol was just about to pass us. "Damn! He's the one that gave a drubbing to Archanbeau."

"And he's holding a MAT-49." Because we were inside the base, both Marchi and I were unarmed.

The Senegalese driver left his companions and came in our direction with a firm step. He had recognized me.

"What do you intend to do?" Marchi asked.

"Too late," I snorted.

The Senegalese stopped three meters from us. "Corporal, I come to greet you," he said. I returned his salute. "What do you want?"

"Come with me, I buy you a drink," he invited me, pompously.

"I'm busy on something here. I'll come willingly later on."

"Later on then, at the canteen," he said, continuing at the head of his patrol.

"That was to show him I'm deciding, not him," I said to Marchi.

"For a moment I feared the worst," my friend confessed.

I looked at Marchi, a wry smile on my lips. "Did you have the jitters?" I asked in Italian.

"I thought he would let go a burst for both of us. Now it's me that's offering you a drink."

"And I must accept the Senegalese's invitation, I promised him that."

"If you refuse it will be such an affront for him that he'll never forgive you, he will think about vengeance. But what about the rules? Africans are not allowed to enter the canteen to drink liquors," Marchi reminded me. "That's another problem for you," he said after mulling the matter over for a few moments.

The Senegalese driver was waiting for us at the canteen entrance. I let him come in, leaving the surprised members of his patrol outside. Marchi, who usually didn't drink liquors, ordered a double cognac for himself. Nobody dared oppose the presence of the African who, standing stiffly, was glancing around with pride: he was drinking in the canteen with a corporal and an adjutant.

Once outside, just before parting ways, the Senegalese driver thanked me.

"It's nothing, why are you thanking me?" I asked.

"If you didn't break my nose I would have killed the captain, thanks again." He returned to the head of his patrol, strutting and smiling widely.

"Here's one that will hold you in great esteem," Marchi said.

I nodded, but was not completely convinced by Marchi's prediction.

Old Habits

The ambushes at night and the acts of sabotage in the following weeks occurred with intensifying frequency. Another two soldiers were victims of puncture wounds inflicted by poisoned bamboo tips, hidden in the mud of the rice fields. Village combing and checking operations thus intensified and, as a consequence, a captain recently arrived at the base was assigned to reconnaissance missions. Placed under his command with my entire squad, I gave him my full-hearted support not only because of professional duty but also because that young officer was to my liking. He didn't have much combat experience but he was intelligent and would learn the ropes in a short while: he was of simple demeanour, straightforward, just and courageous.

Late in the afternoon, during his first action, soon after a shooting in a small village, we were getting ready to return to our trucks which were waiting for us on the road at a safe distance. At that moment, Viet Minh rebels sprang into the open, slipping out from their holes when they heard the explosions of their rudimentary mines which had been sparked off harmlessly in the confusion of the battle. After capturing and frisking them, the young captain gave the order to head to the trucks by raising his arms so that everybody could see him — he didn't have time to lower them again. He fell forwards, hit by a bullet in the back. I bent down quickly to give first aid and to help him lay on his side.

"I believe they got me corporal," he murmured, his face locked in a grimace of pain.

"Quick you guys, insert two rifles into the arms of two combat jackets," I ordered my soldiers. I dragged the captain to a relative cover and lay him on that improvised stretcher. Running and shooting backwards, we reached the trucks. At Phu Lo, via a radio message, a helicopter was already waiting to transport the young captain to the hospital in Hanoi.

A couple of days later, Captain Subreroque assumed the duties of his young colleague. "A good officer," he confided, "too bad he died in the helicopter a few minutes before landing."

I was saddened by the news and by not having had the time to get to know him better. I'm certain that, given more time working together, we would have become good friends.

In those days similar actions were a common occurrence and for accurate fire at long distances I was able to obtain a Mauser rifle; for night combat I preferred the MAT-49. Generally, I led my squad during break-through and cover missions and I must say with satisfaction that my soldiers, after our first excursions, understood each other well and were marvellously proficient in their tactics. They had become expert specialists which was a matter greatly appreciated by Captain Subreroque.

Sometimes, as happened in villages supporting the Viet Minh, after having positioned cover at our flanks, my task included concentrating our machine-guns' firepower just after, or sometimes simultaneously with, our mortar fire. This combination of weaponry proved lethal to the enemy. On one such mission, after an hour of break-through fire, we took up position for close proximity fighting near a village when the policemen of Lieutenant Moreau, chief of the Second Bureau and commander of the Vietnamese Police, entered the first huts. To get a better view of the surroundings, I drifted off about one-hundred paces and climbed a tall hut constructed of dried mud-and-straw bricks, lifting myself with finger holds offered by crevices in the wall and stepping onto the roof. At the sight of two armed rebels carrying grenades running in my direction, on the path passing the hut, I jumped down and, hidden in the shadow of the wall, waited until the shuffling of their sandals was near. I stretched out a leg, tripping the first rebel who rolled to the ground. The second, surprised by my rapid action, stood with a blank look on his face until I adjusted it with a well-placed blow from the butt of my Mauser. Then I forced them to get onto their feet, arms behind their heads, before removing the grenades from their belts and motioning for them to step away from their rifles, which I unloaded and gave back to them to carry. Walking behind my prisoners, prodding them from time to time with my Mauser to keep them moving, I made my way across the village to Lieutenant Moreau who was still busy wrapping up the search with his policemen. As soon as he saw us arriving, the lieutenant grabbed his carbine with the intention to opening fire but stopped in the nick of time when he saw that I was behind them.

"What in the hell are you doing there?" Moreau said crossly. "Don't you see they're still armed? Why didn't you take away their weapons?" he shouted.

"It's normal to force them to carry their own," I replied.

"Are you mad? Where did you learn such nonsense?"

With the Waffen SS at Kolberg, I would have liked to have answered but refrained myself. He didn't have the benefit of training at Sankt Andreas and Sennheim, nor had he fought in Pomerania. Perhaps to tell him that I had would have aroused his animosity.

Respect for a Brave Soldier

As was usual on a night raid, I placed my soldiers a few steps in front of the huts of a village. Once the operation was finished, I found Lieutenant Moreau and his men busy poking the ground with poles, advancing step by step, searching for traps and holes leading to tunnels. Meanwhile, with two Senegalese *tirailleurs*, I took care of the captured Viet Minh and removed their military papers which I would refer to when making my report. A Vietnamese adjutant of a supplementary section attached to the French army attracted my attention as he interrogated a prisoner. Not getting any answer whatsoever, he pulled out a long and sharp knife and cut off the prisoner's ear. Blood flowed profusely from the wound. At the Second Bureau they didn't use torture but they often resorted to rough actions and the other prisoners didn't wait for long before talking. In this way Lieutenant Moreau learned that a Viet Minh divisional commander was in the village, probably hiding in some tunnel. "We must flush him out at all costs," he told me, "we have already found ninety percent of their lairs, and now the only thing left is to wait." Lieutenant Moreau had patience to spare, the more so when, foreseeing a prolonged action, the provisions I ordered an hour earlier arrived by truck. A piglet was roasted which we ate with rice and local vegetables and a swig of *choum* while discussing the best way to drive out the rebel commander. A while later, a couple of *tirailleurs* located the tunnel leading to the main chamber of a Viet Mihn hideout and, after discharging a few magazines from their machine guns, they tried in vain to dislodge the occupants with hand grenades. An oppressive calm then weighed down on the village which a few hours earlier had been rocked by explosions and gunfire. Lieutenant Moreau, wiping his fat, short neck that barely emerged from his wide shoulders, wasn't in a hurry so I sat down on a little mound of soil after warning my soldiers to be on their guard against the Viet Minh still in the tunnel.

When we grew tired of waiting for the Viet Mihn to emerge from their hiding place, Leutenant Moreau and I went to join the men guarding the entrance of the tunnel. "The rebel is safe at the bottom of his den," Lieutenant Moreau said, "you know how well they construct them." He brought his hands to his mouth, and yelled down the tunnel, "Come out! Nobody will harm you. I'll keep the soldiers in check. Come out slowly and with your arms above your head." An obstinate silence followed. Grenades were useless against the occupants of these underground chambers; each horizontal access tunnel was dug on two levels with a short vertical section connecting them, thus isolating the main chamber from the detonation of a grenade. So Moreau decided to intervene in a more effective way. "Dig a vertical shaft to the center of that rebel-built bowel!" he ordered. As the digging got underway, Moreau stepped back and lit up his pipe which he smoked serenely as the excavation progressed.

Suddenly a shadow appeared in the tunnel, lunging at Lieutenant Moreau. We were caught by surprise but our reaction was prompt and we fired off our pistols and rifles. The Viet Minh commander returned fire with an American pistol in his hand. Bent forward, he zigzagged, shooting. Bullets smacked into his body and he fell but continued to drag himself towards the lieutenant when a Senegalese *tirailleur* finished him off with a point-blank burst from a machine gun. The brave Viet Minh officer fell to the side, his body shredded and bleeding.

"That's one less!" Lieutenant Moreau announced, returning his pipe to his mouth.

"He would have been more useful alive," I dared say.

"Alive or dead, what does it matter? This is the end for communists like him," Moreau answered disdainfully.

I was disgusted at the Lieutenant's attitude. OK, so he was right about communists but I had hoped the rebel commander would survive — he deserved it, given the courage he had shown.

Shambles on Patrol

Captain Subreroque was always busy organizing both complex and simple operations but every time we went out on missions led by him, we returned to Phu Lo with captured Viet Minh soldiers and boxes of arms and ammunition taken from the enemy and often too with information of vital importance. He had a good nose for flushing out communist rebels. And so, confident about the confessions extracted from them, he assembled a small expedition with a truck, two 6X6s, a Jeep and as many Senegalese *tirailleurs* as could fit aboard the vehicles. The purpose of this operation, the most dynamic he could muster, was to take by surprise a group of Viet Minh, that we had been hunting for quite a while without success.

It was raining when we left the base some hours before dawn. The driver of the truck I was travelling in with Lieutenant Moreau stopped the vehicle in front of the exit gate but Lieutenant Moreau gave the order to proceed. When I reminded him that we were waiting for the captain to arrive in his jeep, Lieutenant Moreau looked at me with still sleepy eyes, shrugged his shoulders and didn't answer. And so, without our captain, the small convoy headed into the night. After just a few minutes on the road, one of the small 6X6 trucks skidded on the muddy road and slid down the embankment, overturning with the *tirailleurs* still sitting in the box. The racket woke up the entire village of Phu Lo. Dogs barked furiously, alerting any Viet Minh in the area to our presence. The operation had failed even before it had begun. Captain Subreroque arrived in his jeep and, barely containing his rage, asked me to investigate why the truck had left the road. I went down the embankment and almost into the sludge of the paddy field where the small truck was stuck fast. Lieutenant Moreau climbed out of the truck to investigate. "Even those mangy dogs have to be there! What a barking mess," he cursed as he panted with the effort of walking back up the slope.

"They're on the Viets' side," I replied politely before we encountered the enraged Captain Subreroque, who seemed on the point of strangling Moreau with his own hands.

"The gunky soil…" the lieutenant started to justify himself.

"Shut up you piece of idiot!" the captain interrupted. After a brief pause, and unable to refrain himself further, the captain put his hands on his hips and looked the lieutenant up and down. "Why did your good mother make such a twerp!"

Lieutenant Moreau swallowed forcibly. "But, *mon capitaine…*"

"You're a disgrace to this Company, if you really must know!"

The expedition was suspended and, after aiding those injured by the tumbling truck, we returned to the base.

A week went by before the next operation, in part because Captain Subreroque studied the plan of attack in minute detail and also because he requested tank support which took a few days to show up. Once the preparations were complete, our column left early in the morning, heading towards 1st Company's base. The aim was to surprise the Viet Minh as they returned from their night excursion. It was still dark and still more than an hour before dawn. As we approached the 'crossroads of death', I sat with the captain near the turret of the tank second in the convoy, my eyes peering into the surrounding darkness. A blinding flash silhouetted the tank in front and an almost simultaneous blast of blisteringly hot air blew me to the ground. Stunned and unable to hear a thing except for a high-pitched whistle, I staggered to my feet rubbing dust from my eyes. The lead tank had come to a halt with the track on one side ripped from its wheels. Amidst the thick smoke vomiting from the open turret, two of the crew emerged, one after the other while the muzzle-flashes of the enemy's automatic weapons sparkled in the darkness.

"Ambush!" I screamed, barely able to hear my own voice as our soldiers jumped from the following trucks, firing into the paddy field to our left. As my hearing returned, I heard the groans of a wounded comrade and saw Captain Subreroque lying on his back at the foot of the embankment, his hands pressed against his eyes. I rushed over to him and pulled his hands from his bloodied face to see the extent of the damage. Finding that he was not gravely wounded, I hoisted his now inert body to my shoulder and, pursued by sweeps of machine-guns bursts, carried him to a Jeep whose driver was firing from behind his vehicle. I laid the captain on the back seats and pressed a field dressing on his face to control the bleeding. "Jump in...drive on!" I yelled to the driver.

The driver stopped firing for a moment. "But we're under fire."

"We'll drive him back, now!" Seeing that the driver was still refusing to move, I grabbed his collar with my blood-soaked hands and dragged him behind the steering wheel.

"I can't, I can't," he repeated, lowering his head and covering his neck with his hands. Bullets hissed through the air around us and a few pattered into the jeep's bodywork.

I pulled him into a sitting position. "You're wasting time!"

"I'm wounded," the driver moaned, showing me his blood stained hands.

"It's the captain's blood you wimp! If he dies on me I'll cut your throat!"

The driver tried manoeuvring on the narrow road but stopped as panic overwhelmed him. I pushed him from the jeep and jumped behind the steering wheel, revving the engine and spinning the wheels as I accelerated towards Phu Lo at full throttle while our tanks opened up with their cannons, their projectiles exploding violently amidst the flashes of fire from Viet Minh machine guns.

I was mad-angry as I drove at high speed into the emerging dawn, my thoughts shouting in condemnation of our own soldiers who blasted away without taking up proper positions. If it had not been for the support of our tanks the Viets would have slaughtered us all. I glanced over my shoulder to see the captain lying prone, his face in the pool of blood gathering under his forehead. I cursed the cowardly driver aloud. "Idiot of a driver...with him at the wheel I could have helped you, *mon capitaine*. Hold on...a few more minutes and we're there!"

At the infirmary at Phu Lo, the medical team had been alerted by radio and was already waiting for the arrival of casualties from the skirmish. As soon as they lifted the captain from the rear seats of the jeep, I pressed the accelerator and spun it towards the exit gate. A mad drive over the bumpy road took me back to the 'crossroads of death' where the fighting continued. I slammed on the brakes and left the jeep to rejoin our soldiers.

A soldier from my own squad greeted me. "Corporal, you're alive!"

"Casualties?"

"One wounded," replied the soldier.

The Senegalese *tirailleurs*, covered by the machine-gun fire from the tanks and the rifle fire of men taking cover near the trucks, tossed hand grenades into the enemy's positions. The sporadic fire from the enemy stopped suddenly as dawn broke, the rebels retreating, vanishing into morning mist.

Captain Subreroque's wound was more serious than I had anticipated but he began to recover in a few days, thanks to his strong constitution. His nose was under a thick wad of gauze that reached up to a bandage covering his head and half his face. He looked like an Egyptian mummy but he was far from silent when he summoned the NCOs from the 4th Company that had followed the tanks during the failed operation. I too was in his office, at the back of the group gathered in a semi-circle in front of his desk, waiting for his dressing-down.

"Adjutant Nogaroud! Where were you during the ambush?" the captain hissed through his superficial calmness.

"I, *mon capitaine*, was at the back of the column."

"And you, Chief Sergeant Padovani?"

"Busy at the flanks, *mon capitaine*."

"How silly of me...you were all at your posts." The captain raised his voice. "But nobody happened to be at correct spot. I was informed that there was chaos, panic among the *tirailleurs*. Shame on you! How long did it take for you to get a grip on the situation?"

Nobody answered.

"And you, Sergeant Tixier, my invisible sergeant, where were you?"

"*Mon capitaine*, I was waiting for your orders at the center of the alignment."

"And if the orders don't come, if your captain is out of the picture, how long does it take for you to react to the situation?"

Sergeant Tixier bowed his head. As the end of the debriefing drew near, I waited for my turn to be addressed by the captain, thinking that my actions were at least worthy of recognition if not praise. I felt left aside, almost ignored. Maybe he wasn't in the mood for dishing out praise with the others looking on. In absolute silence, he pulled open a drawer, took out a small wooden chest and held it tight in his hand. Shuddering with rage, he hurled it onto his desk with such force that the chest burst upon, scattering its contents across the polished surface.

The captain looked at us one by one, staring into our eyes for a brief, searching moment. "Look at them," he said, his palms facing upwards in a bitter invitation. "Medals sent by the General Staff. They were destined for heroes, for the most deserving ones." With a detached and ice-cold tone in his voice he continued, "Well I, Captain Subreroque, inform you that they will rust in this drawer before being attached to the chest of any commander of the 4th Company."

At the canteen that evening there was much bitter reflection amongst my comrades.

Sorrows and Celebrations

When on leave, I spent money as if I were a reincarnation of Croesus, the legendary and fabulously wealthy King of Lydia, ordering the best bottles of Champagne restaurants had to offer, buying the best brands of cigarettes and liquors and attracting the attention of the prettiest girls. But these things were small expenditures, nothing compared to the sum I had stashed away for my future. I would have liked to have celebrated my good fortune with Adjutant Marchi and other companions sympathetic to me but I had to proceed cautiously and refrain from spending money at a rate not justifiable by my income. I had also become a little restless, worried about what would happen to the money if something unfortunate was to happen to me. I dare not tell anybody about it, nor could I send it home or deposit it in a local bank without the risk of raising too many questions. Then worries about the exchange rate, which was working against me, came into play. On 10 May 1953, a piaster was valued at just ten francs; it had already devalued by seven franks since I confiscated it from the young Viet Minh woman and this left me with the nagging thought that I had taken two steps forward and one back.

On return from my umpteenth reconnaissance mission, there was a letter addressed to me. It came from Paris and the postmark over the stamp carried the maxim 'Tell it with flowers'. I turned the letter over in my hands for more than ten minutes, smoothing it and bringing it to my nose to inhale the delicate, residual perfume of violets. I prolonged, as long as I could bear it, the moment of happiness I anticipated on opening it. A letter from someone you know, that you care about, after so much time and from so far away, would have lifted any soldier's morale. The news was heartbreaking: the girl I kept so close to my heart and whom I dated just before my departure, had written to tell me she had left me for another man, a professional, a respectable person.

Embittered and demoralised by losses financial and romantic, I headed to the canteen intending to indulge in a good swig, to forget, to drown my sorrows. I leaned my MAT-49 at the entrance and took a seat on a barstool to order a cognac, which was served by a Vietnamese of a rather frail build. I gulped it down then ordered another two; then another two, paying promptly and without disturbing anybody, absorbed in my thoughts. Eventually, the barman told me that he would serve me no more. Affronted by this insult, I gave him a slap on the head causing him to collapse to the floor, where he stayed with his arms and legs spread out. Everyone present stood to get a better view, their hands leaning on the tables. The veterans, companions in so many skirmishes, looked at me with forlorn expressions on their faces. They knew well who I was and were used to my volatile character and so most sat down again to avoid becoming a new focus for my anger. A sergeant among those left standing, wearing a neat, white uniform, fresh from France, complained arrogantly, "Hei! Take it easy, corporal. Kids like you should learn how to behave!"

Squinting my eyes, I asked, "You…you…have you ever even fired a rifle in battle?"

"That's really none of your business kid."

"I have…twenty-three months…in Tonkin…do you know what that means?" I slurred. Menacingly, I detached myself from the counter.

The sergeant turned to the rest of the soldiers present. "The only choice left is to throw him in a punishment cell," he said, losing his patience.

I remained still for some seconds, the time necessary to assimilate the words 'punishment cell'. That sergeant should never have proffered them. I got up from the stool and went to the entrance to pick up my MAT-49 and, holding it under my arm, returned to the counter. "Everybody! Face against the wall!" I said curtly and loudly but without yelling, still calm. They knew I wasn't joking and so they complied without a word, including the novice sergeant who was visibly shaken by my reaction.

"My glass, the one that I haven't got yet!" I said to the Vietnamese barman, who had in the meantime recovered from his slap. He poured me a cognac, his hands trembling with fear. I savoured the liquor and, keeping my weapon pointed at those facing the wall, ordered another.. "So you want to throw me in a cell, eh?" I said, addressing the sergeant. "Come to fetch me if you have the courage… come! What are you waiting for?"

The door opened at that moment. Adjutant Marchi stopped after two paces; he understood immediately the situation. "Paul! What in the hell are you coming up with now?" he said, raising his arms.

"Move toward the wall," I pressed him. My friend obeyed. The others started to show signs of nervousness, knowing that I wouldn't have hesitated to shoot if provoked. "Oh, is it my sub-machine gun that scares you?" I said to the sergeant in white livery. I put the MAT-49 on the counter. "Now I'll move ten paces away from it, is that enough?"

The sergeant, his face now as white as his uniform, nodded.

"Good, now try to arrest me if you want to die a hero," I declared.

A subdued murmur rose from those lined with their faces to the wall; two of them turned to look at me, their expressions contorted with anxiety.

"So," I said after a long ten seconds, "it is as I feared, you don't even have a drop of courage!" I went back to the counter, grabbed my MAT-49 and ordered two more drinks. I savoured the liquor with short sips, appreciating fully the calm and silence that now prevailed in the canteen. Slowly, I headed to the exit, lowering my weapon. "I thank you," I said, without hiding my satisfaction, "I really needed a bit of tranquillity and a good swig." I then gave a 'see you later' wave to my friend, Adjutant Marchi, who returned the farewell with an awkward-looking nod.

Back at base, one of the Senegalese *tirailleurs* I had chosen to join the police patrol asked me to read a letter he had just received from home. I had read aloud similar letters in the past to soldiers whose 'sight was poor' but were in fact illiterate, and so too were many of their wives who employed a scribe to write them. Their husbands' cheques and letters were often addressed to the scribe and, I was told, in order to get them the wives sometimes spent the night with him. My Senegalese *tirailleurs* trusted only me to read their letters from home to them and it was evident that many had been written by the same person, such was the similarity in their calligraphy and content. However, the letter I read to this particular Senegalese policeman was a little different from the others. It began: *your brother is sick, your sister doesn't improve, the harvesting was scarce, the old father suffers from back pains, my uncle, my mother and the kids say bye to you and...* The letter was so laden with bad news I stopped right there, wondering if I should continue. As his comrades gathered round to listen, the Senegalese urged me to finish reading the letter. "Tell me something," I said, "how long is it since you left your wife at the village?"

He did a laborious calculation, counting on his fingers and then answered triumphantly, "I'm here since almost three years. Why do you ask Corporal Paul?"

"Well...I don't know what to say but...

The Senegalese's brow furrowed. "Bad news, Corporal Paul?"

"I think so but...hei, there is always the canteen for a good swig to lift your spirits high, if you want to." I tried in this way to prepare him to receive the strange news.

"What does the letter say about my wife, Corporal Paul?"

There was no way to mitigate the disappointment he would feel on hearing the news — as I had discovered to my cost when I opened the letter from my girlfriend — so I gave it to him straight. "She says she had a baby three months ago."

He opened his shiny, black eyes wide; his naturally cavernous nostrils flared as he gave me a questioning look and I nodded to confirm what I had just told him. To my astonishment, a bright smile lit his face. "A baby...a baby," he screamed jubilantly to his countrymen. They stood up together, his comrades congratulating the policeman and encircling me as they danced and sang in rhythm with their steps in a disarming display of glee and contentment.

"Corporal Paul, please read again where my wife writes about the baby."

"You are happy, eh?"

"Good omen, Corporal Paul. Good sign of prosperity in my family," he answered with enthusiasm, his eyes sparkling with sheer joy.

I re-read the letter and then let them drag me to the canteen for a good drink.

Hierarchies

At the Phu Lo base, a French soldier arrived as substitute for the radio operator; he was young and personable and his affable nature soon earned my friendship and the esteem of his comrades. He was sympathetic, courteous and a tolerant optimist. One day, on patrol with a radio installed in his jeep, he ran over a mine that exploded, hurtling the vehicle and soldier into the air. He was transported to Phu Lo by his companions, where he waited to be sent to Hanoi's hospital and so, together with Adjutant Marchi, I paid him a visit in the infirmary.

"Don't stress yourself," Marchi told the youngster as we sat at his bedside.

"Ahh…they got me," whispered the injured soldier with great effort. His stomach had been riddled by shrapnel and, despite the nurses' best attempts to stop him haemorrhaging, blood seeped through his bandages. I tried to cheer him up with the story about the Senegalese policeman's dance but he stopped me with a tired motion of his hand and an insipid smile. "I know I'm done for," he said with resignation, and then joked, "there's nothing they can do except arrest me for illegal transport of scrap metal."

He died the next day at the hospital.

I was designated to command the guard of honour at his funeral and so I arrived at the chapel bringing a wreath from the battalion.

"Was he promoted or a private?" the chaplain asked in the sacristy, slipping a surplice over his captain's uniform.

"What difference does it make?" I asked.

"Six candles for a promoted soldier, three for a private."

"If my friend could talk he would say 'six or three who cares, since I'm dead' don't you think?"

The chaplain looked askance at me, and then placed six candles around the baldaquin before reciting a prayer. *Who knows how many candles a general is entitled to*, I thought.

After the ceremony, a French flag was laid over the coffin before it was lifted onto the back of a truck. At the head of the squad I presented the last honours to that unlucky young man before he was transported to the military cemetery and his final place of rest.

In the evening, after dinner and the last inspection of the guards at their posts, I retired to my room which was separated by a brick wall from the rest of the dormitory where eight Senegalese *tirailleurs* had their cots. I pulled the mosquito net across the doorway and sat down at my desk to write a letter home. At about ten, somebody knocked on the still open door. "Come in," I said despite the late hour, looking up from the desk besides my cot.

"Corporal Martelli," a Senegalese *tirailleur* belonging to another squad said as he lifted the mosquito net. He was holding a loaded MAT-49, balancing it on his arm. He smelled of rancid alcohol.

"What do you want?" I asked gently, glancing across the room to make sure my MAT-49 was in its usual place, leaning against the opposite wall.

He opened his mouth to talk but closed it again without a sound.

"What do you want?" I repeated, as calmly as possible.

He pointed his weapon, ready to shoot. "It's an injustice!" he said, drawling.

"All right, an injustice," I concurred. I couldn't have avoided a burst.

"It hurts in the heart, the injustice."

"You can't find the words, eh? Let's see if I can help you out," I hastened to say, without taking my eyes off his face.

"We suffer injustices, we."

"You mean because you are African?" I cast a rapid glance at my MAT-49 which I knew still had twenty-five rounds in the magazine.

"We do more than you Frenchmen."

"Ah, you mean about the draft?" I said, calculating that my weapon was too far away to reach before he fired.

"We stay longer than you."

"It's the legal length of time for…"

"We get less pay than you, French soldiers," he whined, interrupting me.

"I know, you are right, but the type of duties call for…"

"We eat less than you, whites. No access to canteen for black soldiers."

I continued the dialogue, which seemed the most appropriate course of action given the delicacy of the moment. "The situation is unjust, you are right. But what can I do?" That type of weapon has a hair trigger — a slight touch and it would spray bullets. I thought I was about to pay in person for the inequalities perpetrated by the French colonial authorities.

"Black soldiers…black skin…yours is white."

"You're not wrong there," I said.

"It's difficult…in front of the whites…" he slurred, his hands tightening their grip on his MAT-49.

"You can't find the proper words, right? It's only an inferiority complex, nothing serious."

The drunkard moved one step forward, pointing the barrel at my throat, one meter from me.

"You see," I continued with utmost patience, speaking almost as a friend might, "the good Lord created men; he made them black, white, red, yellow — it's His will, not mine."

"Of all colours," he babbled, fumbling for words. He seemed touched by the apparent logic of my speech.

"Of all sorts," I affirmed. Catching the moment of bewilderment in the black man's clouded eyes, I got up and calmly took a cigarette from my pack. As I inhaled a lungful of the soothing smoke, I looked at my weapon leaning against the wall and figured that the Senegalese would mow me down even before I sprang into action. Talking and gesticulating slowly in front of his eyes with the lighted cigarette, I stepped towards him. *There would be only this one, fleeting chance,* I thought. I leapt forward pushing the barrel of the machine gun away with my left hand. Three cracks of gunfire followed in quick succession. I hit him in his face with a powerful right. At my second punch he fell backwards onto the hard floor and I took the chance to grab my own MAT-49. The pool of blood around the downed man shocked the Senegalese *tirailleurs* of his squad who had rushed in at the sound of the gunshots, so much so that they broke into a sort of aggressive dance while complaining loudly about their unconscious comrade.

"Come closer and you're dead men!" I warned them. They believed me, they knew who I was. Interrupting their babbling of their native tongue, I ordered one of them to inform the nurses.

The lieutenant doctor arrived after a quarter of an hour to verify the circumstances of the drunken soldier's fall. The base of the Senegalese's cranium had been cracked, he told me, and he had signed a statement permitting the unfortunate man to return to his native country.

Zouk To

The Phu Lo Battalion commander was replaced by a new officer, a fellow called Valliet. I detested him from the moment I met him, when I was summoned to his office. Heavily built and tall, his beady and inquisitive eyes continually danced in their sockets. *He would,* I thought, *have seemed more at ease in a police office interrogating criminals rather than leading a battalion.* "What am I going to do with you?" he said to me crossly.

"I don't understand, *mon commandant*," I answered, genuinely surprised and puzzled by his question that carried with it the undertones of accusation.

"Send you to the court martial? That's exactly how I should proceed with your case!"

"My case, *mon commandant*?"

"You've ruined that African, do you understand, Corporal Martelli?" His voice had the roughness of a rasp at work on a piece of hardwood.

"I have the right to defend myself when threatened by someone with a loaded submachine gun," I replied.

"Shut up! What right? You have no valid reason and no excuse for behaving in that violent manner. You should have followed proper procedures…asked his name, registration number and…"

"With a MAT-49 under my nose? Absurd!" I snorted, having now lost my patience.

"Do you want to rot for the rest of your days at Poulo Condor, Corporal Martelli?"

That threat touched a tender spot. I was still extremely sensitive to words such as 'prison' and 'court martial'. I bit my lip in a failed effort to subdue the anger that was building up a head of steam. Then I exploded in front of the cantankerous officer. "I'll desert before I'm dragged in front of a court martial. The Viets will make me a commander, at the least!" I barked at him.

"Get out of here!" Valliet growled angrily.

I gave an impeccable salute and turned to leave, eager to breathe fresh air. "What kind of buffoon is that," I mumbled, "things are going from bad to worse on this base."

Captain Subreroque had unwittingly contributed to this worsening situation: during an assault operation on a fortified Viet Minh village, he suffered a bullet wound to his shoulder and was transferred to the hospital and then sent back to France. Comments were made, maligning the captain by saying that it was a fortunate wound, not serious but with all advantages of a good pension and a medal for valour — but not in my presence.

Captain Subreroque's unexpected departure left the door open for Captain Rigasse. He was a slow and flaccid fatty, with lines of fear etched into his face. As it happened, Rigasse arrived just before Lieutenant Moreau received intelligence of an imminent attack on the tower at fort Zouk To, and agreed to send in reinforcements. Consequently, together with my squad and Adjutant Marchi, I ended up at the post, which was on the road to the Phuc Yen sector. Given Valliet didn't place me under arrest after our squabble, I figured that this was his way of punishing me, through Rigasse, and at the same time getting rid of me from Phu Lo. Maybe so, but being chosen for such a mission was also a mark of esteem as far as my Senegalese *tirailleurs* were concerned; they had excelled in several previous expeditions without suffering fatalities or seriously wounded soldiers. Our deployment could however also have been taken for tacit recognition that my efficient, tight-knit, reliable and, when needed, lethal squad, was the best available. That the operational command had been entrusted to Adjutant Marchi gave me great satisfaction, not only because of our mutual esteem and friendship, but also because he was suited to the task. So, even though the operation seemed quite risky, there was nothing to cause me any great concern.

In the Tonkin district, the Viet Minh were becoming increasingly bold and, whenever they suffered a defeat, sought alternative strategies, as happened in February of the previous year when our troops had to evacuate Hoa Binh, just three months after capturing it, because the rebels moved their Chinese supplies by another route, negating our victory. And also, during December 1952 at Na San, following our counterattack and victory, General Giap changed tactics by concentrating his forces against our secondary bases to avoid our artillery. He went hiding into Laos, invading it in April 1953 having been defeated at Vihn Yen, and at Mao Khe, before I arrived in Hanoi. To alleviate the pressure on his own troops, General Giap ordered local groups to harass our forces. In the meantime he was trying, first with General de Lattre de Tassigny's forces and then with General Salan's, and again in January with Navarre's, to draw our Expeditionary army into battles on terrain that was out of range of our heavy artillery. The supply routes available to him also influenced General Giap's tactics and our aerial attack on his supply depots at Lang Son must have caused him considerable frustration. It seemed therefore that the Viet Mihn, in the area north of Hanoi, was in turmoil but the intelligence obtained by Lieutenant Moreau regarding the attack on Zouk To implied a massive assault by a well-organized force of at least battalion strength.

At the little fort of Zouk To, *after* our arrival, our total force consisted of five Europeans, thirty Vietnamese and twenty Senegalese *tirailleurs*, the whole unit commanded by Adjutant Marchi, a sergeant already there and by me.

I thought I had left my work as a builder-engineer at Phu Lo behind after Captain Subreroque's repatriation but when I realized the precarious situation outside the little fort I buckled down to work immediately. I deployed rolls of barbed wire and selected the zones to be mined around the three reinforced concrete block houses located at the tips of the usual triangle. These were connected with a network of underground tunnels which followed a zigzag course so that they could be defended by just a few men in case of a breach.

"When do you think they'll attack?" I asked Marchi when the work was complete.

"Very soon, at night time as always."

"They want to wear us down, make us anxious," I said.

"Maybe," agrees Marchi, "but one thing is certain…according to my experience they'll exploit fully the surprise factor, you'll see!"

The other French sergeant, a man with an angelic face and an abundance of patience, slept in the top floor of the tower in the middle of the fort with his dog and a Vietnamese woman who, he told me, was about to leave to visit her family in the mountains. The operations room was also located in the tower and together with the sergeant, Adjutant Marchi, a fellow from Brittany nicknamed 'Breton' and another who was nearing the end of his draft and therefore referred to as 'Demob', I spent my days and nights scanning the surroundings with my binoculars and the beam of our searchlight. To maintain contact, the Peripheral Quarter called us by radio every two hours but after a few days of mounting tension, there was still no sign of the Viet Minh. Marchi was beginning to harbour doubts about the intelligence gathered by Moreau and was of the opinion that it was planted by Viet spies for the purpose of dividing our forces.

With the continued absence of Viet Minh activity, we began to relax our surveillance though the guards at the blockhouses were kept on utmost alert. In the evening, the sergeant invited all the Europeans to the operations room in the tower to keep each other company and talk about life back home in France over a few drinks. The sergeant's dog settled down soon after our arrival but then began to show signs of nervousness; every other moment he would prick up his ears, circle the room or growl and show his fangs.

"He senses that something's wrong out there," I remarked.

"He's always like this with unfamiliar people," the sergeant assured me.

I looked out from the window into the compound's yard, trusting more in the dog's instinct than the sergeant's. Outside, absolute silence reigned as it did on previous nights and there was no tangible reason for my unease. We continued drinking, especially the surly Breton, a well-muscled man of imposing aspect with a large face and thick eyebrows.

"Too bad we can't use the searchlight," Demob said in a soprano voice that betrayed his apprehension. He was a young, wiry soldier with a pointed chin and intelligent eyes.

"No lights…these are the orders. The patrol soldiers from Phu Lo are nearby and don't want to be given away by being caught accidentally in the beam," the sergeant reminded us.

The sergeant looked at his watch and then reminded Breton that it was his turn to substitute the guard. The dog bristled for the umpteenth time. Breton rose from his chair but the sergeant, on seeing that Breton was unsteady on his feet, announced that he would go instead to the roof of the tower to keep watch. It was almost two in the morning, a little more than two hours and that night too would have been spent without incident.

The sergeant's lack of concern about the attack predicted by Lieutenant Moreau was probably well-founded. I had made substantial improvements to the defenses around the blockhouses but our main defense was the support of our artillery which protected three designated ranging zones around the fort. Zone One extended for a radius of 100m around the fort; this was the target area of the artillery based at Phu Lo whose shells exploded in mid-air at a height of fifteen to twenty meters, spraying attackers with a rain of shrapnel. It was practically impossible to get close to the tower with fire over Zone One in action. Getting farther away in concentric circles, Zone Two extended the ranging area another 200m and Zone Three an additional 300m. It was up to the 105mm cannons to cover these last two areas and their projectiles didn't leave anything standing. Each of the three blockhouses was equipped with two machine guns and, from the embrasures, the line of sight extended in all directions: from any one of these block houses we could, in fact, shoot against the attackers of the remaining two and of the tower. In short, we had an excellent defensive system.

I climbed up the roof to take a breath of fresh air. "Any activity?" I asked the sergeant.

"Absolutely nothing. Everything is still."

"Your dog is still nervous," I remarked. "He's grumbling and growling again. There must be something strange down there," I said looking into the darkness of the surrounding terrain. In fact, I was as apprehensive as the dog, troubled by a premonition of danger such as I had felt at Körlin and at Kolberg.

The sergeant brought his binoculars to his eyes. "Nothing to worry about," he reafirmed, scanning all around.

"If we could use the searchlight..."

"How would I square that with the orders from Phu Lo?"

"Only for brief moments," I suggested. "I don't trust the area to the north of us."

"Remember," said the sergeant, "there are men on patrol in the area."

"They'll have returned to their base by this time, I'm sure of it. Even so they are not as exposed as we are." I said.

The sergeant switched on the searchlight. Its white shaft of light cut through the night, lighting up a blockhouse. Then he shone it farther afield, into the ranging zones.

"Damn!" I exclaimed.

"*Mon Dieu*! It's the end. They are a thousand of the devils," the sergeant gasped. As he switched off the searchlight, flares hissed into the night sky then hung on their little parachutes to light up the compound. A pandemonium of bursts, bangs and thuds was unleashed against the tower's exterior walls.

I ran back to the operations room to find Marchi already plummeting down the steps in long leaps. I followed him. Bullets smashed against the walls making the sound of a storm of giant hailstones on glass. Breton, now suddenly completely sober, gave orders to the Vietnamese and to Demob who was running in the opposite direction, upstairs towards the radio room. "Tell them they're everywhere, call for fire to Zone One!"

I heard a series of detonations, mines — the Viets were already close to the blockhouses.

"*Porco boia!* They're over-running us!" Marchi screamed. "Let's go hard at it, Paul!"

"Count on me...this will be a good tango." I ran through the tunnel heading to Blockhouse 3, the one entrusted to me, where I found my squad of Senegalese *tirailleurs* already shooting. "Good! Continue firing!" I yelled. They reacted to my words with a brief 'thumbs up' sign; they didn't need encouragement, they knew their business off pat. The Vietnamese soldiers on the other hand gave some cause for concern and needed more detailed instructions. "Ready with the back-up ammo rolls and maga-zines," I ordered to two of them. When I moved toward an embrasure to check the situation I saw Viet Minh soldiers, lit by the staccato flashes of explosions, working at our barbed wire entanglements. I redirected the machine-gunners' fire which imme-diately swept out a dozen of the rebels who were sliding charges under the defense wire. The Viet soldiers charged in silence, whining briefly when hit and unable to gain ground. Then the enemy launched their reserves with orders screamed in their shrill, chanting language. I heard them between blasts, as if they were only a few meters from me. I saw them fall in droves, decimated by our bursts, but they had already opened three long gaps in our wire. Against a dozen Viet Minh advancing with mines on the end of long bamboo sticks, I let go two MAT-49 sweeps, mowing down half of them. Then I aimed at the mines on the ground and was able to hit one which exploded and triggered the others. The Viet Minh carrying out this bold manoeuver were blown, dismembered, into the air. I fired another couple of magazines with my MAT-49 and then handed over my position at the embrasure to a Senegalese while I took charge of the Vietnamese attendants, urging them to make sure they kept the *tirailleurs* supplied with ammo. When I returned to an embrasure to see what was happening outside, I noticed many shadows scurrying, running through the gaps in the wire. "Don't let them come any closer…fire at will!" I yelled. The Viet Minh charged, blindly launching grenades that didn't reach us as they fell under the rifle fire from the Senegalese. Acrid smoke from the frenzy of explosions infiltrated through our embrasures, stinging our nostrils, compelling the machine gunners to cover their noses with handkerchiefs tied behind their necks.

The 105mm projectiles from our artillery hissed overhead then exploded with a contin-uous roar, cutting down scores of Viet Minh soldiers but falling too wide, near Zone Three, when they were really needed in the inner zone, despite the risk to ourselves. To remedy the situation, I made my way back to the tower to tell Demob to contact the artil-lery commander so he could tell him to redirect his fire inside the inner zone. I ran upstairs and burst into the radio room. "Where's Demob?"

Breton, his brow damp with sweat, looked up from the radio operator's desk. "In my blockhouse."

"Tell the artillery to redirect their fire to Zone One," I told Breton.

"I am trying Paul, but the officer in charge says it's too dangerous."

"Let me try to reason with him."

Breton passed me the earphones and left to return to the blockhouse under his command. "Zouk To calling artillery section Phu Lo. Answer, over," I called impatiently.

"We are listening Zouk To, over," the voice on the radio crackled.

"The Viets are at the base of the tower, clear with heavy fire on Zone One, over."

There was electrical interference, a sort of frying noise, and then somebody else answered. "Too risky. We'll continue with blasting charges over Zone One and short fire from the 105s, over."

"You are making a big racket for nothing! It's in Zone One they're pushing," I shouted at the top of my voice.

"Do not insist Zouk To, we'll think of something else. We'll call you, over and out."

I punched the radio in frustration. "It's idiots I have to deal with." I yelled at the blameless radio apparatus.

The French sergeant meanwhile, giving a good example to his Vietnamese soldiers, hurled grenades from the tower's embrasures. His soldiers, unfamiliar with the blasts from 105mm projectiles, seemed rather disoriented: two of them, frozen with fear, had taken shelter under the sergeant's cot. I went over to kick them, forcing them to their duty before peering through a small window. My heart sank. On the barrier wall, in front of the tower, the Viet Minh were scaling a bamboo ladder. A quick-witted Vietnamese behind an embrasure on the tower launched a grenade which exploded directly under the ladder, reducing it to splinters.

I ran downstairs to the blockhouse under my command to find that my *tirailleurs* were now mere shadows in a smog of irritant fumes released by exploding grenades. They were fighting valiantly, keeping a level head and, up to that moment, had withstood waves of ferocious Viet Minh attacks concentrated on this particular blockhouse. I took up position at one of the embrasures, spitting bursts from my sub-machine gun against the relentless assailants. The ground trembled; streams of concrete dust fell from the ceiling of the blockhouse. The continuous roar of explosions, the crackling of machine-gun fire and the combatants' frantic screams merged into a hellish cacophony of battle and I was at the exhilarating, terrifying epicenter of the action.

"Direct fire to Blockhouse 1," I yelled. I took over one of the two heavy machine guns and aimed it at the wave of Viet Minh attacking Demob's blockhouse. Marchi must have simultaneously had the same thought and the lethal cross fire from our two blockhouses cut the attackers to shreds. They enemy, pursued by our efficient bursts, retreated but regrouped immediately to launch another attack in platoons of thirty or forty but they too were repelled by our defensive fire. I knew I had a couple of minutes before the next attack and ordered the machine gunner back to his position before running through the zigzagging tunnel to Blockhouse 1.

"Like bees around honeycomb!" Demob smiled when he saw me. "They must have a grudge against me."

"I was thinking the worst," I said, still panting from my rush through the tunnel.

"Don't say that, for goodness sake," Demob groaned. "In a couple of days I'm due back home. I don't want to die in this hole, that's for sure!"

Breton was firing nearby, besides an embrasure. "Go back and forth between emplacements when you can…keep an eye on the overall situation," I told him.

"Understood, Paul. Every five minutes if the Viets let me."

I laid a hand on Demob's shoulder. "You'll make it through," I said before turning to leave.

"Thanks for the help, Paul!" Demob shouted at the end of a burst, just as I was about to slip into the tunnel to return to my own blockhouse.

I reached my embrasure just in time to make out six Viet Minh still standing after a furious attack against Blockhouse 2, defended by Marchi. They raged against its openings despite my fire catching them sideways, felling two of them. With the force of desperation and a mad courage, the surviving Viets advanced on all fours until they were able to launch an explosive charge into the blockhouse. They fell an instant before the blast, mowed by Marchi's machine gunners.

"Bastards!" I exclaimed. "All fire on Blockhouse 2," I ordered my gunners before slipping into the tunnel leading to that blockhouse. The generator must have taken a hit because the lights in the tunnel were down but coming towards me was the glare of a flashlight. It was Breton.

"Paul! I was coming to tell you they got Marchi!" he shouted.

"Is it serious?"

"He's not responding!"

"Damn!" I cursed at the thought of my wounded friend. I followed Breton back to Marchi's blockhouse and found him slumped on the floor, a couple of meters from his wounded gunners who were moaning with pain. One of the machine guns, its barrel busted, hung from its tripod and the other, crumpled by the explosion, had fallen onto the floor. I ordered the Vietnamese present to provide immediate aid for the wounded while Breton made his presence felt with a MAT-49, through the twisted iron grate of the small window. The grate of another opening, torn from the concrete, had been hurled outside, leaving a larger hole to which I sent a *tirailleur* to assist Breton.

Marchi began complaining, "My shoulder!"

The words brought me comfort. He was still alive and had just regained consciousness. "Don't move!" I urged.

"It's smashed," he mumbled in Italian, pressing a hand over his profusely bleeding wounds.

"Don't talk," I said to him, holding up his head with one hand.

"Keep the bastards out," he muttered.

"I know, I know! Don't think about it, I'll see to it."

I told Breton to find every possible soldier and bring them to the damaged blockhouse which would almost certainly form the focus of the Viets next attack. Then, in the yellow beam of a flashlight, Breton and I carried Marchi through the tunnel to the foundations of the tower where we laid him down.

Breton shook his head mournfully. "Paul, he's unconscious again."

"Try to stop the bleeding, I'll go upstairs for bandages," I said.

The thick external walls of the tower, shuddering under the continuous impact of light mortar grenades, threatened to give way. The whole building shook, as if in an earthquake, as I ran up the stairs, passing the Vietnamese firing from the embrasures. Sweat oozed from every pore in my body by the time I reached the sergeant in the radio room. "Marchi's blockhouse," I shouted, "it's been hit!"

"I've already alerted the artillery — it's under aim." The sergeant spoke into the microphone. "Five or six rounds. Same position, over."

I was desperate to see the Viet Minh attack punished. "Ask for the heavy pills, I'll give the order to evacuate Blockhouse 2," I suggested.

"Calm down Paul, the artillery boys are very accurate in their aim. There's no need to evacuate…the air bursts will prove effective, you'll see."

"You think we can hold till dawn?"

"We should get air support by then…I've informed the aviation center at Gia Lam."

"Tanks…what about tanks?" I asked as I searched for gauze and bandages.

The sergeant didn't answer; he was trying to call Phuc Yen again.

"We need tanks!" I repeated.

The sergeant took off his earphones. "The commander isn't available and the second in command doesn't want to assume responsibility for sending them in," he explained.

The tower shuddered under another barrage of mortar grenades. "Those idiots! We'll die here…martyrs for the country," I yelled.

The sergeant stood up from his desk "They'll have us, *mon Dieu* they'll have us!"

I left the radio room, leaping down the steps four at a time, until I reached the basement where Breton and the wounded Marchi, now made feeble by the loss of blood, were waiting.

"He's come round," Breton said, smiling.

"Here," I said, handing Breton a fistful of bandages, "press down on the wound and stay with him." At each strike of a projectile, vibrations coursed through foundations of the tower, plaster fell from the walls and smoke was beginning to penetrate the tunnel. I knelt beside Marchi. "Once repatriated you'll be a hero," I said, trying to comfort him.

"You'll have it, the *Croix de Guerre*," Breton added.

"And the wooden cross," the wounded Marchi said in a faint voice.

I left Breton with Marchi at the basement of the tower and returned to Blockhouse 3 to oversee our defense. Two hours passed in an instant and we were almost at dawn and running low on ammunition. The Viet Minh, frustrated by our fierce resistance, became more bold and fanatical. They were attacking in waves now, shooting randomly and screaming like madmen. They fell on top of their dead and wounded comrades as they charged, forming piles that gave cover to those still to join the attack in a scene that reminded me of the Russians during the battle at Körlin — the same stupid tactic, the same use of dead soldiers' bodies. And so, despite the ferocity of their assaults, we repulsed the Viets time after time. However, Blockhouse 2 was the weak point in our defense so I ordered its evacuation and the retrieval of any remaining ammunition. It made sense to stop wasting firepower trying to protect it when a single soldier in each of the tunnels could stall incursions into the other blockhouses.

Breton arrived from the basement of the tower. His voice carried an unmistakable tremor of panic. "Paul! The adjutant is worsening…he's raving like a maniac when he's not unconscious."

"Have him carried here, quick!" I wanted him in the safety of my own blockhouse in case the Viet breached Blockhouse 2, opening their way to the tower. Breton arrived soon after carrying Marchi with the aid of two Vietnamese and they laid him at the entrance of my emplacement, in the safety of a corner.

"I'll defend the tunnel here," I told Breton, "keep the situation under control at my back and at Blockhouse 1." Accompanied by two Vietnamese and a *tirailleur*, I took up position ten meters inside the tunnel, at the zigzag angle nearest Marchi's evacuated blockhouse — now overrun by Viet Minh soldiers — and fired off a burst to declare my presence. The Viets returned fire but didn't dare advance. The two Vietnamese looked at me with terror in their eyes, pulling back some steps towards the ammunition stacked on the floor. In no uncertain terms I persuaded them to reload the MAT-49s, refill empty magazines and to be ready with hand grenades. Their fear evaporated and they carried out my orders with relative calm, their minds occupied by the task of preparing for our defense. As I gave the Vietnamese instructions on what to do in case of a Viet Minh break-through, Breton appeared in the tunnel.

"Blockhouse 1 is resisting," he reported. "Our 105 candies are hitting the Viets hard but they don't give up."

"Stay here," I told Breton, "give the men here a hand and don't let the enemy pass."

"And you?"

"I'm going to check out the tower...to see if there is news of tank support."

In the radio room, the sergeant was in mid-sentence. "...they must hurry, there isn't a second to waste, over."

All around the compound our artillery shells exploded in a continuous thunder. "The Viets won't retreat! Blockhouse 2 is out of action and Marchi has nasty wounds," I shouted to the sergeant.

"Hear these drums outside? The artillery have already doubled their firing rate," the sergeant said to me as he donned the earphones again. He spoke into the microphone, his voice loud and frantic. "Fifteen minutes max...we cannot resist for longer. Hurry up for the love of God, over."

"Tanks?" I asked hopefully.

Sweat was running like tears down the sergeant's cheeks. "It's becoming critical, Paul. I'm waiting for confirmation but if they don't arrive on time we're burnt toast."

The radio crackled again: "Zouk To, Zouk To, green light...tanks will be with you shortly...resist. A lieutenant is in overall command, over."

"When will they be here? Verify, Verify! Over." The sergeant shouted, verging on hysteria.

"Zouk To. Estimate arrival at 0440 hours...resist...over and out."

"Finally," the sergeant sighed, loosening his sweat-soaked collar. "How are you doing down there in your blockhouse?"

"Short on ammo," I said. "If the tanks don't arrive on time it will be a massacre."

"*Mon Dieu!*" The sergeant stared at me, horrified by my stark prediction.

Flashes of light from the continuing explosions shot through the embrasures of the tower. It was here that the Viet Minh were now concentrating their fanatical assaults. They were aiming at the top of the tower, increasing their fire power. On the wall around the tower, bamboo ladders appeared one after another. The Viet Minh soldiers boldly climbed them only to be repulsed by the dull thuds of grenades thrown by our Vietnamese and Senegalese soldiers.

Suddenly, a loudspeaker blared out of the darkness, above the din of our exploding artillery shells. The ladder assaults came to an abrupt halt. A nasal voice, distorted by the amplification, spoke in French: "Give yourselves up, do not fight against your brothers. Do not serve the cause of colonialism and capitalism! Lay down your weapons, brothers. Surrender yourselves, French soldiers." The voice continued in the local tongue but was drowned by a rain of bullets as we gave our answer by firing with increased intensity.

"Paul! They're breaching the mouth of the tunnel at Blockhouse 2!" Breton yelled from the bottom of the tower's stairway.

I charged down the tower's stairs at full speed then headed for the zigzag in the tunnel where the *tirailleurs* were already firing and tossing grenades around the corner.

"We can't last much longer, Paul," Breton warned.

"You're right. What time do you make it?"

"About 0430 hours, why?"

"Go see what's happening in Blockhouse 3," I ordered him.

Breton disappeared deeper into the tunnel, behind the faint beacon of his flashlight while we at the zigzag continued to fire sub-machine guns and toss grenades. When he returned, Breton was puffing heavily. "Paul! They've no munitions left."

"Inform the sergeant to radio for all the artillery support they can provide," I urged him. Brenton turned to run again, this time to the tower. I gave the order to the Vietnamese and Senegalese soldiers to retire to Blockhouse 3 while I covered their retreat. The fire from Viet Minh beyond the zigzag increased in intensity with bullets hammering the concrete walls of the tunnel close to me into a choking dust. I discharged a last burst and turned to run down the tunnel towards Blockhouse 2. In the gloomy, dust filled air I saw that two of our Vietnamese had waited to assist me; one held out a hand to take my MAT-49 as I passed, the other pressed a hand grenade into my fist. I pushed my two loyal soldiers away looking them hard in the eyes to ensure their obedience. They bowed their heads, pressed their palms together as if in prayer of thanks and then turned to disappear into the shadows of the tunnel. As I prepared to toss the grenade into the path of the pursuing Viet Minh, the shock waves from our artillery's exploding 105s came to a sudden end; the patter of machine-gun fire and the voices of the Viet Minh faded to nothing.

Breton's joyful voice broke the eerie silence. "Paul! Tanks...they've arrived!"

I left Breton at my position to maintain a defense presence in the tunnel while I returned to the tower. There the sergeant, who quite suddenly seemed ten years younger, looked at me with eyes shining with tears of relief. "They're retreating," he said, "scooting! He summoned me with a gesture towards the embrasure in the room. We looked out to see the Viet Minh scattering in all directions, towards the mountains. Our tanks loosed off a few rounds into their midst; our planes zoomed overhead pursuing the rebels, strafing them. We had survived the bitter onslaught.

Aided by Breton and Demob I helped carry Adjutant Marchi, who was in shock because of massive blood loss, into the open where nurses arranged for his immediate transfer to

Phu Lo. But my work was not yet finished; under the protection of the tanks, I was part of a squad assembled to secure the surrounding area. Judging from the piles of corpses scattered around the blockhouses and as far as the outer limit of firing Zone Three, the Viet Minh had suffered grave losses. Farther out we discovered a rudimentary switchboard in a hollow in the ground that was the Viet Minh command post with telephone wires fanning out into the surrounding countryside.

As I returned to the compound, I thought about how close we had been to disaster. Our ammunition was almost done; a few more minutes and we were destined to succumb to the overwhelming force of our communist enemies. In the most absolute silence, the Viet Minh had strung out their telephone cables, dug foxholes, set up their mortars — all of this right under our noses. And we had played right into their hands with the order not to use the searchlight in case we accidentally disclosed the position of a patrol on night reconnaissance, a patrol that probably didn't even come within a kilometer of our base. Had enemy spies, after having spread the news of an impending assault, induced us to send a patrol out of Phu Lo to test if we would keep the searchlight switched off? Or was that simply a fortunate coincidence in favor of the Viet Minh? In the end, though, despite them having all the time available to prepare for a surprise attack, they had under-evaluated our strength and our will to resist to the end.

I gathered the bamboo sticks used to push the explosive charges until under our barbed wire and then, after piling up the grenades abandoned by the fleeing Viet Minh, I rejoined the Senegalese *tirailleurs* from my squad who were congratulating one another, smiling and laughing, hopping back and forth in a haphazard, dis-coordinated dance of joy.

Towards mid-morning, military journalists following a brigade general arrived at the battle site. The general congratulated us for the good results of the battle, for our combat skills and for the strenuous defense we put up; he shook hands with everybody and assigned the *Croix de Guerre* to Adjutant Marchi who in the meantime had been transferred to the military hospital in Hanoi. Our Vietnamese privates were deservedly decorated for their loyalty to the French Army but I was stunned and incredulous when I saw the same medals being pinned onto the chests of their sergeant and corporal major, the same ones I had kicked for hiding under a cot. These two smiled, thanked the general and played the part of heroes in front of French and Vietnamese photographers and war reporters. I shook my head, sickened by that farce.

One thing continued to trouble me though: I couldn't avoid thinking about the French sergeant's woman who a couple of days before the attack had left the tower to visit her family in the mountains. Some days later, on surveillance duty at the Viet Minh prison camp at Phu Lo, my suspicions were confirmed: I discovered that, since the attack, the Vietnamese woman had been seen neither by her family nor the French sergeant.

Spies Everywhere

One of my duties was to lead a squad that escorted Viet Minh prisoners to Phu Lo in the evenings. It was at such times that bitterness and disillusionment again threatened to overwhelm me. Captain Subreroque and Adjutant Marchi had both been wounded and evacuated leaving me without anyone with whom I could 'shoot the breeze' or share my innermost thoughts. To exacerbate matters, it seemed I was living among idiots. The truck that picked us up in the evening, for example, was never on time because the driver invariably got involved in absurd quarrels. On one occasion, when the truck was exceptionally late, I took the decision to march the prisoners back to the base and lined them up by rows of four on the road. I told their chief, a fellow called To Van Phuc, to translate my words to his men. I began with: "I don't shoot prisoners attempting to escape."

To Van Phuc's soldiers looked at me with their mouths drooping open in astonishment.

"But," I continued, "I shoot *all* the remaining ones. There are twenty-five of you and my MAT-49 has thirty-two rounds in the magazine."

To Van Phuc translated again. This time the prisoners stared coldly at me: we understood each other perfectly.

At Phu Lo, one evening, To Van Phuc approached me, bending in a deep bow, the gesture that preceded a request for the granting of a favor. I peered into his glassy eyes. "Well?"

"A prisoner man, having his family not far from here, just on the road past the market, asks permission to visit his wife, almost due to give birth," he explained, speaking slowly and in a detached manner.

"Out of the question! Forget it," I replied.

To Van Phuc thanked me, kowtowing, bowing again before turning to leave.

"Wait! Who are we talking about?" I asked. An idea had flashed in my mind, a damned idea, reckless to the limit of idiocy but I wanted to try something, almost as an act of defiance against myself. To Van Phuc told me the name of the prisoner on whose behalf he had asked the favor — a good worker.

"It is a big event for our families," To Van Phuc said humbly.

In the morning three days after that request, a Chinese truck headed to the market slowed before entering our base. I quickly summoned the prisoner mentioned by To Van Phuc and urged him to follow me. We both jumped into the truck's box, amidst Vietnamese farmers, women, children and pigs destined to be sold at the market. The passengers, with the exception of the pigs perhaps, were astounded at the sight of a lone soldier among them.

When we jumped from the truck, I told the prisoner in my best Vietnamese that we were going to visit his wife. He understood, smiled at me and bowed to thank me. "Quick! We have no time to waste," I warned.

The market stretched along the road and was in the vicinity of a village that routinely sheltered Viet Minh, some of whom strolled about freely. My arrival with the prisoner was a surprise for everybody.

I held my arm towards the prisoner and tapped my wristwatch. "You have exactly twenty minutes." The prisoner nodded once then bowed before disappearing into a hut. I sat down on a hammock outside, accepting the hospitality offered by the prisoner's aged father-in-law; a tray of local food, Gotab cigarettes (a luxury brand for them) and a cup of tea.

After twenty minutes, I called for the prisoner who came promptly and walked beside me at a brisk pace along the dirt trail connecting the village to the main road. Exotic flowers by the wayside, their perfume and vivid colours lifted my spirits, reminding me of happier moments but I was too battle-hardened to think that this place was as heavenly as it appeared and so stepped up the pace. In less than an hour we were back at the camp at Phu Lo where the prisoner rejoined his compatriots. This bold sortie succeeded without incident because I undertook it without telling anybody else of my intentions, without the chance of an informer warning the Viet Minh.

The next day, To Van Phuc came to me. He put in my hand, wrapped in a large banana tree leaf, a small terracotta jar filled with *choum* saying, "From the prisoner and his new born baby. His family and I say many thanks." He bowed to me, this time in a genuine, natural manner. *Hmm*, I thought…*choum…the Viet Minh spies know us down to the finest details*.

Restlessness

Captain Rigasse requested the support of my squad, which he treated as his personal body-guard, for every sortie he led. In military uniform, and I suspect anywhere else, he looked like a fish out of water. Always anxious and worried about his safety, he certainly did not have the aura of an intrepid warlord.

In a mission I recall clearly, when we were in the cover of an embankment not far from a small village where the effectives of the 1st Company exchanged fire with a group of Viet Minh, the captain demanded artillery fire over those few fleeing rebels. This encounter with the enemy, one without any great importance, ended with many expensive shells exploding ineffectually on rice fields. To be fair, Rigasse probably wasn't completely incompetent as a desk-bound officer but fear gripped him on the battlefield and this undermined the confidence, and therefore the safety, of the men under his command.

Captain Rigasse drank vast quantities of Évian bottled water to replace the sweat that constantly dripped from his forehead and floppy double chin and was usually accompanied by a Vietnamese whose task it was to carry a stock of the water. When the Vietnamese water carrier was on other duties, Rigasse was known to 'request' a swig from soldiers he saw with this particular brand of water. This opened my eyes to a vulnerability that would allow me to play a little trick on the captain as a 'reward' for sending my squad into the cauldron of Zouk To. On a stiflingly hot day, I purchased a small jug of *choum* at the nearby village and poured it into an empty Évian bottle that I had brought with me. Once back at the base, I waited with the Évian bottle, filled with *choum*, until Rigasse happened to pass nearby and offered him a sip.

"Why not?" the captain said.

I passed him the bottle which he opened and put to his lips. The fat on his chin wobbled as the *choum* gurgled down his throat. Suddenly, he threw the bottle to the ground, his small round eyes stared at the sky, his face turned purple and then he let go a blood curdling yell as his hands went to his throat. "Poison," he screamed in a shrill, squawking voice, "I'm poisoned!"

Not surprisingly, Rigasse got rid of me that April by transferring me to the peripheral advance post of Dac Tai, commanded by Lieutenant Cozach. There, given that the Viet Minh were becoming increasingly stronger and bolder, I asked for, and was given, the important task of improving the defenses. During the preceding December, in 1953, the Viet Minh targeted the bases at Dien Bien Phu and now the situation was deteriorating quickly after a further attack in March on three airfields, the closest of which was at Gia Lam.

At Dac Tai, Lieutenant Cozach entrusted a 57mm cannon — installed on a movable turret on top of a blockhouse — to my tender command. I then made the acquaintance of a skinny, middle aged sergeant, a Paris firefighter veteran whose attitude to life astounded me. He was convinced that death stalked him and lived in a constant state of anxiety and, as a consequence of this, arranged all his movements with the purpose of avoiding a sad ending. Often, he beseeched me to take his place in patrol operations, advancing some childish pretexts for his requests. For me, to go on reconnaissance a turn earlier or later made no difference whatsoever, but for him it became a question of life or death. He did strange calculations, interpreted abstruse dreams, compared probabilities; he was always thinking, weighing and evaluating incidents that occurred during previous patrols, convinced that he had it in his power to circumvent fate, if only he could choose the right course of action. I patiently tolerated his strange behaviour because I felt sorry for him seeing him wear himself out in such a way. "Fate is fate, you cannot change it, no matter what you do," I told him one day, during his umpteenth substitution request.

"Just for this one, last time and then I won't bother you again, Paul." he implored me.

And so, I agreed once more to the sergeant's request. "All right, then," I answered, "but it *is* for the last time. Tonight I'll take your place, tomorrow you take mine." He thanked me, patting my shoulder.

Then I thought about the route the patrol would take which extended to the dreaded 'crossroads of death', close to the 1st Company's post and my nerves jangled at the thought. *Shit*, I thought, *the sergeant's anxiety has infected me.* But then again, I had fought with the *Waffen SS* and came out of a world war unscathed so it was unthinkable that I would croak here. And then I recalled the comforting words of the Chinese fortune teller I had consulted in Saigon, soon after disembarking, who had predicted with astounding accuracy a long series of events in my life. No, said the fortune teller, there was no trace of death in the turtle's shell nor among the jangling coins I had thrown in front of him; he was sure of it! I trusted him but never discussed my visit to him with anybody.

A Senegalese sergeant attached to the patrol I had missed explained to me what had happened. When they left Dac Tai base, two soldiers stopped at the first *bouchon*, two at the second and the remainder continued to the 1st Company's base where the superstitious French sergeant, who was in charge of the patrol, paused for a swig at the canteen and for a chat with colleagues he knew. In the evening, he ordered the Senegalese sergeant to lead the patrol on the return march to Dac Tai while he would follow later by taking advantage of a ride on a truck heading in that direction. He thought this would be safer, given that the patrol risked attack at any moment, but the truck ran over a mine which exploded.

Once on the spot, I surveyed the damage to the truck which had been torn in half. At the distance of about thirty meters from the stricken vehicle, lay the superstitious sergeant's body. I retrieved his gold watch, its hands locked at the moment of the blast. From that evening on, I suffered nightmares and headaches and lost my faith in the prediction of the old Chinese fortune teller. With about three months before the end of my draft, enough time for misfortune to finally catch me up, I became increasingly irritable and restless.

Two Traps

Fortunately, the benevolence of the army intervened to distract me from my gloomy thoughts. The women from the military brothel regularly stayed for two or three days at each base and, when they arrived at Dac Tai, I reserved one for the night, paying in advance the arranged amount — but not for her customary services. I had her search my wardrobe for clothes in need of fixing, a service which she carried out very willingly while entertaining me with chat about her companions whose aim was, she told me, to earn as much money as possible before returning home to their families. With her tasks complete, I slipped a good tip into her hand. She looked enquiringly into my eyes, questioning my desires but I dismissed her without hesitation and with good cause. A while earlier, the *tholang* of the nearby village of Dac Tai had been obliged to make available to the garrison a certain number of helpers for the daily corvée duties. Among them was a beautiful and coy Vietnamese girl with big, dark eyes. I liked everything about her; her clear and bright voice, her crystalline laughter and elegant demeanour. At night, I would think of her innocent glances and disarming smile and made up my mind to try to develop a relationship with her. Soon, my brief encounters with her were not enough. I yearned to see her without having to part in haste and so we arranged to meet at her home in the village. I left the base in the evening, promising the sentry, who I knew well, that I would return early in the morning before the change of guard. At the village, she was waiting for me with an oil lamp in her hand and in its faint yellow glow led me to a hut where her family welcomed me with a plate of delicious spring rolls. Each time we parted, I could hardly wait to see her again and my visits soon became a habit. But this risky play had the potential to prove very dangerous and so, as precautions, when I met her I always carried my pistol tucked inside my belt and made a point of arriving earlier or later than planned, often by several hours. On several occasions I even decided to miss a planned meeting completely.

One night, after dinner, while lying on a woven bamboo mat beside her in her family's hut, I detected a slight uneasiness in her eyes which she passed off as a sign of her headache. I caressed her cheek and she curled up beside me, her face hidden by the cascade of her jet-black hair. As usual, I made sure my pistol was at hand next to my pillow and lay there, awake, wondering what might happen between us. Then I realized she was only pretending to sleep. My mind began to race as I lay, face down on the pillow looking towards the door which had been left slightly ajar to allow the cool night air to circulate. In the darkness outside the hut, I thought I saw a shadow slinking towards the entrance and I too feigned sleep, breathing slowly and regularly though my heart was pounding. Someone was crawling across the floor, towards me. I moved casually, as if in a deep sleep, bringing my hand surreptitiously over my pistol's grip. In a smooth movement I disengaged the safety catch and, rolling suddenly to the side, fired three shots into the shadows in rapid sequence but the intruder was able to escape through the open door. My girlfriend sprang to her feet and screaming shrilly ran outside. I grabbed my flashlight, which I had left beside my pistol, and as I went outside noticed large spots of blood on the dry dust at the entrance of the hut. Sensing that further dangers lay ahead, I dressed and left to return to the base before the *tholang* and the inhabitants of the neighbouring dwellings had time to investigate.

From time to time at Dac Tai, a patrol was formed with the mission of fostering and maintaining good relations with the civilian population and, by coincidence, one had been planned for the morning after to the village where my shooting incident took place. I was part of that delegation and was naturally extremely curious to find out exactly what had happened. When we arrived at the village, the old *tholang* received us with the usual bows and with much courtesy, demonstrating admirable coolness. The officer in charge foolishly asked him point-blank if there were any Viet Minh in the village. There were not, swore the chief of the village, bowing.

After mutual exchange of niceties with the *tholang*, I left him with the officer and made my way to the hut where I had spent the night to look for my beautiful Vietnamese girl. At the entrance, there was no sign of the spots of blood that I had seen only a few hours earlier. The bamboo mat on which I had slept had been removed and replaced by a larger one covering the entire floor. Outside, an old woman I had never before seen was boiling tea but there was no trace of the girl and her family. When I returned to the officer, who was still in conversation with the villagers, I heard them swear that the old woman had been living in that hut for many years, as if my beautiful Vietnamese girlfriend never existed. This of course was to be expected if she was indeed a spy for the Viet Minh and her absence left me with a great deal to ponder.

At the moment of our patrol's departure, the old *tholang* deliberately passed close in front of me. His eyebrows formed little arches of triumph and on his wrinkled lips an enigmatic smile formed. Oh, he knew the military rules, the ones concerning soldiers' night leave; his secret was safe with me.

My beautiful Vietnamese girlfriend had vanished like a treasure left behind in a dream. For days afterwards, I thought about her and the aura of tranquility that surrounded her. When she was beside me, the nightmares that had plagued me melted into the night but now that she was gone they returned to torment me. During the following nights, I wakened with startling suddenness, drenched in sweat and every muscle quivering. Peaceful sleep deserted me; my thoughts inexorably transporting me back to recent, dangerous sorties. I thought also about the night I drove a heavy truck, dead-slow, lights off, on roads between rice fields infested by rebels. It was Captain Rigasse who gave me the order to turn at the 'crossroads of death' because the pathway on top of the embankment was too narrow for a U-turn. On the return journey, I discovered that my soldiers had left, taken back, Marchi told me later, to the base by smaller trucks on the order of the captain who, panicking, had a 'premonition' of an imminent Viet Minh attack. He was seeing them everywhere, Adjutant Marchi said to me one evening at the canteen. He reminded the captain that I would have arrived back in a matter of minutes but Rigasse brushed my friend's concerns aside: "He'll never come back. Paul is done for, lost; don't you see we're surrounded by rebel forces? I cannot sacrifice all my men for him alone," he told Marchi. Marchi had never before seen the captain in such a state of agitation and anxiety. Certainly there was some truth in what the captain had said; there *was* very little hope for a solitary soldier going up to the 'crossroads of death' and coming back on the same route without encountering the Viet Minh who, as was their habit, would already be busy laying mines along the road. Nobody should have been expected to risk their life on Colonial Route Number Three in darkness without the support of half a Company. I sweated blood that night with only my MAT-49, my pistol and two grenades for protection. For an interminable half-hour, I was on the edge of panic, of madness. I preferred fighting the Russians in Pomerania, the Popovs of Rokossowski and Zhukov who at least I could see. Here, on this lonely road, in a trap created by my commander's cowardice and surrounded by darkness as deep as the inky night sky, the Viet Minh were invisible.

Anyone can make a Mistake

From Phu Lo, Commander Valliet ordered us to rely more upon Senegalese sergeants in a bid to dispel their inferiority complex. This meant that we would send out patrols made up entirely of African soldiers. Experience forced me to accept this directive with scepticism, particularly since it was not long before that we had received news of the disastrous debacle at Dien Bien Phu. Valliet was taking a risk with everyone's life by abandoning a proven patrolling system for the sole purpose of avoiding injury to the sensibilities of a few African NCOs.

The following morning, a patrol consisting of thirty Senegalese *tirailleurs* left on a reconnaissance mission to the area around the 'crossroads of death'. About a kilometer from Dac Tai, the road passed between two hills, an ideal spot for ambush though it was within range of the 57mm cannon on the turret of the blockhouse at the base. As I shaved my thoughts were with those *tirailleurs* from my squad who had been attached to the patrol. Suddenly, an attendant cleaning the floor upstairs where the cannon was installed, called out as he descended the metal ladder at breakneck speed. "Corporal! Corporal Paul! The Viets!" he shouted.

I splashed water over my face and turned from the mirror, "Are they attacking?"

"No, no. Over the hills!"

I raced up the ladder to the top floor and grabbed my binoculars. As I scanned the section of road between the hills, I was alarmed by the ferocity of the chaotic skirmish that was taking place. The Viet Minh, some brandishing cutlasses or bayonets, others shooting and launching grenades, were pursuing the Senegalese soldiers. I looked around, hoping to see Lieutenant Cozach without whose explicit order I was forbidden to fire the cannon but there was no sign of him. With the situation already critical there was no time to waste. As soon as I jumped into the turret, the attendant handed me a projectile. I slammed it into the breach, calculated the elevation and fired the first of seventeen projectiles.

Lieutenant Cozach stomped into the upper floor of the blockhouse. He stretched his neck towards the turret. "Are you mad? What possessed you to blast away...you cretin." I waited until he pulled himself into the turret and then moved aside, allowing him to observe the disaster through my binoculars. The corners of his mouth tightened. "Nobody is moving!" he said with a grimace of disgust. "Do you realize, wretched imbecile, that you have decimated, wiped out our patrol?"

I remained silent, fearing the worse, thinking that I had been too hasty in firing the cannon with such intensity.

"I hold you entirely responsible for this massacre and its consequences!" Lieutenant Cozach barked.

In silence, I followed my commander from the blockhouse to the courtyard where the remaining Senegalese *tirailleurs* had taken up their positions on our defenses believing an enemy assault was imminent. As Lieutenant Cozach visited each position to tell them to stand down, their eyes turned in my direction, staring and hostile. For the first time in my life, I felt the burden of guilt. I went to the gate, to stare out across the rice fields.

A movement in the distance attracted my attention; it was one of the Senegalese soldiers from the patrol, running with the staggering gait of an exhausted man. The guards opened the perimeter gate to receive their comrade who, chest heaving, came to a halt in front of the soldiers gathering to hear news of the patrol. He was a sorry sight; his shirt was ripped and splattered with blood and he had lost a boot and his weapon. There was a look of dismay on the man's face when he gasped, "Dead...all dead."

Lieutenant Cozach stepped towards me. His unpleasant breath wafting over my face as he sneered, "You see now corporal...it's a slaughter, complete carnage!"

A shudder of disappointment ran through my body. Based on my experience in Pomerania, I thought I had trained my soldiers how to survive a barrage of shells.

"All dead," the Senegalese *tirailleur* repeated, between long gasps for air.

"Just a moment," I said, pointing to the road. A handful of soldiers were assisting a wounded comrade as they approached the camp. In a trickle, other elements of the patrol appeared, some unscathed but soiled with blood and mud, some with superficial cuts. In the end, every man in the patrol found his way back to the base.

As soon as the Senegalese sergeant who led the patrol learned that I had fired the cannon, he threw his arms around my neck. "You deserve a drink, devil of a corporal! Without your cannon it would have been the end for all of us!"

My feelings of guilt evaporated in an instant. I took a deep breath. Every one of the *tirailleurs* from my squad who had been on the patrol had come through without even a scrape. My bombing had forced the Viet Minh to flee to the hills, ruining their ambush. Still, I was relieved and surprised that my shelling had not hit any of the Senegalese in the patrol.

"You were just lucky corporal," my commander said, gritting his teeth.

"Of course I was," I answered, incapable of holding back a smile. I was sure he was reflecting that it would have been much better for him if he had given the order to fire on time. Later, face to face, he thanked me but only as a matter of duty. His eyes told a different story; one of contempt for a mere corporal.

Threat of Violence

Later that evening, I was summoned to a briefing for a sortie which was to be commanded by a novice sergeant, recently arrived from NCO school. The purpose of the operation was to ambush the Viet Minh as they ferried supplies and ammunition from one of their depots to another under the cover of darkness. By now, I was very familiar with the terrain in the area and as soon as the commander traced the route we were to follow on a map, I knew in which places we would be at any given moment of the sortie. When the sergeant bent over the map spread across the table, trying to assimilate the route and some referral points, I rose from my chair to go out and instruct my *tirailleurs*.

"One moment, corporal!" Lieutenant Cozach said. "It is essential that you remain on our side of the creek, otherwise you run the risk of being wiped out by our mortar shots when you call for supporting fire. Do not cross the creek, is that clear?"

"Yes, *mon commandant*, I know where it is," I reassured him.

We left the base at 23.30 hours. Accompanying me and the sergeant were five Senegalese *tirailleurs* and eight Vietnamese soldiers who followed my steps through the tall grass. The NCO had the command but in practice I was the one leading the patrol. I proceeded confidently but with caution, knowing where to set foot to avoid stepping onto one of the Viet Minh's pointed, poisoned sticks.

"Hei corporal! We've reached the creek, we must lie here in wait," the sergeant said.

"This is only a rivulet," I explained. "The creek is further on." My soldiers sensed that I was in mood for adventure that night and played along to see how the new sergeant would hack it. I guided them for another half-kilometer, looking over my shoulder from time to time at the sergeant's worried face. At the moment of leaving the fort I had seen him load a magazine into his MAT-49 and slip another into his pocket. He should have carried at least five of them, like the rest of us, but was probably aiming to avoid the exertion of carrying the magazines which were stuffed with heavy, 9mm cartridges but I was too polite to impose on him with remarks about his judgement. I positioned my soldiers behind a hump in open terrain that offered an open field of fire and crouched beside the sergeant to wait. A couple of hours went by before a shadow emerged from the bush; a wobbling figure coming along the trail towards us. It was a farmer carrying two jars hanging from the hooks of a wooden yoke across his shoulders. The sergeant stiffened, preparing himself for firing. I laid my hand on his sub-machine gun and motioned him to wait. He obeyed me, hesitating, betraying his edginess. A second figure, also carrying containers hanging from a yoke, followed the first. It was an old trick: the Viet Minh had the farmers precede them, loaded with supplies, as trailblazers. If we stopped them, they would simply justify their presence by claiming they were intending to reach the market at the break of dawn. A Viet Minh vanguard usually trailed behind, at a distance of some tens of meters, armed and silent.

The sergeant pointed his weapon at a third wobbling figure approaching us and when he was just about to fire I lowered his barrel with my hand once more. He looked at me, surprised and alarmed. I raised my index finger to my lips. Then the vanguard came into the open ground, the first five members advancing watchfully, keeping to the cover of bushes. Their stride was different; longer than the farmers'. I kept my free hand on the sergeant's lowered weapon knowing that the bulk of the rebels would soon appear but the sergeant was able to free the barrel from my grip to let go a burst. In response, tongues of fire leapt from the muzzles of the enemy's machine guns. Exploding grenades lit up the darkness with their stroboscope-like flashes.

"Fire!" I ordered. "Keep to your positions!" I screamed above the din of the shooting. Beside me, the sergeant was scrambling to launch a white signal rocket so to call for mortar support. "No! Not yet," I yelled. I gave the order to pull back, given the failed surprise and the unknown number of Viet Minh. We continued our retreat towards the creek, turning to fire from time to time to slow the enemy's pursuit.

The sergeant, hesitant and confused, had emptied his two magazines. "Corporal! Pass me some ammo," he ordered.

"Not on your life!" I answered curtly. *This was a lesson he must learn for his own good,* I thought.

"What did you say, Corporal?"

"What did you learn at the NCO's school?"

"Never mind that...I asked you for a magazine!"

"Forget it!"

"It's an order!"

I didn't bother to answer him. I continued the withdrawal from the creek to get out of our mortar zone of fire.

The sergeant was losing patience. "Pass me a magazine. That's a direct order," he said, his words choking in his throat.

"Cut it out! Next time you'll know what to do!" I answered.

The sergeant fired the signal rocket that would bring in the mortar fire. "It doesn't end here, corporal!" he muttered.

The Viet Minh disappeared, swallowed up by the forest, when our mortars rumbled. By now, the moon was shining its cold, white light through the clouds to expose our positions and so we returned to the base where the sergeant jotted down a nasty report about my conduct.

Inevitably, early in the morning, the commander gave me a speech about fellowship, camaraderie, reciprocal help during combat and the respect that a corporal should demonstrate towards his superiors.

"Nowhere have I read that a corporal should be a porter for his sergeant," I said, sure of my ground. Nevertheless, another unflattering note found its way into my personal file. I knew my worth as a fighting soldier and had proved it on many occasions and so took this stain on my character with anger and indignation. When I next met the sergeant, I took the opportunity to let him know what I thought of him. "You are not a man of value, nor a soldier of valour," I told him, "and if you endanger the lives of my *tirailleurs* again, I'll slit your damned throat with great pleasure."

The Boaster

I glanced over at my table where I had left my companion, a young radio operator.

The Vietnamese girl in my arms looked up from her embrace. "Something the matter, soldier? Don't I dance well?"

"No, no! On the contrary. I like the orchestra too, they're very good musicians," I said. The dancer looked me in the eyes, not at all convinced, and tightened her embrace, pulling me closer to her firm body. And she was a good dancer, she had to be, it was her profession. She must have sensed my continuing apprehension and asked, "You not like this bar?"

"Sure sure! Intimate, nice ambience, just what I like," I said absentmindedly.

She pressed her soft, delicate cheek against my neck. "How many ticket you buy?"

Her perfume had all the heady scents of the summer forest, a fresh and exotic fragrance. "About twenty...I am in a mood to move my legs this evening."

"Your friend, he dance too?"

"Doesn't know how to."

"He make up for it with drink."

"He certainly does, damn him!" I glanced over to the table where my young companion, who had begged me to go with him to the night club, was finishing off a bottle of champagne. The girl nestled against me. I pulled her tight, my hands on her back, my fingers running over her tight, silky, emerald-green dress. I felt light-headed, lost in her kitten-like eyes, fascinated by her provocative glances and the swaying, languorous music. She was very experienced and it felt good, her body pressing against mine. I was in a serene, sensual heaven on earth.

The radio operator shattered my dream. He was standing, holding the empty champagne bottle upside down to let the last drops dribble into his mouth. Satisfied that it was empty, he tried to stand the bottle on the table but it wobbled and fell and rolled onto the floor towards a nearby table where five legionnaires were drinking. I had listened to them speak before I started dancing and recognised them as a pair of Slavs, two Spaniards and a Frenchman. The dancer, sensing my distraction, guided me towards the opposite side of the hall. "I hope he doesn't stir up trouble," I told her. She put a finger on my lips and brushed her cheek against mine. I was in ecstasy.

Alcohol induced euphoria now had the young radio operator in its grip. He was on the dance floor, dancing alone with unsteady steps, obstructing other couples and annoying customers. One of the five legionnaires at the nearby table approached him, grabbed him by the collar and, after slapping him smartly on the face, hurled him under a table. A few customers made for the door.

"That idiot!" I hurried to give my dancer a ticket, which she would exchange for cash, and went to the table under which the radio telephonist sprawled. I helped him out. "You deserve it. You promised to behave but you can't take a beating just like that without defending yourself," I rebuked him. I was dragging him to our table when another of the legionnaires approached us.

"Señor, you want some too?" he said, his stubbly chin thrust forward.

My innocent smile did nothing to placate the Spaniard who was already raising his fist. I pre-empted his blow with an uppercut that caught his chin and sent him rolling. The orchestra stopped playing as the dancers cleared the floor and the other four legionnaires prepared to attack. I backed up to a corner near the band and then suddenly launched myself forward, arms flailing and feet flying. My antagonists didn't have time to react and it didn't take too long before all five of them were on the floor. As the Spaniard got to his knees, I was over him in no time, locking his arm against his back.

"*Bueno, amigo!*" he shouted.

I yanked him to his feet and then pushed him in the orchestra's direction. I nodded to the conductor as I slipped back into the arms of the dancer and said: "Tango, please." My whole body was alive, tingling from the excitement of the scuffle. At the end of the dance, as I returned to my table, the legionnaires were making their way towards the exit, chatting among themselves while the young radio operator massaged his slap-reddened face.

A voice called from behind in a commanding tone. When I turned, I saw a lieutenant from the engineering unit inviting me with a gesture to join him at his table. As I sat opposite him, he said in a friendly manner, "Well, we don't see something like that every day. I witnessed the whole thing from the start and I want to tell you that I admire your courage," he said with enthusiasm. "Very well done! I practised sport you know, I can throw a punch or two. If you need my help to get out of here or to get rid of those legionnaires I am at your side."

"Thank you," I said, "I hope to avoid another scuffle but I appreciate your offer and your sportsman-like spirit."

At the exit, the five legionnaires were waiting. I passed them without looking, holding my companion from behind, my arms under his armpits, and whistled to a rickshaw that was parked on the opposite side of the street. As soon as it reached us, I laid my drunken companion on the seat. The driver, with an energetic push on the pedals, turned in the direction of the Commissariat's depot — he knew without being told where to go. The legionnaires surrounded me, firing insults of every sort while the Slavs rolled up their sleeves. Meanwhile, the night club's customers were coming out to enjoy what promised to be an interesting spectacle. I felt my muscles tighten, an innate response to my predicament. "You want another dose? Come on! Who's the first to square up?" My reaction caught the legionnaires by surprise and I took advantage of their moment of indecision to jump on a passing rickshaw.

Back at Phu Lo the next day, before returning to Dac Tai after our brief off-base leave, I saw the radio operator sitting at a table in the mess, in animated conversation with some comrades. As I approached him from behind, I heard him boast: "What a memorable fight! I knocked down one with a blow from my elbow, another with a kick in the face and one more with a punch on the nose. Paul helped me fixing the other two and..." I tapped on the young man's shoulder, interrupting his description of the scuffle.

Without saying anything, I dragged him from the table and directed him towards the door with light kicks on his butt.

A Little Understanding

The itinerant cinema finally arrived at Dac Tai, the last stop on its tour of the bases north of Hanoi, with an escort of women soldiers. With them was a chaplain, taking advantage of the free ride on the truck. To escort him and the women for the return trip, as far as the 'crossroads of death', ten Senegalese *tirailleurs* were chosen. In the proximity of the valley between the two hills, a little more than a kilometer from the base, they were fired on by Viet Minh hiding in the bushes. Fortunately, they were able to take up positions and return fire but experience told us that they might need help. In the courtyard I jumped on a jeep at the head of a hastily gathered reinforcement column and urged the driver to step on the gas.

"Judging from their fire they are not many," he observed.

"We'll scare them away just with our presence," I said. In fact, at our arrival, the rebels were already scattering, shooting here and there until the last moment, as was their habit. I found the chaplain in the open, over the edge of the embankment, appealing for a truce. With his hands raised up in a majestic movement, his face looking at the sky, he said in a loud voice, "I offer you peace, brothers! Peace…the most precious gift that…" He fell forward, first to his knees, then heavily, slamming his face into the ground.

When the firing stopped, one of the *tirailleurs* examined the chaplin's body. "A bullet in the forehead," he reported.

Assured of the complete Viet Minh retreat, the *tirailleurs* returned to their truck which was riddled by bullets. As I was driven back to the base in the jeep, I thought about the chaplain's sudden death. I was reliving the incident as if it was happening over and over again in front of my eyes. I had seen many soldiers hit during combat, seen them fall and die in all manners but the vision of that chaplain, intrepid, indifferent to the danger of the whistling bullets, silhouetted against the sky, stuck in my mind. That vision of sacrifice by the chaplain troubled my dreams during the following nights. In them, his face was a picture of serenity which only served to inflame my anger towards the Viet Minh rebels who were becoming increasingly cocky in their attacks.

The incident with the chaplain was, I suppose, symbolic of my increasingly sceptical view of the war in Vietnam. Victory was slipping from the French Government's hand. I had already tasted the bitter medicine of defeat despite my personal efforts to be a good soldier and recoiled at the thought of finding myself once more in that situation. This time however, it was not the overwhelming power of our enemy that caused our resistance to buckle but the cringing incompetence of our commanders and it was *this* that made my anger rise up like a black, tumultuous cloud. Courage and loyalty count for nothing when soldiers are led by incompetent commanders. The stark, naked fact that I too was powerless in this situation gnawed at my mind like a malignant worm; an irritant that I could do nothing about. And this frustration, at the slightest provocation, took hold of me, boiling into raw anger. I had become a dangerous character, young and exceptionally strong; a man whose temper balanced on a hair-trigger. This trait did not go unnoticed by my commander. As a consequence, one morning Lieutenant Cozach summoned me to his office. I went unwillingly, in a foul mood, wondering what misdemeanor of mine had provoked the commander.

Lieutenant Cozach looked up at me from his desk. "Corporal, anyone can see you are in a deplorable state. You're scruffy, sloppy in your uniform and of sickly appearance despite your good health."

Another bollocking, I thought. "But…"

My commander silenced me with a hand gesture. "I have taken a decision," he said, "With Commander Valliet's approval, I am sending you for a month's rest at Dalat, in the mountains, in the company of the Muong people. Pull yourself back onto your feet. I cannot let you return to France in such a miserable condition. Is that clear?"

I was dumbfounded, incapable of an answer; I was expecting a punishment and instead Lieutenant Cozach had granted me a long leave, a vacation. I thought it was probably a cruel joke but he had talked seriously. I mumbled my thanks and left.

The following morning, before I left the base, the commander approached me.

"So corporal, everything in order?"

I nodded, hoping he hadn't found an excuse to keep me there.

Lieutenant Cozach pointed into the distance. "Look at that hill. There's something on top. I tried to see what it was using my binoculars but with no luck."

There was a hint of humour, of respect in his voice, respect for me.

"I just don't understand it," said the commander theatrically.

"It looks like a pole," I said, half-smiling.

He looked intently into my eyes. "Yes! It is a pole," he said, "a pole with a French flag. Now, I wonder how that got there?"

"Boh!" I exclaimed, nonchalantly. With the help of two Vietnamese soldiers I had, during the night, hoisted the French standard on top of the highest hill, in Viet Minh territory, re-entering the base just in time for the muster. I wanted to pull a crazy stunt before departing for leave but this was also my peculiar, personal way of thanking my superior officer who, in spite of our mutual animosity, had demonstrated an understanding of the reasons behind my volatile temper.

Just Rewards

I was in the canteen bar, not so much for a drink, but to reminisce.

"Paul!"

I turned to see my comrade, Marchi. He had recovered well from the wounds he took in the defense of Zouk To and, thanks no doubt to his excellent physique, had evidently resumed his duties.

"Marchi, you old fox," I called. "How is your wound?"

"Ready for another but this shoulder still gives me some pain. What are you doing here at Phu Lo?"

"I've just handed in a request at the orderly room," I told him.

"Paul...one suggestion...don't stir up a hornets' nests when you're so close to demobilization."

Marchi was well-acquainted with my temper but this time he had nothing to worry about. "It was to ask to be demobilized here in Vietnam," I explained.

"What in the hell are you thinking of? Ah, a beautiful girl…of course, a Meo! Those mountains! I heard you had a month at Dalat," Marchi said, looking at me with an expecting glance, waiting for me to continue talking.

"A paradise, that place. I've just arrived back."

"So. Is she at least pretty?"

I shook my head. "It's nothing to do with women, my friend."

"Ah!" Marchi sighed, disappointed. "Tell me about this paradise, at least there you'll have found some cute ones, no?" He ordered two cognacs, doubles.

It seemed to me that my friend's hair was sparser, perhaps a result of the physical stress he had suffered. "It's a dream place…fresh air, delicious courses in the restaurants, as much drink as a man could wish for and girls too, all nurses, always smiling. Then there was the night club on a lake with a bamboo gangway and a Corsican owner who listens only when his customers talk about money."

"Hum! Interesting. Much better than the hospital I was in," he sighed with a hint of envy.

"But I haven't told you the good news yet." I raised my glass, clinked it against his. "Santé!"

"So…what's the mystery?"

"I made the acquaintance of a devil of a Chinese entrepreneur, a rich businessman." I gulped down another cognac. "He has a big construction company, and all the contracts for the French Government."

"Interesting. And then?"

"He has something like 3000 coolies working for him and needs somebody who is able to manage the whole thing."

"And that somebody would be you."

"Precisely! He's well aware of my work in here and at the other bases…he trusts my experience."

"And the pay?" Marchi asked, intrigued.

"One-hundred and twenty-thousand piasters per month, plus free lodging, personal cook and tailor, oh, and a car and various other benefits and privileges."

Marchi gave a high-pitched whistle.

"I've found the chicken that lays the golden egg," I continued, thinking about my diminishing stash of piasters, two-thirds of which I had already spent at Dalat.

"My friend, if it is as you say, then I wish you a nice stay in Vietnam. You'll be filthy rich!"

"I really hope so. I have to think about my future you know."

"Well, I'm in a less envious position," Marchi sighed.

"You'll have a nice pension, with your years of service and the wound," I said.

The general who commanded the Phuc Yen sector arrived at Dac Tai with an escort of armoured vehicles. He had heard about my episode with the 57mm cannon during the ambush of our Senegalese patrol and Lieutenant Cozach informed me that the general had asked to see me in action.

"At ease, at ease, corporal. I've come to see how you shoot with the turret cannon," he said kindly when I was presented to him in the grounds of the Dac Tai fort in the presence of his wife, orderly officers, film makers and members of the propaganda and news services.

"At your command, *mon général*," I answered with confidence. "Where do you wish me to take aim?"

He turned towards the hills, scanned them up and down with his binoculars before deciding. "Those two rocks protruding from the trees, you see them? One near the other."

I trotted off to the blockhouse and climbed into the turret. Proud of my new role as a celebrity, I rotated the cannon towards the target, calculated the distance and adjusted the elevation — spot on! A Vietnamese attendant handed me a projectile which I loaded into the breech in a smooth movement. I confidently snapped the breechblock shut and grabbed the firing lever with my left hand, preparing to release the shot. Without warning, the barrel of the cannon swung downwards causing me to lose my balance. Instinctively, my right hand shot out to grab something and that something was the firing lever. The shot left with a loud bang followed by an almost instantaneous explosion — I had forgotten to lock the barrel in position. I dared to look towards the assembled dignitaries only when the cries of panic had died down and the smoke of the exploded shell had vanished. Everyone in the general's entourage, including his wife, were staggering to their feet, brushing dust from their clothes. They looked at me, stunned and hardly believing their eyes as, undaunted, I cranked the wheel that raised the barrel, this time locking it into position. After checking the aim, I fired, now scoring a direct hit on the target on the hill. When I smugly looked towards the general's entourage, I saw that every one of them had again dived to the ground. Shamefacedly, I left the blockhouse to report to my commander who, like everyone else, was vigorously dusting off his clothes.

"Firing carried out, target destroyed!" I reported.

"This will suffice, corporal," the commander said with a withering stare.

After the general and his staff left, I was slapped with yet another critical entry in my personal file but I consoled myself with the thought that more than one of the general's escort had at last seen action at close hand, and perhaps had lost control of the bodily functions.

The following days went by without incident but we received strange orders from the General Staff; shooting the Viet Minh was prohibited unless they demonstrated open hostility, surveillance of the hills and mountains was to be cut back and those on patrol were told to fire only if their lives were in danger. Soon afterwards, the news of a possible armistice and of some accords signed in Geneva arrived too. As a consequence we found five French soldiers who had been prisoners of the Viet Minh, released in the middle of a rice field. They wore green fabric pants and large, conic, bamboo hats. The commander sent them to Phu Lo for debriefing.

❦—❦

With the end of my draft approaching, I counted down the remaining days, eagerly anticipating my freedom and the smell of the Chinese entrepreneur's money. Meeting him had been a stroke of exceptionally good luck and I was becoming anxious to learn the outcome of my request to stay in Vietnam. Finally, I was able to hitch a ride on one of our trucks to Phu Lo, where I called in at the orderly room to find if there had been any news of the matter.

"No! Nothing yet," the quartermaster said.

"But my permit should surely have been approved by now," I insisted.

"Paul…" the quartermaster whispered, hesitating, "promise you won't say anything to anybody!"

"I promise."

"You see, your request never left this office," the quartermaster revealed in a low voice.

"Are you joking? Everything's in order…a secure job, excellent pay. What in damnation are they playing at!"

"Paul, calm down! I did everything I could but that's the way things are."

"Impossible…idiots…bastards," I cursed. I left the orderly room seething with rage, heading for the base canteen where I found Marchi leaning on the counter.

"Bad news, Paul?" he asked, seeing me black-browed.

"You can say that! I wasn't expecting such a kick in the guts. Valliet denied my permit to stay in Vietnam…how dare he, that turd of a commander," I thumped the counter with a clenched fist. "What did I do to that bastard?"

"Personal spite, maybe," Marchi suggested. "You've always been a thorn in his side, you know that, right? Or perhaps it was because of your negligence… that incident with the cannon…who knows?" He passed me a glass of cognac. "Take this, drink a sip."

The enormity of my loss was seeping in. "If they don't let me stay here my agreement with the Chinese boss goes up in smoke."

"Better not think about it, Paul."

My mind would not let the matter rest. "It's envy of my good fortune that made him refuse my request. But why ruin my future by crushing me like this? I can't swallow it."

Marchi offered some explanations. "Maybe the General Staff orders are formulated so as not to allow situations like yours, or to discourage similar adventures...maybe Commander Valliet has his hands tied."

One question burned in my mind. "Did he even examine my request?"

"What difference would have it made?"

"Consideration, my friend...to be treated as is fitting. Instead they've completely ignored me...the imbeciles, incompetent dullards, cretins, good for nothings!"

"Just to cheer you up, Paul," Marchi said, laying a hand on my shoulder in consolation, "I was denied my return to France. They want to keep me here until the end of my draft."

"It went wrong for you too, eh?"

"Well, thinking about it, for me it makes no difference. It's all right."

"Bourbaki's army!"

Marchi looked at me, puzzled.

"The *Armée de l'Est* led by Bourbaki in the Franco-German War ...a *Sturmmann* at Greifenberg talked about it... it was a shambles but this one is worse!"

We continued drinking, I to drown my rage and he to try to cheer me up until we parted company with a good handshake.

Return to France – Goodbye and Welcome

Aligned in the courtyard at Phu Lo base, amidst a dozen other demobs, I stood for the last time at attention. Commander Valliet reviewed us quickly, then he made a brief farewell speech. "Life continues for you," he said, "in the civilian environment, among your families which you will see soon enough. You will continue to be good French citizens and to serve the Motherland with the same spirit of self-sacrifice you have demonstrated here in Vietnam. I wish you good luck and I hope that the things you have learned here will be useful to you in your civilian life." He moved along the line stopping to shake hands and exchange a few words with each soldier but when he came in front of me, he stood with his arm stretched and the palm of his hand open. My arms remained steadfastly by my sides.

"Come now, Paul," he urged.

"There isn't one regulation obliging a troop soldier to shake hands with an officer," I replied curtly, ending his embarrassment.

"You'll never change," he remarked coldly.

"That would be impossible!" I retorted, scathingly.

As the officer continued to exchange pleasantries with the other demobilizing soldiers, chatting and smiling, I had tears in my eyes because of the turmoil of rage that swelled inside me. So my draft was ending. This, a shake of the hand, was how I was to be thanked after enduring deadly combat, patrols and ambushes. After all my sacrifices over three years of hard work, after having risked my life on countless occasions, I had been denied the possibility of staying in Vietnam as a civilian worker. My time, the last of my youth, had been wasted. Anger gave way to an infinite, pervading sadness as bitter disillusionment crushed my heart. My life as a soldier with *Corps Expéditionnaire Français en Extrême-Orient* had ended in failure. Once again I was on the losing side. I closed my eyes to contain the tears of sorrow as my thoughts drifted back to those few true friends with whom I had come through the hell of Kolberg, and to that swearing in ceremony in the ranks of the *Waffen SS*. We were prepared to die for the 'New Europe' and many of my comrades fell on the battlefields for this idea. Within the *Waffen SS* strict, iron-fist discipline ruled, our commanders respected every soldier; we were valued members of the squad, the platoon, the section, always ready to protect each other. And every one of us was suited to the arduous task ahead. We had an unbreakable *esprit de corps*. Our capitulation with 'Charlemagne' was without shame, we fought until the last moment, with pride and dignity. Defeat then had been much nobler than here, in Vietnam. This guerrilla war had been carried forward without enthusiasm, with incompetents both on the battlefield and at the negotiation table. Now here I was, standing at attention in front of an officer I hated, who represented not only authority, but also the failure of the French Army and of France.

Two sailors from the aircraft carrier *Arromanches* came to say goodbye to me at the pier where the *Pasteur* was moored. I had met them a few days before while awaiting embarkation at Saigon. One of the fellows was a licenced mechanic, the other a nurse and both were about my age. My head was aching, throbbing in the strong sunshine. "Well! I hope you'll remember me," I joked.

"I'll remember the swigs together for sure," the mechanic answered.

"Boys, what a binge that was," the nurse said. "You must have had a lot of things to forget, Paul."

"But I do seem to recall that when I left, you were hardly able to stand," I retorted.

The mechanic chipped in, "But what about that blond girl you left the night club with… where did you end up?"

"In a scullery," I said, smiling. That was one of the few things I remembered for certain after leaving the night club where we celebrated my demob.

The mechanic scratched his head as if trying to jog his memory. "Oh yes, that Chinese guy, the one at the wall of death. When he saw you ride that motor bike he asked you to work for him, don't you remember Paul."

"I can't accept his offer. The French authorities won't allow me to stay in Vietnam."

"You were a hit with the crowd," said the nurse. "He wanted to hire you on the spot… he would have paid you in gold."

"Too bad," I answered wryly. I was still feeling pretty bitter about having to pass up the chance of a lucrative post offered by the Chinese entrepreneur so the loss of this modest offer, which I had completely forgotten about, had no effect on me. "But it was a great binge," I added. I shook both of them by the hand and turned for the gangway.

"It'll be hot in that ship," the mechanic said, a comment that suddenly made my headache feel ten times worse.

"Good luck to you, Paul," the nurse called.

The mechanic was correct — it was stiflingly humid in the crowded cabins and corridors which were cluttered with bags and suitcases and people trying to sleep on the deck. From below, where a hospital had been set up, hot air carrying a sickly sweet smell wafted through the ship. The wounded there had a resigned appearance, as if they were unhappy about returning home. After a brief religious service, those who died on the voyage were committed to the deep by lowering them to sea level, young men — comrades in arms — thrown to the fish. A deep melancholy entered my heart.

Just before entering port, tugboats hooked up to the *Pasteur*, guiding it to the dock. Two gangways were lowered to the crowded pier. Bunting fluttered on lines strung up on the dockside buildings; a military band played the *Marseillaise* while a squad of legionnaires wearing white kepis saluted in the sunshine. I suppose the tune was intended to stir afresh an empathy with the Motherland, but it left me feeling cold and detached from everything around me, just as it had done on my return from Germany to Belgium.

The first of the demobilized soldiers disembarked. They were heartily received by the authorities, with smiles and handshakes, as they were paraded in front of them. As I waited patiently for my turn, I noticed there was a paratrooper at my side, pressed against the ship's handrail. He was waving half-heartedly to a middle-aged couple and a young woman on the pier; his parents and girlfriend, or wife perhaps. "Hei! You ought to be happy," I said cheerfully, to enthuse him.

He pointed his thumb downwards. "I haven't told them," he said.

Then I saw that a leg had been amputated above the knee. "I'm sorry, really sorry," I babbled. Unable to face witnessing the inevitable shock reaction of his relatives, I drifted away from the paratrooper, towards the stern of the ship.

From the second gangway the seriously wounded, carried on stretchers, bypassed the homecoming welcome by the military and civil authorities to be received by Red Cross attendants who took them quickly to waiting ambulances, as if to deliberately avoid the eyes of the crowd. When things quietened down a little, I went down the gangway towards the dwindling crowd on the pier. There was nobody waiting for me — I didn't expect anybody. As I looked around, trying to gather my bearings, two extremely attractive Red Cross nurses dressed in sexy, skin-tight uniforms came up to me wearing big, white smiles. Naturally, being a young, vigorous man, I returned their smiles when they offered me a pack of Gauloises cigarettes. As I opened the pack, my eyes were drawn to a movie camera catching the happy homecoming moment. *So, this is my last duty*, I thought, *posing as soldier arriving home from Indochina in good shape and perfect health.* This was precisely the image sought for the purposes of political propaganda. Once again I felt I had been used. But at least I was more fortunate than many others on that ship; I was still in one piece.

Disappointments

Three months after my return home, my carefully chosen and sealed treasure chest containing the last 200,000 piasters I had seized from the Viet Minh rebel arrived intact at the station in Longwy. It had travelled from Saigon without attracting the attention of the authorities; my just reward for the sacrifices I had made in the name of the Motherland but I still had to convert it to Francs and so I travelled to Paris, to the Bank of Indochina.

"How many piasters do you wish to exchange?" a clerk asked, leaning forward until his nose almost touched the glass screen of a counter.

"About 50,000."

"Where did you acquire the cash?" the clerk asked, leaning forward again.

"In Hanoi," I answered, after a moment's hesitation.

"Can you legally prove your last transaction or their origin?"

"Yes, I think so, sure!" His questions made me feel ill at ease.

The clerk slipped a form under the glass screen. "You have to fill this up completely. Try to be as accurate as possible. You can only exchange 10,000 piasters, it is the limit imposed by law," he explained in a monotone voice.

"Only 10,000?" I muttered.

"Exactly so, not a piaster more."

I felt my adrenalin rise. "It doesn't matter, I've changed my mind...thanks anyway," I said and then left in a hurry. My head was in turmoil. I threw a punch against a lamp-post as I passed. "Damn!" I cursed loudly. It was beginning to look as if the piasters were worthless, fit only for papering my bedroom walls. Once more I felt a victim of misfortune, of a world that seemed determined to undermine every effort I made.

A few days later, having come to accept the possibility that my piasters were mere scraps of paper, I entered the center for demobilization in Metz where I hoped to exercise my right as an ex-soldier to secure employment. With four years in the French Army behind me and decorations for valour and outstanding performance in sports, I was confident that my request for a five-year contract with civil engineering department would be granted as a matter of formality.

A colonel received me in his office. "My dear young man," he said in a loud voice and with a good-natured expression, "it is not possible. All openings for municipal engineers are already filled."

I had the disagreeable sensation of sweat running down my brow, yet my lips seemed frozen, unable to move. I needed that job but it appeared that my country was now in no need of me.

"But if you wish to consider it," the colonel continued, "there are always openings in Tunisia…"

"Right! For Tunisia," I interrupted angrily, "things are becoming serious down there, eh?"

The colonel looked at me, surprised by my reaction. "That is a possibility."

I rose from the chair, thanked him and left.

Fortunately, I still had another prospect of employment: the admission exam for the Security Republican Service, motorcycles special section. My *Croix de Guerre* put me automatically fourteen points up the ranking, without counting my contribution to the Indochina campaign and the medals I won in various sport disciplines. I came out from the oral test with a mark far above the average but the words of the officer in charge soon deflated my spirits: "Everything went all right but your condemnation from the tribunal counts against you. I don't mean to add weight to your membership of the *Waffen SS*, no, good heavens no. Let's consider that as a sin of youth but the conviction remains. I'm sure you understand."

I understood. Another good possibility had slipped beyond my grasp.

In Paris, at a barracks for international troops most of whom were Americans on leave from the Châteauroux-Déols Air Depot, I asked at the entrance door if work was available. An English soldier accompanied me to the personnel office where a sergeant raised his face from the stack of papers on his desk. "There is an opening as dish-washer in the American kitchen," he said.

"All right," I answered, "I'll take it."

I started work immediately; piles of dishes, trays and big pots arrived continuously so I had to work at good pace but for me it was an easy job. Soon, I made a good impression on the American cooks and a captain from the U.S. Marines in charge of the kitchens and mess held me in high regard. Some of the cooks spoke Spanish and thus I wasn't completely left out of their conversations.

However, two months of scrubbing marmites was more than enough for my patience, especially since the French Government kept a large percentage of my pay by following to the letter the small print in my work contract. I decided therefore to leave Paris and head for Marseille to look for work. During the first days, I wandered about keeping my eyes and ears open for chances that might present themselves. The port was swarming with people; peddlers pushing American cigarettes, smugglers selling almost anything, and fools who fell victim to thieves and crooks. Life there had not changed much at all since my last visit, except that it was now even more frenetic. But the work that I hoped to find there did not exist and I was forced to consider my next step. I even thought of turning to thieving to see me through from day to day but discarded that desperate occupation as far too demeaning. In the end, after much thought and counter thought, I resorted to the only sure prospect, the one purposely kept as back-up in case of desperation — enlistment in the Foreign Legion.

Reflections

I showed up at a fort in front of the old port, where I was very cordially received. At the recruiting office a sergeant explained to me that he had to verify the past of every aspiring legionnaire and that research would take a few days so, for the time being, I was assigned to kitchen duties together with a young Mexican from a respectable family who had enlisted against his wealthy father's wishes. The two of us were also responsible for the smooth functioning of the mess and that included surveillance of the legionnaires coming at the mealtimes and the control of their behaviour. These were from every provenance: failed doctors dreaming of a medical career by tending soldiers' wounds; men who, for any of a thousand reasons, were disgusted with civilian life; German ex-officers; refugees; delinquents of every kind and poor sods who wished only to secure a roof over their heads and enough food to keep them alive.

On my first leave, while returning to the fort in the depth of night, I was walking briskly alongside the pier with the Mexican. Ahead were five legionnaires who occupied all the width of the sidewalk. I slipped between them, moving one of them to the side. I had been a bit rough of manners but I was in a hurry. The brawl that followed was brief and harsh and, as happened at the night club in Hanoi, I left them on the ground, beaten and bruised. The Mexican didn't even have time to give me a hand because my rapid attack had played once more in my favor.

The next day, in the newspaper, an article described the cowardly assault from behind by a pack of criminals at the expenses of five NCO legionnaires, one of whom was in a rather serious condition. At that news, I regretted my arrogant gesture but the legionnaires didn't give me the opportunity or time to apologize which I would have done willingly.

I continued my work at the mess and in the kitchen, making an effort in the hope that everything would go smoothly, but even there arguments broke out and dishes thrown in anger flew across the room — as happened one time, at supper. Some, mainly young German, legionnaires were passing in front of the marmite counter, carrying trays and spoons for their rations. Suddenly, a pile of trays at the beginning of the queue crashed onto the floor with a deafening racket.

"Gather everything," I ordered to the young blond fellow who had caused the fall with a push against the fellow in front.

"Go to hell!" he answered in his native German.

I lobbed a punch on his chin, slamming him against a wall. "I saved your mother's life fighting against the Russians!" I roared in his face. In the meantime, a legionnaire leapt from behind, onto my shoulders. I bent forward sharply so that he flew over my head in a fall that ended on the hard floor. I never tolerated that type of attack, from my back. When another young German lunged at me, I simply moved aside, helping him to land face-down in a marmite full of soup.

"Calm down! Nobody move!" A guard rushed over, pointed a bayonet between my shoulder blades.

"I am calm, perfectly tranquil," I said.

"Walk forward without turning," the guard ordered.

The prison cell they put me in was narrow and had a very low ceiling so that I could barely stand up. From the small glassless window with massive iron bars I could see the old port, smell the familiar odours rising up from the darkening streets. Nevertheless, considering my precarious financial situation, I was ready to endure that confinement in order to continue with the Foreign Legion. *That bare cell was only a temporary setback*, I thought, *one which I could easily endure and which would soon be forgotten.*

Towards ten in the evening, I was still there, my nose between the bars, admiring the beauty of the kaleidoscope in the harbour where the reflections from the lampposts and brightly coloured neon signs of restaurants and shops overlapped, fragmented, or overtook one another as if in a living painting. Somewhere, not too far off, music was playing; couples were dancing, holding each other close. I was entranced by the melody. The melancholy I had fallen into evaporated. My spirit soared through the small window of the prison cell to become at one with the music. Something awakened in my soul, a realization that there was so much more to enjoy life, that I was wasting my time again. I took a drastic decision — the Foreign Legion wasn't for me.

❦—❦

When I was called to the recruiting office, a lieutenant informed me, with a sincere smile, "The searches done on your past, your *Croix de Guerre*, your citations and experience in Indochina are all excellent guaranties. It is men like you the Legion needs; you are cut out to be a good NCO."

"There is one thing I have to tell you, *lieutenant*, and I feel sorry because in here I already feel like a member of this glorious corps," I answered. This was a momentous decision for me, one that would affect the course of my life from that point on. I hesitated but was determined not to backtrack on the decision I had taken in the confinement of the prison cell.

"Yes?"

"I have changed my mind and regret having given you this trouble for nothing."

"On the contrary! It has not been a waste of time, neither for you, nor for us," said the lieutenant. "There is always room here for someone who has fought in two wars at such a young age. Think about it, Paul."

"I have considered it, and…"

"Maybe you need some more time. Think it over. Today is Saturday, you have until Monday to make your choice," he proposed, not at all surprised by my indecision.

On Monday morning, as I promised myself, I left from the main entrance where I encountered one of the NCOs I had roughed up at the pier who at that moment was on duty as the orderly at the guard house.

"You!" he said. "Where are you from? Marseille?"

I hesitated to answer. I didn't wish another scuffle so said nothing and handed him my papers, stamped by the lieutenant at the recruiting office.

"Paul Martelli. Ah! Italian eh?"

"Yes, I'm Italian!" I answered him in my Abruzzi accent.

"Hum! And yet… you look like…"

"Like whom?"

"Strange! I'm never wrong about ugly faces."

I snatched my papers from the orderly's hand while he was still looking at me, trying to figure out where he had seen me, and gave him a smart salute before leaving the fort. *It's behind me*, I thought, taking a deep breath. I took a pack of cigarettes from my pocket, pulled one out and lit up. I flicked the match into the dirty water of the old port, the same water on which vivid colours had waltzed just a few hours before, and drew in a welcome lungful of soothing smoke. It was time for my own, internal reflections.

So, I had fought in Pomerania against the Russian communists as a *Waffen SS* soldier for the good of Europe, and lost. For three years, I was a member of the French Expeditionary Corps in the Far East, fighting against the communist Viet Minh, for the good of France, Vietnam and the entire world, and lost. And now, almost twenty six years old, I was unemployed. Yes, I could have continued fighting, this time with the Foreign Legion and that would have been the natural course for me, and the easiest, but I wanted something more from life. What that something was, remained a mystery to me then, but I knew deep down that my life as a soldier was over. *Maybe*, I thought, *I would find a ship bound for the South Pacific, one I could board as a deck hand or even as a stowaway. I would seek out a place where there were no wars — an island lost in the vastness of the Pacific Ocean, one where I was a stranger, would be perfect.*